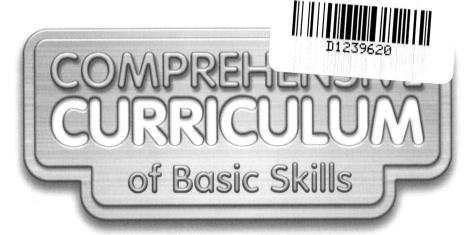

GRADE 3

American Education Publishing™
An imprint of Carson-Dellosa Publishing LLC
Greensboro, North Carolina

American Education Publishing™
An imprint of Carson-Dellosa Publishing LLC
P.O. Box 35665
Greensboro, NC 27425 USA

ISBN 978-1-60996-332-3

06-020141151

READING

- Phonics 7
- Syllables 11
- Compound Words 13
- Vocabulary 15
- Multiple-Meaning Words 19
- Sequencing 22
- Following Directions 32
- Main Idea 36
- Noting Details 51
- Inferences 54
- Reading for Information 56
- Fantasy and Reality 61
- Idioms 62
- Analogies 63
- Classifying 65
- Fiction and Nonfiction 76
- Library and Reference Skills 78
- Reading for Information 83
- Compare and Contrast 87
- Cause and Effect 90

READING COMPREHENSION

- Dinosaurs 98
- Sports Figures 109
- Adventurers 118
- Plants 130
- Rainforests 135
- Birds 143
- Our Solar System 151
- Our Body Systems 162
- Early Transportation 170
- Animals 174
- Drawing Conclusions 182

ENGLISH

- Alphabetical Order 192
- Antonyms 196
- Synonyms 200
- Homophones 203
- Nouns 207
- Pronouns 220
- Abbreviations 224
- Adjectives 225
- Prefixes and Suffixes 229
- Verbs 231
- Adverbs 242
- Other Parts of Speech 244

TABLE OF CONTENTS

- Commas and Capitalization 246
- Parts of Speech 251
- Subjects 255
- Predicates 259
- Types of Sentences 269
- Punctuation 278
- Parts of a Paragraph 282
- Poetry 286

SPELLING

- Vocabulary 290
- Verbs 297
- Homophones 317
- Short Vowels 323
- Long Vowels 326
- Adjectives 329
- C, K, CK Words 334
- S and C Words 342
- Words With Suffixes 346
- Words With Prefixes 351
- Synonyms and Antonyms 354
- Contractions 360

MATH

- Addition and Subtraction 364
- Place Value 366
- Regrouping 377
- Rounding 380
- Multiplication 383
- Division 389
- Fractions 400
- Decimals 404
- Patterns 408
- Geometry 410
- Map Scales 421
- Graphs 423
- Measurement 425
- Time 433
- Money 438
- Review 442
- Problem-Solving 449

APPENDIX

- Glossary 454
- Answer Key 460
- Teaching Suggestions 533
- Index 543

READING

Crocodile
Tears
& other
stories

My Story

Directions: Fill in the blanks. Use these sentences to write a story about yourself.

I feel happy when _____.

I feel sad when _____.

I am good at _____.

Words that describe me: _____ _____

_____ _____ _____.

I can help at home by _____.

My friends like me because _____.

I like to _____.

My favorite food is _____.

My favorite animal is _____.

Now . . . take your answers and write a story about **you**!

Name: _____

Phonics

Some words are more difficult to read because they have one or more silent letters. Many words you already know are like this.

Examples: wrong and **night**.

Directions: Circle the silent letters in each word. The first one is done for you.

(w)rong	answer	autumn	whole
knife	hour	wrap	comb
sigh	straight	knee	known
lamb	taught	scent	daughter
whistle	wrote	knew	crumb

Directions: Draw a line between the rhyming words. The first one is done for you.

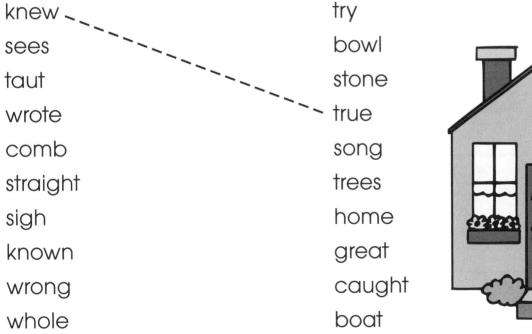

knew	try
sees	bowl
taut	stone
wrote	true
comb	song
straight	trees
sigh	home
known	great
wrong	caught
whole	boat

Name: _____

Phonics

Sometimes letters make sounds you don't expect. Two consonants can work together to make the sound of one consonant. The **f** sound can be made by **ph**, as in the word **elephant**. The consonants **gh** are most often silent, as in the words **night** and **though**. But they also can make the **f** sound as in the word **laugh**.

Directions: Circle the letters that make the **f** sound. Write the correct word from the box to complete each sentence.

ele(ph)ant	cough	laugh	telephone	phonics
dolphins	enough	tough	alphabet	rough

1. The **dolphins** were playing in the sea.

2. Did you have _____ time to do your homework?

3. A cold can make you _____ and sneeze.

4. The _____ ate peanuts with his trunk.

5. The road to my school is _____ and bumpy.

6. You had a _____ call this morning.

7. The _____ meat was hard to chew.

8. Studying _____ will help you read better.

9. The _____ has 26 letters in it.

10. We began to _____ when the clowns came in.

Name: _____

Phonics

There are several consonants that make the **k** sound: **c** when followed by a, o or u as in **cow** or **cup**; the letter **k** as in **milk**; the letters **ch** as in **Christmas** and **ck** as in **black**.

Directions: Read the following words. Circle the letters that make the **k** sound. The first one is done for you.

a(ch)e	school	market	comb
camera	deck	darkness	Christmas
necklace	doctor	stomach	crack
nickel	skin	thick	escape

Directions: Use your own words to finish the following sentences. Use words with the **k** sound.

1. If I had a nickel, I would _____ .

2. My doctor is very _____ .

3. We bought ripe, juicy tomatoes at the _____ .

4. If I had a camera now,
   I would take a picture of _____ .

5. When my stomach aches, _____ .

Grade 3 - Comprehensive Curriculum

Name: _____

Phonics

In some word "families," the vowels have a long sound when you would expect them to have a short sound. For example, the **i** has a short sound in **chill**, but a long sound in **child**. The **o** has a short sound in **cost**, but a long sound in **most**.

Directions: Read the words in the word box below. Write the words that have a long vowel sound under the word **LONG**, and the words that have a short vowel sound under the word **SHORT**. (Remember, a long vowel says its name—like **a** in **ate**.)

old	odd	gosh	gold	sold	soft	toast	frost	lost	most
doll	roll	bone	done	kin	mill	mild	wild	blink	blind

LONG

bone _____ _____

_____ _____

_____ _____

_____ _____

SHORT

doll _____ _____

_____ _____

_____ _____

_____ _____

Name: _____

Syllables

All words can be divided into **syllables**. Syllables are word parts which have one vowel sound in each part.

Directions: Draw a line between the syllable part and write the word on the correct line below. The first one is done for you.

lit|tle	bumblebee	pillow
truck	dazzle	dog
pencil	flag	angelic
rejoicing	ant	telephone

1 SYLLABLE   **2 SYLLABLES**   **3 SYLLABLES**

_____   little   _____

_____   _____   _____

_____   _____   _____

_____   _____   _____

Syllables

When the letters **le** come at the end of a word, they sometimes have the sound of **ul**, as in raffle.

Directions: Draw a line to match the syllables so they make words. The first one is done for you.

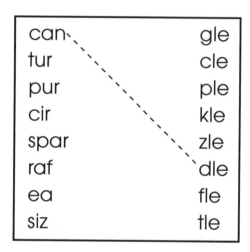

can	gle
tur	cle
pur	ple
cir	kle
spar	zle
raf	dle
ea	fle
siz	tle

Directions: Use the words you made to complete the sentences. One is done for you.

1. Will you buy a ticket for our school <u>raffle</u>?

2. The _____ pulled his head into his shell.

3. We could hear the bacon _____ in the pan.

4. The baby had one _____ on her birthday cake.

5. My favorite color is _____.

6. Look at that diamond _____!

7. The bald _____ is our national bird.

8. Draw a _____ around the correct answer.

Compound Words

A compound word is two small words put together to make one new word. Compound words are usually divided into syllables between the two words.

Directions: Read the words. Then divide them into syllables. The first one is done for you.

1. playground   <u>play   ground</u>   11. hilltop   _____

2. sailboat   _____   12. broomstick   _____

3. doghouse   _____   13. sunburn   _____

4. dishpan   _____   14. oatmeal   _____

5. pigpen   _____   15. campfire   _____

6. outdoors   _____   16. somewhere   _____

7. beehive   _____   17. starfish   _____

8. airplane   _____   18. birthday   _____

9. cardboard   _____   19. sidewalk   _____

10. nickname   _____   20. seashore   _____

Name: _____

Compound Words

Directions: Read the compound words in the word box. Then use them to answer the questions. The first one is done for you.

sailboat	blueberry	bookcase	tablecloth	beehive
dishpan	pigpen	classroom	playground	bedtime
broomstick	treetop	fireplace	newspaper	sunburn

Which compound word means . . .

1. a case for books?   bookcase

2. a berry that is blue?

3. a hive for bees?

4. a place for fires?

5. a pen for pigs?

6. a room for a class?

7. a pan for dishes?

8. a boat to sail?

9. a paper for news?

10. a burn from the sun?

11. the top of a tree?

12. a stick for a broom?

13. the time to go to bed?

14. a cloth for the table?

15. ground to play on?

Name: _____

Transportation Vocabulary

Directions: Unscramble the words to spell the names of kinds of transportation. The first one is done for you.

behelwworar   wheel <u>b</u> <u>a</u> <u>r</u> <u>r</u> <u>o</u> w

anirt   t __ __ __ n

moobattor   moto __ __ __ __ t

crattor   t __ __ c __ __ __

ceicbly   b __ __ __ __ __ e

tocker   r __ __ __ __ t

etobimuloa   aut __ __ __ __ __ __ e

rilanape   a __ __ p __ __ __ e

Directions: Use a word from above to complete each sentence.

1. My mother uses a _____ to move dirt to her garden.

2. The _____ blasted the spaceship off the launching pad.

3. We flew on an _____ to visit my aunt in Florida.

4. My grandfather drives a very old _____.

5. We borrowed Fred's _____ to go water skiing.

6. You should always look both ways when crossing a _____ track.

7. I hope I get a new _____ for my birthday.

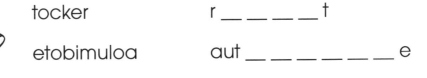

Space Vocabulary

Directions: Unscramble each word. Use the numbers below the letters to tell you what order they belong in. Write the word by its definition.

i r t b o
4 2 5 3 1

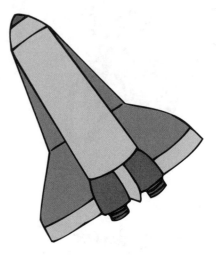

u t o n c w d n o
3 5 7 9 1 8 6 4 2

u l e f
2 4 3 1

a t s r a t n o u
7 9 2 4 1 3 6 5 8

t e h t s u l
5 7 2 4 1 3 6

A member of the team that flies a
spaceship.   _____

A rocket-powered spaceship that
travels between Earth and space. _____

The material, such as gas, used for
power.   _____

The seconds just before
take-off.   _____

The path of a spaceship as it goes
around Earth.   _____

Name: _____

Weather Vocabulary

Directions: Use the weather words in the box to complete the sentences.

sunny	temperature	foggy	puddles	rainy
windy	rainbow	cloudy	lightning	snowy

1. My friends and I love _____ days, because we can have snowball fights!

2. On _____ days, we like to stay indoors and play board games.

3. Today was hot and _____ , so we went to the beach.

4. We didn't see the sun at all yesterday. It was _____ all day.

5. _____ weather is perfect for flying kites.

6. It was so _____ , Mom had to use the headlights in the car so we wouldn't get lost.

7. While it was still raining, the sun began to shine and created a beautiful _____ .

8. We like to jump in the _____ after it rains.

9. _____ flashed across the sky during the thunderstorm.

10. The _____ outside was so low, we needed to wear hats, mittens and scarves.

Name: _____

Vocabulary Word Lists

Directions: Complete the vocabulary word lists. Be creative!

Drinks
chocolate milk

Lights
flashlight

Pets
dogs

School Supplies
paper

What other things can you think of to list?

_____

Name: _____

Multiple-Meaning Words

Many words have more than one meaning. These words are called **multiple-meaning words**. Think of how the word is used in a sentence or story to determine the correct meaning.

Directions: The following baseball words have multiple meanings. Write the correct word in each baseball below.

play	bat	ball	fly	run

This word means . . .

_____
1. a flying mammal
2. a special stick used in baseball

This word means . . .

_____
1. a small insect
2. to soar through the air

This word means . . .

_____
1. a big dance
2. a round object used in sports

This word means . . .

_____
1. a performance
2. to amuse oneself

Which word is left? _____ Write sentences using two different meanings of the word.

1._____

2._____

Name: _____

Multiple-Meaning Words

Directions: Complete each sentence on pages 20 and 21 using one of the words below. Each word will be used only twice.

bank   ball   park   run   play   kid   fly   bat

1. The kitten watched the _____ crawl slowly up the wall.

2. "You wouldn't _____ me, would you?" asked Dad.

3. Do you think Aunt Donna and Uncle Mike will come to my school _____ ?

4. He hit the ball so hard it broke the _____ .

5. "My favorite part of the story is when the princess goes to the _____ ," sighed Veronica.

6. My brother scored the first _____ in the game.

Name: _____

Multiple-Meaning Words

7. We will have to _____ quietly while the baby is sleeping.

8. Before we go to the store, I want to get some coins out of my _____.

9. The nature center will bring a live _____ for our class to see.

10. We sat on the _____ as we fished in the river.

11. The umpire decided the pitcher needed a new _____.

12. We will _____ in a race tomorrow.

13. "Can we please go to the _____ after I clean my room?" asked Jordan.

14. That boomerang can really_____!

15. Is it okay to _____ my bike here?

16. The baby goat, or _____, follows its mother everywhere.

Name: _____

Sequencing

Directions: Fill in the blank spaces with what comes next in the series. The first one is done for you.

year	Wednesday	day	sixth	large
twenty	February	night	seventeen	mile
paragraph	winter	ocean		

1. Sunday, Monday, Tuesday, _____Wednesday_____

2. third, fourth, fifth, _____

3. November, December, January, _____

4. tiny, small, medium, _____

5. fourteen, fifteen, sixteen, _____

6. morning, afternoon, evening, _____

7. inch, foot, yard, _____

8. day, week, month, _____

9. spring, summer, autumn, _____

10. five, ten, fifteen, _____

11. letter, word, sentence, _____

12. second, minute, hour, _____

13. stream, lake, river, _____

Sequencing

When words are in a certain order, they are in sequence.

Directions: Complete each sequence using a word from the box. There are extra words in the box. The first one has been done for you.

below	three	fifteen	December	twenty	above
after	go	third	hour	March	yard

1. January, February, **March**

2. before, during, _____

3. over, on, _____

4. come, stay, _____

5. second, minute, _____

6. first, second, _____

7. five, ten, _____

8. inch, foot, _____

Name: _____

Sequencing: Smallest to Largest

Directions: Rearrange each group of words to form a sequence from smallest to largest.

Example:

minute, second, hour   <u>second, minute, hour</u>

1. least, most, more   _____

2. full, empty, half-full   _____

3. month, day, year   _____

4. baseball, golf ball, soccer ball   _____

5. penny, dollar, quarter   _____

6. $4.12, $3.18, $3.22   _____

7. boy, man, infant   _____

8. mother, daughter, grandmother   _____

Name: _____

Sequencing

Directions: Read each story. Circle the phrase that tells what happened before.

1. Beth is very happy now that she has someone to play with. She hopes that her new sister will grow up quickly!

   A few days ago . . .

   Beth was sick.

   Beth's mother had a baby.

   Beth got a new puppy.

2. Sara tried to mend the tear. She used a needle and thread to sew up the hole.

   While playing, Sara had . . .

   broken her bicycle.

   lost her watch.

   torn her shirt.

3. The movers took John's bike off the truck and put it in the garage. Next, they moved his bed into his new bedroom.

   John's family . . .

   bought a new house.

   went on vacation.

   bought a new truck.

4. Katie picked out a book about dinosaurs. Jim, who likes sports, chose two books about baseball.

   Katie and Jim . . .

   went to the library.

   went to the playground.

   went to the grocery.

Sequencing

Directions: Read each story. Circle the sentence that tells what might happen next.

1. Sam and Judy picked up their books and left the house. They walked to the bus stop. They got on a big yellow bus.

   What will Sam and Judy do next?

   They will go to school.

   They will visit their grandmother.

   They will go to the store.

2. Maggie and Matt were playing in the snow. They made a snowman with a black hat and a red scarf. Then the sun came out.

   What might happen next?

   It will snow again.

   They will play in the sandbox.

   The snowman will melt.

3. Megan put on a big floppy hat and funny clothes. She put green make-up on her face.

   What will Megan do next?

   She will go to school.

   She will go to a costume party.

   She will go to bed.

4. Mike was eating a hot dog. Suddenly he smelled smoke. He turned and saw a fire on the stove.

   What will Mike do next?

   He will watch the fire.

   He will call for help.

   He will finish his hot dog.

Name: _____

Sequencing

Directions: Number these sentences from 1 to 5 to show the correct order of the story.

Building a Treehouse

_____ They had a beautiful treehouse!

_____ They got wood and nails.

__1__ Jay and Lisa planned to build a treehouse.

_____ Now, they like to eat lunch in their treehouse.

_____ Lisa and Jay worked in the backyard for three days building the treehouse.

A School Play

_____ Everyone clapped when the curtain closed.

_____ The girl who played Snow White came onto the stage.

_____ All the other school children went to the gym to see the play.

_____ The stage curtain opened.

__1__ The third grade was going to put on a play about Snow White.

Name: _____

Sequencing

Directions: Number these sentences from 1 to 8 to show the correct order of the story.

_____ Jack's father called the family doctor.

_____ Jack felt much better as his parents drove him home.

_____ Jack woke up in the middle of the night with a terrible pain in his stomach.

_____ The doctor told Jack's father to take Jack to the hospital.

_____ Jack called his parents to come help him.

_____ At the hospital, the doctors examined Jack. They said the problem was not serious. They told Jack's parents that he could go home.

_____ Jack's mother took his temperature. He had a fever of 103 degrees.

_____ On the way to the hospital, Jack rested in the backseat. He was worried.

Name: _____

Sequencing: A Story

This is a story from *The McGuffey Second Reader*. This is a very old book your great-great-grandparents may have used to learn to read.

Directions: Read the story on pages 29 and 30, then answer the questions on page 31.

The Crow and the Robin

One morning in the early spring, a crow was sitting on the branch of an old oak tree. He felt very ugly and cross and could only say, "Croak! Croak!" Soon, a little robin, who was looking for a place to build her nest, came with a merry song into the same tree. "Good morning to you," she said to the crow.

But the crow made no answer; he only looked at the clouds and croaked something about the cold wind. "I said, 'Good morning to you,'" said the robin, jumping from branch to branch.

"I wonder how you can be so merry this morning," croaked the crow.

"Why shouldn't I be merry?" asked the robin. "Spring has come and everyone ought to be happy."

"I am not happy," said the crow. "Don't you see those black clouds above us? It is going to snow."

"Very well," said the robin, "I shall keep on singing until the snow comes. A merry song will not make it any colder."

"Caw, caw, caw," croaked the crow. "I think you are very foolish."

Name: _____

Sequencing: A Story

The Crow and the Robin

The robin flew to another tree and kept on singing, but the crow sat still and made himself very unhappy. "The wind is so cold," he said. "It always blows the wrong way for me."

Very soon the sun came out, warm and bright, and the clouds went away, but the crow was as cross as ever.

The grass began to spring up in the meadows. Green leaves and flowers were seen in the woods. Birds and bees flew here and there in the glad sunshine. The crow sat and croaked on the branch of the old oak tree.

"It is always too warm or too cold," said he. "To be sure, it is a little pleasant just now, but I know that the sun will soon shine warm enough to burn me up. Then before night, it will be colder than ever. I do not see how anyone can sing at such a time as this."

Just then the robin came back to the tree with a straw in her mouth for her nest. "Well, my friend," asked she, "where is your snow?"

"Don't talk about that," croaked the crow. "It will snow all the harder for this sunshine."

"And snow or shine," said the robin, "you will keep on croaking. For my part, I shall always look on the bright side of things and have a song for every day in the year."

Which will you be like—the crow or the robin?_____

Name: _____

Sequencing: The Story

These sentences retell the story of "The Crow and the Robin" but are out of order.

Directions: Write the numbers 1 through 10 on the lines to show the correct sequence. The first one has been done for you.

____ Although the sun came out and the clouds went away, the crow was still as cross as ever.

____ "I shall always . . . have a song for every day in the year," said the robin.

__1__ The crow sat on the branch of an old oak tree and could only say, "Croak! Croak!"

____ "This wind is so cold. It always blows the wrong way," the crow said.

____ The crow said, "It is going to snow."

____ The robin said good morning to the crow.

____ The crow told the robin that he thought she was very foolish.

____ The grass began to spring up in the meadows.

____ The robin was jumping from branch to branch as she talked to the crow.

____ The robin came back with straw in her mouth for her nest.

Name: _____

Following Directions

Directions: Learning to follow directions is very important. Use the map to find your way to different houses.

1. Color the start house yellow.
2. Go north 2 houses, and east two houses.
3. Go north 2 houses, and west 4 houses.
4. Color the house green.

5. Start at the yellow house.
6. Go east 1 house, and north 3 houses.
7. Go west 3 houses, and south 3 houses.
8. Color the house blue.

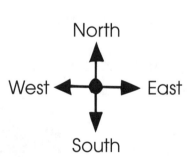

Name: _____

Following Directions

Directions: Read each sentence and do what it says to do.

1. Count the syllables in each word. Write the number on the line by the word.
2. Draw a line between the two words in each compound word.
3. Draw a circle around each name of a month.
4. Draw a box around each food word.
5. Draw an **X** on each noise word.
6. Draw a line under each day of the week.
7. Write the three words from the list you did not use. Draw a picture of each of those words.

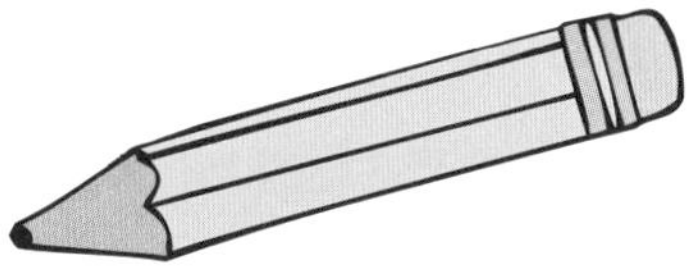

_____ April	_____ vegetable	_____ tablecloth
_____ bang	_____ June	_____ meat
_____ sidewalk	_____ Saturday	_____ crash
_____ astronaut	_____ March	_____ jingle
_____ moon	_____ cardboard	_____ rocket
_____ Friday	_____ fruit	_____ Monday

_____   _____   _____

Name: _____

Following Directions: A Recipe

Following directions means doing what the directions say to do. Following directions is an important skill to know. When you are trying to find a new place, build a model airplane or use a recipe, you should follow the directions given.

Directions: Read the following recipe. Then answer the questions on page 35.

Fruit Salad

1 fresh pineapple	2 oranges
1 cantaloupe	1 pear
2 bananas	1 cup seedless grapes
1 cup strawberries	lemon juice

- Cut the pineapple into chunks.

- Use a small metal scoop to make balls of the cantaloupe.

- Slice the pear, bananas and strawberries.

- Peel the oranges and divide them into sections. Cut each section into bite-sized pieces.

- Dip each piece of fruit in lemon juice, then combine them in a large bowl.

- Cover and chill.

- Pour a fruit dressing of your choice over the chilled fruit, blend well and serve cold.

    Makes 4 large servings.

Name: _____

Following Directions: A Recipe

Directions: Using the recipe on page 34, answer the questions below.

1. How many bananas does the recipe require? _____

2. Does the recipe explain why you must dip the fruit in lemon juice? _____

   Why would it be important to do this? _____

   _____

3. Would your fruit salad be as good if you did not cut the pineapple or section

   the oranges? Why or why not? _____

   _____

4. Which do you do first?

   (Check one.)

   ____ Pour dressing over the fruit.

   ____ Slice the pear.

   ____ Serve the fruit salad.

5. Which three fruits do you slice?

   _____

   _____

   _____

Name:_____

Main Idea

The main idea of a story is what the story is mostly about.

Directions: Read the story. Then answer the questions.

A tree is more than the enormous plant you see growing in your yard. A large part of the tree grows under the ground. This part is called the roots. If the tree is very big and very old, the roots may stretch down 100 feet!

The roots hold the tree in the ground. The roots do another important job for the tree. They gather minerals and water from the soil to feed the tree so it will grow. Most land plants, including trees, could not live without roots to support and feed them.

1. The main idea of this story is:

   The roots of a tree are underground.
   The roots do important jobs for the tree.

2. Where are the roots of a tree? _____

Circle the correct answer.

3. The roots help to hold the tree up.   True   False

4. Name two things the roots collect from the soil for the tree.

   1) _____ 2) _____

Main Idea

Directions: Read about spiders. Then answer the questions.

Many people think spiders are insects, but they are not. Spiders are the same size as insects, and they look like insects in some ways. But there are three ways to tell a spider from an insect. Insects have six legs, and spiders have eight legs. Insects have antennae, but spiders do not. An insect's body is divided into three parts; a spider's body is divided into only two parts.

1. The main idea of this story is:

   Spiders are like insects.
   Spiders are like insects in some ways, but they are not insects.

2. What are three ways to tell a spider from an insect?

   1) _____

   2) _____

   3) _____

Circle the correct answer.

3. Spiders are the same size as insects.   True   False

Name: _____

Main Idea

Directions: Read about the giant panda. Then answer the questions.

Giant pandas are among the world's favorite animals. They look like big, cuddly stuffed toys. There are not very many pandas left in the world. You may have to travel a long way to see one.

The only place on Earth where pandas live in the wild is in the bamboo forests of the mountains of China. It is hard to see pandas in the forest because they are very shy. They hide among the many bamboo trees. It also is hard to see pandas because there are so few of them. Scientists think there may be less than 1,000 pandas living in the mountains of China.

1. Write a sentence that tells the main idea of this story:

   _____

   _____

2. What are two reasons that it is hard to see pandas in the wild?

   1)_____

   2)_____

3. How many pandas are believed to be living in the mountains of China?

   _____

Name: _____

Main Idea

Directions: Read the story. Then answer the questions.

Because bamboo is very important to pandas, they have special body features that help them eat it. The panda's front foot is like a hand. But, instead of four fingers and a thumb, the panda has five fingers and an extra-long wrist bone. With its special front foot, the panda can easily pick up the stalks of bamboo. It also can hold the bamboo more tightly than it could with a hand like ours.

Bamboo stalks are very tough. The panda uses its big heavy head, large jaws and big back teeth to chew. Pandas eat the bamboo first by peeling the outside of the stalk. They do this by moving their front feet from side to side while holding the stalk in their teeth. Then they bite off a piece of the bamboo and chew it with their strong jaws.

1. Write a sentence that tells the main idea of this story.

_____

2. Instead of four fingers and a thumb, the panda has

_____

3. Bamboo is very tender.   True   False

Name: _____

Main Idea

Directions: Read each main idea sentence on pages 40 and 41. Then read the detail sentences following each main idea. Draw a ✓ on the line in front of each detail that supports the main idea.

Example: Niagara Falls is a favorite vacation spot.

   ✓   There are so many cars and buses that it is hard to get around.
         My little brother gets sick when we go camping.
   ✓   You can see people there from all over the world.

1. Hummingbirds are interesting birds to watch.

   ___   They look like tiny helicopters as they move around the flowers.

   ___   One second they are "drinking" from the flower; the next, they are gone!

   ___   It is important to provide birdseed in the winter for our feathered friends.

2. Boys and girls look forward to Valentine's Day parties at school.

   ___   For days, children try to choose the perfect valentine for each friend.

   ___   The school program is next Tuesday night.

   ___   Just thinking about frosted, heart-shaped cookies makes me hungry!

Main Idea

3. In-line skating has become a very popular activity.

___ Bicycles today are made in many different styles.

___ It is hard to spend even an hour at a park without seeing children and adults skating.

___ The stores are full of many kinds and colors of in-line skates.

4. It has been a busy summer!

___ Dad built a new deck off the back of our house, and everyone helped.

___ Our next-door neighbor needed my help to watch her three-year-old twins.

___ We will visit my relatives on the East coast for Christmas this year.

Main Idea

The **main idea** of a paragraph is the most important point. Often, the first sentence in a paragraph tells the main idea. Most of the other sentences are details that support the main idea. One of the sentences in each paragraph below does not belong in the story.

Directions: Circle the sentence that does not support the main idea.

My family and I went to the zoo last Saturday. It was a beautiful day. The tigers napped in the sun. I guess they liked the warm sunshine as much as we did! Mom and Dad laughed at the baby monkeys. They said the monkeys reminded them of how we act. My sister said the bald eagle reminded her of Dad! I know I'll remember that trip to the zoo for a long time. My cousin is coming to visit the weekend before school starts.

Thanksgiving was a special holiday in our classroom. Each child dressed up as either a Pilgrim or a Native American. My baby sister learned to walk last week. We prepared food for our "feast" on the last day of school before the holiday. We all helped shake the jar full of cream to make real butter. Our teacher cooked applesauce. It smelled delicious!

Name: _____

Main Idea

Directions: Circle the sentence in each paragraph that does not support the main idea.

The school picnic was so much fun! When we arrived, we each made a name tag. Then we signed up for the contests we wanted to enter. My best friend was my partner for every contest. The hen laid so many eggs that I needed a basket to carry them. All that exercise made us very hungry. We were glad to see those tables full of food.

The storm howled outside, so we stayed in for an evening of fun. The colorful rainbow stretched across the sky. The dining room table was stacked with games and puzzles. The delightful smell of popcorn led us into the kitchen where Dad led a parade around the kitchen table. Then we carried our bowls of popcorn into the dining room. We laughed so hard and ate so much, we didn't care who won the games. It was a great evening!

The city championship game would be played on Saturday at Brookside Park. Coach Metzger called an extra practice Friday evening. He said he knew we were good, because we had made it this far. He didn't want us to get nervous and forget everything we knew. School starts on Monday, but I'm not ready to go back yet. After working on some drills, Coach told us to relax, get lots of rest and come back ready to play.

Detail Sentences

In most paragraphs, the main idea is stated in the first sentence. The other sentences in the paragraph should give details to support that main idea. These are **detail sentences**.

Example: My calico cat was a good mother to her new kittens.
        a. Each day she made sure they were well fed.
        b. It was fun to watch her play with them.

Directions: Write two detail sentences to support each main idea.

1. Christopher loved his new bike.

    a. _____

    b. _____

2. Kim had trouble deciding what to get her mom for Mother's Day.

    a. _____

    b. _____

3. The picnic was canceled due to rain.

    a. _____

    _____

    b. _____

    _____

Name: _____

Main Idea: The Inventor

Directions: Read about Thomas Jefferson, then answer the questions.

Thomas Jefferson was the third president of the United States. He was also an inventor. That means he created things that had never been made before. Thomas Jefferson had many inventions. He built a chair that rotated in circles. He created a rotating music stand. He also made a walking stick that unfolded into a chair. Thomas Jefferson even invented a new kind of plow for farming.

1. The main idea is: (Circle one.)

   Thomas Jefferson was very busy when he was president.

   Thomas Jefferson was a president and an inventor.

2. What do we call a person who has new ideas and makes things that no one else has made before? _____

3. List three of Thomas Jefferson's inventions.

1) _____

2) _____

3) _____

Name: _____

Main Idea: Inventing the Bicycle

Directions: Read about the bicycle, then answer the questions.

One of the first bicycles was made out of wood. It was created in 1790 by an inventor in France. The first bicycle had no pedals. It looked like a horse on wheels. The person who rode the bicycle had to push it with his/her legs. Pedals weren't invented until nearly 50 years later.

Bikes became quite popular in the United States during the 1890s. Streets and parks were filled with people riding them. But those bicycles were still different from the bikes we ride today. They had heavier tires, and the brakes and lights weren't very good. Bicycling is still very popular in the United States. It is a great form of exercise and a handy means of transportation.

1. Who invented the bicycle? _____

2. What did it look like? _____

_____

3. When did bikes become popular in the United States? _____

4. Where did people ride bikes? _____

5. How is biking good for you? _____

6. How many years have bikes been popular in the United States? _____

Name: _____

Main Idea: Chewing Gum

Directions: Read about chewing gum, then answer the questions.

Thomas Adams was an American inventor. In 1870, he was looking for a substitute for rubber. He was working with chicle (chick-ul), a substance that comes from a certain kind of tree in Mexico. Years ago, Mexicans chewed chicle. Thomas Adams decided to try it for himself. He liked it so much he started selling it. Twenty years later, he owned a large factory that produced chewing gum.

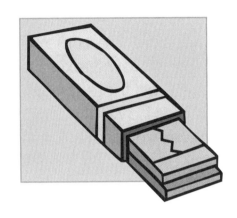

1. Who was the American inventor who
   started selling chewing gum? _____

2. What was he hoping to invent? _____

3. When did he invent chewing gum? _____

4. Where does the chicle come from? _____

5. Why did Thomas Adams start
   selling chewing gum? _____

6. How long was it until Adams owned a large
   factory that produced chewing gum? _____

Name: _____

Main Idea: The Peaceful Pueblos

Directions: Read about the Pueblo Native Americans, then answer the questions.

The Pueblo (pooh-eb-low) Native Americans live in the southwestern United States in New Mexico and Arizona. They have lived there for hundreds of years. The Pueblos have always been peaceful Native Americans. They never started wars. They only fought if attacked first.

The Pueblos love to dance. Even their dances are peaceful. They dance to ask the gods for rain or sunshine. They dance for other reasons, too. Sometimes the Pueblos wear masks when they dance.

1. The main idea is: (Circle one.)

   Pueblos are peaceful Native Americans who still live in parts of the United States.

   Pueblo Native Americans never started wars.

2. Do Pueblos like to fight? _____

3. What do the Pueblos like to do? _____

Name: _____

Main Idea: Clay Homes

Directions: Read about adobe houses, then answer the questions.

Pueblo Native Americans live in houses made of clay. They are called adobe (ah-doe-bee) houses. Adobe is a yellow-colored clay that comes from the ground. The hot sun in New Mexico and Arizona helps dry the clay to make strong bricks. The Pueblos have used adobe to build their homes for many years.

Pueblos use adobe for other purposes, too. The women in the tribes make beautiful pottery out of adobe. While the clay is still damp, they form it into shapes. After they have made the bowls and other containers, they paint them with lovely designs.

1. What is the subject of this story? _____

2. Who uses clay to make their houses? _____

3. How long have they been building adobe houses? _____

4. Why do adobe bricks need to be dried? _____

5. How do the Pueblos make pottery from adobe? _____

Name: _____

Main Idea: George Washington

Directions: Read about George Washington, then answer the questions.

George Washington was the first president of the United States. An old story proclaimed that he was very honest. It said that when Washington was just six years old, he cut down a cherry tree on the farm where he lived. The story said Washington could not lie about it. He told his father he cut down the tree. But George Washington did not chop down a cherry tree. People have since discovered that the story was invented. They say a man named Parson Weems wrote one of the first books about George Washington. He liked Washington so much, he made up that story.

1. The main idea of this story is: (Circle one.)

   George Washington cut down a cherry tree.

   George Washington did not cut down a cherry tree.

2. Is the story of George Washington chopping down a cherry tree true or false? (Circle one.)
   True or False

3. Who made up the story about George Washington? _____

4. When did the story say George Washington
   cut down the tree?   _____

5. Where was the tree supposedly
   cut down by Washington? _____

6. How did Parson Weems tell people the story? _____

Name: _____

Noting Details

Directions: Read the story. Then answer the questions.

Thomas Edison was one of America's greatest inventors. An **inventor** thinks up new machines and new ways of doing things. Edison was born in Milan, Ohio in 1847. He went to school for only three months. His teacher thought he was not very smart because he asked so many questions.

Edison liked to experiment. He had many wonderful ideas. He invented the light bulb and the phonograph (record player).

Thomas Edison died in 1931, but we still use many of his inventions today.

1. What is an inventor?

_____

2. Where was Thomas Edison born?

_____

3. How long did he go to school?

_____

4. What are two of Edison's inventions?

_____

Name: _____

Noting Details

Directions: Read the story. Then answer the questions.

The giant panda is much smaller than a brown bear or a polar bear. In fact, a horse weighs about four times as much as a giant panda. So why is it called "giant"? It is giant next to another kind of panda called the red panda.

The red panda also lives in China. The red panda is about the size of a fox. It has a long, fluffy, striped tail and beautiful reddish fur. It looks very much like a raccoon.

Many people think the giant pandas are bears. They look like bears. Even the word panda is Chinese for "white bear." But because of its relationship to the red panda, many scientists now believe that the panda is really more like a raccoon!

1. Why is the giant panda called "giant"?

   _____

2. Where does the red panda live?

   _____

3. How big is the red panda?

   _____

4. What animal does the red panda look like?

   _____

5. What does the word panda mean?

   _____

Name: _____

Noting Details

Directions: Read the story. Then answer the questions.

Giant pandas do not live in families like people do. The only pandas that live together are mothers and their babies. Newborn pandas are very tiny and helpless. They weigh only five ounces when they are born—about the weight of a stick of butter! They are born with their eyes closed, and they have no teeth.

It takes about three years for a panda to grow up. When full grown, a giant panda weighs about 300 pounds and is five to six feet tall. Once a panda is grown up, it leaves its mother and goes off to live by itself.

1. What pandas live together? _____

_____

2. How much do pandas weigh when they are born?_____

_____

3. Why do newborn pandas live with their mothers? _____

_____

4. When is a panda full grown? _____

_____

5. How big is a grown-up panda? _____

Name: _____

Inference

Inference is using logic to figure out what is not directly told.

Directions: Read the story. Then answer the questions.

In the past, many thousands of people went to the National Zoo each year to see Hsing-Hsing, the panda. Sometimes, there were as many as 1,000 visitors in one hour! Like all pandas, Hsing-Hsing spent most of his time sleeping. Because pandas are so rare, most people think it is exciting to see even a sleeping panda!

1. Popular means well-liked. Do you think giant pandas are popular?

_____

2. What clue do you have that pandas are popular?

_____

3. What did most visitors see Hsing-Hsing doing?

_____

Name: _____

Inference

Directions: Read the messages on the memo board. Then answer the questions.

1. What kind of lesson does Katie have? _____

2. What time is Amy's birthday party? _____

3. What kind of appointment does Jeff have on September 3rd? _____

4. Who goes to choir practice? _____

5. Where is Dad's meeting? _____

6. What time does Jeff go to the doctor? _____

Name:_____

Reading for Information

Directions: Read the story. List the four steps or changes a caterpillar goes through as it becomes a butterfly. Draw the stages in the boxes at the bottom of the page.

The Life Cycle of the Butterfly

One of the most magical changes in nature is the metamorphosis of a caterpillar. There are four stages in the transformation. The first stage is the embryonic stage. This is the stage in which tiny eggs are deposited on a leaf. The second stage is the larvae stage. We usually think of caterpillars at this stage. Many people like to capture the caterpillars hoping that while they have the caterpillar, it will turn into pupa. Another name for the pupa stage is the cocoon stage. Many changes happen inside the cocoon that we cannot see. Inside the cocoon, the caterpillar is changing into an adult. The adult breaks out of the cocoon as a beautiful butterfly!

1._____

2._____

3._____

4._____

Life Cycle of the Butterfly

Name: _____

Reading for Information

Telephone books contain information about people's addresses and phone numbers. They also list business addresses and phone numbers. The information in a telephone book is listed in alphabetical order.

Directions: Use your telephone book to find the following places in your area. Ask your mom or dad for help if you need it.

Can you find . . .

	Name	Phone number
. . . a pizza place?	_____	_____
. . . a bicycle store?	_____	_____
. . . a pet shop?	_____	_____
. . . a toy store?	_____	_____
. . . a water park?	_____	_____

What other telephone numbers would you like to have?

_____

Name: _____

Reading for Information: Dictionaries

Dictionaries contain meanings and pronunciations of words. The words in a dictionary are listed in alphabetical order. Guide words appear at the top of each dictionary page. They help us know at a glance what words are on each page.

Directions: Place the words in alphabetical order.

APPLE	CRAB	CRIB	FROG
_____	_____	_____	_____
_____	_____	_____	_____
_____	_____	_____	_____

apple   dog   crab   ear

book   atlas   cake   frog

egg   drip   coat   crib

Name: _____

Reading for Information: Newspapers

A newspaper has many parts. Some of the parts of a newspaper are:

- banner — the name of the paper
- lead story — the top news item
- caption — sentences under the picture which give information about the picture
- sports — scores and information on current sports events
- comics — drawings that tell funny stories
- editorial — an article by the editor expressing an opinion about something
- ads — paid advertisements
- weather — information about the weather
- advice column — letters from readers asking for help with a problem
- movie guides — a list of movies and movie times
- obituary — information about people who have died

Directions: Match the newspaper sections below with their definitions.

banner   an article by the editor

lead story   sentences under pictures

caption   movies and movie times

editorial   the name of the paper

movies   information about people who have died

obituary   the top news item

Newspaper Writing

A good news story gives us important information. It answers the questions:

WHO?   WHY?   WHAT?

WHERE?   HOW?   WHEN?

Directions: Think about the story "Little Red Riding Hood." Answer the following questions about the story.

Who are the characters? _____

_____

What is the story about? _____

_____

Why does Red go to Granny's house? _____

_____

Where does the story take place? _____

_____

When did she go to Granny's house? _____

_____

Where did the Wolf greet Red? _____

_____

Name: _____

Fantasy and Reality

Something that is **real** could actually happen. Something that is **fantasy** is not real. It could not happen.

Examples: Real: Dogs can bark.
           Fantasy: Dogs can fly.

Directions: Look at the sentences below. Write **real** or **fantasy** next to each sentence.

1. My cat can talk to me.   _____

2. Witches ride brooms and cast spells.   _____

3. Dad can mow the lawn.   _____

4. I ride a magic carpet to school.   _____

5. I have a man-eating tree.   _____

6. My sandbox has toys in it.   _____

7. Mom can bake chocolate chip cookies. _____

8. Mark's garden has tomatoes and corn in it._____

9. Jack grows candy and ice cream   _____
   in his garden.

10. I make my bed everyday.   _____

Write your own **real** sentence._____

_____

Write your own **fantasy** sentence._____

_____

Name: _____

Idioms

Idioms are a colorful way of saying something ordinary. The words in idioms do not mean exactly what they say.

Directions: Read the idioms listed below. Draw a picture of the literal meaning. Then match the idiom to its correct meaning.

Jump on the bandwagon! ●   ● She doesn't eat very much.

She eats like a bird. ●   ● Keep the secret.

Don't cry over spilled milk! ●   ● Make sure you don't miss an opportunity.

Don't let the cat out of the bag! ●   ● Get involved!

You are the apple of my eye. ●   ● Don't worry about things that have already happened.

Don't miss the boat. ●   ● I think you are special.

Analogies

Analogies compare how things are related to each other.

Directions: Complete the other analogies.

Example: Finger is to **hand** as **toe** is to **foot**.

1. Apple is to tree   as   flower is to _____ .

2. Tire is to car   as   wheel is to _____ .

3. Foot is to leg   as   hand is to _____ .

Name: _____

Analogies

Directions: Complete each analogy using a word from the box. The first one has been done for you.

week	bottom	month	tiny	sentence	lake	out	eye

1. **Up** is to **down**   as   **in** is to ___out___ .

2. **Minute** is to **hour**   as   **day** is to _____ .

3. **Month** is to **year**   as   **week** is to _____ .

4. **Over** is to **under**   as   **top** is to _____ .

5. **Big** is to **little**   as   **giant** is to _____ .

6. **Sound** is to **ear**   as   **sight** is to _____ .

7. **Page** is to **book**   as   **word** is to _____ .

8. **Wood** is to **tree**   as   **water** is to _____ .

Name: _____

Classifying: Seasons

Directions: Each word in the box can be grouped by seasons. Complete the pyramids for each season with a word from the box.

July 4	hot	football	bike rides
kite	froze	sled ride	swimming
snowman	bunnies	ice	jack-o-lantern
windy	baseball	leaves	Thanksgiving

1. Spring

k
w
b
b

2. Summer

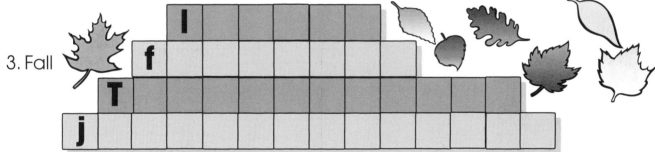

h
J
s
b

3. Fall

l
f
T
j

4. Winter

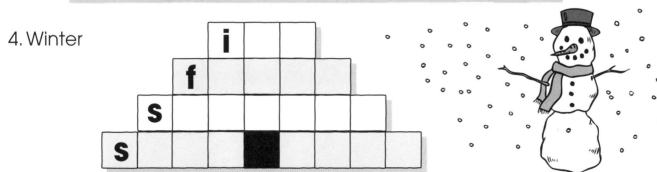

i
f
s
s

Name: _____

Classifying

Directions: Write each word from the box in the correct category.

Trees

robin	elm
buckeye	willow
sunflower	bluejay
canary	oak
rose	wren
tulip	morning glory

Birds

Flowers

Classifying

Directions: Look at the three words in each box and add one more that is like the others.

cars trucks airplanes _____		cows pigs chickens _____	
bread bagels muffins _____		pens pencils paints _____	
square triangle rectangle _____		violets tulips iris _____	
milk yogurt cheese _____		mom dad sister _____	
merry-go-round swings sandbox _____		snowpants boots jacket _____	

Challenge: Can you list the theme of each group?

_____   _____

_____   _____

_____   _____

_____   _____

Name: _____

Classifying

Directions: Write a word from the word box that is described by the four words in each group.

cake flower	farm dishes	sick puppy	winter storm	kite ocean	car book

leaves petals stem roots _____	sand shells waves fish _____	snow wind cold ice _____	string tail wind fly _____
fever headache pills sneeze _____	rain thunder wind hail _____	soft furry playful small _____	sugar butter flour chocolate _____
tractor animals barn plow _____	cup plate bowl platter _____	pages words pictures cover _____	tires seats windows trunk _____

Classifying

Directions: Write a word from the word box to complete each sentence. If the word you write names an article of clothing, write **1** on the line. If it names food, write **2** on the line. If it names an animal, write **3** on the line. If the word names furniture, write **4** on the line.

jacket	chair	shirt	owl	mice
bed	cheese	dress	bread	chocolate

__1__ 1. Danny tucked his _____ into his pants.

_____ 2. _____ is my favorite kind of candy.

_____ 3. The wise old _____ sat in the tree and said, "Who-o-o."

_____ 4. We can't sit on the _____ because it has a broken leg.

_____ 5. Don't forget to wear your _____ because it is chilly today.

_____ 6. Will you please buy a loaf of _____ at the store?

_____ 7. She wore a very pretty _____ to the dance.

_____ 8. The cat chased the _____ in the barn.

_____ 9. I was so sleepy that I went to _____ early.

_____ 10. We put _____ in the mouse trap to help catch the mice.

Name: _____

Classifying

Directions: Write the word from the word box that tells what kinds of things are in each sentence.

birds	toys	states	insects	women
men	numbers	animals	flowers	letters

1. A father, uncle and king are all _____.

2. Fred has a wagon, puzzles and blocks. These are all _____.

3. Iowa, Ohio and Maine are all _____.

4. A robin, woodpecker and canary all have wings. They are kinds of _____.

5. Squirrels, rabbits and foxes all have tails and are kinds of _____.

6. Roses, daisies and violets smell sweet. These are kinds of _____.

7. A, B, C and D are all _____. You use them to spell words.

8. Bees, ladybugs and beetles are kinds of _____.

9. Mother, aunt and queen are _____.

10. Seven, thirty and nineteen are all _____.

Name: _____

Classifying: Comparisons

Directions: Compare the people of Wackyville to each other. Read the sentences and answer the questions. The first one has been done for you.

1. Wanda cooks fast. Joe cooks faster than Wanda. Who cooks faster?

   _____ *Joe* _____

2. Mr. Green plants many flowers. Mrs. Posy plants fewer flowers than Mr. Green. Who plants more flowers?

   _____

3. Hugo weighs a lot. Edward weighs less. Who weighs more?

   _____

4. Sheila has 3 cats. Billy has 2 cats, 1 dog and 1 bird. Who has more pets?

   _____

5. Ms. Brown has many trees. Mr. Smith has fewer trees than Ms. Brown. Who has more trees?

   _____

6. An elephant moves slowly. A snail moves even slower. Which animal moves quicker?

   _____

Classifying

Directions: Read each animal story. Then look at the fun facts. Write an **H** for horse, **P** for panda or **D** for dog next to each fact.

Horses

Horses are fun to ride. You can ride them in the woods or in fields. Horses usually have pretty names. Sometimes, if they are golden, they are called Amber. Horses swish their tails when it is hot. That keeps the flies away from them.

Pandas

Pandas are from China. They like to climb trees. They scratch bark to write messages to their friends in the trees. When pandas get hungry, they gnaw on bamboo shoots.

Dogs

Dogs are good pets. People often call them by names like Spot or Fido. Sometimes they are named after their looks. For example, a brown dog is sometimes named Brownie. Some people have special, small doors for their dogs to use.

Fun Facts

_____ 1. My name is often Spot or Fido.

_____ 2. I am from China.

_____ 3. I make a good house pet.

_____ 4. I like to carry people into the fields.

_____ 5. My favorite food is bamboo.

_____ 6. Flies bother me when I am hot.

_____ 7. Amber is often my name when I am golden.

_____ 8. I leave messages for my friends by scratching bark.

_____ 9. Sometimes I have my own special door on a house.

Name: _____

Webs

Webs are another way to classify information. Look at the groups below. Add more words in each group.

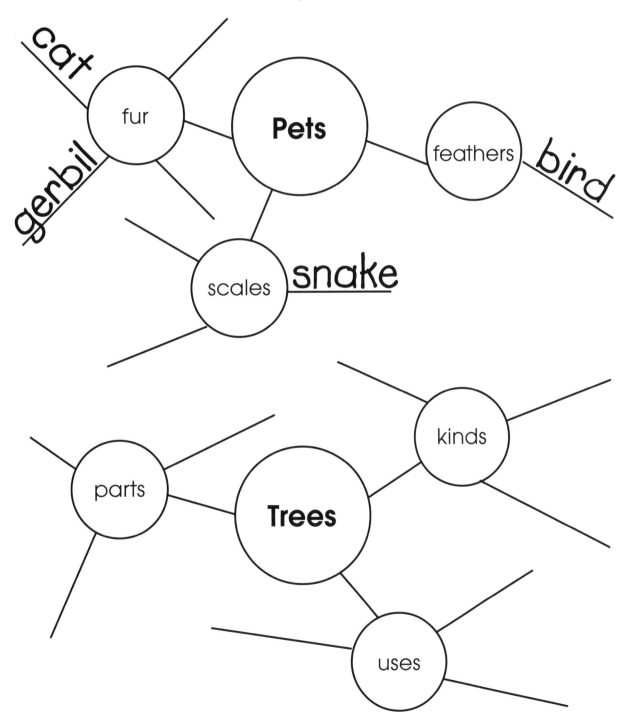

Story Webs

All short stories have a plot, characters, setting and a theme.

The **plot** is what the story is about.

The **characters** are the people or animals in the story.

The **setting** is where and when the story occurs.

The **theme** is the message or idea of the story.

Directions: Use the story "Snow White" to complete this story web.

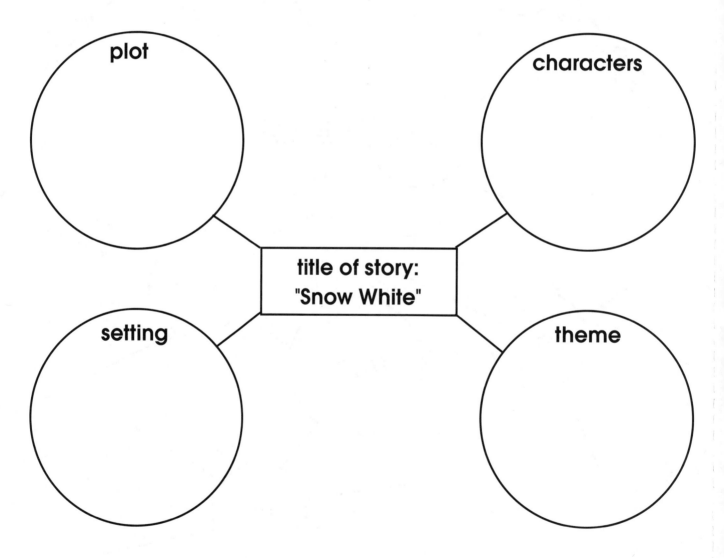

plot

characters

title of story:
"Snow White"

setting

theme

Name: _____

Types of Books

A **fiction** book is a book about things that are made up or not true. Fantasy books are fiction. A **nonfiction** book is about things that have really happened. Books can be classified into more types:

Mystery - books that have clues that lead to solving a problem or mystery

Biography - book about a real person's life

Poetry - a collection of poems, which may or may not rhyme

Fantasy - books about things that cannot really happen

Sports - books about different sports or sport figures

Travel - books about going to other places

Directions: Write mystery, biography, poetry, fantasy, sports or travel next to each title.

The Life of Helen Keller _____

Let's Go to Mexico! _____

The Case of the Missing Doll _____

How to Play Golf _____

Turtle Soup and Other Poems _____

Fred's Flying Saucer _____

Name: _____

Fiction and Nonfiction

Fiction writing is a story that has been invented. The story might be about things that could really happen (realistic) or about things that couldn't possibly happen (fantasy). **Nonfiction** writing is based on facts. It usually gives information about people, places or things. A person can often tell while reading whether a story or book is fiction or nonfiction.

Directions: Read the paragraphs below and on page 77. Determine whether each paragraph is fiction or nonfiction. Circle the letter **F** for fiction or the letter **N** for nonfiction.

"Do not be afraid, little flowers," said the oak. "Close your yellow eyes in sleep and trust in me. You have made me glad many a time with your sweetness. Now I will take care that the winter shall do you no harm." **F N**

The whole team watched as the ball soared over the outfield fence. The game was over! It was hard to walk off the field and face parents, friends and each other. It had been a long season. Now, they would have to settle for second place. **F N**

Be careful when you remove the dish from the microwave. It will be very hot, so take care not to get burned by the dish or the hot steam. If time permits, leave the dish in the microwave for 2 or 3 minutes to avoid getting burned. It is a good idea to use a potholder, too. **F N**

Name: _____

Fiction and Nonfiction

Megan and Mariah skipped out to the playground. They enjoyed playing together at recess. Today, it was Mariah's turn to choose what they would do first. To Megan's surprise, Mariah asked, "What do you want to do, Megan? I'm going to let you pick since it's your birthday!" **F N**

It is easy to tell an insect from a spider. An insect has three body parts and six legs. A spider has eight legs and no wings. Of course, if you see the creature spinning a web, you will know what it is. An insect wouldn't want to get too close to the web or it would be stuck. It might become dinner! **F N**

My name is Lee Chang, and I live in a country that you call China. My home is on the other side of the world from yours. When the sun is rising in my country, it is setting in yours. When it is day at your home, it is night at mine. **F N**

Henry washed the dog's foot in cold water from the brook. The dog lay very still, for he knew that the boy was trying to help him. **F N**

Library Skills

A library is a place filled with books. People can borrow the books and take them home. When they are finished reading them, people return the books to the library. Most libraries have two sections: One is for adult books and one is for children's books. A librarian is there to help people find books.

Directions: Read the title of each library book. On each line, write **A** if the book is written for an adult or **C** if it is written for a child.

1. Sam Squirrel Goes to the City _____

2. Barney Beagle Plays Baseball _____

3. Sammy's Silly Poems _____

4. Understanding Your Child . . . _____

5. Learn to Play Guitar _____

6. Bake Bread in Five Easy Steps _____

7. The Selling of the President _____

8. Jenny's First Party _____

Name: _____

Library Skills: Alphabetical Order

Ms. Ling, the school librarian, needs help shelving books. Fiction titles are arranged in alphabetical order by the author's last name. Ms. Ling has done the first set for you.

__3__ Silverstein, Shel   __1__ Bridwell, Norman   __2__ Farley, Walter

Directions: Number the following groups of authors in alphabetical order.

_____ Bemelmans, Ludwig   _____ Perkins, Al

_____ Stein, R.L.   _____ Dobbs, Rose

_____ Sawyer, Ruth   _____ Baldwin, James

_____ Baum, L. Frank   _____ Kipling, Rudyard

The content of some books is also arranged alphabetically.

Directions: Circle the books that are arranged in alphabetical order.

T.V. guide   dictionary   encyclopedia   novel

almanac   science book   Yellow Pages   catalog

Write the books you circled in alphabetical order.

1._____

2._____

3._____

Name: _____

Reference Books

Reference books are books that tell basic facts. They usually cannot be checked out from the library. Dictionaries and encyclopedias are reference books. A dictionary tells you about words. Encyclopedias give you other information, such as when the president was born, what the Civil War was and where Eskimos live. Encyclopedias usually come in sets of more than 20 books. Information is listed in alphabetical order, just like words are listed in the dictionary. There are other kinds of reference books, too, like books of maps called atlases. Reference books are not usually read from cover to cover.

Directions: Draw a line from each sentence to the correct type of book. The first one has been done for you.

DICTIONARY

1. I can tell you the definition of **divide**. ———

A-D

E-G

2. I can tell you when George Washington was born.

H-J

3. I can give you the correct spelling for many words.

K-M

4. I can tell you where Native Americans live.

N-P

5. I can tell you the names of many butterflies.

Q-S

6. I can tell you what **modern** means.

T-V

7. I can give you the history of dinosaurs.

W-Y

8. If you have to write a paper about Eskimos, I can help you.

Z

Name: _____

Periodicals

Libraries also have periodicals such as magazines and newspapers. They are called **periodicals** because they are printed regularly within a set period of time. There are many kinds of magazines. Some discuss the news. Others cover fitness, cats or other topics of special interest. Almost every city or town has a newspaper. Newspapers usually are printed daily, weekly or even monthly. Newspapers cover what is happening in your town and in the world. They usually include sections on sports and entertainment. They present a lot of information.

Directions: Follow the instructions.

1. Choose an interesting magazine.

   What is the name of the magazine? _____

   List the titles of three articles in the magazine.

   _____

   _____

   _____

2. Now, look at a newspaper.

   What is the name of the newspaper? _____

   The title of a newspaper story is called a headline.

   What are some of the headlines in your local

   newspaper?

   _____

   _____

Grade 3 - Comprehensive Curriculum

References

Paul and Maria want to learn about the Moon. They go to the library. Where should they look while they are there?

Directions: Answer the questions to help Paul and Maria find information about the Moon.

1. Should they look in the children's section or in the adult's section?

   _____

2. Should they look for a fiction book or a nonfiction book?

   _____

3. Who at the library can help them?

   _____

4. What reference books should they look at?

   _____

5. Where can they find information that may have been in the news?

   _____

6. What word would they look up in the encyclopedia to get the information they need?

   _____

Name: _____

Reading a Schedule

There are many different kinds of reading. When reading a magazine, you probably skim over pictures, captions and headlines. You stop to read carefully when you see something of interest. If your teacher assigns a chapter in a science textbook, you read it carefully so you don't miss important details. A **schedule** is a chart with lists of times. Would you read slowly or quickly to get information from a schedule? If you did not read carefully, you might get on the wrong bus or miss the bus altogether!

Directions: Look carefully at the bus schedule, then answer the questions.

	City Transit System				
Bus		**Leaves**		**Arrives**	
#10	Pine Street	7:35 A.M.	Oak Street	7:58 A.M.	
#17	James Road	7:46 A.M.	Main Street	8:10 A.M.	
#10	Oak Street	8:05 A.M.	Charles Road	8:25 A.M.	
#29	Pine Street	9:12 A.M.	Oak Street	9:35 A.M.	

1. Which bus goes to Main Street in the morning? _____

2. If you miss the #10 bus to Oak Street, could you still get there by noon? _____ How? _____

3. What time does bus #29 arrive at Oak Street? _____

4. Can you travel from Pine Street to Charles Road? _____ On which bus? _____

5. Bus #17 leaves _____ at 7:46 A.M. and arrives at Main Street at _____ A.M.

Name: _____

Reading a Schedule

Here is a schedule for the day's activities at Camp Do-A-Lot. Lisa and Jessie need help to decide what they will do on their last day.

Directions: Use this schedule to answer the questions on page 85.

CAMP DO-A-LOT

Saturday, July 8, 2000

Breakfast	6:30 A.M.	Dining Hall
Archery	7:30 A.M.	Field behind the Hall
Canoeing	7:30 A.M.	Blue Bottom Lake
Landscape Painting	7:30 A.M.	Rainbow Craft Shed
Horseback Riding	8:45 A.M.	Red Barn
Landscape Painting	8:45 A.M.	Rainbow Craft Shed
Scavenger Hunt	8:45 A.M.	Dining Hall
Cabin Clean-up	10:45 A.M.	Assigned Cabins
Lunch	11:45 A.M.	Dining Hall
Canoeing	1:00 P.M.	Blue Bottom Lake
Archery	1:00 P.M.	Field behind the Hall
Scavenger Hunt	1:00 P.M.	Dining Hall
Awards Ceremony	2:45 P.M.	Outdoor Theater
Dismissal	3:30 P.M.	

Reading a Schedule

Directions: Use the schedule of activities on page 84 to answer the questions.

1. Where do Lisa and Jessie need to go to take part in archery?

   _____

2. Both girls want to go canoeing. What are the two times that canoeing

   is offered? _____ and _____

3. Lisa and Jessie love to go on scavenger hunts. They agree to go on the hunt

   at 1:00 P.M. When will they have to go canoeing? _____

4. Only one activity on the last day of camp takes place at the Outdoor

   Theater. What is it?_____

5. What happens at 10:45 A.M.? _____

6. If you went to the Rainbow Craft Shed at 7:30 A.M., what activity would you

   find there?_____

Pretend you are at Camp Do-A-Lot with Lisa and Jessie. On the line next to
each time, write which activity you would choose to do.

7:30 A.M.   _____

              _____

8:45 A.M.   _____

              _____

1:00 P.M.   _____

              _____

Name: _____

Reading a Schedule

Special Saturday classes are being offered to students of the county schools. They will be given the chance to choose from art, music or gymnastics classes.

Directions: Read the schedule, then answer the questions.

Saturday, November 13		
Art	**Music**	**Gymnastics**
8:00 A.M. Watercolor—Room 350 Clay Sculpting—Room 250	Island Rhythms—Room 54 Orchestra Instruments—Stage	Floor Exercises—W. Gym Parallel Bars—E. Gym
Break (10 minutes)		
10:00 A.M. Painting Stills—Room 420 Watercolor—Room 350	Percussion—Room 54 Jazz Sounds—Stage	Uneven Bars—N. Gym _____
Break (10 minutes)		
11:00 A.M. Oils on Canvas—Room 258 _____	Island Rhythms—Room 54 Create Your Own Music— Room 40	Uneven Bars—N. Gym Balance Beam—W. Gym

1. Where would you meet to learn about Jazz Sounds? _____

2. Could a student sign up for Watercolor and Floor Exercises? _____
   Explain your answer. _____

3. Which music class would a creative person enjoy? _____

   _____

4. Could a person sign up for an art class at 11:00? _____

5. What time is the class on clay sculpting offered? _____

Name: _____

Compare and Contrast

To **compare** means to discuss how things are similar. To **contrast** means to discuss how things are different.

Directions: Compare and contrast how people grow gardens. Write at least two answers for each question.

Many people in the country have large gardens. They have a lot of space, so they can plant many kinds of vegetables and flowers. Since the gardens are usually quite large, they use a wheelbarrow to carry the tools they need. Sometimes they even have to carry water or use a garden hose.

People who live in the city do not always have enough room for a garden. Many people in big cities live in apartment buildings. They can put in a window box or use part of their balcony space to grow things. Most of the time, the only garden tools they need are a hand trowel to loosen the dirt and a watering can to make sure the plant gets enough water.

1. Compare gardening in the country with gardening in the city.

   _____

   _____

2. Contrast gardening in the country with gardening in the city.

   _____

   _____

Name: _____

Compare and Contrast

Directions: Look for similarities and differences in the following paragraphs. Then answer the questions.

Phong and Chris both live in the city. They live in the same apartment building and go to the same school. Phong and Chris sometimes walk to school together. If it is raining or storming, Phong's dad drives them to school on his way to work. In the summer, they spend a lot of time at the park across the street from their building.

Phong lives in Apartment 12-A with his little sister and mom and dad. He has a collection of model race cars that he put together with his dad's help. He even has a bookshelf full of books about race cars and race car drivers.

Chris has a big family. He has two older brothers and one older sister. When Chris has time to do anything he wants, he gets out his butterfly collection. He notes the place he found each specimen and the day he found it. He also likes to play with puzzles.

1. Compare Phong and Chris. List at least three similarities.

_____

_____

_____

2. Contrast Phong and Chris. List two differences.

_____

_____

_____

Compare and Contrast: Venn Diagram

Directions: List the similarities and differences you find below on a chart called a **Venn diagram**. This kind of chart shows comparisons and contrasts.

Butterflies and moths belong to the same group of insects. They both have two pairs of wings. Their wings are covered with tiny scales. Both butterflies and moths undergo metamorphosis, or a change, in their lives. They begin their lives as caterpillars.

Butterflies and moths are different in some ways. Butterflies usually fly during the day, but moths generally fly at night. Most butterflies have slender, hairless bodies; most moths have plump, furry bodies. When butterflies land, they hold their wings together straight over their bodies. When moths land, they spread their wings out flat.

1. List three ways that butterflies and moths are alike.

   _____

   _____

   _____

2. List three ways that butterflies and moths are different.

   _____

   _____

   _____

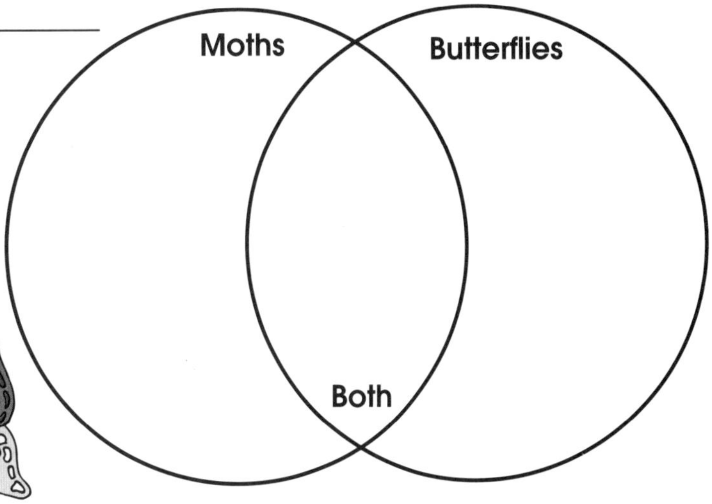

3. Combine your answers from questions 1 and 2 into a Venn diagram. Write the differences in the circle labeled for each insect. Write the similarities in the intersecting part.

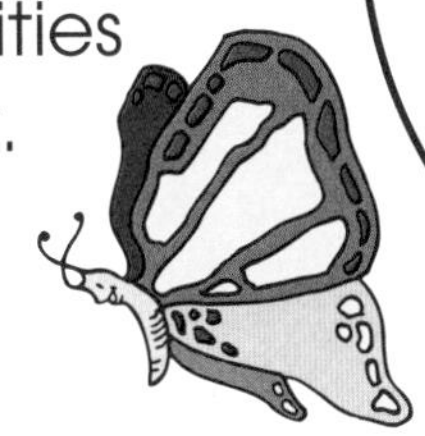

Moths   Butterflies

Both

Name: _____

Cause and Effect

A **cause** is the reason for an event. An **effect** is what happens as a result of a cause.

Directions: Circle the cause and underline the effect in each sentence. They may be in any order. The first one has been done for you.

1. (The truck hit an icy patch) and <u>skidded off the road</u>.

2. When the door slammed shut, the baby woke up crying.

3. Our soccer game was cancelled when it began to storm.

4. Dad and Mom are adding a room onto the house since our family is growing.

5. Our car ran out of gas on the way to town, so we had to walk.

6. The home run in the ninth inning helped our team win the game.

7. We had to climb the stairs because the elevator was broken.

8. We were late to school because the bus had a flat tire.

Name: _____

Cause and Effect

Cause and effect sentences often use clue words to show the relationship between two events. Common clue words are because, so, when and since.

Directions: Read the sentences on pages 91 and 92. Circle each clue word. The first one has been done for you.

1. I'll help you clean your room, (so) we can go out to play sooner.

2. Because of the heavy snowfall, school was closed today.

3. She was not smiling, so her mother wanted her school pictures taken again.

4. Mrs. Wilderman came to school with crutches today, because she had a skating accident.

5. When the team began making too many mistakes at practice, the coach told them to take a break.

Name: _____

Cause and Effect

6. Our telephone was not working, so I called the doctor from next door.

7. The police officer began to direct traffic, since the traffic signal was not working.

8. The class will go out to recess when the room is cleaned up.

9. "I can't see you because the room is too dark," said Jordan.

10. He has to wash the dishes alone because his sister is sick.

11. Since the bus had engine trouble, several children were late to school.

12. Monday was a holiday, so Mom and Dad took us to the park.

Name: _____

Cause and Effect

Directions: Draw a line to match each phrase to form a logical cause and effect sentence.

1. Dad gets paid today, so   because she is sick.

2. When the electricity went out,   we're going out for dinner.

3. Courtney can't spend the night   so she bought a new sweater.

4. Our front window shattered   we grabbed the flashlights.

5. Sophie got $10.00 for her birthday,   when the baseball hit it.

Directions: Read each sentence beginning. Choose an ending from the box that makes sense. Write the correct letter on the line.

1. Her arm was in a cast, because ____

2. They are building a new house on our street, so ____

3. Since I'd always wanted a puppy, ____

4. I had to renew my library book, ____

5. My parents' anniversary is tomorrow, ____

> A. we all went down to watch.
> B. so my sister and I bought them some flowers.
> C. since I hadn't finished it.
> D. she fell when she was skating.
> E. Mom gave me one for my birthday.

Causes

Directions: Complete each sentence by writing a possible cause.

1. I bought my best friend this book _____

   _____.

2. Dad's back was really sore because_____

   _____.

3. Our school bus was late this morning since _____

   _____.

4. We don't have any homework this weekend so _____

   _____.

Write two sentences that show a cause-and-effect relationship.

1. _____

   _____.

2. _____

   _____

   _____

   _____.

Effects

Directions: Complete each sentence by writing a possible effect.

1. The front door was locked, so _____

   _____.

2. Because of the heavy rains last night, _____

   _____.

3. Since I spent all my money, _____

   _____.

4. When my alarm clock did not wake me this morning, _____

   _____.

Review

Directions: Read the story. Then answer the questions.

There are many different kinds of robots. One special kind of robot takes the place of people in guiding airplanes and ships. They are called "automatic pilots." These robots are really computers programmed to do just one special job. They have the information to control the speed and direction of the plane or ship.

Robots are used for many jobs in which a person can't get too close because of danger, such as in exploding a bomb. Robots can be controlled from a distance. This is called "remote control." These robots are very important in studying space. In the future, robots will be used to work on space stations and on other planets.

1. The main idea of this story is:

_____

_____

2. Why are robots good in dangerous jobs?

_____

3. What is "remote control"?

_____

4. What will robots be used for in the future?

_____

What would you have a robot do for you?

_____

Main Idea: Iguanodon

Millions of years ago, many kinds of dinosaurs roamed the Earth. The name of one kind of dinosaur was Iguanodon (ee-gwan-eh-don). The Iguanodon looked like a giant lizard. It had tough skin. The Iguanodon's skin must have felt like leather! Iguanodons ate plants.

Directions: Answer these questions about Iguanodons.

1. Circle the main idea:

    The Iguanodon's skin was like leather.

    The Iguanodon was a plant-eating dinosaur with tough skin.

2. What kind of food did Iguanodons eat?

    _____

3. What animal living today did the Iguanodon look like?

    _____

Making Inferences: Dining Dinosaurs

Brontosaurus dinosaurs lived in the swamps. Swamps are water areas where many plants grow. Here are the names of the other kinds of dinosaurs that lived in the swamps. Diplodocus (dip-low-dock-us), Brachiosaurus (bracky-o-saur-us) and Cetiosaurus (set-e-o-saur-us). These dinosaurs had small heads and small brains. They weighed 20 tons or more. They grew to be 60 feet long! These animals did not need to have sharp teeth.

Directions: Answer these questions about Brontosaurus and other big dinosaurs.

1. These big dinosaurs did not have sharp teeth. What did they eat?

   _____

2. Why were swamps a good place for these big dinosaurs to live?

   _____

   _____

3. These big dinosaurs had small brains. Do you think they were smart? Why?

   _____

   _____

4. Name the three kinds of dinosaurs that lived in swamps.

   _____

   _____

Comprehension: Tyrannosaurus Rex

One of the biggest dinosaurs was Tyrannosaurus Rex (ty-ran-oh-saur-us recks). This dinosaur walked on its two big back legs. It had two small, short front legs. From the top of its head to the tip of its tail, Tyrannosaurus Rex measured 50 feet long. Its head was 4 feet long! Are you taller than this dinosaur's head? Tyrannosaurus was a meat eater. It had many small, sharp teeth. Its favorite meal was a smaller dinosaur that had a bill like a duck. This smaller dinosaur lived near water.

Directions: Answer these questions about Tyrannosaurus Rex.

1. What is the story about?

   _____

2. What size was this dinosaur?

   _____

   _____

3. When this dinosaur was hungry, what did it eat?

   _____

   _____

4. Where did this dinosaur find its favorite meal?

   _____

   _____

5. Why did this dinosaur need many sharp teeth?

   _____

   _____

Comprehension: Triceratops

Triceratops was one of the last dinosaurs to develop. It lived in the Cretaceous (kre-tay-shus) period of history. It was in this time that the dinosaurs became extinct. Triceratops means "three-horned lizard." It was a strong dinosaur and able to defend itself well since it lived during the same time period as Tyrannosaurus Rex.

Triceratops was a plant-eating dinosaur. Its body was 20 feet long, and its head, including the three horns and bony "frill," was another 6½ feet.

Directions: Answer these questions about Triceratops.

1. Dinosaurs became extinct during the _____ period of history.

2. What does **Triceratops** mean?

   _____

3. What information above tells you that Triceratops was able to defend itself?

   _____

   _____

Comprehension: Stegosaurus

The Stegosaurus was a well-equipped fighter. It was covered with large, bony plates and had a spiked tail. As you can probably imagine, this spiked tail was a very important part of its defense. This was another large dinosaur, the same size as Triceratops. It had four legs, but the two front legs were smaller than the two hind legs, and it had a very small head compared to its body. Have you ever seen a walnut? The brain of Stegosaurus was about the same size.

Stegosaurus was one of the many plant-eating dinosaurs. I guess you could call it a vegetarian (veg-e-tair-ee-un). Vegetarians only eat plants like vegetables, leaves and grass! Stegosaurus lived in the Jurassic period, the middle period of dinosaur history.

Directions: Answer these questions about Stegosaurus.

1. Write three things that are the same size as Stegosaurus' brain.

   1) _____ 2) _____ 3) _____

2. The _____ of this dinosaur was a very important part of its defense.

3. Which set of legs, the front legs or the hind ones, do you think the Stegosaurus

   used more?_____

   Why do you think so? _____

   _____

Recalling Details: Dinosaur Chart

Directions: Use the pages about Tyrannosaurus Rex, Stegosaurus and Triceratops to help you fill in the chart below.

	Period of History	What It Ate	Size
T-Rex			
Triceratops			
Stegosaurus			

Directions: Use the chart to answer these questions.

1. Did Triceratops and Stegosaurus live on Earth at the same time?

       Yes   No

2. Which dinosaur was the largest of the three?

_____

3. Which two of these dinosaurs were plant eaters?

   1) _____   2) _____

Comprehension: Cold-Blooded Animals

Like snakes, dinosaurs were cold-blooded. Cold-blooded animals cannot keep themselves warm. Because of this, dinosaurs were not very active when it was cold. In the early morning they did not move much. When the sun grew warm, the dinosaurs became active. When the sun went down in the evening, they slowed down again for the night. The sun warmed the dinosaurs and gave them the energy they needed to move about.

Directions: Answer these questions about dinosaurs.

1. Why were dinosaurs inactive when it was cold?

   _____

   _____

2. What time of day were the dinosaurs active?

   _____

   _____

3. What times of day were the dinosaurs not active?

   _____

   _____

4. Why did dinosaurs need the sun?

   _____

   _____

Comprehension: Sizes of Dinosaurs

There were many sizes of dinosaurs. Some were as small as dogs. Others were huge! The huge dinosaurs weighed 100,000 pounds. Some dinosaurs ate meat, including other dinosaurs. Some dinosaurs, like the Iguanodon, ate only plants. Meat-eating dinosaurs had sharp teeth. Plant-eating dinosaurs had flat teeth. If you had lived long ago, would you have gotten close enough to look at their teeth?

Directions: Answer these questions about dinosaurs.

1. What size were the small dinosaurs?

   _____

2. How much did the big dinosaurs weigh?

   _____

3. Name two things the different kinds of dinosaurs ate.

   1) _____ 2) _____

4. What kind of teeth did meat-eating dinosaurs have?

   _____

5. What kind of teeth did plant-eating dinosaurs have?

   _____

Comprehension: Dinosaur Fossils

Dinosaurs roamed the Earth for 125 million years. Can you imagine that much time? About 40 years ago, some people found fossils of dinosaur tracks in Connecticut. Fossils are rocks that hold the hardened bones, eggs and footprints of animals that lived long ago. The fossil tracks showed that many dinosaurs walked together in herds. The fossils showed more than 2,000 dinosaur tracks!

Directions: Answer these questions about fossils.

1. What did the people find in the fossils?

   _____

2. In what state were the fossils found?

   _____

3. How many tracks were in the fossils?

   _____

4. What did the tracks show?

   _____

5. How long did dinosaurs roam the Earth?

   _____

Main Idea: Dinosaur Models

Some people can build models of dinosaurs. The models are fakes, of course. But they are life-size and they look real! The people who build them must know the dinosaur inside and out. First, they build a skeleton. Then they cover it with fake "skin." Then they paint it. Some models have motors in them. The motors can make the dinosaur's head or tail move. Have you ever seen a life-size model of a dinosaur?

Directions: Answer these questions about dinosaur models.

1. Circle the main idea:

   Some models of dinosaurs have motors in them.

   Some people can build life-size models of dinosaurs that look real.

2. What do the motors in model dinosaurs do?

   _____

   _____

3. What is the first step in making a model dinosaur?

   _____

   _____

4. Why do dinosaur models look real?

   _____

   _____

Review

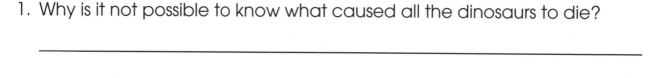

There are no dinosaurs alive today. They became extinct (ex-tinkt) millions of years ago. This was before people lived on Earth. When animals are extinct, they are gone forever. No one knows exactly why dinosaurs became extinct. Some scientists say that a disease may have killed them. Other scientists say a huge hot rock called a comet hit the Earth. The comet caused a big fire. The fire killed the dinosaurs' food. Still other scientists believe that the Earth grew very cold. The dinosaurs died because they could not keep warm. Many scientists have ideas, but no one can know for sure exactly what happened.

Directions: Answer these questions about dinosaurs becoming extinct.

1. Why is it not possible to know what caused all the dinosaurs to die?

   _____

   _____

2. Circle the main idea:

   The dinosaurs died when a comet hit the Earth and caused a big fire.

   There are many ideas about what killed the dinosaurs, but no one knows for sure.

3. What does **extinct** mean?

   _____

   _____

4. Who are the people with ideas about what happened to dinosaurs?

   _____

Name: _____

Comprehension: Kareem Abdul-Jabbar

Have you heard of a basketball star named Kareem Abdul-Jabbar? When he was born, Kareem's name was Lew Alcindor. He was named after his father. When he was in college, Kareem changed his religion from Christianity to Islam. That was when he took the Muslim name of Kareem Abdul-Jabbar.

Directions: Answer these questions about Kareem Abdul-Jabbar.

1. What was Kareem Abdul-Jabbar's name when he was born?

_____

2. Who was Kareem named after?

_____

3. When did Kareem become a Muslim?

_____

4. When did he change his name to Kareem Abdul-Jabbar?

_____

Grade 3 - Comprehensive Curriculum

Name: _____

Comprehension: Kareem Abdul-Jabbar

Kareem Abdul-Jabbar grew up to be more than 7 feet tall! Kareem's father and mother were both very tall. When he was 9 years old, Kareem was already 5 feet 4 inches tall. Kareem was raised in New York City. He went to Power Memorial High School and played basketball on that team. He went to college at UCLA. He played basketball in college, too. At UCLA, Kareem's team lost only two games in 3 years! After college, Kareem made his living playing basketball.

Directions: Answer these questions about Kareem Abdul-Jabbar.

1. Who is the story about?

   _____

2. For what is this athlete famous?

   _____

3. When did Kareem reach the height of 5 feet 4 inches?

   _____

4. Where did Kareem go to college?

   _____

5. Why did Kareem grow so tall?

   _____

   _____

6. How did Kareem make his living?

   _____

   _____

Name: _____

Comprehension: Michael Jordan

Michael Jordan was born February 17, 1963, in Brooklyn, New York. His family moved to North Carolina when he was just a baby. As a young boy, his favorite sport was baseball, but he soon found that he could play basketball as well. At age 17, he began to show people just how talented he really was.

Throughout his basketball career, Michael Jordan has won many scoring titles. Many boys and girls look up to Michael Jordan as their hero. Did you know he had a hero, too, when he was growing up? He looked up to his older brother, Larry.

Michael Jordan, a basketball superstar, is not just a star on the basketball court. He also works hard to raise money for many children's charities. He encourages children to develop their talents by practice, practice, practice!

Directions: Answer these questions about Michael Jordan.

1. Michael says children can develop their talents by lots of _____.

2. Who was Michael's hero when he was growing up?

   _____

3. Where was Michael Jordan born?

   _____

4. At first, he played _____ instead of basketball.

Comprehension: Mary Lou Retton

Mary Lou Retton became the first U.S. woman to win Olympic gold in gymnastics. She accomplished this at the 1984 Olympics held in Los Angeles, when she was 16 years old. "Small but mighty" would certainly describe this gymnast.

She was the youngest of five children—all good athletes. She grew up in Fairmont, West Virginia, and began her gymnastic training at the age of 7.

Most women gymnasts are graceful, but Mary Lou helped open up the field of gymnastics to strong, athletic women. Mary Lou was 4 feet 10 inches tall and weighed a mere 95 pounds!

Directions: Answer these questions about Mary Lou Retton.

1. Circle the main idea:

    Mary Lou loved performing.

    Mary Lou is a famous Olympic gymnast.

2. She was born in _____.

3. At what age did she begin her gymnastics training? _____

4. Mary Lou won a gold medal when she was _____ years old.

Comprehension: Troy Aikman

Troy Aikman, Dallas Cowboy, was born on November 21, 1966. As a young boy, he enjoyed doing the usual things, like fishing or hunting with his dad. He also loved playing sports with his friends.

Troy Aikman knows a lot about change. When he was a young boy of 12 living in a city, he knew he wanted to be a baseball player. But when his family moved to a 172-acre ranch near Henryetta, Oklahoma, he felt like he would have to give up that dream. He soon learned that the people of Oklahoma loved football more than any other sport. Troy soon learned to love football, too. And he learned he was very good at it.

You can be a champion, too, in spite of changes in your life. You just have to be willing to make those changes work for you!

Directions: Answer these questions about Troy Aikman.

1. Why did Troy Aikman change from playing baseball to playing football?

_____

2. How old was he when his family moved?

_____

3. For what NFL team does he play?

_____

4. How can changes in your life be a good thing?

_____

_____

Comprehension: Babe Ruth

A great baseball champion, Babe Ruth, was born in Baltimore, Maryland, on February 6, 1895. He could hit a ball farther than most major-league players when he was only 13 years old. He did not have a very good home life, so he spent most of his early years living in a school for boys. He played baseball whenever he could, so he became very good at it.

George Ruth (his real name) was given the nickname, Babe, when he was 19 years old. A minor-league team manager, Jack Dunn, became his legal guardian. The other players on the team called him "Jack's Babe." Later, it was shortened to "Babe."

Directions: Answer these questions about Babe Ruth.

1. When was Babe Ruth born?

_____

2. Where was he born?

_____

3. What was Babe's original nickname?

_____

4. How old was Babe when he got his nickname?

_____

Name: _____

Comprehension: Babe Ruth

Babe Ruth began playing as a pitcher for the Boston Red Sox in 1915. He switched to the outfield in 1918 because his manager wanted him to bat more often. Everyone soon found out what a good hitter he was!

Yankee Stadium became known as "The House That Ruth Built" because he was such a popular player and so many people came to the baseball games. New York City was able to have a new baseball stadium because he was so popular. This left-handed baseball superstar drew large crowds to ballparks wherever his team played. Even if he didn't hit a home run, the fans were just excited to have the chance to see him.

Directions: Answer these questions about Babe Ruth.

1. Does the story let you know whether Babe is still living? _____

   How old would he be if he were still alive?

   _____

2. What is another name for Yankee Stadium?

   _____

3. In 1915, he began playing for the _____ as a pitcher.

4. Why did his manager switch him to the outfield?

   _____

   _____

Recalling Details: The Home Run Race

The summer of 1998 was exciting for the sport of baseball. Even if you were not a big fan of this sport, you couldn't help but hear about two great sluggers—Mark McGwire and Sammy Sosa. By mid-summer, many baseball fans realized that several men were getting close to the home run record. The record of 61 home runs in a single season had been set by Roger Maris 37 years before!

On Tuesday, September 8, 1998, that record was broken. Mark McGwire, who plays for the St. Louis Cardinals, hit his 62nd home run in a game with the Chicago Cubs.

To make the home run race more interesting, a player for the Chicago Cubs, Sammy Sosa, was also close to breaking the 61 home run record. On Sunday, September 13, Sammy Sosa also hit his 62nd home run.

Directions: Write the letter of the correct answer in the blanks.

A. Sept. 13   B. McGwire   C. 37   D. Maris   E. Chicago Cubs

1. Had the home run record _____

2. First to hit 62 home runs _____

3. Sosa broke the home run record _____

4. Years record had stood _____

5. Sosa's team _____

Recalling Details: Venn Diagram

A **Venn diagram** is a diagram used to compare two things. The Venn diagram below is comparing a cat and a dog.

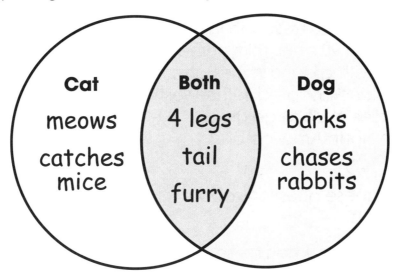

Directions: Use **The Home Run Race** (page 116) to complete the Venn diagram comparing Mark McGwire and Sammy Sosa.

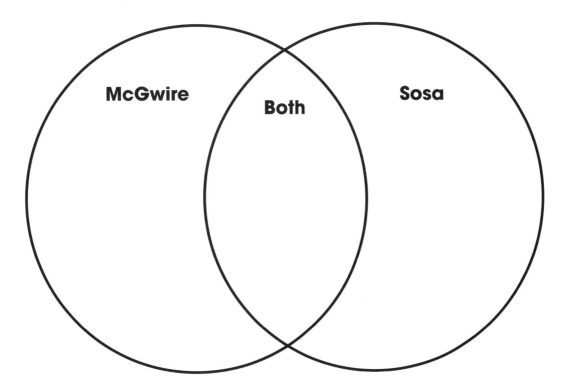

Comprehension: Christopher Columbus

What do you know about Christopher Columbus? He was a famous sailor and explorer. Columbus was 41 years old when he sailed from southern Spain on August 3, 1492, with three ships. On them was a crew of 90 men. Thirty-three days later, he landed on Watling Island in the Bahamas. The Bahamas are islands located in the West Indies. The West Indies are a large group of islands between North America and South America.

Directions: Answer these questions about Christopher Columbus.

1. How old was Columbus when he set sail from southern Spain?

   _____

2. How many ships did he take?

   _____

3. How many men were with him?

   _____

4. How long did it take him to reach land?

   _____

5. Where did Columbus land?

   _____

6. What are the West Indies?

   _____

Comprehension: Christopher Columbus

Columbus was an explorer. He wanted to find out what the rest of the world looked like. He also wanted to make money! He would sail to distant islands and trade with the people there. He would buy their silks, spices and gold. Then he would sell these things in Spain. In Spain, people would pay high prices for them. Columbus got the queen of Spain to approve his plan. She would pay for his ships and his crew. He would keep 10 percent of the value of the goods he brought back. She would take the rest. Columbus and the queen had a business deal.

Directions: Answer these questions about Christopher Columbus.

1. Which statement is correct?

   Columbus and the queen of Spain were friends.

   Columbus and the queen of Spain were business partners.

2. Write two reasons why Columbus was an explorer.

   1) _____

   2) _____

3. What was Columbus' business deal with the queen of Spain?

   1) Columbus would get _____

   _____.

   2) In return for paying his expenses, the queen would get

   _____

   _____.

Comprehension: Lewis and Clark

In 1801, President Thomas Jefferson chose an army officer named Meriwether Lewis to lead an expedition through our country's "new frontier." He knew Lewis would not be able to make the journey by himself, so he chose William Clark to travel with him. The two men had known each other in the army. They decided to be co-leaders of the expedition.

The two men and a group of about 45 others made the trip from the state of Missouri, across the Rocky Mountains all the way to the Pacific Coast. They were careful in choosing the men who would travel with them. They wanted men who were strong and knew a lot about the wilderness. It was also important that they knew some of the Native American languages.

Directions: Answer these questions about Lewis and Clark.

1. Which president wanted an expedition through the "new frontier"?

   _____

2. Look at a United States map or a globe. In what direction did Lewis and Clark travel? (Circle one.)

   north   south   east   west

3. About how many people made up the entire expedition, including Lewis and Clark?

   _____

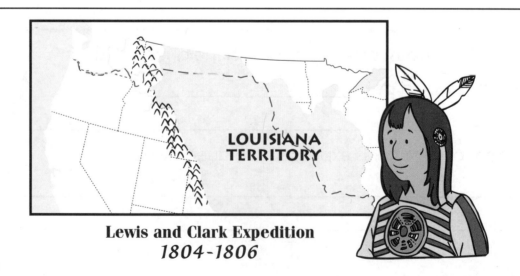

Lewis and Clark Expedition
1804-1806

Comprehension: Lewis and Clark

The two explorers and their men began their trip in 1804. They had camped all winter across the river from St. Louis, Missouri. While camping, they built a special boat they would need for the first part of their trip. This boat, called a keelboat, was 55 feet long. It could be rowed or sailed. If the men needed to use it like a raft, they could do that, too.

Besides flour, salt and cornmeal, they took along medicines and weapons. They knew they would meet Native Americans as they traveled to the "new frontier," so they also brought colored beads and other small gifts to give to them.

Directions: Answer these questions about Lewis and Clark.

1. Lewis, Clark and the others began their trip in _____.

2. What is the name of the special boat that they built for their trip?

_____

3. Why did they take along small gifts and colored beads?

_____

_____

Comprehension: Boats for the Expedition

The men were not able to take the keelboat the whole way on their trip. The Missouri River became too narrow for this boat, so Lewis and Clark had to send some of the men back to St. Louis with it. More canoes were built with the help of some friendly Native Americans. These were used for travel since they no longer had the keelboat.

Directions: Answer these questions about Lewis and Clark's boats.

1. Why couldn't Lewis and Clark use the keelboat for the entire trip?

   _____

   _____

2. What did they do with it?

   _____

3. Why did they need to build more canoes?

   _____

   _____

Find a picture of a keelboat or canoe. Draw a picture of it below.

Comprehension: Hardships of the Expedition

Lewis and Clark and their men had seen large grizzly bears as they traveled through the West. They were thankful they had their weapons with them. But meeting the grizzlies was not the hardest part of the journey. It was also hard to cross the Rocky Mountains. It took the explorers and their "party" a month to make this part of their trip. The friendly Shoshone tribe was very helpful in telling them how they could cross the mountains.

There were many reasons why this part of the trip was difficult. The steep, narrow pathways sometimes caused the horses to fall over the cliffs to their deaths. Many times the men had to lead the horses. There were also fewer wild animals for the men to hunt for food.

Directions: Answer these questions about the hardships of the expedition.

1. What was the hardest part of the trip?

_____

2. Lewis and Clark got help from which friendly Native American tribe?

_____

3. What word in the story means "a group of people traveling together"?

_____

4. What caused some of the horses to fall to their deaths?

_____

Name: _____

Comprehension: End of the Journey

New canoes had to be built for the last part of the trip. The men traveled along the Clearwater River to get to the Columbia River, and finally the Pacific Coast. They reached the Northwest Coast in November 1805.

President Jefferson was glad he had chosen Lewis and Clark to lead the expedition. They were able to make the trip successfully and could now claim the Oregon region for the United States.

Directions: Answer these questions about Lewis and Clark's expedition.

1. What two rivers did Lewis and Clark travel on the last part of their journey?

   1) _____

   2) _____

2. When did they reach the Pacific Coast? _____

3. What season of the year is that? _____

4. Circle the words below that would describe the journey:

   dangerous   quick   not planned   successful

5. This expedition allowed the United States to claim _____

   _____.

Comprehension: George Washington

George Washington was the first president of the United States. He was born in Wakefield, Virginia, on February 22, 1732. His father was a wealthy Virginia planter. As he grew up, George Washington became interested in surveying and farming. When George was only 11 years old, his father died. George moved in with his older brother, Lawrence.

Even if he had not become the country's first president, he would have been well known because of his strong military leadership. Washington was a good leader because of his patience and his ability to survive hardships.

George Washington became president in 1789. At that time there were only 11 states in the United States. He served two terms (4 years each) as our first president. After his second term, he returned to a former home at Mt. Vernon. He died there in 1799 after catching a cold while riding around his farm in the wind and snow.

Directions: Answer these questions about George Washington.

1. In what year did George Washington become president? _____

2. Besides being our country's first president, how else did he serve our country?

_____

_____

3. Where was he born?

_____

Comprehension: Robin Hood

Long ago in England there lived a man named Robin Hood. Robin lived with a group of other men in the woods. These woods were called Sherwood Forest.

Robin Hood was a thief—a different kind of thief. He stole from the rich and gave what he stole to the poor. Poor people did not need to worry about going into Sherwood Forest. In fact, Robin Hood often gave them money. Rich people were told to beware. If you were rich, would you stay out of Sherwood Forest?

Directions: Answer these questions about Robin Hood.

1. What was the name of the woods where Robin Hood lived?

   _____

2. What did Robin Hood do for a living?

   _____

3. What was different about Robin Hood?

   _____

4. Did poor people worry about going into Sherwood Forest? Why or why not?

   _____

5. Do you think rich people worried about going into Sherwood Forest? Why?

   _____

Making Inferences: Robin Hood and the King

Everyone in England knew about Robin Hood. The king was mad! He did not want a thief to be a hero. He sent his men to Sherwood Forest to catch Robin Hood. But they could not catch him. Robin Hood outsmarted the king's men every time!

One day, Robin Hood sent a message to the king. The message said, "Come with five brave men. We will see who is stronger." The king decided to fool Robin Hood. He wanted to see if what people said about Robin Hood was true. The king dressed as a monk. A monk is a poor man who serves God. Then he went to Sherwood Forest to see Robin Hood.

Directions: Circle the correct answer to these questions about the king's meeting with Robin Hood.

1. If the stories about Robin Hood were true, what happened when the king met Robin Hood?

   Robin Hood robbed the king and took all his money.

   Robin Hood helped the king because he thought he was a poor man.

2. Why didn't the king want Robin Hood to know who he was?

   He was afraid of Robin Hood.

   He wanted to find out what Robin Hood was really like.

3. Why couldn't the king's men find Robin Hood?

   Robin Hood outsmarted them.

   They didn't look in Sherwood Forest.

Making Inferences: Robin Hood and the King

The king liked Robin Hood. He said, "Here is a man who likes a good joke." He told Robin Hood who he really was. Robin Hood was not mad. He laughed and laughed. The king invited Robin Hood to come and live in the castle. The castle was 20 miles away. Robin had to walk south, cross a river and make two left turns to get there. He stayed inside the castle grounds for a year and a day.

Then Robin grew restless and asked the king for permission to leave. The king did not want him to go. He said Robin Hood could visit Sherwood Forest for only one week. Robin said he missed his men but promised to return. The king knew Robin Hood never broke his promises.

Directions: Answer these questions about Robin Hood and the king.

1. Do you think Robin Hood returned to the castle? _____

2. Why do you think Robin Hood laughed when the king told him the truth?

   _____

3. Give directions from Sherwood Forest to the king's castle.

   _____

   _____

   _____

4. Circle the main idea:

   The king liked Robin Hood, but Robin missed his life in Sherwood Forest.

   Robin Hood thought the castle was boring.

Comprehension: Benjamin Franklin

Benjamin Franklin was born in Boston, Massachusetts, on January 17, 1706. Even though he only attended school to age 10, he worked hard to improve his mind and character. He taught himself several foreign languages and learned many skills that would later be a great help to him.

Ben Franklin played a very important part in our history. One of his many accomplishments was as a printer. He was a helper (apprentice) to his half-brother, James, and later moved to the city of Philadelphia where he worked in another print shop.

Another skill that he developed was writing. He wrote and published Poor Richard's Almanac in December 1732. Franklin was also a diplomat. He served our country in many ways, both in the United States and in Europe. As an inventor he experimented with electricity. Have you heard about the kite and key experiment? Benjamin Franklin was able to prove that lightning has an electrical discharge.

Directions: Answer these questions about Benjamin Franklin.

1. Circle the main idea:

    Benjamin Franklin was a very important part of our history.

    Benjamin Franklin wrote Poor Richard's Almanac.

    He flew a kite with a key on the string.

2. How old was Ben Franklin when he left school? _____

3. Write three of Ben Franklin's accomplishments.

    1) _____

    2) _____

    3) _____

Comprehension: Morning Glories

Have you ever seen morning glories? They begin to bloom in mid-May. Morning glory flowers grow on vines. They trail over the ground. Sometimes the vines twine over other plants. They will grow over walls and fences. The vines on morning glory plants can grow to be 10 feet long! Morning glory flowers are bell-shaped. The flowers are white, pink or blue. There are more than 200 different kinds of morning glory flowers!

Directions: Answer these questions about morning glories.

1. When do morning glories begin to bloom?

   _____

2. Morning glories grow on

   stems.

   vines.

3. What shape are morning glory flowers?

   _____

4. How many different kinds of morning glory flowers are there?

   _____

Following Directions: How Plants Get Food

Every living thing needs food. Did you ever wonder how plants get food? They do not sit down and eat a bowl of soup! Plants get their food from the soil and from water. To see how, cut off some stalks of celery. Put the stalks in a clear glass. Fill the glass half full of water. Add a few drops of red food coloring to the water. Leave it overnight. The next day you will see that parts of the celery have turned red! The red lines show how the celery "sucked up" water.

Directions: Answer these questions about how plants get food.

1. Name two ways plants get food.

   1) _____

   2) _____

2. Complete the four steps for using celery to see how plants get food.

   1) Cut off some stalks of _____.

   2) Put the stalks in _____.

   3) Fill the glass _____.

   4) Add a few drops of _____.

3. What do the red lines in the celery show?

   _____

   _____

Making Inferences: Fig Marigolds

Fig marigolds are beautiful! The flowers stay closed unless the light is bright. These flowers are also called by another name—the "mid-day flower." Mid-day flowers have very long leaves. The leaves are as long as your finger!

There is something else unusual about mid-day flowers. They change color. When the flowers bloom, they are light yellow. After two or three days, they turn pink.

Mid-day flowers grow in California and South America where it is hot. They do not grow in other parts of the United States.

Directions: Answer these questions about fig marigolds.

1. Why do you think fig marigolds are also called mid-day flowers?

   _____

   _____

2. How long are the leaves of the mid-day flower?

   _____

3. Why do you think mid-day flowers do not grow all over the United States?

   _____

   _____

Main Idea: Unusual Plants

Do you have a cat? Do you have catnip growing around your home? If you don't know, your cat probably does. Cats love the catnip plant and can be seen rolling around in it. Some cat toys have catnip inside them because cats love it so much.

People can enjoy catnip, too. Some people make catnip tea with the leaves of the plant. It is like the mint with which people make tea.

Another refreshing drink can be made with the berries of the sumac bush or tree. Native Americans would pick the red berries, crush them and add water to make a thirst-quenching drink. The berries were sour, but they must have believed that the cool, tart drink was refreshing. Does this remind you of lemonade?

Directions: Answer these questions about unusual plants.

1. What is the main idea of the first two paragraphs above?

   _____

   _____

2. Write two ways cats show that they love catnip.

   1) _____

   2) _____

3. How can people use catnip?

   _____

   _____

Comprehension: Dangerous Plants

You may have been warned about some plants. Poison ivy and poison oak are plants we usually learn about at an early age. The itching and burning some people get from touching or even being around these plants is enough to make them extra careful. Have you ever walked through a field and felt like you had been stung? You probably touched the stinging nettle. This plant with jagged edges is a good one to avoid, too.

Other plants can be more dangerous. You should not pick and eat any berries, seeds or nuts without first checking to make sure they are safe. You could get very sick or even die if you ate from one of these poisonous plants. Rhubarb and cherries are two common pie-making ingredients, but never eat the leaves of the rhubarb plant. The cherry leaves and branches have poison in them.

Directions: Answer these questions about dangerous plants.

1. You should not pick and eat any _____, _____

   or _____ without first making sure they are safe.

2. _____ and _____ might make your skin

   itch and burn.

3. What would happen if you touched a stinging nettle plant?

   _____

   _____

Comprehension: Rainforests

The soil in rainforests is very dark and rich. The trees and plants that grow there are very green. People who have seen one say a rainforest is "the greenest place on Earth." Why? Because it rains a lot. With so much rain, the plants stay very green. The earth stays very wet. Rainforests cover only 6 percent of the Earth. But they are home to 66 percent of all the different kinds of plants and animals on Earth! Today, rainforests are threatened by such things as acid rain from factory smoke emissions around the world and from farm expansion. Farmers living near rainforests cut down many trees each year to clear the land for farming. I wish I could see a rainforest. Do you?

Directions: Answer these questions about rainforests.

1. What do the plants and trees in a rainforest look like?

   _____

2. What is the soil like in a rainforest?

   _____

3. How much of the Earth is covered by rainforests?

   _____

4. What percentage of the Earth's plants and animals live there?

   _____

Comprehension: The Rainforest Lizard

Many strange animals live in the rainforest. One kind of strange animal is a very large lizard. This lizard grows as large as a dog! It has scales on its skin. It has a very wide mouth. It has spikes sticking out of the top of its head. It looks scary, but don't be afraid! This lizard eats mostly weeds. This lizard does not look very tasty, but other animals think it tastes good. Snakes eat these lizards. So do certain birds. Some people in the rainforest eat them, too! Would you like to eat a lizard for lunch?

Directions: Answer these questions about the rainforest lizard.

1. What is the size of this rainforest lizard?

   _____

2. Where do its scales grow?

   _____

3. Which kind of food does the lizard eat?

   _____

4. Who likes to eat these lizards?

   _____

5. Would you like to see this lizard?

   _____

Comprehension: The Sloth

The sloth spends most of its life in the trees of the rainforest. The three-toed sloth, for example, is usually hanging around, using its claws to keep it there. Because it is in the trees so much, it has trouble moving on the ground. Certainly it could be caught easily by other animals of the rainforest if it was being chased. The sloth is a very slow-moving animal. Do you have any idea what the sloth eats? The sloth eats mostly leaves it finds in the treetops.

Have you ever seen a three- or two-toed sloth? If you see one in a zoo, you don't have to get close enough to count the toes. You can tell these two "cousins" apart in a different way—the three-toed sloth has some green mixed in with its fur because of the algae it gets from the trees.

Directions: Answer these questions about the sloth.

1. How does the three-toed sloth hang around the rainforest?

    a. by its tail, like a monkey

    b. by its claws, or toes

2. The main diet of the sloth is _____.

3. Why does the sloth have trouble moving around on the ground?

    _____

    _____

Comprehension: The Kinkajou

If you have ever seen a raccoon holding its food by its "hands" and carefully eating it, you would have an idea of how the kinkajou (king-kuh-joo) eats. This animal of the rainforest is a "cousin" of the raccoon. Unlike its North American cousin, though, it is a golden-brown color.

The kinkajou's head and body are 17 to 22 inches long. The long tail of the kinkajou comes in handy for hanging around its neighborhood! If you do some quick mental math you can get a good idea of its size. It weighs very little—about 5 pounds. (You may have a 5-pound bag of sugar or flour in your kitchen to help you get an idea of the kinkajou's weight.)

This rainforest animal eats a variety of things. It enjoys nectar from the many rainforest flowers, insects, fruit, honey, birds and other small animals. Because it lives mostly in the trees, the kinkajou has a ready supply of food.

Directions: Answer these questions about the kinkajou.

1. The kinkajou is a "cousin" to the _____.

2. Do you weigh more or less than the kinkajou? _____

3. Write three things the kinkajou eats.

   1) _____

   2) _____

   3) _____

Comprehension: The Jaguar

The jaguar weighs between 100 and 250 pounds. It can be as long as 6 feet! This is not your ordinary house cat!

One strange feature of the jaguar is its living arrangements. The jaguar has its own territory. No other jaguar lives in its "home range." It would be very unusual for one jaguar to meet another in the rainforest. One way they mark their territory is by scratching trees.

Have you ever seen your pet cat hide in the grass and carefully and quietly sneak up on an unsuspecting grasshopper or mouse? Like its gentler, smaller "cousin," the jaguar stalks its prey in the high grass. It likes to eat small animals, such as rodents, but can attack and kill larger animals such as tapirs, deer and cattle. It is good at catching fish as well.

Directions: Answer these questions about the jaguar.

1. The jaguar lives:

    a. in large groups

    b. alone

    c. under water

2. This large cat marks its territory by:

    a. black marker

    b. roaring

    c. scratching trees

3. What does the jaguar eat?

    _____

4. How much does it weigh?

    _____

Comprehension: The Toucan

One interesting bird of the rainforest is the toucan. This bird has a very large bill which is shaped like a canoe. Sometimes the toucan's bill can be as large as its body! The toucan's bill is colorful and hard, but flexible. You can also tell a toucan by its colorful feathers. They are mostly blue or black but also include red, yellow and orange.

The heavy growth in the rainforest provides protective covering for this colorful bird. The toucan lives in the layer of the rainforest called the "canopy." Here, high in the trees, it can use its large, hooked bill to find the berries and fruits that it loves to eat.

Directions: Answer these questions about the toucan.

1. Circle three characteristics of the toucan's bill.

   colorful   large

   brittle   pointed

   small   soft

   hooked

2. In what layer of the rainforest does the toucan live?

   _____

3. What does the toucan love to eat?

   1) _____

   2) _____

4. What colors are the toucan's feathers?

   _____

Comprehension: Visiting the Rainforest

Many people travel to the rainforest each year. Some go by car, some go by train and some go by school bus! You don't even need a passport—the only thing you need is a field-trip permission slip.

If you are lucky enough to live in the Cleveland, Ohio area, you might get to take a class trip to the rainforest there. It is next to the Cleveland Zoo. This "rainforest" is a building that contains all the sights, sounds, smells and temperatures of the real rainforest. You will get to see many of the animals, big and small, that you could see if you went to Central or South America. The plants that grow there also grow in the rainforest. It is an interesting way to get an idea of what life is like in that part of the world!

Directions: Answer these questions about visiting the "rainforest."

1. If you lived in northern Ohio, name three ways you could get to the

   "rainforest." _____

2. In this "rainforest" you can see _____ and _____
   that are found in the real rainforest.

3. Do you think it would be hot or cold in this "rainforest" building?

   hot   cold

4. The real rainforest is located in both _____

   and _____.

Grade 3 - Comprehensive Curriculum

Name: _____

Making Inferences: Unusual Flowers

You can grow many kinds of flowers in a garden. Here are the names of some—trumpet vine, pitcher plant and bird-of-paradise. The flowers that grow on these plants form seeds. The seeds can be used to grow new plants. The bird-of-paradise looks as if it has wings! The pitcher plant is very strange. It eats insects! The trumpet vine grows very long. It trails around fences and other plants. These plants are very different. Together, they make a pretty flower garden.

Bird of Paradise

Directions: Answer these questions about unusual flowers.

1. What do you think a pitcher plant looks like?

   _____

2. What do you think a trumpet vine looks like?

   _____

3. Name two of the three plants that grow seeds in their flowers.

   1) _____

   2) _____

4. What can the seeds be used for?

   _____

5. What could you plant in a garden to get rid of insects?

   _____

Name: _____

Making Inferences: State Bird — Arizona

Have you ever traveled through Arizona or other southwestern states of the United States? One type of plant you may have seen is the cactus. This plant and other desert thickets are homes to the cactus wren, the state bird of Arizona. It is interesting how this bird (which is the size of a robin) can roost on this prickly plant and keep from getting stuck on the sharp spines. The cactus wren builds its nest on top of these thorny desert plants.

The cactus wren's "song" is not a beautiful, musical sound. Instead, it is compared to the grating sound of machinery. You can also identify the bird by its coloring. It has white spots on its outer tail feathers and white eyebrows. The crown (head) of the cactus wren is a rusty color.

Directions: Answer these questions about the cactus wren.

1. In what part of the United States would you find the cactus wren?

   _____

2. What does **prickly** mean?

   a. soft   b. green   c. having sharp points

3. Do you think you would like to hear the "song" of the cactus wren? Why or why not?

   _____

   _____

   _____

Comprehension: State Bird — Louisiana

Along the sandy coastline of Louisiana you may see the brown pelican. It is not hard to identify this large bird with a throat pouch. When it is young, the brown pelican has a dark-brown body and head. If you see this bird with a brown body and a white head, you are looking at an adult.

Do you know what the brown pelican uses its large throat pouch for? If you said the pouch is used for carrying the fish it catches, you would be wrong. Many people think that is how the pouch is used, but the pouch is really used for separating the fish from the water. Just imagine how much water the brown pelican can scoop up as it fishes!

Directions: Answer these questions about the brown pelican.

1. The brown pelican is found mostly along the _____ of Louisiana.

2. How does it catch its food?

   _____

   _____

3. How is a young pelican's coloring different from the adult pelican?

   _____

   _____

   _____

4. What does **pouch** mean?

   a. catch   b. pocket   c. fish

Comprehension: State Bird — Maine

The chickadee may visit your bird feeder on a regular basis if you live in Maine. This bird seems to have a feeding schedule so it doesn't miss a meal! The chickadee can be tamed to eat right out of your hand. If this bird sees some insect eggs on a tree limb, it even will hang upside down to get at this treat.

The chickadee lives in forests and open woodlands throughout most of the year, but when winter comes, it moves into areas populated by people. It is colored gray with a black cap and white on its underside and cheeks.

The chickadee lives in the northern half of the United States and in southern and western Canada. The western part of Alaska is also home to this curious and tame little bird.

Directions: Answer these questions about the chickadee.

1. What does **curious** mean?

   a. underside   c. tame

   b. questioning   d. schedule

2. What does the chickadee do when winter comes?

   _____

   _____

3. One of the chickadee's favorite treats is _____.

4. Where does the chickadee live?

   _____

   _____

   _____

Comprehension: State Bird — Ohio

The cardinal is the state bird of Ohio. You probably know that the cardinal is red, but do you know how this bright red bird (males are red; females are brown with some red) got its name? Its name came from the bright red robes of the Roman Catholic cardinals.

Cardinals live in gardens as well as brushy swamps, thickets and the edges of woodlands. This bird can be found, year-round, in the eastern half of the United States. Some parts of southern California and Arizona are also home to this bird.

If you have a bird feeder, you have probably seen a cardinal there. Its main diet is seeds, but it also sometimes eats insects. The song of the cardinal can be heard throughout the year, so you don't have to wait for the warmer weather of spring.

Directions: Answer these questions about the cardinal.

1. Which paragraph tells you where the cardinal lives?

    a. paragraph 1

    b. paragraph 2

    c. paragraph 3

2. What do cardinals eat?

    _____

3. How did this bird get its name?

    _____

    _____

4. Which is red in color, the male or female cardinal?

    _____

Main Idea: Hawks

Hawks are birds of prey. They "prey upon" birds and animals. This means they kill other animals and eat them. The hawk has long pointed wings. It uses them to soar through the air as it looks for prey. It looks at the ground while it soars.

When it sees an animal or bird to eat, the hawk swoops down. It grabs the animal in its beak and and claws then carries it off and eats it. The hawk eats birds, rats, ground squirrels and other pests.

Directions: Answer these questions about hawks.

1. Circle the main idea:

   Hawks are mean because they swoop down from the sky and eat animals and birds.

   Hawks are helpful because they eat sick birds, rats, ground squirrels and other pests.

2. What kind of wings does a hawk have?

   _____

3. How does the hawk pick up its prey?

   _____

4. What does "prey upon" mean?

   _____

Comprehension: Birds' Homing Instinct

What is instinct (in-stinkt)? Instinct is knowing how to do something without being told how. Animals have instincts. Birds have an amazing instinct. It is called the "homing instinct." The homing instinct is birds' inner urge to find their way somewhere. When birds fly south in the winter, how do they know where to go? How do they know how to get there? When they return in the spring, what makes them return to the same place they left? It is birds' homing instinct. People do not have a homing instinct. That is why we get lost so often!

Directions: Answer these questions about birds' homing instinct.

1. What word means knowing how to do something without being told?

   _____

2. What is birds' inner urge to find their way somewhere called?

   _____

3. Which direction do birds fly in the winter?

   _____

4. Do people have a homing instinct?

   _____

5. When do birds return home?

   _____

Comprehension: Pet Crickets

Did you know that some people keep crickets as pets? These people always keep two crickets together. That way, the crickets do not get lonely!

Crickets are kept in a flowerpot filled with dirt. The dirt helps the crickets feel at home. They are used to being outside. Over the flowerpot is a covering that lets air inside. It also keeps the crickets in! Some people use a small net; others use cheesecloth. They make sure there is room under the covering for crickets to hop!

Pet crickets like to eat bread and lettuce. They also like raw hamburger meat. Would you like to have a pet cricket?

Directions: Answer these questions about pet crickets.

1. Where do pet crickets live?

   _____

2. Why should you put dirt in with the crickets?

   _____

3. What is placed over the flowerpot?

   _____

4. Write three things pet crickets like to eat. _____

   _____

   _____

Making Inferences: Pussy Willow Poem

Directions: Read the poem about the pussy willow plant. Then answer the questions.

I have a little pussy,
Her coat is silver gray.
She's in a great wide meadow,
She never runs away.
She'll always be a pussy,
She'll never be a cat.
'Cause she's a pussy willow!
What do you think of that?

1. Why does a pussy willow never run away?

   _____

2. Why will this pussy never grow to be a cat?

   _____

3. Really, what is the "coat of silver gray"?

   _____

Comprehension: Our Solar System

There are nine planets in our solar system. All of them circle the Sun. The planet closest to the Sun is named Mercury. The Romans said Mercury was the messenger of the gods. The second planet from the Sun is named Venus. Venus shines the brightest. Venus was the Roman goddess of beauty. Earth is the third planet from the Sun. It is about the same size as Venus. After Earth is Mars, which is named after the Roman god of war. The other five planets are Jupiter, Saturn, Uranus, Neptune and Pluto. They, too, are named after Roman gods.

Directions: Answer these questions about our solar system.

1. How many planets are in our solar system?

   _____

2. What do the planets circle?

   _____

3. What are the planets named after?

   _____

4. Which planet is closest to the Sun?

   _____

5. Which planet is about the same size as Earth?

   _____

6. Which planet comes after Earth in the solar system?

   _____

Name: _____

Comprehension: Mercury

In 1974, for the first time, a U.S. spacecraft passed within 400 miles of the planet Mercury. The name of the spacecraft was Mariner 10. There were no people on the spacecraft, but there were cameras that could take clear pictures from a long distance. What the pictures showed was interesting. They showed that Mercury's surface was a lot like the surface of the Moon. The surface of Mercury is filled with huge holes called craters. A layer of fine dust covers Mercury. This, too, is like the dust on the Moon. There is no life on either Mercury or the Moon.

Directions: Answer these questions about Mercury.

1. What was the name of the spacecraft that went near Mercury?

   _____

2. What was on the spacecraft?

   _____

3. Write two ways that Mercury is like the Moon.

   1) _____

   2) _____

4. Is there life on Mercury?

   _____

Main Idea: Venus

For many years, no one knew much about Venus. When people looked through telescopes, they could not see past Venus' clouds. Long ago, people thought the clouds covered living things. Spacecraft radar has shown this is not true. Venus is too hot for life to exist. The temperature on Venus is about 900 degrees! Remember how hot you were the last time it was 90 degrees? Now imagine it being 10 times hotter. Nothing could exist in that heat. It is also very dry on Venus. For life to exist, water must be present. Because of the heat and dryness, we know there are no people, plants or other life on Venus.

Directions: Answer these questions about Venus.

1. Circle the main idea:

   We cannot see past Venus' clouds to know what the planet is like.

   Spacecraft radar shows it is too hot and dry for life to exist on Venus.

2. What is the temperature on Venus? _____

3. This temperature is how many times hotter than a hot day on Earth?

   6 times hotter

   10 times hotter

4. In the past, why did people think life might exist on Venus?

   _____

   _____

Comprehension: Earth

One planet in our solar system certainly supports life—Earth. Our planet is the third planet from the Sun and takes 365 days, or 1 year, to orbit the Sun. This rotation makes it possible for most of our planet to have four seasons—winter, spring, summer and fall.

Besides being able to support life, our planet is unique in another way—Earth is 75% covered by water. No other planet has that much, if any, liquid on its surface. This liquid and its evaporation help provide the cloud cover and our climate patterns.

Earth has one natural satellite—the Moon. Scientists and other experts all over the world have created and sent into orbit other satellites used for a variety of purposes—communication, weather forecasting, and so on.

Directions: Answer these questions about Earth.

1. How much of Earth is covered by water? _____

2. The Moon is a _____ of Earth.

3. How long does it take Earth to orbit the Sun? _____

4. How does water make Earth the "living planet"?

_____

_____

Comprehension: Mars

The U.S. has sent many unmanned spacecrafts to Mars since 1964. (**Unmanned** means there were no people on the spacecraft.) That's why scientists know a lot about this planet. Mars has low temperatures. There is no water on Mars. There is only a gas called water vapor. There is also ice on Mars. Scientists have also learned that there is fog on Mars in the early morning! Do you remember when you last saw fog here on Earth? Scientists say the fog on Mars looks the same. As on Earth, the fog occurs in low-lying areas of the ground.

Another interesting thing about Mars is that it is very windy. The wind blows up many dust storms on this planet. A spacecraft called Mariner 9 was the first to take pictures of dust storms. Later, the unmanned Viking spacecraft landed on the surface of Mars.

Directions: Answer these questions about Mars.

1. On Mars, it is   cold.

                 hot.

2. When there are no people on a spacecraft, it is _____.

3. Mars and Earth both have _____ in the early morning in low-lying areas.

4. These are caused by all the wind on Mars.

   _____

5. This spacecraft took pictures of dust storms on Mars.

   _____

Comprehension: Jupiter

Jupiter, the fifth planet from the Sun, is circled by a ring of dark particles. It takes this planet almost 12 years to orbit the Sun. Jupiter's ring is very difficult to see from Earth without using special equipment. Jupiter is the largest planet in our solar system. It is 11 times bigger than Earth!

Scientists have been able to learn much about this planet because of the information received from Voyager 1 in 1979. They know that we cannot send a spacecraft to land on the surface of Jupiter as we have done with the Moon. The surface of Jupiter is not solid. The outer "shell" of Jupiter is gas.

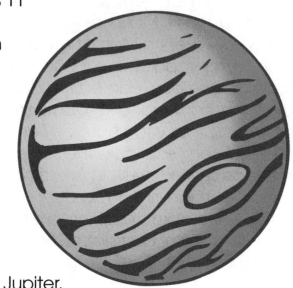

Directions: Answer these questions about Jupiter.

1. In what year did Voyager 1 send us more information about Jupiter?

   _____

2. Why can't we send a spacecraft to land on Jupiter?

   _____

   _____

3. The ring that circles Jupiter is made of _____.

4. What is the largest planet in our solar system?

   _____

5. Jupiter is the _____ planet from the Sun.

Name: _____

Comprehension: Saturn

Have you looked at Saturn through a strong telescope? If you have, you know it has rings. Saturn is the most beautiful planet to see! It is bright yellow. It is circled by four rings. Two bright rings are on the outside of the circle. Two dark rings are on the inside. The rings of Saturn are made of billions of tiny bits of ice and rock. The ice and rocks travel around the planet in a swarm. They keep their ring shape as the planet travels around the Sun. These rings shine brightly, and so does the planet Saturn. Both reflect the rays of the Sun. The Sun is 885 million miles away from Saturn. It takes Saturn 29 $\frac{1}{2}$ years to travel around the Sun!

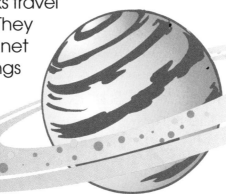

Directions: Answer these questions about Saturn.

1. How many rings does Saturn have? _____

2. Where are Saturn's dark rings?

   _____

3. Where are Saturn's bright rings?

   _____

4. What are Saturn's rings made of?

   _____

5. What causes Saturn and its rings to shine?

   _____

6. How far away from the Sun is Saturn?

   _____

Comprehension: Uranus

William Herschel discovered the planet Uranus in 1781. As has happened many times throughout history with other scientists, inventors and explorers, he didn't realize he had found a planet—he thought it was a comet. Scientists didn't know too much about this planet, though, until 1986 when the U.S. spacecraft Voyager 2 flew past it.

Do you think the planet Earth is big? Well, the planet Uranus is four times bigger! Uranus is another planet that has rings. While Saturn's rings are made of ice and rock, the rings of Uranus are made of dark particles the size of boulders. Earth has one natural satellite—the Moon—but Uranus has 15 natural satellites. It takes Earth 1 year to circle the Sun, but Uranus takes 84 years! Uranus is the seventh planet from the Sun.

Directions: Answer these questions about Uranus.

1. This story tells about two planets that have rings. They are:

   1) _____   2) _____

2. Who was William Herschel?

   _____

3. Which planet is bigger, Earth or Uranus? How much bigger?

   _____

Comprehension: Neptune

Neptune is the eighth planet from the Sun. Because of its location, it takes Neptune 168 years to orbit the Sun. It is closely related to Uranus, one of its neighbors in the solar system. Scientists have noticed that its coloring and appearance look very similar to that of Uranus.

Neptune was discovered by Galle in 1846. It is almost four times bigger than Earth. Neptune has two known satellites—the larger is named Triton and the smaller is named Nereid. Some scientists have noticed that the orbit of the larger satellite is getting closer and closer to the planet. It will eventually crash into the surface of Neptune. However, you and I won't be able to watch this happen. Scientists predict it will happen in 100 million years!

Directions: Answer these questions about Neptune.

1. Why does it take Neptune 168 years to orbit the Sun?

_____

2. What are the names of Neptune's two satellites?

1) _____ 2) _____

3. Which word in the last paragraph means "to tell about something that will happen"?

_____

4. Who discovered the planet Neptune?

_____

Comprehension: Pluto

Pluto is the ninth planet in our solar system. It is 3,700 million miles from the Sun. It cannot be seen from Earth without a telescope. Maybe that is why it was named Pluto. Pluto was the Roman god of the underworld. For years, scientists suspected there was a ninth planet. But it was not until 1930 that a young scientist proved Pluto existed. His name was Clyde Tombaugh. He compared pictures of the sky near Pluto taken at different times. He noticed one big "star" was in a different place in different pictures. He realized it was not a star. It was a planet moving around the Sun.

Directions: Answer these questions about Pluto.

1. Who discovered Pluto? _____

2. When did he discover Pluto? _____

3. Why was the new planet named Pluto?

   _____

   _____

4. How was Pluto discovered? _____

   _____

5. What is Pluto's distance from the sun? _____

Comprehension: Moon

Our moon is not the only moon in the solar system. Some other planets have moons also. Saturn has 10 moons! Our moon is Earth's closest neighbor in the solar system. Sometimes our moon is 225,727 miles away. Other times, it is 252,002 miles away. Why? Because the Moon revolves around Earth. It does not go around Earth in a perfect circle. So, sometimes its path takes it further away from our planet.

When our astronauts visited the Moon, they found dusty plains, high mountains and huge craters. There is no air or water on the Moon. That is why life cannot exist there. The astronauts had to wear space suits to protect their skin from the bright Sun. They had to take their own air to breathe. They had to take their own food and water. The Moon was an interesting place to visit. Would you want to live there?

Directions: Answer these questions about the Moon.

1. Circle the main idea:

   The Moon travels around Earth, and the astronauts visited the Moon.

   Astronauts found that the Moon—Earth's closest neighbor— has no air or water and cannot support life.

2. Write three things our astronauts found on the Moon.

   1) _____ 2) _____ 3) _____

3. Make a list of what to take on a trip to the Moon.

   _____

   _____

Comprehension: Your Heart

Make your hand into a fist. Now look at it. That is about the size of your heart! Your heart is a strong pump. It works all the time. Right now it is beating about 90 times a minute. When you run, it beats about 150 times a minute.

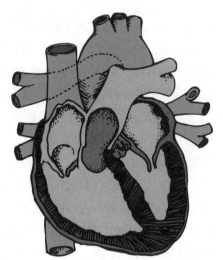

Inside, your heart has four spaces. The two spaces on the top are called atria. This is where blood is pumped into the heart. The two spaces on the bottom are called ventricles. This is where blood is pumped out of the heart. The blood is pumped to every part of your body. How? Open and close your fist. See how it tightens and loosens? The heart muscle tightens and loosens, too. This is how it pumps blood.

Directions: Answer these questions about your heart.

1. How often does your heart work?

   _____

2. How fast does it beat when you are sitting?

   _____

3. How fast does it beat when you are running?

   _____

4. How many spaces are inside your heart?_____

5. What are the heart's upper spaces called? What are the lower spaces called?

   _____   _____

Making Inferences: Your Bones

Are you scared of skeletons? You shouldn't be. There is a skeleton inside of you! The skeleton is made up of all the bones in your body. These 206 bones give you your shape. They also protect your heart and everything else inside. Your bones come in many sizes. Some are short. Some are long. Some are rounded. Some are very tiny. The outside of your bones looks solid. Inside, they are filled with a soft material called marrow. This is what keeps your bones alive. Red blood cells and most white blood cells are made here. These cells help feed the body and fight disease.

Directions: Answer these questions about your bones.

1. Do you think your leg bone is short, long or rounded?

   _____

2. Do you think the bones in your head are short, long or rounded?

   _____

3. What is the size of the bones in your fingers?

   _____

4. What is the "something soft" inside your bones?

   _____

5. How many bones are in your skeleton?

   _____

Comprehension: Your Muscles

Can you make a fist? You could not do this without muscles. You need muscles to make your body move. You have muscles everywhere. There are muscles in your legs. There are even muscles in your tongue!

Remember, your heart is a muscle. It is called an "involuntary muscle" because it works without help from you. Your stomach muscles are also involuntary. You don't need to tell your stomach to digest food. Other muscles are called "voluntary muscles." You must tell these muscles to move. Most voluntary muscles are hooked to bones. When the muscles squeeze, they cause the bone to move. Without your muscles, you would be nothing but a "bag of bones"!

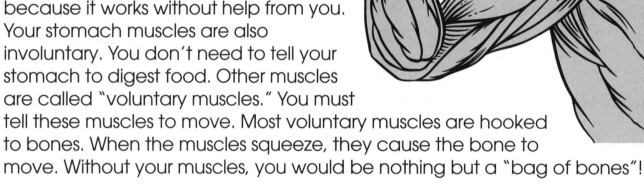

Directions: Answer these questions about your muscles.

1. What are involuntary muscles?

_____

2. What are voluntary muscles?

_____

3. These muscles are usually hooked to bones:

    involuntary muscles

    voluntary muscles

4. What causes bones to move?

_____

Name: _____

Comprehension: Your Hands

Wiggle your fingers. Now clap your hands. That was easy, wasn't it? But it wasn't as easy as you think! Each of your hands has 27 bones. Eight of the 27 bones are in your wrist. There are five bones in each of your palms. Your hands have many muscles, too. It takes 30 muscles to wiggle your fingers. When you use your hands, the bones and muscles work together. Remember this the next time you cut your meat. You will use your wrist bones and muscles. You will use your finger bones and muscles. Cutting your meat seems easy. It is—thanks to your muscles and bones!

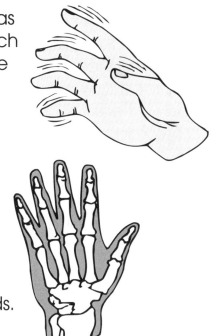

Directions: Answer these questions about your hands.

1. How many bones are in each of your wrists?

   _____

2. How many bones are in each of your hands?

   _____

3. How many muscles does it take to wiggle your fingers?

   _____

4. How many bones are in each of your palms?

   _____

5. Add together the palm bones and wrist bones. Subtract from the total number of bones in the hand. How many bones are left?

   _____

Comprehension: Your Digestive System

The digestive system begins in your mouth. (And you thought you were just enjoying that salad and slice of pizza!) The teeth begin the process by slicing and chewing the food you eat. Usually adults have 32 teeth to help do this. Saliva enters the mouth, too, and helps soften the food so it can be swallowed easily. Now, your salad and pizza move through a short tube called the esophagus onward to the stomach.

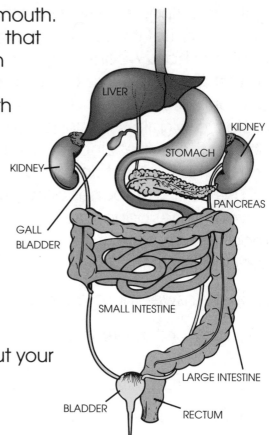

Directions: Answer these questions about your digestive system.

1. What does saliva do?

_____

_____

2. Where does the digestive system begin?

_____

3. What do your teeth do?

_____

4. The _____ is a short tube that brings food to the stomach.

Comprehension: Your Digestive System

It's here in the stomach that food is stored long enough to let it mix with 6 pints of gastric juices. These important juices help kill bacteria and break down food into nutrients that your body needs.

Next, the food moves into the small intestine. This section of the digestive system helps to continue breaking down the food into nutrients needed by your body. From here, most of the nutrients needed are absorbed.

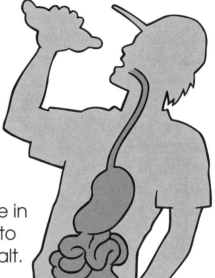

The final stage of the digestive system takes place in the large intestine, or colon. The colon helps send into the body any leftover usable products, water and salt.

Directions: Answer these questions about your digestive system.

1. How do the gastric juices help digestion?

_____

_____

What is their function?

_____

2. Where does the final stage of digestion take place?

_____

3. Number the order of where digestion takes place.

_____ large intestine   _____ mouth   _____ esophagus

_____ small intestine   _____ stomach

Main Idea: Your Lungs

Imagine millions of teeny, tiny balloons joined together. That is what your lungs are like. When you breathe, the air goes to your two lungs. One lung is located on each side of your chest. The heart is located between the two lungs. The lungs are soft, spongy and delicate. That is why there are bones around the lungs. These bones are called the rib cage. The rib cage protects the lungs so they can do their job. The lungs bring oxygen (ox-i-gin) into the body. They also take waste out of the body. This waste is called carbon dioxide. We could not live without our lungs!

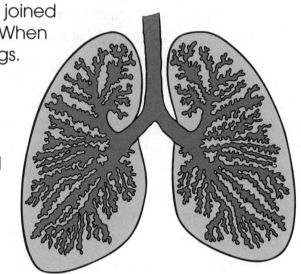

Directions: Answer these questions about your lungs.

1. Circle the main idea:

   The lungs are spongy and located in the chest. They are like small balloons.

   The lungs bring in oxygen and take out carbon dioxide. We could not live without our lungs.

2. What is the name of the bones around your lungs?

   _____

3. What is located between the lungs?

   _____

4. What goes into your lungs when you breathe?

   _____

5. Why are there bones around your lungs?

   _____

Comprehension: Your Brain

When you are grown, your brain will weigh only 3 pounds. But what an important 3 pounds! Billions of brain cells are packed into your brain. The cells make up the three areas of the brain. One part does your thinking and feeling. Another part of the brain helps you move your body. It also helps you keep your balance. A third part of the brain keeps you alive! It keeps your heart beating and your lungs working so you don't have to think about these things. This part of your brain is called the medulla (ma-dool-la). As long as you are alive, the medulla never rests.

Directions: Answer these questions about your brain.

1. What do you think would happen if the medulla stopped working?

   _____

2. What do you think would happen if something happened to the part of your brain that helps you move your body?

   _____

   _____

3. Circle the main idea:

   The brain has lots of cells. Three billion cells are packed into the brain.

   The brain has three areas. Each area has a very important job to do.

4. What directions does the medulla give the heart and lungs?

   _____

   _____

Comprehension: Horseless Carriage

Do you know how people traveled before cars? They rode horses! Often the horses were hooked up to wagons. Some horses were hooked up to carriages. Wagons were used to carry supplies. Carriages had covered tops. They were used to carry people. Both wagons and carriages were pulled by horses.

The first cars in the United States were invented shortly before the year 1900. These cars looked a lot like carriages. The seats were high off the ground. They had very thin wheels. The difference was that they were powered by engines. Carriages were pulled by horses. Still, they looked alike. People called the first cars "horseless carriages."

Directions: Answer these questions about "horseless carriages."

1. Write one way wagons and carriages were the same.

   _____

2. When were the first cars invented?

   _____

3. Why were the first cars called "horseless carriages"?

   _____

4. What was the difference between a carriage and a "horseless carriage"?

   _____

   _____

Comprehension: Giant Snowblower

A snowblower is used to blow snow off sidewalks and driveways. It is faster than using a shovel. It is also easier! Airports use snowblowers, too. They use them to clear the runways that planes use. Many airports use a giant snowblower. It is a type of truck. This snowblower weighs 30,000 pounds! It can blow 100,000 pounds of snow every minute. It cuts through the snow with huge blades. The blades are over 6 feet tall.

Directions: Answer these questions about snowblowers.

1. Why do people use snowblowers instead of shovels?

_____

2. What do airports use snowblowers for?

_____

3. How much do some airport snowblowers weigh?

_____

4. How much snow can the airport snowblower blow every minute?

_____

5. What does the snowblower use to cut through snow?

_____

Comprehension: Early Trucks

What would we do without trucks? Your family may not own a truck, but everyone depends on trucks. Trucks bring our food to stores. Trucks deliver our furniture. Trucks carry new clothes to shopping centers. The goods of the world move on trucks.

Trucks are harder to make than cars. They must be sturdy. They carry heavy loads. They cannot break down.

The first trucks were on the road in 1900. Like trains, they were powered by steam engines. They did not use gasoline. The first trucks did not have heavy wheels. Their engines often broke down.

Trucks changed when the U.S. entered World War I in 1917. Big, heavy tires were put on trucks. Gasoline engines were used. Trucks used in war had to be sturdy. Lives were at stake!

Directions: Answer these questions about the first trucks.

1. What powered the first trucks?

   _____

2. When did early trucks begin using gasoline engines?

   _____

3. How do trucks serve us?

   _____

   _____

4. Why did trucks used in war have to be sturdy?

   _____

Comprehension: The First Trains

Trains have been around much longer than cars or trucks. The first train used in the United States was made in England. It was brought to the U.S. in 1829. Because it was light green, it was nicknamed the Grasshopper. Unlike a real grasshopper, this train was not fast. It only went 10 miles an hour.

That same year, another train was built by an American. Compared to the Grasshopper, the American train was fast. It went 30 miles an hour. People were amazed. This train was called the Rocket. Can you guess why?

Directions: Answer these questions about the first trains.

1. Where was the first train made that was used in the U.S.?

   _____

2. What did people call this train?

   _____

3. How fast did it travel?

   _____

4. What year did the Grasshopper arrive in the U.S.?

   _____

5. What American train was built that same year?

   _____

Comprehension: Beavers

Have you ever been called a "busy beaver"? You may not know what this expression means, but read the paragraphs below to find out.

Most animals cannot change where they live. A bird can build a nest and a mole can burrow into the ground, but the beaver can do more than that. If it likes a certain area but finds that the water is not deep enough, do you know what it can do? The beaver "gets busy" and starts cutting down trees to build a dam so that the area covered by water is deeper and larger.

The beaver does this using its sharp teeth. After it gnaws on a tree, it cuts away until the tree starts to fall. The beaver makes sure to get out of the way! It then trims off the branches and bark. Without using a chainsaw, as a person would do, the beaver cuts the wood into smaller pieces.

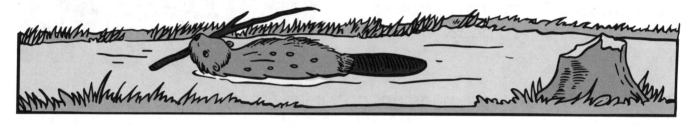

Directions: Answer these questions about the beaver.

1. What does the beaver use to chop down a tree?

   _____

2. After the tree has fallen, what does the beaver do?

   _____

   _____

3. How did the term **busy beaver** come about?

   _____

   _____

   _____

Comprehension: Beavers

The beaver is not only a great lumberjack, it can also swim quite well. Its special fur helps to keep it warm; its hind legs work like fins; its tail is used as a rudder to steer it through the water. The beaver can hold its breath under water for 15 minutes, and its special eyelids are transparent, so they work like goggles!

Even though the beaver is a very good swimmer and can stay under water for a long time, it does not live under water. When the beaver builds a dam it also builds a lodge. A lodge is a dome-shaped structure above water level in which the beaver lives. The beaver enters its lodge through underwater tunnels. The lodge provides a place for the beaver to rest, eat and raise young.

Directions: Answer these questions about the beaver.

1. What is the main idea of the first paragraph?

   _____

   _____

2. Which word in the first paragraph means "able to see through"?

   _____

3. How long can the beaver hold its breath under water?

   _____

4. How does a beaver enter his lodge?

   _____

Comprehension: Cows

Thousands of years ago, people domesticated (tamed) cows. If you live on or near a farm, you may see cows every day. You may know what it is like to hear their mooing sounds when they are ready to be fed or milked.

Cows are raised for meat and milk. If a cow is raised for the sole purpose of providing milk, it is called a dairy cow. Some common breeds of dairy cows are Holstein-Friesians (hole-steen free-zhunz), Jerseys, Brown Swiss and Guernseys (gurn-zeez). Cows raised for their meat are Herefords (her-ferdz).

Cows use their long tails to swat flies and other bothersome bugs. Cows chew cud. This is a portion of their food that has already been chewed a little. It is swallowed, then brought back up after it has been combined with liquid. The cow has four stomachs which make this possible. What do you think of chewing cud? Yuck!

Directions: Answer these questions about cows.

1. Holstein-Friesians and Guernseys are two kinds of _____ cows.

2. Cows have _____ stomachs.

3. Another word for tamed is _____.

4. A common breed of cow raised for meat is _____.

Making Inferences: Sheep

Sheep like to stay close together. They do not run off. They move together in a flock. They live on sheep ranches. Some sheep grow 20 pounds of fleece each year. After it is cut off, the fleece is called wool. Cutting off the wool is called "shearing." It does not hurt the sheep to be sheared. The wool is very warm and is used to make clothing.

Female sheep are called ewes ("yous"). Some types of ewes have only one baby each year. The baby is called a lamb. Other types of ewes have two or three lambs each year.

Directions: Answer these questions about sheep.

1. Why is sheep's behavior helpful to sheep ranchers?

   _____

2. If you were a sheep farmer, would you rather own the kind of sheep that has one baby each year, or one that has two or three?

   _____

   Why?

   _____

3. When it is still on the sheep, what is wool called?

   _____

4. What is a group of sheep called?

   _____

Making Inferences: Sheep

Farmers shear sheep at the time of the year when the climate is warm. Shearing is usually done in May in the northern states and as early as February or March in the warmer southern states.

Whether in a small or large flock, sheep must be watched more carefully than cattle. Herders take care of sheep on the open range. The herders live in tents, campers or camp wagons and take care of 500–2,000 sheep. As the sheep get larger, the herder must make sure that there is plenty of grass for the herd to graze.

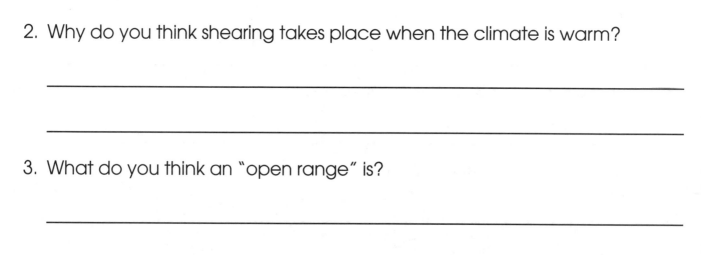

Directions: Answer these questions about sheep.

1. What does **graze** mean?

    a. run

    b. eat

    c. like

2. Why do you think shearing takes place when the climate is warm?

    _____

    _____

3. What do you think an "open range" is?

    _____

    _____

Comprehension: Rhinos

Rhinos are the second largest land animal. Only elephants are bigger.

Most people think rhinos are ugly. Their full name is "rhinoceros" (rhy-nos-ur-us). There are five kinds of rhinos—the square-lipped rhino, black rhino, great Indian rhino, Sumatran (sue-ma-trahn) rhino and Javan rhino.

Rhinos have a great sense of smell, which helps protect them. They can smell other animals far away. They don't eat them, though. Rhinos do not eat meat. They are vegetarians.

Directions: Answer these questions about rhinos.

1. What is the largest land animal?

_____

2. What are the five kinds of rhinos?

1) _____

2) _____

3) _____

4) _____

5) _____

3. What is a "vegetarian"?

_____

_____

Comprehension: Robins

Have you ever heard this old song? "Oh, the red, red robin goes bob-bob-bobbin' along!" It's hard not to smile when you see a robin. Robins were first called "redbreasts." If you have seen one, you know why! The fronts of their bodies are red. Robins are cheerful-looking birds.

Robins sing a sweet, mellow song. That is another reason why people like robins. The female robin lays two to six eggs. She sits on them for 2 weeks. Then the father and mother robin both bring food to the baby birds. Robins eat spiders, worms, insects and small seeds. Robins will also eat food scraps people put out for them.

Directions: Answer these questions about robins.

1. Write one reason people like robins.

_____

2. How many eggs does a mother robin lay?

_____

3. What do robins eat?

_____

4. Who sits on the robin's eggs?

_____

Comprehension: Rodents

You are surrounded by rodents (row-dents)! There are 1,500 different kinds of rodents. One of the most common rodents is the mouse. Rats, gophers (go-furs) and beavers are also rodents. So are squirrels and porcupines (pork-you-pines).

All rodents have long, sharp teeth. These sharp teeth are called incisors (in-size-ors). Rodents use these teeth to eat their food. They eat mostly seeds and vegetables. There is one type of rodent some children have as a pet. No, it is not a rat! It is the guinea (ginney) pig.

Directions: Answer these questions about rodents.

1. How many different kinds of rodents are there?

   _____

2. Name seven kinds of rodents.

   1) _____

   2) _____

   3) _____

   4) _____

   5) _____

   6) _____

   7) _____

3. What are rodents' sharp teeth called?

   _____

4. What rodent is sometimes a pet?

   _____

Making Inferences: Dictionary Mystery

Directions: Below are six dictionary entries with pronunciations and definitions. The only things missing are the entry words. Write the correct entry words. Be sure to spell each word correctly.

Entry word:

_____

(rōz)
A flower that grows on bushes and vines.

Entry word:

_____

(ra bət)
A small animal that has long ears.

Entry word:

_____

(fäks)
A wild animal that lives in the woods.

Entry word:

_____

(pē än ō)
A musical instrument that has many keys.

Entry word:

_____

(lāk)
A body of water that is surrounded by land.

Entry word:

_____

(bās bȯl)
A game played with a bat and a ball.

Directions: Now write the entry words in alphabetical order.

1. _____
2. _____
3. _____
4. _____
5. _____
6. _____

Drawing Conclusions

Drawing a conclusion means to use clues to make a final decision about something. To draw a conclusion, you must read carefully.

Directions: Read each story carefully. Use the clues given to draw a conclusion about the story.

The boy and girl took turns pushing the shopping cart. They went up and down the aisles. Each time they stopped the cart, they would look at things on the shelf and decide what they needed. Jody asked her older brother, "Will I need a box of 48 crayons in Mrs. Charles' class?"

"Yes, I think so," he answered. Then he turned to their mother and said, "I need some new notebooks. Can I get some?"

1. Where are they? _____

2. What are they doing there? _____

3. How do you know? Write at least two clue words that helped you.

_____

Eric and Randy held on tight. They looked around them and saw that they were not the only ones holding on. The car moved slowly upward. As they turned and looked over the side, they noticed that the people far below them seemed to be getting smaller and smaller. "Hey, Eric, did I tell you this is my first time on one of these?" asked Randy. As they started down the hill at a frightening speed, Randy screamed, "And it may be my last!"

1. Where are they? _____

2. How do you know? Write at least two clue words that helped you.

_____

Drawing Conclusions: The Jitterbug

Directions: Read about the jitterbug, then answer the questions.

The music is playing loudly. Paul and Mary are facing each other. They hold hands. They are going to do something called the jitterbug. Paul starts bouncing back and forth, first on one foot, then on the other. Mary starts doing the same thing. They are "keeping time" to the beat of the music. Then they start moving around a lot. Mary ducks under Paul's arm. They are laughing because they are having fun.

1. What are Paul and Mary doing? _____

2. What clue words helped you to know? _____

3. Why are Paul and Mary laughing? _____

Drawing Conclusions: A Colorful Yard

Directions: Read the story, then answer the questions.

Mrs. Posy plants roses everywhere. She plants yellow roses near her front porch. She plants red roses near the back door. There are also pink roses and white roses in her yard. Every time the postal carrier comes to her house, he sneezes. "You should not plant so many flowers," he tells Mrs. Posy. Mrs. Posy just smiles.

1. What are Mrs. Posy's favorite flowers? _____

2. Why do you think the postal carrier tells Mrs. Posy, "You should not plant so

   many flowers"? _____

   _____

3. Why does Mrs. Posy smile? _____

   _____

Drawing Conclusions: Mrs. Posy's Roses

Directions: Read more about Mrs. Posy, then answer the questions.

Mrs. Posy is working in her rose garden. She is trimming the branches so that the plants will grow better. Mrs. Posy is careful, because rose bushes have thorns on them. "Hello, Mrs. Posy!" calls Ann as she rides her bicycle down the street. "Hi, Ann!" replies Mrs. Posy. Then she yells, "Ouch!" She runs inside the house and stays there for a few minutes. When Mrs. Posy comes back outside, she has a bandage on one finger.

1. Why is Mrs. Posy careful when she works with rose bushes?

   _____

2. Why does Mrs. Posy look up from her work? _____

   _____

3. Why did Mrs. Posy yell, "Ouch!"? _____

   _____

4. Why did Mrs. Posy run into the house? _____

   _____

Name: _____

Drawing Conclusions: What's Hiding?

Directions: Read about caterpillars, then answer the questions.

Some people do not like caterpillars. Caterpillars look like fuzzy worms. They have many legs and they creep and crawl on trees and leaves. But a caterpillar is really the beginning of something else. After the caterpillar is very large, it spins a cocoon. It stays inside the cocoon for a few months. When the cocoon opens, something else is inside. It is very beautiful. It flies away.

1. Why would people dislike caterpillars? _____

_____

2. What happens while the caterpillar is in the cocoon? _____

_____

3. When does the cocoon open? _____

_____

4. What comes out of the cocoon? _____

_____

Drawing Conclusions: Butterflies

Directions: Read about butterflies, then answer the questions.

Butterflies are many different colors. They have different designs on them, too. These colors and designs help them. When some butterflies are resting, they look like leaves. Animals cannot see them. Other butterflies smell funny. Animals do not like the smell.

1. How do the different colors and designs help protect butterflies?

   _____

2. Why do they need protection from other animals? _____

   _____

3. How does looking like leaves protect butterflies? _____

   _____

4. What else might protect some butterflies? _____

   _____

Drawing Conclusions: Eskimos

Directions: Read about the traditional lives of Eskimos, then answer the questions.

Eskimos live in Alaska. A long time ago, Eskimos lived in houses made of snow, dirt or animal skins. They moved around from place to place. The Eskimos hunted and fished. They often ate raw meat because they had no way to cook it. When they ate meat raw, they liked it dried or frozen. Eskimos used animal skins for their clothes. They used fat from whales, seals and other animals to heat their houses.

1. Why did the Eskimos make houses out of snow? _____

_____

2. How did they prepare their raw meat? _____

_____

3. How might they use animal fat to heat their houses? _____

_____

Drawing Conclusions: Eskimos

Directions: Read about today's Eskimos, then answer the questions.

Today, many Eskimos live in villages or towns instead of moving from place to place. They work at jobs, instead of hunting and fishing. Eskimo children go to school, too. Their houses are heated by oil from the ground instead of animal oil. Many Eskimos use snowmobiles instead of dogs and sleds. In the winter, they wear coats that are very warm.

1. Name two things Eskimos may have learned from other people.

   _____

   _____

2. Why do they use snowmobiles instead of dogs and sleds? _____

   _____

3. Why do Eskimos wear warm coats? _____

   _____

ENGLISH

highest

higher

high

Name: _____

Alphabetical Order

Alphabetical order (or ABC order) is the order of letters in the alphabet. When putting words in alphabetical order, use the first letter of each word.

Directions: Number the words in each list from 1 to 5 in alphabetical order.

___ happy   ___ zebra   ___ banana

___ scared   ___ gorilla   ___ kiwi

___ worried   ___ monkey   ___ apple

___ amused   ___ hyena   ___ peach

___ excited   ___ kangaroo   ___ lemon

Name: _____

Alphabetical Order

Directions: Alphabetical order is putting words in the order in which they appear in the alphabet. Put the eggs in alphabetical order. The first and last words are done for you.

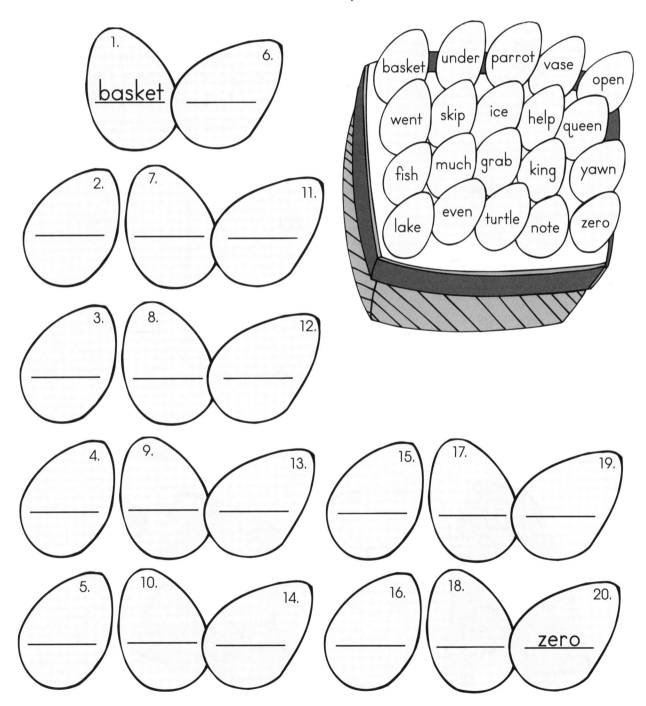

1. basket

6. _____

2. _____

7. _____

11. _____

3. _____

8. _____

12. _____

4. _____

9. _____

13. _____

15. _____

17. _____

19. _____

5. _____

10. _____

14. _____

16. _____

18. _____

20. zero

Words in basket: basket, under, parrot, vase, open, went, skip, ice, help, queen, fish, much, grab, king, yawn, lake, even, turtle, note, zero

Grade 3 - Comprehensive Curriculum

Alphabetical Order

The words in these lists begin with the same letter.

Directions: Use the second or third letters of each word to put the lists in alphabetical order.

Example:

tiger	3	tiger
tape	1	tape
tide	2	tide

All three words begin with the same letter (**t**), so look at the second letters. The letter **a** comes before **i**, so **tape** comes first. Then look at the third letters in **tiger** and **tide** to see which word comes next.

___ glad

___ goat

___ gasoline

___ gentle

___ grumble

___ answer

___ about

___ ask

___ around

___ against

___ tape

___ taste

___ table

___ talent

___ taught

Alphabetical Order

Alphabetical order is the order in which letters come in the alphabet.

Directions: Write the words in alphabetical order. If the first letter is the same, use the second letter of each word to decide which word comes first. If the second letter is also the same, look at the third letter of each word to decide.

Example: wish   wasp   won't

1. w**a**sp
2. w**i**sh
3. w**o**n't

bench   flag   bowl   egg   nod   neat

1. _____   1. _____

2. _____   2. _____

3. _____   3. _____

dog   dart   drag   skipped   stairs   stones

1. _____   1. _____

2. _____   2. _____

3. _____   3. _____

ENGLISH

Antonyms

An **antonym** is a word that means the opposite of another word.

Examples:

child  adult  hot 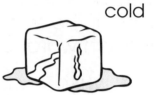 cold

Directions: Match the words that have opposite meanings. Draw a line between each pair of antonyms.

thaw	same
huge	sad
crying	friend
happy	open
enemy	freeze
asleep	thin
closed	hide
fat	tiny
seek	awake
different	laughing

Name: _____

Antonyms

Directions: Complete each sentence with an antonym pair from page 196. Some pairs will not be used.

Example: Usually we wear <u>different</u> clothes, but today we are dressed the <u>same</u>.

1. A _____ is allowed in the museum if he/she is with an _____.

2. Mom was _____ it rained since her garden was very dry, but I was _____ because I had to stay inside.

3. The _____ crowd of people tried to fit into the _____ room.

4. The _____ baby was soon _____ and playing in the crib.

5. We'll _____ the meat for now, and Dad will _____ it when we need it.

6. The windows were wide _____, but the door was _____.

Now, write your own sentence using one of the antonym pairs.

_____

_____

_____

Antonyms

Antonyms are words that are opposites.

Example: hairy   bald

Directions: Choose a word from the box to complete each sentence below.

open	right	light	full	late	below
hard	clean	slow	quiet	old	nice

Example:

My car was **dirty**, but now it's **clean**.

1. Sometimes my cat is naughty, and sometimes she's _____.

2. The sign said, "Closed," but the door was _____.

3. Is the glass half empty or half _____?

4. I bought new shoes, but I like my _____ ones better.

5. Skating is easy for me, but _____ for my brother.

6. The sky is dark at night and _____ during the day.

7. I like a noisy house, but my mother likes a _____ one.

8. My friend says I'm wrong, but I say I'm _____.

9. Jason is a fast runner, but Adam is a _____ runner.

10. We were supposed to be early, but we were _____.

Name: _____

Antonyms

Directions: Write the antonym pairs from each sentence in the boxes.

Example: Many things are bought and sold at the market.

bought	sold

1. I thought I lost my dog, but someone found him.

2. The teacher will ask questions for the students to answer.

3. Airplanes arrive and depart from the airport.

4. The water in the pool was cold compared to the warm water in the whirlpool.

5. The tortoise was slow, but the hare was fast.

Name: _____

Synonyms

Synonyms are words with nearly the same meaning.

Directions: Draw a line to match each word on the left with its synonym on the right.

infant	hello
forest	coat
bucket	grin
hi	baby
bunny	woods
cheerful	fall
jacket	repair
alike	small
smile	same
autumn	hop
little	skinny
thin	top
jump	rabbit
shirt	pail
fix	happy

Name: _____

Synonyms

Directions: Read each sentence. Choose a word from the box that has the same meaning as the bold word. Write the synonym on the line next to the sentence. The first one has been done for you.

skinniest	biggest	jacket	little	quickly	woods	joyful
grin	alike	trip	rabbit	fix	autumn	infant

1. The deer ran through the **forest**. _____woods_____

2. White mice are very **small** pets. _____

3. Goldfish move **fast** in the water. _____

4. The twins look exactly the **same**. _____

5. Trees lose their leaves in the **fall**. _____

6. The blue whale is the **largest** animal on Earth. _____

7. We will go to the ocean on our next **vacation**. _____

8. The **bunny** hopped through the tall grass. _____

9. The **baby** was crying because it was hungry. _____

10. Put on your **coat** before you go outside. _____

11. Does that clown have a big **smile** on his face? _____

12. That is the **thinnest** man I have ever seen. _____

13. I will **repair** my bicycle as soon as I get home. _____

14. The children made **happy** sounds when they won. _____

Name: _____

Synonyms

Directions: Match the pairs of synonyms.

delight •   • discover
speak •   • tidy
lovely •   • start
find •   • talk
nearly •   • beautiful
neat •   • almost
big •   • joy
sad •   • unhappy
begin •   • large

Directions: Read each sentence. Write the synonym pairs from each sentence in the boxes.

1. That unusual clock is a rare antique.

2. I am glad you are so happy!

3. Becky felt unhappy when she heard the sad news.

Name: _____

Homophones

Homophones are words that sound the same but are spelled differently and have different meanings.

Example:

 **sew**   **sow**    **so**

Directions: Read the sentences and write the correct word in the blanks.

Example:

blue	**blew**	She has **blue** eyes.
		The wind **blew** the barn down.
eye	**I**	He hurt his left _____ playing ball.
		_____ like to learn new things.
see	**sea**	Can you _____ the winning runner from here?
		He goes diving for pearls under the _____ .
eight	**ate**	The baby _____ the banana.
		Jane was _____ years old last year.
one	**won**	Jill _____ first prize at the science fair.
		I am the only _____ in my family with red hair.
be	**bee**	Jenny cried when a _____ stung her.
		I have to _____ in bed every night at eight o'clock.
two **to** **too**		My father likes _____ play tennis.
		I like to play, _____ .
		It takes at least _____ people to play.

Name: _____

Homophones

Directions: Circle the correct word to complete each sentence. Then write the word on the line.

1. I am going to _____ a letter to my grandmother.
   right, write

2. Draw a circle around the _____ answer.
   right, write

3. Wait an _____ before going swimming.
   our, hour

4. This is _____ house.
   our, hour

5. He got a _____ from his garden.
   beat, beet

6. Our football team _____ that team.
   beat, beet

7. Go to the store and _____ a loaf of bread.
   by, buy

8. We will drive _____ your house.
   by, buy

9. It will be trouble if the dog _____ the cat.
   seas, sees

10. They sailed the seven _____ .
    seas, sees

11. We have _____ cars in the garage.
    to, too, two

12. I am going _____ the zoo today.
    to, too, two

13. My little brother is going, _____ .
    to, too, two

Name: _____

Homophones

Homophones are words that sound the same but have different spellings and meanings.

Directions: Complete each sentence using a word from the box.

blew	night	blue	knight	hour	in	ant	inn
our	aunt	meet	too	two	to	meat	

1. A red _____ crawled up the wall.

2. It will be one _____ before we can go back home.

3. Will you _____ us later?

4. We plan to stay at an _____ during our trip.

5. The king had a _____ who fought bravely.

6. The wind _____ so hard that I almost lost my hat.

7. His jacket was _____.

8. My_____ plans to visit us this week.

9. I will come _____ when it gets too cold outside.

10. It was late at _____ when we finally got there.

11. _____ of us will go with you.

12. I will mail a note _____ someone at the bank.

13. Do you eat red _____?

14. We would like to join you, _____.

15. Come over to see _____ new cat.

Grade 3 - Comprehensive Curriculum

Name: _____

Homophones

Directions: Circle the words that are not used correctly. Write the correct word above the circled word. Use the words in the box to help you. The first one has been done for you.

road	see	one	be	so	I	brakes	piece	there
wait	not	some	hour	would	no	deer	you	heard

Jake and his family were getting close to Grandpa's. It had taken them

hour
nearly an (our) to get their, but Jake knew it was worth it. In his mind, he could

already sea the pond and could almost feel the cool water. It had been sew

hot this summer in the apartment.

"Wood ewe like a peace of my apple, Jake?" asked his big sister Clare.

"Eye can't eat any more."

"Know, thank you," Jake replied. "I still have sum of my fruit left."

Suddenly, Dad slammed on the breaks. "Did you see that dear on the rode?

I always herd that if you see won, there might bee more."

"Good thinking, Dad. I'm glad you are a safe

driver. We're knot very far from

Grandpa's now. I can't weight!"

Name: _____

Nouns

Nouns are words that tell the names of people, places or things.

Directions: Read the words below. Then write them in the correct column.

goat	Mrs. Jackson	girl
beach	tree	song
mouth	park	Jean Rivers
finger	flower	New York
Kevin Jones	Elm City	Frank Gates
Main Street	theater	skates
River Park	father	boy

Person

Place

Thing

_____   _____   _____

_____   _____   _____

_____   _____   _____

_____   _____   _____

_____   _____   _____

_____   _____   _____

Grade 3 - Comprehensive Curriculum

Common Nouns

Common nouns are nouns that name any member of a group of people, places or things, rather than specific people, places or things.

Directions: Read the sentences below and write the common noun found in each sentence.

Example: ___socks___ My socks do not match.

1. _____ The bird could not fly.

2. _____ Ben likes to eat jelly beans.

3. _____ I am going to meet my mother.

4. _____ We will go swimming in the lake tomorrow.

5. _____ I hope the flowers will grow quickly.

6. _____ We colored eggs together.

7. _____ It is easy to ride a bicycle.

8. _____ My cousin is very tall.

9. _____ Ted and Jane went fishing in their boat.

10. _____ They won a prize yesterday.

11. _____ She fell down and twisted her ankle.

12. _____ My brother was born today.

13. _____ She went down the slide.

14. _____ Ray went to the doctor today.

Name: _____

Proper Nouns

Proper nouns are names of specific people, places or things. Proper nouns begin with a capital letter.

Directions: Read the sentences below and circle the proper nouns found in each sentence.

Example: (Aunt Frances) gave me a puppy for my birthday.

1. We lived on Jackson Street before we moved to our new house.

2. Angela's birthday party is tomorrow night.

3. We drove through Cheyenne, Wyoming on our way home.

4. Dr. Charles always gives me a treat for not crying.

5. George Washington was our first president.

6. Our class took a field trip to the Johnson Flower Farm.

7. Uncle Jack lives in New York City.

8. Amy and Elizabeth are best friends.

9. We buy doughnuts at the Grayson Bakery.

10. My favorite movie is *E.T.*

11. We flew to Miami, Florida in a plane.

12. We go to Riverfront Stadium to watch the baseball games.

13. Mr. Fields is a wonderful music teacher.

14. My best friend is Tom Dunlap.

Proper Nouns

Directions: Rewrite each sentence, capitalizing the proper nouns.

1. mike's birthday is in september.

_____

2. aunt katie lives in detroit, michigan.

_____

3. In july, we went to canada.

_____

4. kathy jones moved to utah in january.

_____

5. My favorite holiday is valentine's day in february.

_____

6. On friday, mr. polzin gave the smith family a tour.

_____

7. saturday, uncle cliff and I will go to the mall of america in minnesota.

_____

_____

Proper Nouns

Directions: Write about you! Write a proper noun for each category below. Capitalize the first letter of each proper noun.

1. Your first name: _____

2. Your last name: _____

3. Your street: _____

4. Your city: _____

5. Your state: _____

6. Your school: _____

7. Your best friend's name: _____

8. Your teacher: _____

9. Your favorite book character: _____

10. Your favorite vacation place: _____

Name: _____

Common and Proper Nouns

Directions: Look at the list of nouns in the box. Write the common nouns under the kite. Write the proper nouns under the balloons. Remember to capitalize the first letter of each proper noun.

lisa smith
cats
shoelace
saturday
dr. martin
whistle
teddy bears
main street
may
boy
lawn chair
mary stewart
bird
florida
school
apples
washington, d.c.
pine cone
elizabeth jones
charley reynolds

COMMON NOUNS

PROPER NOUNS

_____   _____

_____   _____

_____   _____

_____   _____

_____   _____

_____   _____

_____   _____

_____   _____

_____   _____

Name: _____

Plural Nouns

A **plural** is more than one person, place or thing. We usually add an **s** to show that a noun names more than one. If a noun ends in **x**, **ch**, **sh** or **s**, we add an **es** to the word.

Example: pizza   pizzas

Directions: Write the plural of the words below.

Example: dog + s = dogs   **Example: peach + es = peaches**

cat   _____   lunch   _____

boot   _____   bunch   _____

house   _____   punch   _____

Example: ax + es = axes   **Example: glass + es = glasses**

fox   _____   mess   _____

tax   _____   guess   _____

box   _____   class   _____

Example: dish + es = dishes

bush   _____

ash   _____   **walrus**

brush   _____   **walruses**

Name: _____

Plural Nouns

To write the plural forms of words ending in **y**, we change the **y** to **ie** and add **s**.

Example: pony ___ponies___

Directions: Write the plural of each noun on the lines below.

berry _____

cherry _____

bunny _____

penny _____

family _____

candy _____

party _____

Now, write a story using some of the words that end in **y**. Remember to use capital letters and periods.

_____

_____

_____

_____

Name: _____

Plural Nouns

Directions: Write the plural of each noun to complete the sentences below. Remember to change the **y** to **ie** before you add **s**!

1. I am going to two birthday _____ this week.
    (party)

2. Sandy picked some _____ for Mom's pie.
    (cherry)

3. At the store, we saw lots of _____.
    (bunny)

4. My change at the candy store was three _____.
    (penny)

5. All the _____ baked cookies for the bake sale.
    (lady)

6. Thanksgiving is a special time for _____ to gather together.   (family)

7. Boston and New York are very large _____.
    (city)

Name: _____

Plural Nouns

Some words have special plural forms.

Example: leaf   leaves

Directions: Some of the words in the box are special plurals. Complete each sentence with a plural from the box. Then write the letters from the boxes in the blanks below to solve the puzzle.

tooth	teeth
child	children
foot	feet
mouse	mice
woman	women
man	men

1. I lost my two front ___ ___ ___ [ ] ___ !

2. My sister has two pet ___ ___ ___ [ ] .

3. Her favorite book is Little ___ ___ ___ [ ] ___ .

4. The circus clown had big ___ ___ ___ [ ] .

5. The teacher played a game with the
___ [ ] ___ ___ ___ ___ ___ .

Take good care of this pearly plural!

___ ___ ___ ___ ___
 1   2   3   4   5

Name: _____

Plural Nouns

Directions: The **singular form** of a word shows one person, place or thing. Write the singular form of each noun on the lines below.

cherries _____

lunches _____

countries _____

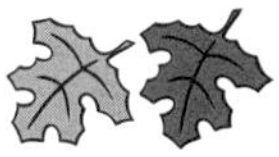

leaves _____

churches _____

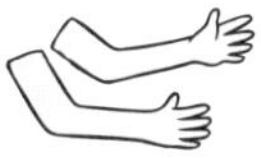

arms _____

boxes _____

men _____

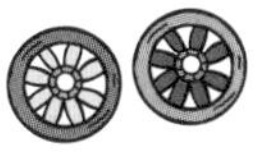

wheels _____

pictures _____

cities _____

places _____

ostriches _____

glasses _____

Name: _____

Possessive Nouns

Possessive nouns tell who or what is the owner of something. With singular nouns, we use an apostrophe **before** the **s**. With plural nouns, we use an apostrophe **after** the **s**.

Example:

singular: one elephant

The **elephant's** dance was wonderful.

plural: more than one elephant

The **elephants'** dance was wonderful.

Directions: Put the apostrophe in the correct place in each bold word. Then write the word in the blank.

1. The **lions** cage was big. _____

2. The **bears** costumes were purple. _____

3. One **boys** laughter was very loud. _____

4. The **trainers** dogs were dancing about. _____

5. The **mans** popcorn was tasty and good. _____

6. **Marks** cotton candy was delicious. _____

7. A little **girls** balloon burst in the air. _____

8. The big **clowns** tricks were very funny. _____

9. **Lauras** sister clapped for the clowns. _____

10. The **womans** money was lost in the crowd. _____

11. **Kellys** mother picked her up early. _____

Name: _____

Possessive Nouns

Directions: Circle the correct possessive noun in each sentence and write it in the blank.

Example: One _____girl's_____ mother is a teacher.

(girl's)   girls'

1. The _____ tail is long.

cat's   cats'

2. One _____ baseball bat is aluminum.

boy's   boys'

3. The_____ aprons are white.

waitresses'   waitress's

4. My _____ apple pie is the best!

grandmother's   grandmothers'

5. My five _____ uniforms are dirty.

brother's   brothers'

6. The _____ doll is pretty.

child's   childs'

7. These_____ collars are different colors.

dog's   dogs'

8. The _____ tail is short.

cow's   cows'

Name: _____

Pronouns

Pronouns are words that are used in place of nouns.
Examples: he, she, it, they, him, them, her, him

Directions: Read each sentence. Write the pronoun that takes the place of each noun.

Example:
   The **monkey** dropped the banana. _It_

1. **Dad** washed the car last night. _____

2. **Mary and David** took a walk in the park. _____

3. **Peggy** spent the night at her grandmother's house. _____

4. The baseball **players** lost their game. _____

5. **Mike Van Meter** is a great soccer player. _____

6. The **parrot** can say five different words. _____

7. **Megan** wrote a story in class today. _____

8. They gave a party for **Teresa**. _____

9. Everyone in the class was happy for **Ted**. _____

10. The children petted the **giraffe**. _____

11. Linda put the **kittens** near the warm stove. _____

12. **Gina** made a chocolate cake for my birthday. _____

13. **Pete and Matt** played baseball on the same team. _____

14. Give the books to **Herbie**. _____

Name: _____

Pronouns

Singular Pronouns

I me my mine
you your yours
he she it her
hers his its him

Plural Pronouns

we us our ours
you your yours
they them their theirs

Directions: Underline the pronouns in each sentence.

1. Mom told us to wash our hands.

2. Did you go to the store?

3. We should buy him a present.

4. I called you about their party.

5. Our house had damage on its roof.

6. They want to give you a prize at our party.

7. My cat ate her sandwich.

8. Your coat looks like his coat.

Pronouns

We use the pronouns **I** and **we** when talking about the person or people doing the action.

Example: **I** can roller skate. **We** can roller skate.

We use **me** and **us** when talking about something that is happening to a person or people.

Example: They gave **me** the roller skates.
They gave **us** the roller skates.

Directions: Circle the correct pronoun and write it in the blank.

Example:

___We___ are going to the picnic together. (We,) Us

1. _____ am finished with my science project. **I, Me**

2. Eric passed the football to _____ . **me, I**

3. They ate dinner with _____ last night. **we, us**

4. _____ like spinach better than ice cream. **I, Me**

5. Mom came in the room to tell _____ good night. **me, I**

6. _____ had a pizza party in our backyard. **Us, We**

7. They told _____ the good news. **us, we**

8. Tom and _____ went to the store. **me, I**

9. She is taking _____ with her to the movies. **I, me**

10. Katie and _____ are good friends. **I, me**

Name: _____

Possessive Pronouns

Possessive pronouns show ownership.

Example: his hat, **her** shoes, **our** dog

We can use these pronouns before a noun:
my, our, you, his, her, its, their

Example: That is **my** bike.

We can use these pronouns on their own:
mine, yours, ours, his, hers, theirs, its

Example: That is **mine**.

Directions: Write each sentence again, using a pronoun instead of the words in bold letters. Be sure to use capitals and periods.

Example:

My **dog's** bowl is brown.   **Its** bowl is brown.

1. That is **Lisa's** book. _____

2. This is **my pencil**. _____

3. This hat is **your hat**. _____

4. Fifi is **Kevin's** cat. _____

5. That beautiful house is **our home**.

_____

6. **The gerbil's** cage is too small.

_____

Name: _____

Abbreviations

An **abbreviation** is the shortened form of a word. Most abbreviations begin with a capital letter and end with a period.

Mr.	Mister	St.	Street
Mrs.	Missus	Ave.	Avenue
Dr.	Doctor	Blvd.	Boulevard
A.M.	before noon	Rd.	Road
P.M.	after noon		

Days of the week: Sun. Mon. Tues. Wed. Thurs. Fri. Sat.
Months of the year: Jan. Feb. Mar. Apr. Aug. Sept. Oct. Nov. Dec.

Directions: Write the abbreviations for each word.

street _____   doctor _____   Tuesday _____

road _____   mister _____   avenue _____

missus _____   October _____   Friday _____

before noon _____   March _____   August _____

Directions: Write each sentence using abbreviations.

1. On Monday at 9:00 before noon Mister Jones had a meeting.

_____

2. In December Doctor Carlson saw Missus Zuckerman.

_____

3. One Tuesday in August Mister Wood went to the park.

_____

Adjectives

Adjectives are words that tell more about nouns, such as a **happy** child, a **cold** day or a **hard** problem. Adjectives can tell how many (**one** airplane) or which one (**those** shoes).

Directions: The nouns are in bold letters. Circle the adjectives that describe the nouns.

Example: Some people have (unusual) **pets**.

1. Some people keep wild **animals**, like lions and bears.

2. These **pets** need special care.

3. These **animals** want to be free when they get older.

4. Even small **animals** can be difficult if they are wild.

5. Raccoons and squirrels are not tame **pets**.

6. Never touch a wild **animal** that may be sick.

Complete the story below by writing in your own adjectives. Use your imagination.

My Cat

My cat is a very_____ animal. She has _____

and _____ fur. Her favorite toy is a _____ ball.

She has _____ claws. She has a _____ tail.

She has a _____ face and _____ whiskers.

I think she is the _____ cat in the world!

Name: _____

Adjectives

Directions: Read the story below and underline the adjectives which are used in the story.

The Best Soup I Ever Had

I woke up one cold winter morning and decided to make a delicious pot of hot vegetable soup. The first vegetables I put in the big grey pot were some sweet white onions. Then I added orange carrots and dark green broccoli. The broccoli looked just like little, tiny trees. Fresh, juicy tomatoes and crisp potatoes were added next. I cooked it for a long, long time. This soup turned out to be the best soup I ever had.

Write two adjectives to describe each of the words below.

cucumber ___ long ___   peas _____

___ green ___   _____

spinach _____   corn _____

_____   _____

Now, rewrite two of the sentences from the story. Substitute your own adjectives for the words you underlined to make your own soup.

_____

_____

_____

Name: _____

Adjectives and Nouns

Directions: Underline the nouns in each sentence below. Then draw an arrow from each adjective to the noun it describes.

Example:

A <u>platypus</u> is a furry <u>animal</u> that lives in <u>Australia</u>.

1. This animal likes to swim.

2. The nose looks like a duck's bill.

3. It has a broad tail like a beaver.

4. Platypuses are great swimmers.

5. They have webbed feet which help them swim.

6. Their flat tails also help them move through the water.

7. The platypus is an unusual mammal because it lays eggs.

8. The eggs look like reptile eggs.

9. Platypuses can lay three eggs at a time.

10. These babies do not leave their mothers for one year.

11. This animal spends most of its time hunting near streams.

Adjectives

A chart of adjectives can also be used to help describe nouns.

Directions: Look at the pictures. Complete each chart.

Example:

Noun	What Color?	What Size?	What Number?
flower	red	small	two

Noun	What Color?	What Size?	What Number?

Noun	What Color?	What Size?	What Number?

Noun	What Color?	What Size?	What Number?

Name: _____

Prefixes

Prefixes are special word parts added to the beginnings of words. Prefixes change the meaning of words.

Prefix	Meaning	Example
un	not	**un**happy
re	again	**re**do
pre	before	**pre**view
mis	wrong	**mis**understanding
dis	opposite	**dis**obey

Directions: Circle the word that begins with a prefix. Then write the prefix and the root word.

1. The dog was unfriendly.   _____ + _____

2. The movie preview was interesting.   _____ + _____

3. The referee called an unfair penalty. _____ + _____

4. Please do not misbehave.   _____ + _____

5. My parents disapprove of that show.   _____ + _____

6. I had to redo the assignment.   _____ + _____

Name: _____

Suffixes

Suffixes are word parts added to the ends of words. Suffixes change the meaning of words.

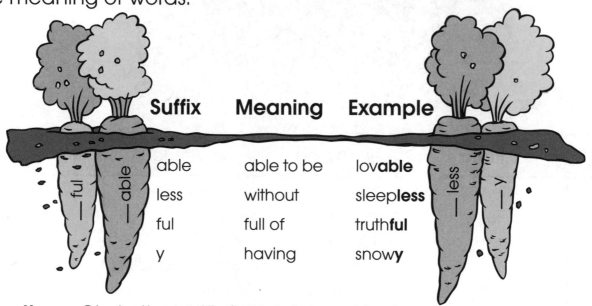

Suffix	Meaning	Example
able	able to be	lov**able**
less	without	sleep**less**
ful	full of	truth**ful**
y	having	snow**y**

Directions: Circle the suffix in each word below.

Example: fluff(y)

rainy	thoughtful	likeable
blameless	enjoyable	helpful
peaceful	careless	silky

Directions: Write a word for each meaning.

full of hope _____   having rain _____

without hope _____   able to break _____

without power _____   full of cheer _____

Name: _____

Verbs

A **verb** is the action word in a sentence, the word that tells what something does or that something exists. **Examples: run, jump, skip**.

Directions: Draw a box around the verb in each sentence below.

1. Spiders spin webs of silk.

2. A spider waits in the center of the web for its meals.

3. A spider sinks its sharp fangs into insects.

4. Spiders eat many insects.

5. Spiders make their nests with silk.

6. Female spiders wrap silk around their eggs to protect them.

Directions: Choose the correct verb from the box and write it in the sentences below.

| hides | swims | eats | grabs | hurt |

1. A crab spider _____ deep inside a flower where it cannot be seen.

2. The crab spider _____ insects when they land on the flower.

3. The wolf spider is good because it _____ wasps.

4. The water spider _____ under water.

5. Most spiders will not _____ people.

Name: _____

Verbs

When a verb tells what one person or thing is doing now, it usually ends in **s**. **Example:** She **sings**.

When a verb is used with **you**, **I** or **we**, we do not add an **s**.

Example: I **sing**.

Directions: Write the correct verb in each sentence.

Example:

I _____write_____ a newspaper about our street.   **writes, write**

1. My sister _____ me sometimes.   **helps, help**

2. She _____ the pictures.   **draw, draws**

3. We _____ them together.   **delivers, deliver**

4. I _____ the news about all the people.   **tell, tells**

5. Mr. Macon _____ the most beautiful flowers.   **grow, grows**

6. Mrs. Jones _____ to her plants.   **talks, talk**

7. Kevin Turner _____ his dog loose everyday.   **lets, let**

8. Little Mikey Smith _____ lost once a week.   **get, gets**

9. You may _____ I live on an interesting street.   **thinks, think**

10. We _____ it's the best street in town.   **say, says**

Name: _____

Helping Verbs

A **helping verb** is a word used with an action verb.

Examples: might, **shall** and **are**

Directions: Write a helping verb from the box with each action verb.

can	could	must	might
may	would	should	will
shall	did	does	do
had	have	has	am
are	were	is	
be	being	been	

Example:

Tomorrow, I _____ might _____ play soccer.

1. Mom _____ buy my new soccer shoes tonight.

2. Yesterday, my old soccer shoes _____ ripped by the cat.

3. I _____ going to ask my brother to go to the game.

4. He usually _____ not like soccer.

5. But, he _____ go with me because I am his sister.

6. He _____ promised to watch the entire soccer game.

7. He has _____ helping me with my homework.

8. I _____ spell a lot better because of his help.

9. Maybe I _____ finish the semester at the top of my class.

    Grade 3 - Comprehensive Curriculum

Name: _____

Past-Tense Verbs

The **past tense** of a verb tells about something that has already happened. We add a **d** or an **ed** to most verbs to show that something has already happened.

Directions: Use the verb from the first sentence to complete the second sentence.

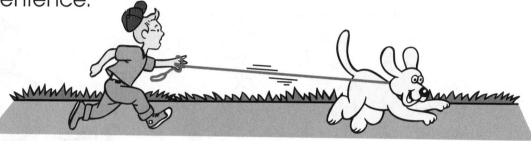

Example:

Please **walk** the dog.   I already __walked__ her.

1. The flowers look good.   They _____ better yesterday.

2. Please accept my gift.   I _____ it for my sister.

3. I wonder who will win.   I _____ about it all night.

4. He will saw the wood.   He _____ some last week.

5. Fold the paper neatly.   She _____ her paper.

6. Let's cook outside tonight.   We _____ outside last night.

7. Do not block the way.   They _____ the entire street.

8. Form the clay this way.   He _____ it into a ball.

9. Follow my car.   We _____ them down the street.

10. Glue the pages like this.   She _____ the flowers on.

Name: _____

Present-Tense Verbs

The **present tense** of a verb tells about something that is happening now, happens often or is about to happen. These verbs can be written two ways: The bird sing**s**. The bird is sing**ing**.

Directions: Write each sentence again, using the verb **is** and writing the **ing** form of the verb.

Example: He cooks the cheeseburgers.

He is cooking the cheeseburgers.

1. Sharon dances to that song.

_____

2. Frank washed the car.

_____

3. Mr. Benson smiles at me.

_____

Write a verb for the sentences below that tells something that is happening now. Be sure to use the verb **is** and the **ing** form of the verb.

Example: The big, brown dog is barking _____ .

1. The little baby _____ .

2. Most nine-year-olds _____ .

3. The monster on television _____ .

Name: _____

Future-Tense Verbs

The **future tense** of a verb tells about something that has not happened yet but will happen in the future. **Will** or **shall** are usually used with future tense.

Directions: Change the verb tense in each sentence to future tense.

Example: She cooks dinner.

_____ She will cook dinner. _____

1. He plays baseball.

   _____

2. She walks to school.

   _____

3. Bobby talks to the teacher.

   _____

4. I remember to vote.

   _____

5. Jack mows the lawn every week.

   _____

6. We go on vacation soon.

   _____

Name: _____

Review

Verb tenses can be in the past, present or future.

Directions: Match each sentence with the correct verb tense.
(**Think:** When did each thing happen?)

It will rain tomorrow.	past	**Past**
He played golf.	present	
Molly is sleeping.	future	**Present**
Jack is singing a song.	past	
I shall buy a kite.	present	**Future**
Dad worked hard today.	future	

Directions: Change the verb to the tense shown.

1. Jenny played with her new friend. (present)

_____

2. Bobby is talking to him. (future)

_____

3. Holly and Angie walk here. (past)

_____

Name: _____

Irregular Verbs

Irregular verbs are verbs that do not change from the present tense to the past tense in the regular way with **d** or **ed**.

Example: sing, **sang**

Directions: Read the sentence and underline the verbs. Choose the past-tense form from the box and write it next to the sentence.

blow — blew	fly — flew
come — came	give — gave
take — took	wear — wore
make — made	sing — sang
grow — grew	

Example:

Dad will <u>make</u> a cake tonight. _____made_____

1. I will probably grow another inch this year. _____

2. I will blow out the candles. _____

3. Everyone will give me presents. _____

4. I will wear my favorite red shirt. _____

5. My cousins will come from out of town. _____

6. It will take them four hours. _____

7. My Aunt Betty will fly in from Cleveland. _____

8. She will sing me a song when she gets here. _____

Name: _____

Irregular Verbs

Directions: Circle the verb that completes each sentence.

1. Scientists will try to (find, found) the cure.

2. Eric (brings, brought) his lunch to school yesterday.

3. Everyday, Betsy (sings, sang) all the way home.

4. Jason (breaks, broke) the vase last night.

5. The ice had (freezes, frozen) in the tray.

6. Mitzi has (swims, swum) in that pool before.

7. Now I (choose, chose) to exercise daily.

8. The teacher has (rings, rung) the bell.

9. The boss (speaks, spoke) to us yesterday.

10. She (says, said) it twice already.

Grade 3 - Comprehensive Curriculum

Name: _____

Irregular Verbs

The verb **be** is different from all other verbs. The present-tense forms of **be** are **am**, **is** and **are**. The past-tense forms of **be** are **was** and **were**. The verb **to be** is written in the following ways:

singular: I am, you are, he is, she is, it is
plural: we are, you are, they are

Directions: Choose the correct form of **be** from the words in the box and write it in each sentence.

| are | am | is | was | were |

Example:

I _____**am**_____ feeling good at this moment.

1. My sister _____ a good singer.

2. You _____ going to the store with me.

3. Sandy_____ at the movies last week.

4. Rick and Tom _____ best friends.

5. He _____ happy about the surprise.

6. The cat_____ hungry.

7. I_____ going to the ball game.

8. They_____ silly.

9. I_____ glad to help my mother.

Name: _____

Linking Verbs

Linking verbs connect the noun to a descriptive word. Linking verbs are often forms of the verb **be**.

Directions: The linking verb is underlined in each sentence. Circle the two words that are being connected.

Example: The (cat) <u>is</u> (fat.)

1. My favorite food <u>is</u> pizza.

2. The car <u>was</u> red.

3. I <u>am</u> tired.

4. Books <u>are</u> fun!

5. The garden <u>is</u> beautiful.

6. Pears <u>taste</u> juicy.

7. The airplane <u>looks</u> large.

8. Rabbits <u>are</u> furry.

Grade 3 - Comprehensive Curriculum

Adverbs

Adverbs are words that describe verbs. They tell where, how or when.

Directions: Circle the adverb in each of the following sentences.

Example: The doctor worked (carefully.)

1. The skater moved gracefully across the ice.

2. Their call was returned quickly.

3. We easily learned the new words.

4. He did the work perfectly.

5. She lost her purse somewhere.

Directions: Complete the sentences below by writing your own adverbs in the blanks.

Example: The bees worked _____busily_____ .

1. The dog barked _____ .

2. The baby smiled _____ .

3. She wrote her name _____ .

4. The horse ran _____ .

Name: _____

Adverbs

Directions: Read each sentence. Then answer the questions on the lines below.

Example: Charles ate hungrily.   who? ___Charles___

what? ___ate___   how? ___hungrily___

1. She dances slowly.   who? _____

what? _____   how? _____

2. The girl spoke carefully.   who? _____

what? _____   how? _____

3. My brother ran quickly.   who? _____

what? _____   how? _____

4. Jean walks home often.   who? _____

what? _____   when? _____

5. The children played there.   who? _____

what? _____   where? _____

Name: _____

Prepositions

Prepositions show relationships between the noun or pronoun and another noun in the sentence. The preposition comes before that noun.

Example: The <u>book</u> is on the table.

Common Prepositions

above	behind	by	near	over
across	below	in	off	through
around	beside	inside	on	under

Directions: Circle the prepositions in each sentence.

1. The dog ran fast around the house.

2. The plates in the cupboard were clean.

3. Put the card inside the envelope.

4. The towel on the sink was wet.

5. I planted flowers in my garden.

6. My kite flew high above the trees.

7. The chair near the counter was sticky.

8. Under the ground, worms lived in their homes.

9. I put the bow around the box.

10. Beside the pond, there was a playground.

Articles

Articles are words used before nouns. **A, an** and **the** are articles. We use **a** before words that begin with a consonant. We use **an** before words that begin with a vowel.

Example: **a peach**    **an apple**

Directions: Write **a** or **an** in the sentences below.

Example: My bike had _____a_____ flat tire.

1. They brought _____ goat to the farm.

2. My mom wears _____ old pair of shoes to mow the lawn.

3. We had _____ party for my grandfather.

4. Everybody had _____ ice-cream cone after the game.

5. We bought _____ picnic table for our backyard.

6. We saw _____ lion sleeping in the shade.

7. It was _____ evening to be remembered.

8. He brought _____ blanket to the game.

9. _____ exit sign was above the door.

10. They went to _____ orchard to pick apples.

11. He ate _____ orange for lunch.

Commas

Commas are used to separate words in a series of three or more.

Example: My favorite fruits are apples, bananas and oranges.

Directions: Put commas where they are needed in each sentence.

1. Please buy milk eggs bread and cheese.

2. I need a folder paper and pencils for school.

3. Some good pets are cats dogs gerbils fish and rabbits.

4. Aaron Mike and Matt went to the baseball game.

5. Major forms of transportation are planes trains and automobiles.

Commas

We use commas to separate the day from the year.
Example: May 13, 1950

Directions: Write the dates in the blanks. Put the commas in and capitalize the name of each month.

Example:

Jack and Dave were born on february 22 1982.

_____ February 22, 1982 _____

1. My father's birthday is may 19 1948.

_____

2. My sister was fourteen on december 13 1994.

_____

3. Lauren's seventh birthday was on november 30 1998.

_____

4. october 13 1996 was the last day I saw my lost cat.

_____

5. On april 17 1997, we saw the Grand Canyon.

_____

6. Our vacation lasted from april 2 1998 to april 26 1998.

_____   _____

7. Molly's baby sister was born on august 14 1991.

_____

8. My mother was born on june 22 1959.

_____

Grade 3 - Comprehensive Curriculum

Name: _____

Articles and Commas

Directions: Write **a** or **an** in each blank. Put commas where they are needed in the paragraphs below.

Owls

_____ owl is _____ bird of prey. This means it hunts

small animals. Owls catch insects fish and birds. Mice are

_____ owl's favorite dinner. Owls like protected places,

such as trees burrows or barns. Owls make noises that sound

like hoots screeches or even barks. _____ owl's feathers

may be black brown gray or white.

 **A Zoo for You**

_____ zoo is _____ excellent place for keeping animals. Zoos have

mammals birds reptiles and amphibians. Some zoos have domestic animals,

such as rabbits sheep and goats. Another name for this type of zoo is _____

petting zoo. In some zoos, elephants lions and tigers live in open country.

This is because _____ enormous animal needs open space for roaming.

Name: _____

Capitalization

The names of **people**, **places** and **pets**, the **days of the week**, the **months of the year** and **holidays** begin with a capital letter.

Directions: Read the words in the box. Write the words in the correct column with capital letters at the beginning of each word.

ron polsky	tuesday	march	april
presidents' day	saturday	woofy	october
blackie	portland, oregon	corning, new york	molly yoder
valentine's day	fluffy	harold edwards	arbor day
bozeman, montana	sunday		

People

_____

_____

_____

Places

_____

_____

_____

Pets

_____

_____

_____

Days

_____

_____

_____

Months

_____

_____

_____

Holidays

_____

_____

_____

Grade 3 - Comprehensive Curriculum

Name: _____

Capitalization and Commas

We capitalize the names of cities and states. We use a comma to separate the name of a city and a state.

Directions: Use capital letters and commas to write the names of the cities and states correctly.

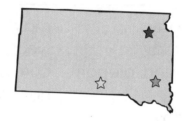

Example:

sioux falls south dakota _Sioux Falls, South Dakota_

1. plymouth massachusetts _____

2. boston massachusetts _____

3. philadelphia pennsylvania _____

4. white plains new york _____

5. newport rhode island _____

6. yorktown virginia _____

7. nashville tennessee _____

8. portland oregon _____

9. mansfield ohio _____

Parts of Speech

Nouns, pronouns, verbs, adjectives, adverbs and prepositions are all **parts of speech**.

Directions: Label the words in each sentence with the correct part of speech.

Example: The cat is fat.
article noun verb adjective

1. My cow walks in the barn.

2. Red flowers grow in the garden.

3. The large dog was excited.

Name: _____

Parts of Speech

Directions: Ask someone to give you nouns, verbs, adjectives and pronouns where shown. Write them in the blanks. Read the story to your friend when you finish.

The _____ **Adventure**
(adjective)

I went for a _____ . I found a really big _____ .
(noun)   (noun)

It was so _____ that I _____ all the
(adjective)   (verb)

way home. I put it in my _____ . To my amazement, it
(noun)

began to _____ . I _____ . I took it to my
(verb)   (past-tense verb)

_____ . I showed it to all my _____ .
(place)   (plural noun)

I decided to _____ it in a box and wrap it up with
(verb)

_____ paper. I gave it to _____ for a
(adjective)   (person)

present. When _____ opened it, _____
(pronoun)   (pronoun)

_____ . _____ shouted, "Thank you!
(past-tense verb)   (pronoun)

This is the best _____ I've ever had!"
(noun)

Name: _____

Parts of Speech

Directions: Write the part of speech of each underlined word.

NOUN PRONOUN VERB ADJECTIVE ADVERB PREPOSITION

① ②
There <u>are</u> many <u>different</u> kinds of animals. Some animals live in the

③
wild. Some animals live in the <u>zoo</u>. And still others live in homes. The animals

④
that <u>live</u> in homes are called pets.

There are many types of pets. Some pets without fur are fish, turtles,

⑤ ⑥
snakes and hermit crabs. Trained birds can fly <u>around</u> <u>your</u> house. Some

⑦
<u>furry</u> animals are cats, dogs, rabbits, ferrets, gerbils or hamsters. Some animals

⑧ ⑨
can <u>successfully</u> learn tricks that <u>you</u> teach them. Whatever your favorite

⑩
animal is, animals can be <u>special</u> friends!

1. _____ 4. _____

2. _____ 5. _____ 7. _____ 9. _____

3. _____ 6. _____ 8. _____ 10. _____

Name: _____

And and But

We can use **and** or **but** to make one longer sentence from two short ones.

Directions: Use **and** or **but** to make two short sentences into a longer, more interesting one. Write the new sentence on the line below the two short sentences.

Example:

The skunk has black fur. The skunk has a white stripe.

The skunk has black fur and a white stripe.

1. The skunk has a small head. The skunk has small ears.

_____

2. The skunk has short legs. Skunks can move quickly.

_____

3. Skunks sleep in hollow trees. Skunks sleep underground.

_____

4. Skunks are chased by animals. Skunks do not run away.

_____

5. Skunks sleep during the day. Skunks hunt at night.

_____

Name: _____

Subjects

A **subject** tells who or what the sentence is about.

Directions: Underline the subject in the following sentences.

Example:

The <u>zebra</u> is a large animal.

1. Zebras live in Africa.

2. Zebras are related to horses.

3. Horses have longer hair than zebras.

4. Zebras are good runners.

5. Their feet are protected by their hooves.

6. Some animals live in groups.

7. These groups are called herds.

8. Zebras live in herds with other grazing animals.

9. Grazing animals eat mostly grass.

10. They usually eat three times a day.

11. They often travel to water holes.

Name: _____

Simple Subjects

A **simple subject** is the main noun or pronoun in the complete subject.

Directions: Draw a line between the subject and the predicate. Circle the simple subject.

Example: The black (bear) lives in the zoo.

1. Penguins look like they wear tuxedos.

2. The seal enjoys raw fish.

3. The monkeys like to swing on bars.

4. The beautiful peacock has colorful feathers.

5. Bats like dark places.

6. Some snakes eat small rodents.

7. The orange and brown giraffes have long necks.

8. The baby zebra is close to his mother.

Name: _____

Compound Subjects

Compound subjects are two or more nouns that have the same predicate.

Directions: Combine the subjects to create one sentence with a compound subject.

Example: Jill can swing.
Whitney can swing.
Luke can swing.

Jill, Whitney and Luke can swing.

1. Roses grow in the garden. Tulips grow in the garden.

_____

2. Apples are fruit. Oranges are fruit. Bananas are fruit.

_____

3. Bears live in the zoo. Monkeys live in the zoo.

_____

4. Jackets keep us warm. Sweaters keep us warm.

_____

Name: _____

Compound Subjects

Directions: Underline the simple subjects in each compound subject.

Example: <u>Dogs</u> and <u>cats</u> are good pets.

1. Blueberries and strawberries are fruit.

2. Jesse, Jake and Hannah like school.

3. Cows, pigs and sheep live on a farm.

4. Boys and girls ride the bus.

5. My family and I took a trip to Duluth.

6. Fruits and vegetables are good for you.

7. Katarina, Lexi and Mandi like to go swimming.

8. Petunias, impatiens, snapdragons and geraniums are all flowers.

9. Coffee, tea and milk are beverages.

10. Dave, Karla and Tami worked on the project together.

Predicates

A **predicate** tells what the subject is doing, has done or will do.

Directions: Underline the predicate in the following sentences.

Example: Woodpeckers <u>live in trees.</u>

1. They hunt for insects in the trees.

2. Woodpeckers have strong beaks.

3. They can peck through the bark.

4. The pecking sound can be heard from far away.

Directions: Circle the groups of words that can be predicates.

have long tongues   pick up insects

hole in bark   sticky substance

help it to climb trees   tree bark

Now, choose the correct predicates from above to finish these sentences.

1. Woodpeckers   _____ .

2. They use their tongues to _____ .

3. Its strong feet   _____ .

Simple Predicates

A **simple predicate** is the main verb or verbs in the complete predicate.

Directions: Draw a line between the complete subject and the complete predicate. Circle the simple predicate.

Example: The ripe apples ⟮fell⟯ to the ground.

1. The farmer scattered feed for the chickens.

2. The horses galloped wildly around the corral.

3. The baby chicks were staying warm by the light.

4. The tractor was baling hay.

5. The silo was full of grain.

6. The cows were being milked.

7. The milk truck drove up to the barn.

8. The rooster woke everyone up.

Compound Predicates

Compound predicates have two or more verbs that have the same subject.

Directions: Combine the predicates to create one sentence with a compound predicate.

Example: We went to the zoo.
We watched the monkeys.
We went to the zoo and watched the monkeys.

1. Students read their books. Students do their work.

_____

2. Dogs can bark loudly. Dogs can do tricks.

_____

3. The football player caught the ball. The football player ran.

_____

4. My dad sawed wood. My dad stacked wood.

_____

5. My teddy bear is soft. My teddy bear likes to be hugged.

_____

Compound Predicates

Directions: Underline the simple predicates (verbs) in each predicate.

Example: The fans <u>clapped</u> and <u>cheered</u> at the game.

1. The coach talks and encourages the team.

2. The cheerleaders jump and yell.

3. The basketball players dribble and shoot the ball.

4. The basketball bounces and hits the backboard.

5. The ball rolls around the rim and goes into the basket.

6. Everyone leaps up and cheers.

7. The team scores and wins!

Name: _____

Subjects and Predicates

Directions: Write the words for the subject to answer the **who** or **what** questions. Write the words for the predicate to answer the **does**, **did**, **is** or **has** questions.

Example:

My friend has two pairs of sunglasses.   who? _My friend_

has? _has two pairs of sunglasses._

1. John's dog went to school with him.   **what?** _____

   did? _____

2. The Eskimo traveled by dog sled.   **who?** _____

   did? _____

3. Alex slept in his treehouse last night.   **who?** _____

   did? _____

4. Cherry pie is my favorite kind of pie.   **what?** _____

   is? _____

5. The mail carrier brings the mail to the door.   **who?** _____

   does? _____

6. We have more than enough bricks to build the wall.   **who?** _____

   has? _____

7. The bird has a worm in its beak.   **what?** _____

   has? _____

Name: _____

Subjects and Predicates

Directions: Every sentence has two main parts—the subject and the predicate. Draw one line under the subject and two lines under the predicate in each sentence below.

Example:

Porcupines are related to mice and rats.

1. They are large rodents.

2. Porcupines have long, sharp quills.

3. The quills stand up straight when it is angry.

4. Most animals stay away from porcupines.

5. Their quills hurt other animals.

6. Porcupines sleep under rocks or bushes.

7. They sleep during the day.

8. Porcupines eat plants at night.

9. North America has some porcupines.

10. They are called New World porcupines.

11. New World porcupines can climb trees.

Name: _____

Subjects and Predicates

Directions: Draw one line under the subjects and two lines under the predicates in the sentences below.

1. My mom likes to plant flowers.

2. Our neighbors walk their dog.

3. Our car needs gas.

4. The children play house.

5. Movies and popcorn go well together.

6. Peanut butter and jelly is my favorite kind of sandwich.

7. Bill, Sue and Nancy ride to the park.

8. We use pencils, markers and pens to write on paper.

9. Trees and shrubs need special care.

Name: _____

Subjects

Directions: Use your own words to write the subjects in the sentences below.

1. _____ landed in my backyard.

2. _____ rushed out of the house.

3. _____ had bright lights.

4. _____ were tall and green.

5. _____ talked to me.

6. _____ came outside with me.

7. _____ ran into the house.

8. _____ shook hands.

9. _____ said funny things.

10. _____ gave us a ride.

11. _____ flew away.

12. _____ will come back soon.

Name: _____

Predicates

Directions: Use your own words to write the predicates in the sentences below.

1. The swimming pool _____ .

2. The water _____ .

3. The sun _____ .

4. I always _____ .

5. My friends _____ .

6. We always _____ .

7. The lifeguard _____ .

8. The rest periods _____ .

9. The lunch _____ .

10. My favorite food _____ .

11. The diving board _____ .

12. We never _____ .

Review

Directions: Use **and** or **but** to make longer, more interesting sentences from two shorter sentences.

1. I have a dog. I have a cat.

_____

2. The sun is shining. The weather is cold.

_____

Directions: Draw one line under the subjects in the sentences. Draw two lines under the predicates.

1. We went on a white water rafting trip.

2. Sam and Ben won the best prize.

3. She painted a picture for me.

4. Those flowers are beautiful.

5. She is a great babysitter.

6. My shoes got wet in the creek.

7. The cows are not in the barn.

8. He has a new shirt for the party.

Name: _____

Word Order

Word order is the logical order of words in sentences.

Directions: Put the words in order so that each sentence tells a complete idea.

Example: outside put cat the

<u>Put the cat outside.</u>

1. mouse the ate snake the

_____

2. dog John his walk took a for

_____

3. birthday Maria the present wrapped

_____

4. escaped parrot the cage its from

_____

5. to soup quarts water three of add the

_____

6. bird the bushes into the chased cat the

_____

Sentences and Non-Sentences

A **sentence** tells a complete idea.

Directions: Circle the groups of words that tell a complete idea.

1. Sharks are fierce hunters.

2. Afraid of sharks.

3. The great white shark will attack people.

4. Other kinds will not.

5. Sharks have an outer row of teeth for grabbing food.

6. When the outer teeth fall out, another row of teeth moves up.

7. Keep the ocean clean by eating dead animals.

8. Not a single bone in its body.

9. Cartilage.

10. Made of the same material as the tip of your nose.

11. Unlike other fish, sharks cannot float.

12. In motion constantly.

13. Even while sleeping.

Name: _____

Completing a Story

Directions: Complete the story, using sentences that tell complete ideas.

One morning, my friend asked me to take my first bus trip

downtown. I was so excited I _____

_____ .

At the bus stop, we saw_____ . Our bus driver

_____ .

When we got off the bus_____

_____ . I'd never seen so many

_____ .

My favorite part was when we _____

_____ .

We stopped to eat _____

_____

_____ . I bought a _____

_____ .

When we got home, I told my friend, "_____

_____

_____ ."

Name: _____

Complete the Sentences

Directions: Write your own endings to make the sentences tell a complete idea.

Example:

The Wizard of Oz is a story about <u>Dorothy and her dog, Toto</u>.

1. Dorothy and Toto live on _____.

2. A big storm _____.

3. Dorothy and Toto are carried off to _____.

4. Dorothy meets _____.

5. Dorothy, Toto and their friends follow the _____.

6. Dorothy tries to find _____.

7. The Wizard turns out to be _____.

8. A scary person in the story is _____.

9. The wicked witch is killed by _____.

10. The hot air balloon leaves without _____.

11. Dorothy uses her magic shoes to _____.

Name: _____

Complete the Sentences

Directions: Write your own endings to make the sentences tell a complete idea.

Example:

Cinderella is a story about ___Cinderella, her stepmother,___ ___stepsisters and the prince.___

1. Cinderella lives with _____

2. Her stepmother and her stepsisters _____

3. Cinderella's stepsisters receive _____

4. Cinderella cannot go to the ball because _____

_____

5. The fairy godmother comes _____

6. The prince dances with _____

7. When the clock strikes midnight, _____

8. The prince's men look for _____

9. The slipper fits _____

10. Cinderella and the prince live _____

Grade 3 - Comprehensive Curriculum

Statements and Questions

Statements are sentences that tell about something. Statements begin with a capital letter and end with a period. **Questions** are sentences that ask about something. Questions begin with a capital letter and end with a question mark.

Directions: Rewrite the sentences using capital letters and either a period or a question mark.

Example: walruses live in the Arctic

<u>Walruses live in the Arctic.</u>

1. are walruses large sea mammals or fish

_____

2. they spend most of their time in the water and on ice

_____

3. are floating sheets of ice called ice floes

_____

4. are walruses related to seals

_____

5. their skin is thick, wrinkled and almost hairless

_____

Statements and Questions

Directions: Change the statements into questions and the questions into statements.

Example: Jane is happy.   Is Jane happy?
              Were you late?   You were late.

1. The rainbow was brightly colored.

   _____

2. Was the sun coming out?

   _____

3. The dog is doing tricks.

   _____

4. Have you washed the dishes today?

   _____

5. Kurt was the circus ringmaster.

   _____

6. Were you planning on going to the library?

   _____

Name: _____

Exclamations

Exclamation points are used for sentences that express strong feelings. These sentences can have one or two words or be very long.

Example: Wait! or **Don't forget to call!**

Directions: Add an exclamation point at the end of sentences that express strong feelings. Add a period at the end of the statements.

1. My parents and I were watching television

2. The snow began falling around noon

3. Wow

4. The snow was really coming down

5. We turned the television off and looked out the window

6. The snow looked like a white blanket

7. How beautiful

8. We decided to put on our coats and go outside

9. Hurry

10. Get your sled

11. All the people on the street came out to see the snow

12. How wonderful

13. The children began making a snowman

14. What a great day

Name: _____

Review

There are three kinds of sentences.

Statements: Sentences that tell something. Statements end with a period (**.**).

Questions: Sentences that ask a question. Questions end with a question mark (**?**).

Exclamations: Sentences that express a strong feeling. Exclamations end with an exclamation point (**!**).

Directions: Write what kind of sentence each is.

1. _____ What a super day to go to the zoo!

2. _____ Do you like radishes?

3. _____ I belong to the chess club.

4. _____ Wash the dishes.

5. _____ How much does that cost?

6. _____ Apples grow on trees.

7. _____ Look out the window.

8. _____ Look at the colorful rainbow!

Grade 3 - Comprehensive Curriculum

Name: _____

Contractions

Contractions are shortened forms of two words. We use apostrophes to show where letters are missing.

Example: It is = it's

Directions: Write the words that are used in each contraction.

we're _____+_____   they'll _____+_____

you'll _____+_____   aren't _____+_____

I'm   _____+_____   isn't _____+_____

Directions: Write the contraction for the two words shown.

you have _____   have not _____

had not _____   we will _____

they are _____   he is   _____

she had _____   it will _____

I am   _____   is not _____

Name: _____

Apostrophes

Apostrophes are used to show ownership by placing an **s** at the end of a single person, place or thing.

Example: Mary**'s** cat

Directions: Write the apostrophes in the contractions below.

Example: We shouldn' t be going to their house so late at night.

1. We didn t think that the ice cream would melt so fast.

2. They re never around when we re ready to go.

3. Didn t you need to make a phone call?

4. Who s going to help you paint the bicycle red?

Directions: Add an apostrophe and an **s** to the words to show ownership of a person, place or thing.

Example: Jill**'s** bike is broken.

1. That is Holly   flower garden.

2. Mark   new skates are black and green.

3. Mom threw away Dad   old shoes.

4. Buster   food dish was lost in the snowstorm.

Name: _____

Quotation Marks

Quotation marks are punctuation marks that tell what is said by a person. Quotation marks go before the first word and after the punctuation of a direct quote. The first word of a direct quote begins with a capital letter.

Example: Katie said, "Never go in the water without a friend."

Directions: Put quotation marks around the correct words in the sentences below.

Example: "Wait for me, please," said Laura.

1. John, would you like to visit a jungle? asked his uncle.

2. The police officer said, Don't worry, we'll help you.

3. James shouted, Hit a home run!

4. My friend Carol said, I really don't like cheeseburgers.

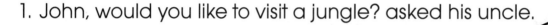

Directions: Write your own quotations by answering the questions below. Be sure to put quotation marks around your words.

1. What would you say if you saw a dinosaur?

   _____

   _____

2. What would your best friend say if your hair turned purple?

   _____

   _____

Quotation Marks

Directions: Put quotation marks around the correct words in the sentences below.

1. Can we go for a bike ride? asked Katrina.

_____

2. Yes, said Mom.

_____

3. Let's go to the park, said Mike.

_____

4. Great idea! said Mom.

_____

5. How long until we get there? asked Katrina.

_____

6. Soon, said Mike.

_____

7. Here we are! exclaimed Mom.

_____

Name: _____

Parts of a Paragraph

A **paragraph** is a group of sentences that all tell about the same thing. Most paragraphs have three parts: a **beginning**, a **middle** and an **end**.

Directions: Write **beginning**, **middle** or **end** next to each sentence in the scrambled paragraphs below. There can be more than one middle sentence.

Example:

___middle___ We took the tire off the car.

___beginning___ On the way to Aunt Louise's, we had a flat tire.

___middle___ We patched the hole in the tire.

___end___ We put the tire on and started driving again.

_____ I took all the ingredients out of the cupboard.

_____ One morning, I decided to bake a pumpkin pie.

_____ I forgot to add the pumpkin!

_____ I mixed the ingredients together, but something was missing.

_____ The sun was very hot and our throats were dry.

_____ We finally decided to turn back.

_____ We started our hike very early in the morning.

_____ It kept getting hotter as we walked.

Name: _____

Topic Sentences

A **topic sentence** is usually the first sentence in a paragraph. It tells what the story will be about.

Directions: Read the following sentences. Circle the topic sentence that should go first in the paragraph that follows.

Rainbows have seven colors.

There's a pot of gold.

I like rainbows.

The colors are red, orange, yellow, green, blue, indigo and violet. Red forms the outer edge, with violet on the inside of the rainbow.

He cut down a cherry tree.

His wife was named Martha.

George Washington was a good president.

He helped our country get started. He chose intelligent leaders to help him run the country.

Mark Twain was a great author.

Mark Twain was unhappy sometimes.

Mark Twain was born in Missouri.

One of his most famous books is *Huckleberry Finn*. He wrote many other great books.

Middle Sentences

Middle sentences support the topic sentence. They tell more about it.

Directions: Underline the middle sentences that support each topic sentence below.

Topic Sentence:

Penguins are birds that cannot fly.

Pelicans can spear fish with their sharp bills.

Many penguins waddle or hop about on land.

Even though they cannot fly, they are excellent swimmers.

Pelicans keep their food in a pouch.

Topic Sentence:

Volleyball is a team sport in which the players hit the ball over the net.

There are two teams with six players on each team.

My friend John would rather play tennis with Lisa.

Players can use their heads or their hands.

I broke my hand once playing handball.

Topic Sentence:

Pikes Peak is the most famous of all the Rocky Mountains.

Some mountains have more trees than other mountains.

Many people like to climb to the top.

Many people like to ski and camp there, too.

The weather is colder at the top of most mountains.

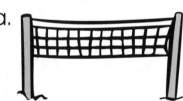

Name: _____

Ending Sentences

Ending sentences are sentences that tie the story together.

Directions: Choose the correct ending sentence for each story from the sentences below. Write it at the end of the paragraph.

A new pair of shoes!
All the corn on the cob I could eat!
A new eraser!

Corn on the Cob

Corn on the cob used to be my favorite food. That is, until I lost my four front teeth. For one whole year, I had to sit and watch everyone else eat my favorite food without me. Mom gave me creamed corn, but it just wasn't the same. When my teeth finally came in, Dad said he had a surprise for me. I thought I was going to get a bike or a new C.D. player or something. I was just as happy to get what I did.

I would like to take a train ride every year.
Trains move faster than I thought they would.
She had brought her new gerbil along for the ride.

A Train Ride

When our family took its first train ride, my sister brought along a big box. She would not tell anyone what she had in it. In the middle of the trip, we heard a sound coming from the box. "Okay, Jan, now you have to open the box," said Mom. When she opened the box we were surprised.

Grade 3 - Comprehensive Curriculum

Name: _____

Alliteration

Alliteration is the repeated use of beginning sounds. Alliterative sentences are sometimes referred to as tongue twisters.

Example:

She sells sea shells by the seashore.
Peter Piper picked a peck of pickled peppers.

Directions: Use alliteration to write your own tongue twisters.

1. _____

_____

_____

2. _____

_____

_____

3. _____

_____

_____

Name: _____

Poetry

Shape poems are words that form the shape of the thing being written about.

Example:

Directions: Create your own shape poem below.

Name: _____

Poetry: Cinquains

A cinquain is a type of poetry. The form is:

Noun
Adjective, adjective
Verb + ing, verb + ing, verb + ing
Four-word phrase
Synonym for noun in line 1.

Example:

Books
Creative, fun
Reading, choosing, looking
I love to read!
Novels

Directions: Write your own cinquain!

_____
noun

_____, _____
adjective   adjective

_____, _____, _____
verb + ing   verb + ing   verb + ing

_____
four-word phrase

_____
synonym for noun in first line

SPELLING

Vocabulary: Beginning and Ending Sounds

Directions: Use the words in the box to answer the questions below.

ax	mix
beach	church
class	kiss
brush	crash

Which word:

begins with the same sound as **breakfast** and ends with the same sound as **fish**? _____

begins with the same sound as **children** and ends with the same sound as **catch**? _____

begins and ends with the same sound as **cuts**? _____

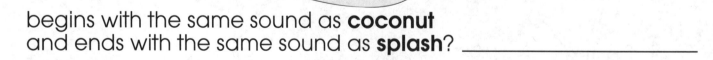

sounds like **acts**? _____

begins with the same sound as **coconut** and ends with the same sound as **splash**? _____

rhymes with **tricks**? _____

has **each** in it? _____

Vocabulary: Sentences

Directions: Use a word from the box to complete each sentence.
Use each word only once.

| ax | mix | beach | church | class | kiss | brush | crash |

1. Those two cars are going to _____ .

2. He chopped the wood with an _____ .

3. Grandma gave me a _____ on my cheek.

4. Before you go, _____ your hair.

5. How many students are in your _____ at school?

6. The waves bring sand to the _____ .

7. To make orange, you _____ yellow and red.

8. On Sunday, we always go to _____ .

Name: _____

Vocabulary: Plurals

A word that names one thing is **singular**, like **house**. A word that names more than one thing is **plural**, like **houses**.

To make a word plural, we usually add **s**.

Examples: one book — two book**s**   one tree — four tree**s**

To make plural words that end in **s**, **ss**, **x**, **sh** and **ch**, we add **es**.

Examples: one fox — two fox**es**   one bush — three bush**es**

Directions: Write the word that is missing from each pair below. Add **s** or **es** to make the plural words. The first one is done for you.

	Singular	**Plural**
	table	tables
	beach	_____
	class	_____
	_____	axes
	brush	_____
	_____	crashes

Name: _____

Vocabulary: Spelling

Directions: Circle the word in each sentence which is not spelled correctly. Then write the word correctly.

1. How many clases are in your school? _____

2. Our town has six chirches. _____

3. Have you been to Maryland's beechs? _____

4. Water mixs with dirt to make mud. _____

5. We need two axs for this tree. _____

6. That car has been in three crashs. _____

7. She gave the baby lots of kises. _____

8. I lost both of my brushs at school. _____

Vocabulary: Nouns and Verbs

A **noun** names a person, place or thing. A **verb** tells what something does or what something is. Some words can be a noun one time and a verb another time.

Directions: Complete each pair of sentences with a word from the box. The word will be a noun in the first sentence and a verb in the second sentence.

mix	kiss	brush	crash

1. Did your dog ever give you a _____?
                               (noun)

   I have a cold, so I can't _____ you today.
                             (verb)

2. I brought my comb and my _____.
                            (noun)

   I will _____ the leaves off your coat.
          (verb)

3. Was anyone hurt in the _____?
                          (noun)

   If you aren't careful, you will _____ into me.
                                   (verb)

4. We bought a cake _____ at the store.
                    (noun)

   I will _____ the eggs together.
          (verb)

Vocabulary: Nouns and Verbs

Directions: Write the correct word in each sentence. Use each word once. Write **N** above the words that are used as nouns (people, places and things). Write **V** above the words that are used as verbs (what something does or what something is).

Example:

I need a ___drink___ . I will ___drink___ milk.

mix	beach	church	class	kiss	brush	crash

1. It's hot today, so let's go to the _____ .

2. The _____ was crowded.

3. I can't find my paint _____ .

4. Will you _____ my finger and make it stop hurting?

5. I will _____ the red and yellow paint to get orange.

6. The teacher asked our _____ to get in line.

7. If you move that bottom can, the rest will

_____ to the floor.

Name: _____

Vocabulary: Sentences

Every sentence must have two things: a **noun** that tells who or what is doing something and a **verb** that tells what the noun is doing.

Directions: Add a **noun** or a **verb** to complete each sentence. Be sure to begin your sentences with capital letters and end them with periods.

Example: reads after school (needs a noun)

Brandy reads after school. _____

1. brushes her dog every day

_____

2. at the beach, we

_____

3. kisses me too much

_____

4. in the morning, our class

_____

5. stopped with a crash

_____

Vocabulary

Directions: Find the picture that matches each sentence below. Then complete each sentence with the word under the picture.

list

spill

search

pound

toast

load

1. I will _____ until I find it.

2. Be careful you don't _____ the paint.

3. Is that _____ too heavy for you?

4. They made _____ for breakfast.

5. Please go to the store and buy a _____ of butter.

6. Is my name on the _____?

Name: _____

Vocabulary

Directions: Find the picture that matches each sentence below. Then complete the sentence with the word under the picture.

hug   **plan**   **clap**

stir   **drag**   **grab**

1. She will _____ where to go on her trip.

2. _____ that big box over here, please.

3. My little brother always tries to _____ my toys.

4. May I help you _____ the soup?

5. I like to _____ my dog because he is so soft.

6. After she played, everyone started to _____ .

Name: _____

Vocabulary: Beginning and Ending Sounds

Directions: Write the words from the box that begin or end with the same sound as the pictures.

| stir | clap | drag | hug | plan | grab |

1. Which word begins with the same sound as each picture?

2. Which word (or words) ends with the same sound as each picture?

_____

_____

_____

_____

_____

_____

Grade 3 - Comprehensive Curriculum

Vocabulary: Explaining Sentences

Directions: Complete each sentence, explaining why each event might have happened.

She hugged me because _____

_____ .

He didn't want to play with us because _____

_____ .

We planned to go to the zoo because _____

_____ .

I grabbed it away from him because _____

_____ .

We clapped loudly because _____

_____ .

Name: _____

Vocabulary: Verbs

Directions: Write the verb that answers each question. Write a sentence using that verb.

stir	clap	drag	hug	plan	grab

Which verb means to put your arms around someone?

_____

_____

Which verb means to mix something with a spoon?

_____

_____

Which verb means to pull something along the ground?

_____

_____

Which verb means to take something suddenly?

_____

_____

Name: _____

Vocabulary: Past-Tense Verbs

The past tense of a verb tells that something already happened. To tell about something that already happened, add **ed** to most verbs. If the verb already ends in **e**, just add **d**.

Examples:

We enter**ed** the contest last week.   We taste**d** the cupcakes.
I fold**ed** the paper wrong.   They decide**d** quickly.
He add**ed** two boxes to the pile.   She share**d** her cupcake.

Directions: Use the verb from the first sentence to complete the second sentence. Add **d** or **ed** to show that something already happened.

Example:

My mom looks fine today. Yesterday, she ____**looked**____ tired.

1. You enter through the middle door.

   We _____ that way last week.

2. Please add this for me. I already _____ it twice.

3. Will you share your cookie with me?

   I _____ my apple with you yesterday.

4. It's your turn to fold the clothes. I _____ them yesterday.

5. May I taste another one? I already _____ one.

6. You need to decide. We _____ this morning.

Name: _____

Vocabulary: Past-Tense Verbs

When you write about something that already happened, you add **ed** to most verbs. For some verbs that have a short vowel and end in one consonant, you double the consonant before adding **ed**.

Examples:

He hug**ged** his pillow.
She stir**red** the carrots.
They clap**ped** for me.

The dog grab**bed** the stick.
We plan**ned** to go tomorrow.
They drag**ged** their bags on the ground.

Directions: Use the verb from the first sentence to complete the second sentence. Change the verb in the second part to the past tense. Double the consonant and add **ed**.

Example:

We skip to school. Yesterday, we _____skipped_____ the whole way.

1. It's not nice to grab things.

   When you _____ my cookie, I felt angry.

2. Did anyone hug you today? Dad _____ me this morning.

3. We plan our vacations every year. Last year, we _____ to go to the beach.

4. Is it my turn to stir the pot? You _____ it last time.

5. Let's clap for Andy, just like we _____ for Amy.

6. My sister used to drag her blanket everywhere.

   Once, she _____ it to the store.

Vocabulary: Past-Tense Verbs

When you write about something that already happened, you add **ed** to most verbs. Here is another way to write about something in the past tense.

Examples: The dog walked.   The dog was walking.
                The cats played.   The cats were playing.

Directions: Write each sentence again, writing the verb a different way.

Example: The baby pounded the pans.

The baby was pounding the pans.

1. Gary loaded the car by himself.

_____

2. They searched for a long time.

_____

3. The water spilled over the edge.

_____

4. Dad toasted the rolls.

_____

Name: _____

Vocabulary: Past-Tense Verbs

Directions: Write sentences that tell about each picture using the words **is, are, was** and **were**. Use words from the box as either nouns or verbs.

pound	spill	toast	list	load	search

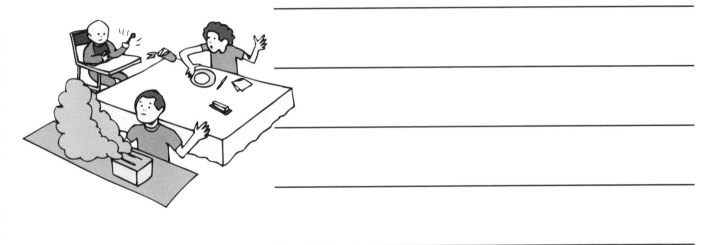

_____

_____

_____

_____

_____

_____

_____

_____

_____

Grade 3 - Comprehensive Curriculum

Vocabulary: Present-Tense Verbs

When something is happening right now, it is in the **present tense**. There are two ways to write verbs in the present tense:

Examples: The dog **walks**.   The cats **play**.
                The dog **is walking**.   The cats **are playing**.

Directions: Write each sentence again, writing the verb a different way.

Example:

He lists the numbers.

He is listing the numbers.
_____

1. She is pounding the nail.

_____

2. My brother toasts the bread.

_____

3. They search for the robber.

_____

4. The teacher lists the pages.

_____

5. They are spilling the water.

_____

6. Ken and Amy load the packages.

_____

Vocabulary: Sentences

Directions: Write a word from the box to complete each sentence.
Use each word only once.

glue	enter	share	add	decide	fold

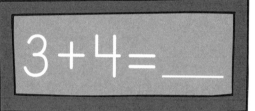

1. I know how to _____ 3 and 4.

2. Which book did you _____ to read?

3. Go in the door that says "_____."

4. I will_____ a yellow circle for the sun onto my picture.

5. I help_____ the clothes after they are washed.

6. She will _____ her banana with me.

Vocabulary

Directions: Follow the directions below.

glue	enter	share	add	decide	fold

1. Add letters to these words to make words from the box.

   old _____   are _____

2. Write the two words from the box that begin with vowels.

   _____   _____

3. Change one letter of each word to make a word from the box.

   food _____   clue _____

4. Change two letters of this word to make a word from the box.

   beside _____

Vocabulary: Statements

A **statement** is a sentence that tells something.

Directions: Use the words in the box to complete the statements below. Write the words on the lines.

glue	decide	add
share	enter	fold

1. It took ten minutes for Kayla to _____ the numbers.

2. Ben wants to _____ his cookies with me.

3. "I can't _____ which color to choose," said Rocky.

4. _____ can be used to make things stick together.

5. "This is how you _____ your paper in half," said Mrs. Green.

6. The opposite of **leave** is _____ .

Write your own statement on the line.

_____

Vocabulary: Questions

Questions are asking sentences. They begin with a capital letter and end with a question mark. Many questions begin with the words **who, what, why, when, where** and **how**. Write six questions using the question words below. Make sure to end each question with a question mark.

1. Who _____

2. What _____

3. Why _____

4. When _____

5. Where _____

6. How _____

Vocabulary: Commands

A **command** is a sentence that tells someone to do something.

Directions: Use the words in the box to complete the commands below. Write the words on the lines.

glue	decide	add	share	enter	fold

1. _____ a cup of flour to the cake batter.

2. _____ how much paper you will need to write your story.

3. Please _____ the picture of the apple onto the paper.

4. _____ through this door and leave through

   the other door.

5. Please _____ the letter and put it into an envelope.

6. _____ your toys with your sister.

Write your own command on the lines.

_____

_____

Name: _____

Vocabulary: Directions

A **direction** is a sentence written as a command.

Directions: Write the missing directions for these pictures. Begin each direction with one of the verbs below.

glue	enter	share	add	decide	fold

How To Make a Peanut Butter and Jelly Sandwich:

1. Spread peanut butter on bread.

2. _____

3. Cut the sandwich in half.

4. _____

How To Make a Valentine:

1. _____

2. Draw half a heart.

3. Cut along the line you drew.

4. _____

Kinds of Sentences

A **statement** is a sentence that tells something.
A **question** is a sentence that asks something.
A **command** is a sentence that tells someone to do something.

Commands begin with a verb or **please.** They usually end with a period. The noun is **you** but does not need to be part of the sentence.

Example: "Come here, please." means "**You** come here, please."

Examples of commands: Stand next to me.
Please give me some paper.

Directions: Write **S** in front of the statements, **Q** in front of the questions and **C** in front of the commands. End each sentence with a period or a question mark.

Example:

_____C_____ Stop and look before you cross the street.

_____ 1. Did you do your math homework

_____ 2. I think I lost my math book

_____ 3. Will you help me find it

_____ 4. I looked everywhere

_____ 5. Please open your math books to page three

_____ 6. Did you look under your desk

_____ 7. I looked, but it's not there

_____ 8. Who can add seven and four

_____ 9. Come up and write the answer on the board

_____ 10. Chris, where is your math book

_____ 11. I don't know for sure

_____ 12. Please share a book with a friend

Name: _____

Kinds of Sentences

Remember: a **statement** tells something, a **question** asks something and a **command** tells someone to do something.

Directions: On each line, write a statement, question or command. Use a word from the box in each sentence.

glue	share	decide
enter	add	fold

Example:

Question:

Can he add anything else?

1. Statement:

_____

2. Question:

_____

3. Command:

_____

4. Statement:

_____

5. Question:

_____

Name: _____

Kinds of Sentences

Directions: Use the group of words below to write three sentences: a **statement**, a **question** and a **command**.

| add | can | these | he | quickly | numbers |

Example:

Statement:

He can add these numbers quickly.

Question:

Can he can add these numbers quickly?

Command:

Add these numbers quickly.

| fold | here | should | we | it |

1. Statement:

_____

2. Question:

_____

3. Command:

_____

Grade 3 - Comprehensive Curriculum

Name: _____

Vocabulary: Completing a Story

Directions: Use verbs to complete the story below. The verbs that tell about things that happened in the past will end in **ed**.

Last week, Amy and I _____

a contest. We were supposed to make a

card to give to a child in a hospital. First, we

_____ a big sheet of white paper

in half to make the card. Then we _____ to draw a

rainbow on the front. Amy started coloring the rainbow all by herself.

"Wait!" I said. "We both _____ the contest. Let me help!"

"Okay," Amy said. "Let's _____ . You _____

a color, and then I'll _____ a color." It was more fun

when we _____ . When we finished making the rainbow,

we _____ to _____ a sun to the picture. I cut

one out of yellow paper. Then Amy _____ it just above

the rainbow. Well, our card didn't win the contest, but it did make

a little boy with a broken leg smile. Amy and I felt so happy! We

_____ to go right home and make some more cards!

Name: _____

Homophones

Homophones are words that sound the same but are spelled differently and have different meanings.

Directions: Use the homophones in the box to answer the riddles below.

main	meat	peace	dear	to
mane	meet	piece	deer	too

1. Which word has the word **pie** in it? _____

2. Which word rhymes with **ear** and is an animal? _____

3. Which word rhymes with **shoe** and means **also**? _____

4. Which word has the word **eat** in it and is something you might eat? _____

5. Which word has the same letters as the word **read** but in a different order? _____

6. Which word rhymes with **train** and is something on a pony? _____

7. Which word, if it began with a capital letter, might be the name of an important street? _____

8. Which word sounds like a number but has only two letters? _____

9. Which word rhymes with and is a synonym for **greet**? _____

10. Which word rhymes with the last syllable in **police** and can mean quiet? _____

Name: _____

Homophones: Sentences

Directions: Write a word from the box to complete each sentence.

main	meat	peace	dear	two
mane	meet	piece	deer	too

1. The horse had a long, beautiful _____ .

   The _____ idea of the paragraph was boats.

2. Let's _____ at my house to do our homework.

   The lion was fed _____ at mealtime.

3. We had _____ kittens.

   Mike has a red bike. Tom does, _____ .

4. The _____ ran in front of the car.

   I begin my letters with " _____ Mom."

Name: _____

Homophones

Directions: Cut out each honeybee at the bottom of the page and glue it on the flower with its homophone.

cut ✂ -

Name: _____

Homophones: Spelling

Directions: Circle the word in each sentence which is not spelled correctly. Then write the word correctly.

1. Please meat me at the park.   _____

2. I would like a peace of pie.   _____

3. There were too cookies left.   _____

4. The horse's main needed to be brushed. _____

5. We saw a dear in the forest.   _____

Grade 3 - Comprehensive Curriculum

Name: _____

Homophones: Rhymes

Directions: Use homophones to create two-lined rhymes.

Example: I found it a **pain**

To comb the horse's **mane**!

1. _____

_____

2. _____

_____

3. _____

_____

Short Vowels

Short vowel patterns usually have a single vowel followed by a consonant sound.

Short a is the sound you hear in the word **can**.

Short e is the sound you hear in the word **men**.

Short i is the sound you hear in the word **pig**.

Short o is the sound you hear in the word **pot**.

Short u is the sound you hear in the word **truck**.

fast	stop
spin	track
wish	lunch
bread	block

Directions: Use the words in the box to answer the questions below.

Which word:

begins with the same sound as **blast** and ends with the same sound as **look**? _____

rhymes with **stack**? _____

begins with the same sound as **phone** and ends with the same sound as **lost**? _____

has the same vowel sound as **hen**? _____

rhymes with **crunch**? _____

begins with the same sound as **spot** and ends with the same sound as **can**? _____

begins with the same sound as **win** and ends with the same sound as **crush**? _____

has the word **top** in it? _____

Short Vowels: Sentences

Directions: Use the words in the box to complete each sentence.

fast	wish	truck	bread	sun
best	stop	track	lunch	block

Race cars can go very_____ .

Carol packs a _____ for Ted before school.

Throw a penny in the well and make a _____ .

The _____ had a flat tire.

My favorite kind of _____ is whole wheat.

Short Vowels: Spelling

Directions: Circle the word in each sentence which is not spelled correctly. Then write the word correctly.

1. Be sure to stopp at the red light. _____

2. The train goes down the trak. _____

3. Please put the bred in the toaster. _____

4. I need another blok to finish. _____

5. The beasst player won a trophy. _____

6. Blow out the candles and make a wiish. _____

7. The truk blew its horn. _____

Name: _____

Long Vowels

Long vowels are the letters **a**, **e**, **i**, **o** and **u** which say the letter name sound.

Long a is the sound you hear in **cane**.

Long e is the sound you hear in **green**.

Long i is the sound you hear in **pie**.

Long o is the sound you hear in **bowl**.

Long u is the sound you hear in **cube**.

lame	goal
pain	few
street	fright
nose	gray
bike	fuse

Directions: Use the words in the box to answer the questions below.

1. Add one letter to each of these words to make words from the box.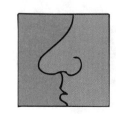

   ray _____ use _____ right _____

2. Change one letter from each word to make a word from the box.

   pail _____ goat _____

   late _____ bite _____

3. Write the word from the box that . . .

   has the long **e** sound. _____

   rhymes with **you**. _____

   is a homophone for **knows**. _____

Name: _____

Long Vowels: Sentences

Directions: Use the words in the box to complete each sentence.

lame	goal	pain	few	bike
street	fright	nose	gray	fuse

1. Look both ways before crossing the _____ .

2. My _____ had a flat tire.

3. Our walk through the haunted house

   gave us such a _____ .

4. I kicked the soccer ball and scored a _____ .

5. The _____ clouds mean rain is coming.

6. Cover your _____ when you sneeze.

7. We blew a _____ at my house last night.

Name: _____

Long Vowels

Directions: Use long vowel words from the box to answer the clues below. Write the letters of the words on the lines.

| few bike dime goal fuse lame street nose fright pain |

1. ___ ___ ___ ___ ___ [ ] (rhymes with **night**)

2. ___ ___ [ ] ___ ___ ___ (could be Main or Maple)

3. ___ [ ] ___ (synonym for **a couple**)

4. ___ ___ [ ] ___ (rhymes with **tame**)

5. ___ ___ ___ [ ] (can be ridden on a trail)

6. ___ ___ ___ ___ [ ] (homophone for **pane**)

7. [ ] ___ ___ ___ (ten of these make a dollar)

8. ___ [ ] ___ ___ (changing one letter of this word makes **goat**)

9. ___ [ ] ___ ___ (has the word **use** in it)

10. ___ ___ [ ] ___ (homophone for **knows**)

Now, read the letters in the boxes from top to bottom to find out what kind of a job you did!

Name: _____

Adjectives

Directions: Use the words in the box to answer the questions below. Use each word only once.

polite	careless	neat	shy	selfish	thoughtful

1. Someone who is quiet and needs some time to make new friends is _____.

2. A person who says "please" and "thank you" is _____.

3. Someone who always puts all the toys away is _____.

4. A person who won't share with others is being _____.

5. A person who leaves a bike out all night is being _____.

6. Someone who thinks of others is _____.

Adjectives

Directions: Use the adjectives in the box to answer the questions below.

| polite | careless | neat | shy | selfish | thoughtful |

1. Change a letter in each word to make an adjective.

near   _____

why   _____

2. Write the word that rhymes with each of these.

fell dish   _____

not full   _____

hair mess   _____

3. Find these words in the adjectives. Write the adjective.

at   _____

are   _____

it   _____

Name: _____

Adjectives: Spelling

Directions: Circle the word in each sentence which is not spelled correctly. Then write the word correctly.

1. John isn't shelfish at all. _____

2. He sharred his lunch with me today. _____

3. I was careles and forgot to bring mine. _____

4. My father says if I planed better,
   that wouldn't happen all the time. _____

5. John is kind of quiet, and I used
   to think he was shie. _____

6. Now, I know he is really thotful. _____

7. He's also very polyte and always
   asks before he borrows anything. _____

8. He would never just reach over
   and grabb something he wanted. _____

9. I'm glad John desided to be my friend. _____

Adjectives: Explaining Sentences

Directions: Use a word from the box to tell about a person in each picture below. Then write a sentence that explains why you chose that word.

| polite neat careless shy selfish thoughtful |

The word I picked: _____

I think so because . . .

_____

The word I picked: _____

I think so because . . .

_____

The word I picked: _____

I think so because . . .

_____

Name: _____

Adjectives

Directions: Look at each picture. Then add adjectives to the sentences. Use colors, numbers, words from the box and any other words you need to describe each picture.

Example:

| polite | neat | careless |
| shy | selfish | thoughtful |

The boy shared his pencil.

The polite boy shared his red pencil.

The girl dropped her coat.

_____

The boy played with cars.

_____

The boy put books away.

_____

Grade 3 - Comprehensive Curriculum

C, K, CK Words: Spelling

Directions: Write the words from the box that answer the questions.

crowd	keeper	cost	pack	kangaroo	thick

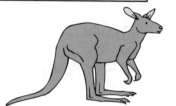

1. Which words spell the **k** sound with a **k**?

_____

2. Which words spell the **k** sound with a **c**?

_____

3. Which words spell the **k** sound with **ck**?

_____

4. Circle the letters that spell **k** in these words:

cook   black   cool   kite

cake   pocket   poke

5. Which words from the box rhyme with each of these?

tossed _____   deeper _____

proud _____   all in blue _____

Name: _____

C, K, CK Words: Sentences

The **k** sound can be spelled with a **c**, **k** or **ck** after a short vowel sound.

Directions: Use the words from the box to complete the sentences. Use each word only once.

crowd	keeper
cost	pack
kangaroo	thick

1. On sunny days, there is always a _____ of people at the zoo.

2. It doesn't _____ much to get into the zoo.

3. We always get hungry, so we _____ a picnic lunch.

4. We like to watch the _____ .

5. Its _____ tail helps it jump and walk.

6. The _____ always makes sure the cages are clean.

Name: _____

C, K, CK Words: Sentences

Remember: every sentence must have a noun that tells who or what is doing something and a verb that tells what the noun is doing.

Directions: Parts of each sentence below are missing. Rewrite each sentence, adding a noun or a verb, periods and capital letters.

Example:

read a book every day (needs a noun)

Leon reads a book every day.

1. packed a lunch

_____

2. the crowd at the beach

_____

3. cost too much

_____

4. kangaroos and their babies

_____

5. was too thick to chew

_____

C, K, CK Words: Joining Sentences

Joining words are words that make two sentences into one longer sentence. Here are some words that join sentences:

and — if both sentences are about the same noun or verb.

> **Example:** Tom is in my class at school, **and** he lives near me.

but — if the second sentence says something different from the first sentence.

> **Example:** Julie walks to school with me, **but** today she is sick.

or — if each sentence names a different thing you could do.

> **Example:** We could go to my house, **or** we could go to yours.

Directions: Join each set of sentences below using the words **and**, **but** or **or**.

1. Those socks usually cost a lot. This pack of ten socks is cheaper.

_____

_____

2. The kangaroo has a pouch. It lives in Australia.

_____

_____

3. The zoo keeper can start to work early. She can stay late.

_____

_____

Name: _____

C, K, CK Words: Joining Sentences

If and **when** can be joining words, too.

Directions: Read each set of sentences. Then join the two sentences to make one longer sentence.

Example: The apples will need to be washed.
The apples are dirty.

The apples will need to be washed
if they are dirty.

1. The size of the crowd grew. It grew when the game began.

_____

_____

2. Be careful driving in the fog. The fog is thick.

_____

_____

3. Pack your suitcases. Do it when you wake up in the morning.

_____

_____

C, K, CK Words: Joining Sentences

Some words that can join sentences are:

when — **When** we got there, the show had already started.

after — **After** I finished my homework, I watched TV.

because — You can't go by yourself, **because** you are too young.

Directions: Use the joining words to make the two short sentences into one longer one.

1.  The keeper opened the door. The bear got out.

_____

_____

 I didn't buy the tickets. They cost too much.

_____

_____

3. 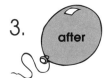 The kangaroo ate lunch. He took a nap.

_____

_____

4. 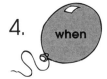 The door opened. The crowd rushed in.

_____

_____

5 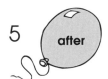 I cut the bread. Everyone had a slice.

_____

_____

C, K, CK Words: Joining Sentences

Directions: Use **because**, **after** or **when** to join each set of sentences into one longer sentence.

1. I pack my own lunch. I always put in some fruit.

_____

_____

2. I would like to be a zoo keeper. I love animals.

_____

_____

3. I was surprised there was such a crowd. It cost a lot.

_____

_____

4. I beat the eggs for two minutes. They were thick and yellow.

_____

_____

C, K, CK Words: Completing a Story

Directions: Use **c**, **k**, or **ck** words to complete this story. Some of the verbs are past tense and need to end with **ed**.

One day, Kevin and I _____ a lunch and went to the

zoo. There was a big _____ of people. Kevin wanted

to see the _____. When we got to the

_____ cage, we met the _____,

whose name was Carla. "How much does it _____ $ to

keep a _____?" Kevin asked the _____.

"Our grass at home is really _____ NOT THIN , and that's

what _____ eat, right?"

"You must have a big cage and clean it every day," Carla the

_____ told Kevin. Kevin got quiet very quickly.

"I'll just keep coming here to see _____ in

the cage you clean," he said.

Name: _____

S Words: Spelling

The **s** sound can be spelled with an **s**, **ss**, **c** or **ce**.

Directions: Use the words from the box to complete the sentences below. Write each word only once.

center	pencil	space
address	police	darkness

1. I drew a circle in the _____ of the page.

2. I'll write to you if you tell me your _____ .

3. She pushed too hard and broke the point on her _____ .

4. If you hear a noise at night, call the _____ .

5. It was night, and I couldn't see him in the _____ .

6. There's not enough _____ for me to sit next to you.

Name: _____

S Words: Spelling

Directions: Write the words from the box that answer the questions.

center	pencil	space	address	police	darkness

1. Which words spell the **s** sound with **ss**?

_____

2. Which words spell **s** with a **c**?

_____

3. Which words spell **s** with **ce**?

_____

4. Write two other words you know that spell **s** with an **s**.

_____

5. Circle the letters that spell **s** in these words.

decide   kiss   careless   ice

cost   fierce   sentence

6. Put these letters in order to make words from the box.

sdsdera _____   sdserakn _____

clipoe _____   clipne _____

capse _____   retnce _____

Name: _____

C Words: Spelling

The letter **c** can make the **k** sound or the **s** sound.

Example: **c**ount, **c**ity

Directions: Write **k** or **s** to show how the **c** in each word sounds.

cave _____   copy _____   force _____

become _____   dance _____   city _____

certain _____   contest _____   cool _____

Directions: Use the words from the box to answer these questions.

| center | pencil | space | address | police | darkness |

1. Which word begins with the same sound as **simple** and ends with the same sound as **fur**? _____

2. Which word begins with the same sound as **average** and ends with the same sound as **circus**? _____

3. Which word begins with the same sound as **popcorn** and ends with the same sound as **glass**? _____

4. Which word begins and ends with the same sound as **pool**?

_____

5. Which word begins with the same sound as **city** and ends with the same sound as **kiss**? _____

6. Which word begins and ends with the same sound as **delicious**?

_____

Review

Directions: Circle the words which are not spelled correctly in the story. Then write each word correctly on the lines below.

One day, Peter and I were sitting on a bench at the park. A polise woman came and sat in the empty spase beside us. "Have you seen a little dog with thik black fur?" she asked. She was very poolite. "Remember that dog?" I asked Peter. "He was just here!" Peter nodded. He was too shie to say anything.

"Give us his adress," I said. "We'll find him and take him home." She got out a pensil and wrote the addres in the senter of a piece of paper. Peter and I desided to walk down the street the way the dog had gone. There was a krowd of people at a cherch we passed, but no dog.

Then it started getting late. "We better go home," Peter said. "I can't see in this drakness, anyway."

As we turned around to go back, there was the little dog! He had been following us! We took him to the adress. The girl who came to the door grabed him and huged him tight. "I'm sorry I let you wander away," she told the dog. "I'll never be so carless again." I thought she was going to kis us, too. We left just in time!

_____ _____ _____

_____ _____ _____

_____ _____ _____

_____ _____ _____

_____ _____ _____

Name: _____

Suffixes

A **suffix** is a word part added to the end of a word. Suffixes add to or change the meaning of the word.

Example: sad + ly = sadly

Below are some suffixes and their meanings.

ment	state of being, quality of, act of
ly	like or in a certain way
ness	state of being
ful	full of
less	without

Directions: The words in the box have suffixes. Use the suffix meanings above to match each word with its meaning below. Write the words on the lines.

friendly	cheerful	safely	sleeveless	speechless
kindness	amazement	sickness	peaceful	excitement

1. in a safe way __ __ __ __ __
   6

2. full of cheer __ __ __ __ __ __ __
   2

3. full of peace __ __ __ __ __ __ __
   4

4. state of being amazed __ __ __ __ __ __ __ __ __
   5

5. state of being excited __ __ __ __ __ __ __ __ __ __
   1

6. without speech __ __ __ __ __ __ __ __ __ __
   3

Use the numbered letters to find the missing word below.

You are now on your way to becoming a

__ __ __ __ __ __ of suffixes!
5   6   3   1   4   2

Name: _____

Suffixes: Adverbs

Adverbs are words that describe verbs. Adverbs tell where, when or how. Most adverbs end in the suffix **ly**.

Directions: Complete each sentence with the correct part of speech.

Example:

| Hank | wrote | here. |
| who? (noun) | what? (verb) | where? (adverb) |

1.

| | was lost | |
| who? (noun) | what? (verb) | where? (adverb) |

2.

| | | quickly. |
| who? (noun) | what? (verb) | how? (adverb) |

3.

| | felt | |
| who? (noun) | what? (verb) | how? (adverb) |

4.

| My brother | | |
| who? (noun) | what? (verb) | when? (adverb) |

5.

| | woke up | |
| who? (noun) | what? (verb) | when? (adverb) |

6.

| | | gladly. |
| who? (noun) | what? (verb) | how? (adverb) |

Name: _____

Suffixes: Sentences

Directions: Use a word from the box to complete each sentence.

| cheerful | softness | encouragement |
| kindness | safely | friendly |

1. The _____ dog licked me and wagged his tail.

2. Jeff is happy and _____ .

3. To ride your bike _____ , you should wear a helmet.

4. My aunt is known for her thoughtfulness and _____ .

5. I love the _____ of my cat's fur.

6. The teacher gave her class a lot of _____ .

Suffixes: Root Words

A **root word** is a word before a suffix is added.

Example: In the word **hope**ful, the root word is **hope**.

DON'T BE CLUELESS!

Directions: Each egg contains a root word. Cut out each egg and match it with a basket so that it forms a new word. Write the new word on the lines on the basket.

I CAN'T STAND THE EGGCITEMENT!

cut ✂ -

friend   cheer   safe   sleeve   speech

kind   amaze   sick   peace

Prefixes

Prefixes are word parts added to the beginning of a root word. Prefixes add to or change the meaning of the word.

Example: remake — to make something again.

re — again   un — not   dis — not or reverse   in — in or not

Directions: Read the meanings on each treasure chest lid. Then glue the correct word onto each treasure chest.

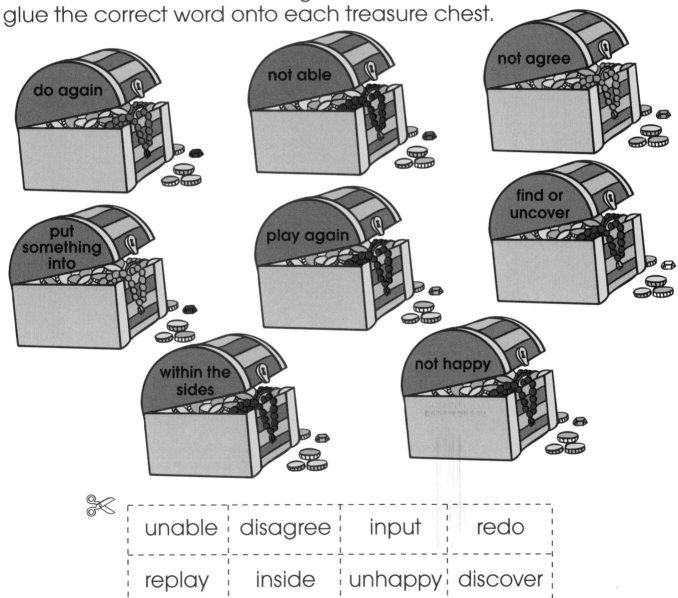

do again

not able

not agree

put something into

play again

find or uncover

within the sides

not happy

| unable | disagree | input | redo |
| replay | inside | unhappy | discover |

Name: _____

Prefixes: Sentences

Directions: Match each sentence with the word which completes it. Then write the word on the line.

1. The farmer was _____ because it •
   didn't rain.

2. The scientist tried to _____ the •
   secret formula.

3. The child _____ his report •
   into the computer.

4. We were _____ to do the •
   work without help.

5. My brother and I _____ about •
   which show to watch.

6. The umpire called for a _____ of •
   the game.

7. We had to stay _____ when •
   it got cold.

8. I spilled my milk on my paper and had to •
   _____ my homework.

• input

• redo

• unhappy

• disagree

• replay

• discover

• inside

• unable

Synonyms

Synonyms are words which mean almost the same thing.

Example: sick — ill

Directions: Use words from the box to help you complete the sentences below.

glad	fast	noisy	filthy	angry

1. When I am mad, I could also say I am _____ .

2. To be _____ is the same as being happy.

3. After playing outside, I thought I was dirty, but Mom said I was

   _____ !

4. I tried not to be too loud, but I couldn't help being a little

   _____ .

5. If you're too _____ , or speedy, you may not do

   a careful job.

Think of another pair of synonyms. Write them on the lines.

_____   _____

Name: _____

Synonyms

Directions: Cut out the sails below. Glue each one to the boat whose synonym matches it.

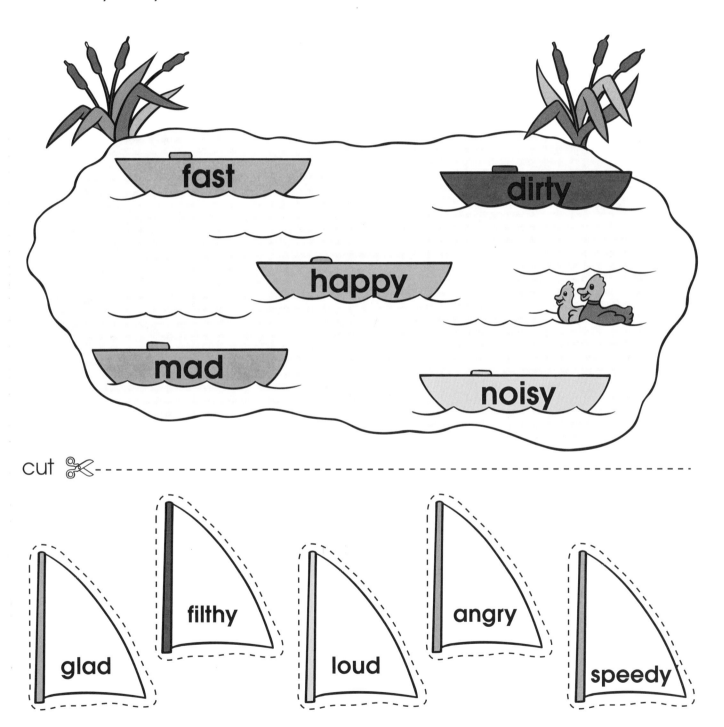

cut ✂ -

Grade 3 - Comprehensive Curriculum

Antonyms

Antonyms are words that have opposite meanings.

Example: neat — sloppy

Directions: Cut out each frog below and glue it to the lily pad with its antonym.

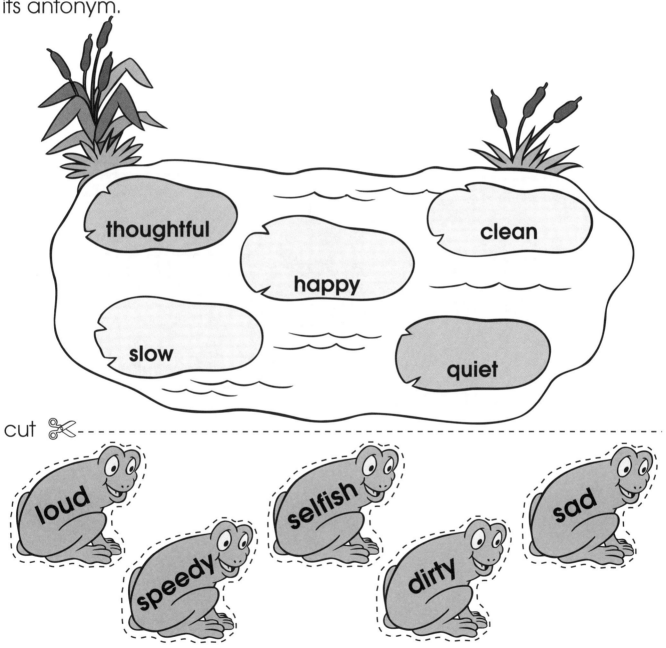

cut ✂ -

Antonyms

Directions: Use antonyms from the box to complete the sentences below.

speedy	clean	quiet	thoughtful	happy

1. If we get too loud, the teacher will ask us to get _____ .

2. She was sad to lose her puppy, but she was _____

   to find it again.

3. Mark got dirty, so he had to scrub himself _____ .

4. Janna was too _____ when

   she did her homework, so she tried

   to be slow when she did it over.

5. Dave was too selfish to share his cookies,

   but Deborah was _____ enough to share hers.

Think of another pair of antonyms. Write them on the lines.

_____   _____

Contractions

A **contraction** is a short way to write two words together. Some letters are left out, but an apostrophe takes their place.

Directions: Write the words from the box that answer the questions.

hasn't	you've	aren't	we've	weren't

1. Write the correct contractions below.

   Example:

   I have _____I've_____   was not _____wasn't_____

   we have _____   you have _____

   are not _____   were not _____

   has not _____

2. Write two words from the box that are contractions using **have**.

   _____   _____

3. Write three words from the box that are contractions using **not**.

   _____   _____   _____

Name: _____

Contractions

Directions: In each sentence below, underline the two words that could be made into a contraction. Write the contraction on the line. Use each contraction from the box only once.

Example: The boys <u>have not</u> gone camping in a long time.

haven't

hasn't	you've	aren't
we've	weren't	

1. After a while, we were not sure it was the right direction.

_____

2. I think we have been this way before. _____

3. We have been waiting, but our guide has not come yet.

_____

4. Did you say you have been here with your sister?

_____

5. You are not going to give up and go back, are you?

_____

Grade 3 - Comprehensive Curriculum

Review

Directions: Circle the two words in each sentence that are not spelled correctly. Then write the words correctly.

1. Arn't you going to shere your cookie with me?

_____ _____

2. We planed a long time, but we still wern't ready.

_____ _____

3. My pensil hassn't broken yet today.

_____ _____

4. We arn't going because we don't have the correct adress.

_____ _____

5. Youve stired the soup too much.

_____ _____

6. Weave tried to be as neet as possible.

_____ _____

7. She hasnt seen us in this darknes.

_____ _____

MATH

Name: _____

Addition

Directions: Add.

Example:

Add the ones.	Add the tens.

$$26$$
$$+21$$
$$7$$

$$26$$
$$+21$$
$$47$$

$$18$$
$$+11$$

$$24$$
$$+35$$

$$38$$
$$+21$$

$$49$$
$$+50$$

$$52$$
$$+33$$

$$75$$
$$+12$$

$$83$$
$$+16$$

$$67$$
$$+32$$

$$44$$
$$+25$$

$$28$$
$$+41$$

68 + 20 = _____   54 + 25 = _____   71 + 17 = _____

The Lions scored 42 points. The Clippers scored 21 points.
How many points were scored in all?   _____

Name: _____

Subtraction

Subtraction means "taking away" or subtracting one number from another to find the difference. For example, 10 - 3 = 7.

Directions: Subtract.

Example:

Subtract the ones.	Subtract the tens.
39 -24 5	39 -24 | 5

48 -35	95 -22	87 -16	55 -43

37 -14	69 -57	44 -23	99 -78

66 - 44 = _____   57 - 33 = _____

The yellow car traveled 87 miles per hour. The orange car traveled 66 miles per hour. How much faster was the yellow car traveling?

_____

Place Value

The place value of a digit, or numeral, is shown by where it is in the number. For example, in the number 1,234, 1 has the place value of thousands, 2 is hundreds, 3 is tens and 4 is ones.

Hundred Thousands	Ten Thousands	Thousands	Hundreds	Tens	Ones
9	4	3	8	5	2

943,852

Directions: Match the numbers in Column A with the words in Column B.

A	B
62,453	two hundred thousand
7,641	three thousand
486,113	four hundred thousand
11,277	eight hundreds
813,463	seven tens
594,483	five ones
254,089	six hundreds
79,841	nine ten thousands
27,115	five tens

Name: _____

Addition: Regrouping

Addition means "putting together" or adding two or more numbers to find the sum. For example, 3 + 5 = 8. To regroup is to use ten ones to form one ten, ten tens to form one 100 and so on.

Directions: Add using regrouping.

Example:

Add the ones.

```
  88
+ 21
   9
```

Add the tens
with regrouping.

```
  88
+ 21
 109
```

```
  37          56          51          37          70
+ 72        + 67        + 88        + 55        + 68
```

```
  93          47          81          23          36
+ 54        + 82        + 77        + 92        + 71
```

92 + 13 = _____   73 + 83 = _____   54 + 61 = _____

The Blues scored 63 points. The Reds scored 44 points.
How many points were scored in all?   _____

Subtraction: Regrouping

Subtraction means "taking away" or subtracting one number from another to find the difference. For example, 10 - 3 = 7. To regroup is to use one ten to form ten ones, one 100 to form ten tens and so on.

Directions: Study the example. Subtract using regrouping.

Example:

$$
\begin{array}{rcl}
32 &=& 2\ \text{tens} + 12\ \text{ones} \\
-13 &=& 1\ \text{ten} + 3\ \text{ones} \\
\hline
19 &=& 1\ \text{ten} + 9\ \text{ones}
\end{array}
$$

```
  33        86        92        71
 -28       -59       -37       -48
```

```
  63        45        31        55
 -47       -18       -22       -39
```

82 - 69 = _____   73 - 36 = _____

The Yankees won 85 games.
The Cubs won 69 games.
How many more games
did the Yankees win?   _____

Name: _____

Addition and Subtraction: Regrouping

Addition means "putting together" or adding two or more numbers to find the sum. Subtraction means "taking away" or subtracting one number from another to find the difference. To regroup is to use one ten to form ten ones, one 100 to form ten tens and so on.

Directions: Add or subtract. Regroup when needed.

$$\begin{array}{r} 92 \\ -47 \\ \hline \end{array} \qquad \begin{array}{r} 58 \\ +26 \\ \hline \end{array} \qquad \begin{array}{r} 63 \\ +18 \\ \hline \end{array} \qquad \begin{array}{r} 77 \\ -38 \\ \hline \end{array}$$

$$\begin{array}{r} 27 \\ -17 \\ \hline \end{array} \qquad \begin{array}{r} 31 \\ +42 \\ \hline \end{array} \qquad \begin{array}{r} 56 \\ -29 \\ \hline \end{array} \qquad \begin{array}{r} 67 \\ +33 \\ \hline \end{array}$$

$$\begin{array}{r} 72 \\ +19 \\ \hline \end{array} \qquad \begin{array}{r} 87 \\ -58 \\ \hline \end{array} \qquad \begin{array}{r} 93 \\ -89 \\ \hline \end{array} \qquad \begin{array}{r} 54 \\ +27 \\ \hline \end{array}$$

The soccer team scored 83 goals this year. The soccer team scored 68 goals last year. How many goals did they score in all? _____

How many more goals did they score this year than last year? _____

Addition: Regrouping

Directions: Study the example. Add using regrouping.

Examples:

Add the ones. Regroup.	Add the tens. Regroup.	Add the hundreds.

<table>
<tr><td>1
156
+267
―――
3</td><td>6
+7
――
13</td><td>1
5
+6
――
12</td><td>11
156
+267
―――
23</td><td>1
156
+267
―――
423</td></tr>
</table>

```
  29        81        52        49
  46        78        67        37       162
 +12       +33       +23       +19      +349
 ———       ———       ———       ———      ————
```

```
 273       655       783       385       428
+198      +297      +148      +169      +122
————      ————      ————      ————      ————
```

Sally went bowling. She had scores of
115, 129 and 103. What was her total
score for three games?   _____

Addition: Regrouping

Directions: Add using regrouping. Then use the code to discover the name of a United States president.

$$\begin{array}{r} 348 \\ +752 \\ \hline 1,100 \end{array}$$
$$\begin{array}{r} 642 \\ +277 \\ \hline \end{array}$$
$$\begin{array}{r} 386 \\ +787 \\ \hline \end{array}$$
$$\begin{array}{r} 184 \\ +875 \\ \hline \end{array}$$
$$\begin{array}{r} 578 \\ +874 \\ \hline \end{array}$$

$$\begin{array}{r} 653 \\ +768 \\ \hline \end{array}$$
$$\begin{array}{r} 653 \\ +359 \\ \hline \end{array}$$
$$\begin{array}{r} 946 \\ +239 \\ \hline \end{array}$$
$$\begin{array}{r} 393 \\ +257 \\ \hline \end{array}$$
$$\begin{array}{r} 199 \\ +843 \\ \hline \end{array}$$

$$\begin{array}{r} 721 \\ +679 \\ \hline \end{array}$$

____. ____ ____ ____ ____ ____ ____ ____ ____ ____

1012	1173	1059	1421	919	650	1452	1042	1100	1400	1185
N	A	S	I	W	T	H	O	G	N	G

Addition: Regrouping

Directions: Study the example. Add using regrouping.

Example:

Steps:
5,356   1. Add the ones.
+3,976   2. Regroup the tens. Add the tens.
9,332   3. Regroup the hundreds. Add the hundreds.
         4. Add the thousands.

```
  6,849          1,846          9,221
 +3,276         +8,384         +6,769
```

```
  2,758          5,299          7,932
 +3,663         +8,764         +6,879
```

A plane flew 1,838 miles on the first day. It flew 2,347 miles on the second day. How many miles did it fly in all?

_____

Name: _____

Addition: Mental Math

Directions: Try to do these addition problems in your head without using paper and pencil.

7	6	8	10	2	6
+4	+3	+1	+ 2	+9	+6

10	40	80	60	50	100
+20	+20	+100	+30	+70	+ 40

350	300	400	450	680	900
+150	+500	+800	+ 10	+100	+ 70

	4,000	300	8,000		7,000
1,000	400	200	500	9,800	300
+ 200	+ 30	+ 80	+ 60	+ 150	+ 30

Name: _____

Subtraction: Regrouping

Directions: Regrouping for subtraction is the opposite of regrouping for addition. Study the example. Subtract using regrouping. Then use the code to color the flowers.

Example:

$$\begin{array}{r} 647 \\ -453 \\ \hline 194 \end{array}$$

Steps:
1. Subtract ones.
2. Subtract tens. Five tens cannot be subtracted from 4 tens.
3. Regroup tens by regrouping 6 hundreds (5 hundreds + 10 tens).
4. Add the 10 tens to the four tens.
5. Subtract 5 tens from 14 tens.
6. Subtract the hundreds.

If the answer has:
1 one, color it red;
8 ones, color it pink;
5 ones, color it yellow.

$$\begin{array}{r} 428 \\ -397 \end{array}$$

$$\begin{array}{r} 368 \\ -173 \end{array}$$

$$\begin{array}{r} 943 \\ -652 \end{array}$$

$$\begin{array}{r} 726 \\ -331 \end{array}$$

$$\begin{array}{r} 637 \\ -242 \end{array}$$

$$\begin{array}{r} 549 \\ -361 \end{array}$$

$$\begin{array}{r} 749 \\ -568 \end{array}$$

$$\begin{array}{r} 528 \\ -270 \end{array}$$

Subtraction: Regrouping

Directions: Study the example. Follow the steps. Subtract using regrouping.

Example:

```
 634
-455
 179
```

Steps:
1. Subtract ones. You cannot subtract five ones from 4 ones.
2. Regroup ones by regrouping 3 tens to 2 tens + 10 ones.
3. Subtract 5 ones from 14 ones.
4. Regroup tens by regrouping hundreds (5 hundreds + 10 tens).
5. Subtract 5 tens from 12 tens.
6. Subtract hundreds.

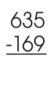

```
 635        553        832        944
-169       -174       -563       -578
```

```
 423        941        733        266
-268       -872       -498       -197
```

```
 387        594        960        887
-198       -385       -759       -598
```

Sue goes to school 185 days a year. Yoko goes to school 313 days a year. How many more days of school does Yoko attend each year?

_____

Subtraction: Regrouping

Directions: Study the example. Follow the steps. Subtract using regrouping. If you have to regroup to subtract ones and there are no tens, you must regroup twice.

Example:

```
 300
-182
 118
```

Steps:
1. Subtract ones. You cannot subtract 2 ones from 0 ones.
2. Regroup. No tens. Regroup hundreds
   (2 hundreds + 10 tens).
3. Regroup tens (9 tens + 10 ones).
4. Subtract 2 ones from ten ones.
5. Subtract 8 tens from 9 tens.
6. Subtract 1 hundred from 2 hundreds.

```
 602        306        600        807        703
-423       -128       -263       -499       -328


 800        206        400        508        909
-557       -137       -224       -379       -769


 207        604        308        700        900
-138       -397       -199       -531       -278
```

Subtraction: Regrouping

Directions: Subtract. Regroup when necessary. The first one is done for you.

7,354 −5,295 2,059	4,214 −3,185	8,437 −5,338	6,837 −4,318
5,735 −3,826	1,036 − 947	6,735 −6,646	3,841 −1,953

Columbus discovered America in 1492. The pilgrims landed in America in 1620. How many years difference was there between these two events?

_____

Grade 3 - Comprehensive Curriculum

Subtraction: Mental Math

Directions: Try to do these subtraction problems in your head without using paper and pencil.

9 - 3	12 - 6	7 - 6	5 - 1	15 - 5	2 - 0
40 -20	90 - 80	100 - 50	20 -20	60 -10	70 - 40
450 -250	500 - 300	250 - 20	690 -100	320 - 20	900 - 600
1,000 - 400	8,000 - 500	7,000 - 900	4,000 -2,000	9,500 - 4,000	5,000 -2,000

Name: _____

Review

Directions: Add or subtract using regrouping.

```
   28        82        33         67
   56        49        75         94
  +93       +51      +128       +248
```

```
  683       756       818        956
 -495      +139      -387       +267
```

```
 1,588     4,675     8,732      2,938
 -  989    -2,976    -5,664     +3,459
```

To drive from New York City to Los Angeles is 2,832 miles. To drive from New York City to Miami is 1,327 miles. How much farther is it to drive from New York City to Los Angeles than from New York City to Miami? _____

Rounding: The Nearest Ten

If the ones number is 5 or greater, "round up" to the nearest 10. If the ones number is 4 or less, the tens number stays the same and the ones number becomes a zero.

Examples: 15 round up to 20 23 round down to 20 47 round up to 50

7	_____	58	_____
12	_____	81	_____
33	_____	94	_____
27	_____	44	_____
73	_____	88	_____
25	_____	66	_____
39	_____	70	_____

Name: _____

Rounding: The Nearest Hundred

If the tens number is 5 or greater, "round up" to the nearest hundred.
If the tens number is 4 or less, the hundreds number remains the same.

REMEMBER... Look at the number directly to the right of the place you are rounding to.

Example:

230 round down to 200

470 round up to 500

150 round up to 200

732 round down to 700

456 _____   120 _____

340 _____   923 _____

867 _____   550 _____

686 _____   231 _____

770 _____   492 _____

Name: _____

Front-End Estimation

Front-end estimation is useful when you don't need to know the exact amount, but a close answer will do.

When we use front-end estimation, we use only the first number, and then add the numbers together to get the estimate.

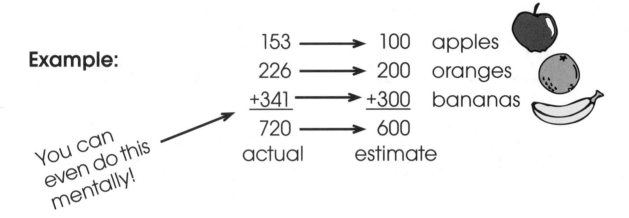

Example:

You can even do this mentally!

153	→	100	apples
226	→	200	oranges
+341	→	+300	bananas
720	→	600	
actual		estimate	

Directions: Estimate the sum of these numbers.

456 →
121 →
+438 → + _____

910 →
280 →
+320 → + _____

686 →
307 →
+711 → + _____

Multiplication

Multiplication is a short way to find the sum of adding the same number a certain amount of times. For example, we write 7 x 4 = 28 instead of 7 + 7 + 7 + 7 = 28.

Directions: Study the example. Multiply.

Example:

There are two groups of seashells.
There are 3 seashells in each group.   2 x 3 = 6
How many seashells are there in all?

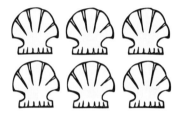

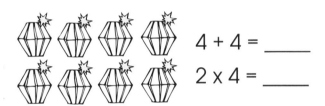   4 + 4 = _____

2 x 4 = _____

   3 + 3 + 3 = _____

3 x 3 = _____

2	3	4	6	7
x3	x5	x3	x2	x3

5	6	4	7	8
x2	x3	x2	x2	x3

5	9	8	6	9
x5	x4	x5	x6	x3

Name: _____

Multiplication

Directions: Multiply.

$$
\begin{array}{r} 3 \\ \times 5 \\ \hline \end{array}
\qquad
\begin{array}{r} 4 \\ \times 6 \\ \hline \end{array}
\qquad
\begin{array}{r} 3 \\ \times 8 \\ \hline \end{array}
$$

$$
\begin{array}{r} 5 \\ \times 5 \\ \hline \end{array}
\qquad
\begin{array}{r} 4 \\ \times 8 \\ \hline \end{array}
\qquad
\begin{array}{r} 5 \\ \times 4 \\ \hline \end{array}
$$

$$
\begin{array}{r} 6 \\ \times 7 \\ \hline \end{array}
\qquad
\begin{array}{r} 3 \\ \times 9 \\ \hline \end{array}
\qquad
\begin{array}{r} 2 \\ \times 8 \\ \hline \end{array}
\qquad
\begin{array}{r} 7 \\ \times 6 \\ \hline \end{array}
\qquad
\begin{array}{r} 9 \\ \times 4 \\ \hline \end{array}
$$

$$
\begin{array}{r} 6 \\ \times 8 \\ \hline \end{array}
\qquad
\begin{array}{r} 5 \\ \times 6 \\ \hline \end{array}
\qquad
\begin{array}{r} 7 \\ \times 7 \\ \hline \end{array}
\qquad
\begin{array}{r} 5 \\ \times 3 \\ \hline \end{array}
\qquad
\begin{array}{r} 8 \\ \times 9 \\ \hline \end{array}
$$

A riverboat makes 3 trips a day every day.
How many trips does it make in a week?

_____

Multiplication

Factors are the numbers multiplied together in a multiplication problem. The answer is called the product. If you change the order of the factors, the product stays the same.

Example:

There are 4 groups of fish.
There are 3 fish in each group.
How many fish are there in all?

$$4 \quad x \quad 3 \quad = 12$$
factor x factor = product

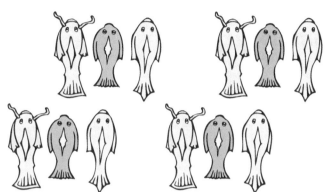

Directions: Draw 3 groups of 4 fish.

$$3 \times 4 = 12$$

Compare your drawing and answer with the example. What did you notice?

Directions: Fill in the missing numbers. Multiply.

5 x 4 = _____   3 x 6 = _____   4 x 2 = _____

4 x 5 = _____   6 x 3 = _____   2 x 4 = _____

3	7	2	9	8	4
x7	x3	x9	x2	x4	x8

5	2	6	3	5	6
x2	x5	x3	x6	x6	x5

Name: _____

Multiplication: Zero and One

Any number multiplied by zero equals zero. One multiplied by any number equals that number. Study the example. Multiply.

Example:

How many full sails are there in all?

2 boats x **1** sail on each boat = **2** sails

How many full sails are there now?

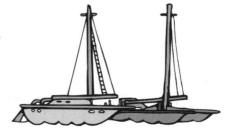

2 boats x **0** sails = **0** sails

Directions: Multiply.

1	2	3	4	0	7
x5	x1	x0	x1	x6	x0

9	8	3	4	7	6
x1	x0	x1	x0	x1	x1

Multiplication

Directions: Time yourself as you multiply. How quickly can you complete this page?

3 x2	8 x7	1 x0	1 x6	3 x4	0 x4
4 x1	4 x4	2 x5	9 x3	9 x9	5 x3
0 x8	2 x6	9 x6	8 x5	7 x3	4 x2
3 x5	2 x0	4 x6	1 x3	0 x0	3 x3

Grade 3 - Comprehensive Curriculum

Multiplication Table

Directions: Complete the multiplication table. Use it to practice your multiplication facts.

X	0	1	2	3	4	5	6	7	8	9	10
0	0										
1		1									
2			4								
3				9							
4					16						
5						25					
6							36				
7								49			
8									64		
9										81	
10											100

Name: _____

Division

Division is a way to find out how many times one number is contained in another number. For example, $28 \div 4 = 7$ means that there are seven groups of four in 28.

Directions: Study the example. Divide.

Example:

There are 6 oars.
Each canoe needs 2 oars.
How many canoes can be used?

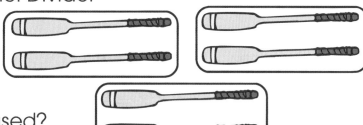

Circle groups of 2.
There are 3 groups of 2.

$$\underset{\text{oars}}{6} \div \underset{\substack{\text{number} \\ \text{of oars} \\ \text{needed} \\ \text{per canoe}}}{2} = \underset{\text{canoes}}{3}$$

$9 \div 3 =$ _____ $8 \div 2 =$ _____ $16 \div 4 =$ _____

$15 \div 5 =$ _____ $18 \div 2 =$ _____ $20 \div 4 =$ _____

$21 \div 7 =$ _____ $24 \div 6 =$ _____ $12 \div 2 =$ _____

Name: _____

Division

Directions: Divide. Draw a line from the boat to the sail with the correct answer.

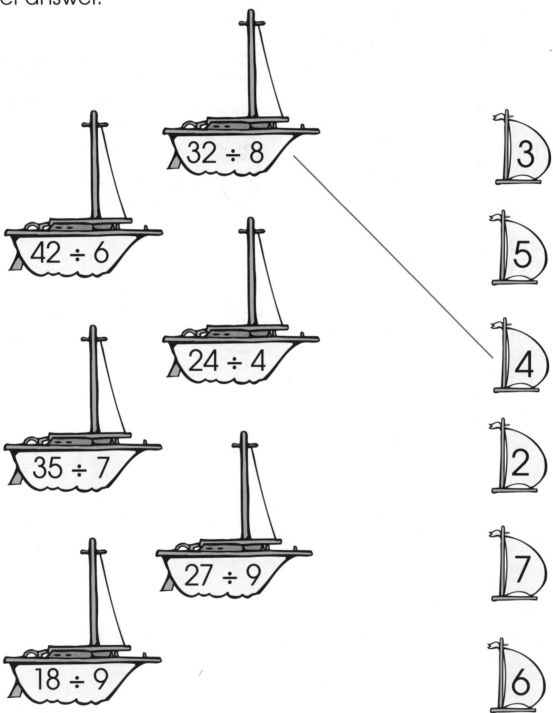

Order of Operations

When you solve a problem that involves more than one operation, this is the order to follow:

( ) Parentheses first
x Multiplication and ÷ division, working from left to right
+ Addition and - subtraction, working from left to right

Example: $2 + (3 \times 5) - 2 = 15$
$2 + 15 - 2 = 15$
$17 - 2 = 15$

Directions: Solve the problems using the correct order of operations.

$(5 - 3) + 4 \times 7 =$ _____ $1 + 2 \times 3 + 4 =$ _____

$6 \times 3 - 1 =$ _____ $(8 \div 2) \times 4 =$ _____

$9 \div 3 \times 3 + 0 =$ _____ $5 - 2 \times 1 + 2 =$ _____

Name: _____

Order of Operations

Directions: Use +, –, x and ÷ to complete the problems so the number sentence is true.

Example: 4 __+__ 2 __–__ 1 = 5

(8 ____ 2) ____ 4 = 8

(1 ____ 2) ____ 3 = 1

9 ____ 3 ____ 9 = 3

(7 ____ 5) ____ 1 = 2

8 ____ 5 ____ 4 = 10

5 ____ 4 ____ 1 = 1

REMEMBER...
USE THE ORDER OF OPERATIONS

Name: _____

Review

Directions: Multiply or divide. Fill in the blanks with the missing numbers or x or ÷ signs. The first one is done for you.

5 <u>x</u> 4 = 20   6 x 8 = _____   7 x _____ = 14

3 _ 6 = 18   7 x 2 = _____   _____ x 3 = 24

6 _ 2 = 3   24 ÷ 6 = _____   6 x 5 = _____

25 _ 5 = 5   49 ÷ 7 = _____   8 x _____ = 32

3 _ 8 = 24   18 ÷ 3 = _____   9 x 5 = _____

12 _ 3 = 4   9 x 8 = _____   6 x _____ = 36

Grade 3 - Comprehensive Curriculum

Division

Division is a way to find out how many times one number is contained in another number. The ÷ sign means "divided by." Another way to divide is to use ⌐. The dividend is the larger number that is divided by the smaller number, or divisor. The answer of a division problem is called the quotient.

Directions: Study the example. Divide.

Example:

quotient

$$20 \div 4 = 5$$

dividend divisor quotient

$$5$$
$$4\overline{)20}$$

divisor dividend

$35 \div 7 =$ _____ $7\overline{)35}$ $42 \div 6 =$ _____ $6\overline{)42}$

$2\overline{)12}$ $3\overline{)18}$ $4\overline{)36}$ $5\overline{)50}$

$6\overline{)24}$ $7\overline{)21}$ $8\overline{)32}$ $9\overline{)27}$

$36 \div 6 =$ _____ $28 \div 4 =$ _____ $15 \div 5 =$ _____ $12 \div 2 =$ _____

A tree farm has 36 trees. There are 4 rows of trees. How many trees are there in each row?   _____

Name: _____

Division: Zero and One

Directions: Study the rules of division and the examples. Divide, then write the number of the rule you used to solve each problem.

Examples:

Rule 1: $1\overline{)5}$ with quotient 5 Any number divided by 1 is that number.

Rule 2: $5\overline{)5}$ with quotient 1 Any number except 0 divided by itself is 1.

Rule 3: $7\overline{)0}$ with quotient 0 Zero divided by any number is zero.

Rule 4: $0\overline{)7}$ You cannot divide by zero.

$1\overline{)6}$ Rule ____ $4 \div 1 = $ ____   Rule ____

$7\overline{)7}$ Rule ____    $9 \div 9 = $ ____   Rule ____

$9\overline{)0}$ Rule ____ $7 \div 1 = $ ____   Rule ____

$1\overline{)4}$ Rule ____ $6 \div 0 = $ ____   Rule ____

Division: Remainders

Division is a way to find out how many times one number is contained in another number. For example, 28 ÷ 4 = 7 means that there are seven groups of four in 28. The dividend is the larger number that is divided by the smaller number, or divisor. The quotient is the answer in a division problem. The remainder is the amount left over. The remainder is always less than the divisor.

Directions: Study the example. Find each quotient and remainder.

Example:

There are 11 dog biscuits. Put them in groups of 3. There are 2 left over.

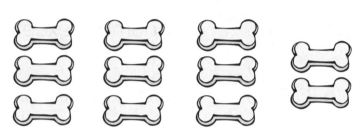

$$\begin{array}{r} 3 \\ 3\overline{)11} \\ \underline{-9} \\ 2 \text{ remainder} \end{array} \qquad \begin{array}{r} 3 \text{ r } 2 \\ 3\overline{)11} \end{array}$$

Remember: The remainder must be less than the **divisor**!

$$3\overline{)13} \qquad 4\overline{)17} \qquad 6\overline{)32} \qquad 5\overline{)26}$$

9 ÷ 4 = _____   12 ÷ 5 = _____   26 ÷ 4 = _____   49 ÷ 9 = _____

The pet store has 7 cats. Two cats go in each cage. How many cats are left over?

_____

Divisibility Rules

A number is divisible... by 2 if the last digit is 0 or even (2, 4, 6, 8).
by 3 if the sum of all digits is divisible by 3.
by 4 if the last two digits are divisible by 4.
by 5 if the last digit is a 0 or 5.
by 10 if the last digit is 0.

Example: 250 is divisible by   2, 5, 10

Directions: Tell what numbers each of these numbers is divisible by.

3,732 _____   439 _____

50 _____   444 _____

7,960 _____   8,212 _____

104,924 _____   2,345 _____

Name: _____

Factor Trees

Factors are the smaller numbers multiplied together to make a larger number. Factor trees are one way to find all the factors of a number.

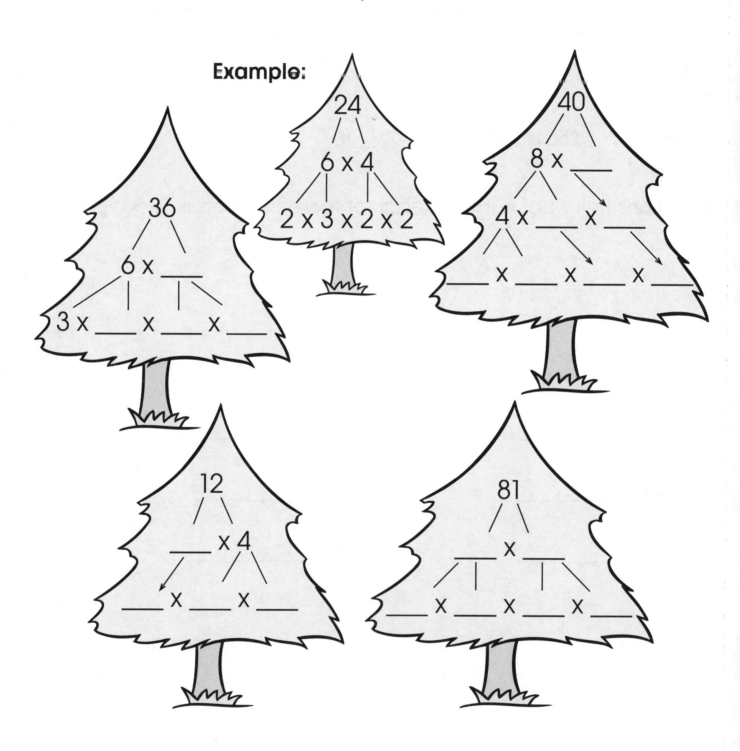

Example:

24
6 x 4
2 x 3 x 2 x 2

36
6 x ___
3 x ___ x ___ x ___

40
8 x ___
4 x ___ x ___
___ x ___ x ___

12
___ x 4
___ x ___

81
___ x ___
___ x ___ x ___

Name: _____

Percentages

A percentage is the amount of a number out of 100. This is the percent sign: %

Directions: Fill in the blanks.

Example: 70% = _____ / 100   _____ % = 40 / 100

30% = _____ / 100   10% = _____ / 100

90% = _____ / 100   40% = _____ / 100

70% = _____ / 100   80% = _____ / 100

_____ % = 20 / 100   _____ % = 60 / 100

_____ % = 30 / 100   _____ % = 10 / 100

_____ % = 50 / 100   _____ % = 90 / 100

Fractions

A fraction is a number that names part of a whole, such as $\frac{1}{2}$ or $\frac{1}{3}$.

Directions: Write the fraction that tells what part of each figure is colored. The first one is done for you.

Example:

2 parts shaded
5 parts in the whole figure

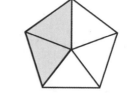

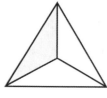

_____

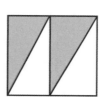

_____

_____

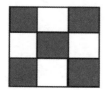

_____

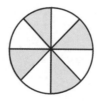

_____

_____

_____

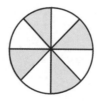

_____

_____

Name: _____

Fractions: Equivalent

Fractions that name the same part of a whole are equivalent fractions.

Example:

$$\frac{1}{2} = \frac{2}{4}$$

Directions: Fill in the numbers to complete the equivalent fractions.

$$\frac{1}{4} = \frac{\boxed{}}{8}$$

$$\frac{2}{3} = \frac{\boxed{}}{6}$$

$$\frac{1}{6} = \frac{\boxed{}}{12}$$

$$\frac{2}{3} = \frac{\boxed{}}{6}$$

$$\frac{1}{3} = \frac{\boxed{}}{12}$$

$$\frac{1}{5} = \frac{\boxed{}}{15}$$

$$\frac{1}{4} = \frac{\boxed{}}{8}$$

$$\frac{1}{2} = \frac{\boxed{}}{6}$$

$$\frac{2}{3} = \frac{\boxed{}}{9}$$

$$\frac{2}{6} = \frac{\boxed{}}{18}$$

Name: _____

Fractions: Division

A fraction is a number that names part of an object. It can also name part of a group.

Directions: Study the example. Divide by the bottom number of the fraction to find the answers.

Example:
There are 6 cheerleaders.
$\frac{1}{2}$ of the cheerleaders are boys.
How many cheerleaders are boys?

6 cheerleaders ÷ 2 groups = 3 boys

$\frac{1}{2}$ of 6 = 3

$\frac{1}{2}$ of 8 = __4__

$\frac{1}{2}$ of 10 = ____

$\frac{1}{3}$ of 9 = ____

$\frac{1}{5}$ of 10 = ____

$\frac{1}{4}$ of 12 = ____

$\frac{1}{8}$ of 32 = ____

$\frac{1}{3}$ of 27 = ____

$\frac{1}{5}$ of 30 = ____

$\frac{1}{2}$ of 14 = ____

$\frac{1}{9}$ of 18 = ____

$\frac{1}{6}$ of 24 = ____

$\frac{1}{3}$ of 18 = ____

$\frac{1}{10}$ of 50 = ____

Name: _____

Fractions: Comparing

Directions: Circle the fraction in each pair that is larger.

Example:

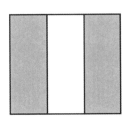
$\left(\dfrac{2}{3}\right)$

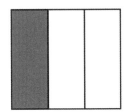
$\dfrac{1}{3}$

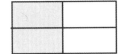
$\dfrac{2}{4}$

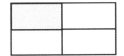
$\dfrac{1}{4}$

$\dfrac{1}{8}$

$\dfrac{2}{8}$

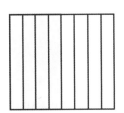
$\dfrac{1}{2}$

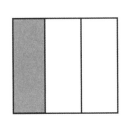
$\dfrac{1}{3}$

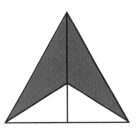
$\dfrac{2}{3}$

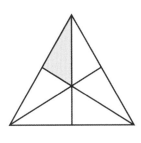
$\dfrac{1}{6}$

$\dfrac{1}{4}$ or $\dfrac{1}{6}$

$\dfrac{1}{5}$ or $\dfrac{1}{7}$

$\dfrac{1}{8}$ or $\dfrac{1}{4}$

Decimals

A decimal is a number with one or more numbers to the right of a decimal point. A decimal point is a dot placed between the ones place and the tens place of a number, such as 2.5.

Example:

$\frac{3}{10}$ can be written as .3   They are both read as three-tenths.

Directions: Write the answer as a decimal for the shaded parts.

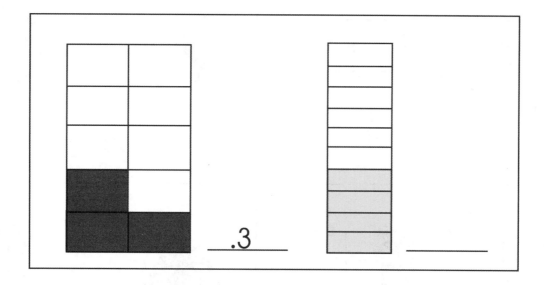

.3 _____   _____

Directions: Color parts of each object to match the decimals given.

.7   .6   .5

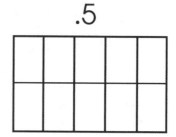

Name: _____

Decimals

A decimal is a number with one or more numbers to the right of a decimal point, such as 6.5 or 2.25. Equivalent means numbers that are equal.

Directions: Draw a line between the equivalent numbers.

.8 $\frac{5}{10}$

five-tenths $\frac{8}{10}$

.7 $\frac{6}{10}$

.4   .3

six-tenths $\frac{2}{10}$

three-tenths $\frac{7}{10}$

.2 $\frac{9}{10}$

nine-tenths $\frac{4}{10}$

Name: _____

Decimals Greater Than 1

Directions: Write the decimal for the part that is shaded.

Example:

$2\frac{4}{10}$

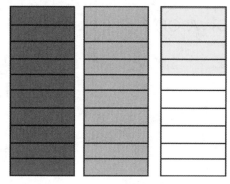

Write: 2.4   Read: two and four-tenths

$1\frac{2}{10}$ = ____

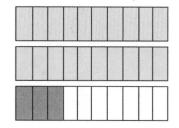

$3\frac{6}{10}$ = ____

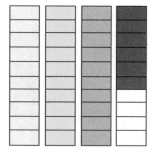

$2\frac{3}{10}$ = ____

$2\frac{7}{10}$ = ____

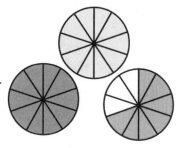

Directions: Write each number as a decimal.

four and two-tenths = ____   seven and one-tenth = ____

$3\frac{4}{10}$ = ____ $6\frac{9}{10}$ = ____ $8\frac{3}{10}$ = ____ $7\frac{5}{10}$ = ____

MATH   Name: _____

Decimals: Addition and Subtraction

Decimals are added and subtracted in the same way as other numbers. Simply carry down the decimal point to your answer.

Directions: Add or subtract.

Examples:

$$\begin{array}{r} 1.3 \\ +2.8 \\ \hline \end{array}$$

$$\begin{array}{r} 4.5 \\ -2.2 \\ \hline \end{array}$$

$$\begin{array}{r} 1.3 \\ +2.2 \\ \hline \end{array}$$

$$\begin{array}{r} 4.6 \\ -3.4 \\ \hline \end{array}$$

$$\begin{array}{r} 5.1 \\ +8.8 \\ \hline \end{array}$$

$$\begin{array}{r} 6.7 \\ -4.3 \\ \hline \end{array}$$

$$\begin{array}{r} 7.9 \\ -3.7 \\ \hline \end{array}$$

$$\begin{array}{r} 6.4 \\ +8.7 \\ \hline \end{array}$$

$$\begin{array}{r} 11.4 \\ -\ 9.5 \\ \hline \end{array}$$

$$\begin{array}{r} 0.5 \\ +3.6 \\ \hline \end{array}$$

9.3 + 1.2 = _____   2.5 - 0.7 = _____   1.2 + 5.0 = _____

Bob jogs around the school every day. The distance for one time around is .7 of a mile. If he jogs around the school two times, how many miles does he jog each day? _____

Name: _____

Patterns

Directions: Write the one that would come next in each pattern.

0   2   0   4   0   6   _____

1   3   5   7   9   11   _____

5   10   20   40   80   _____

   _____

   _____

   _____

1   A   2   B   3   C   _____

A   B   C   1   2   3   _____

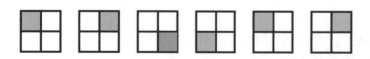   _____

Pattern Maze

Directions: Follow the pattern: ● ■ ▲ ☆ to get through the maze.

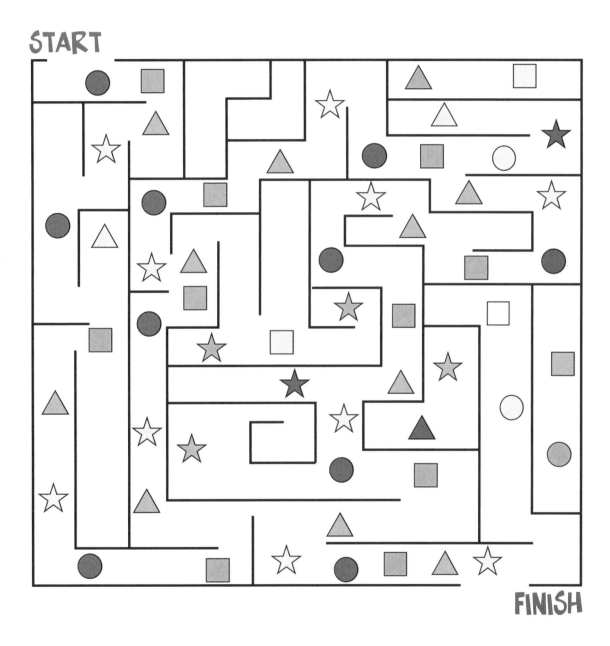

START

FINISH

Name: _____

Geometry

Geometry is the branch of mathematics that has to do with points, lines and shapes.

 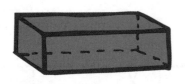 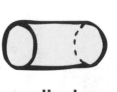 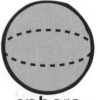

cube　　**rectangular prism**　　**cone**　　**cylinder**　　**sphere**

Directions: Use the code to color the picture.

Color:
cubes — blue
rectangular prisms — red
cones — green
cylinders — yellow
spheres —orange

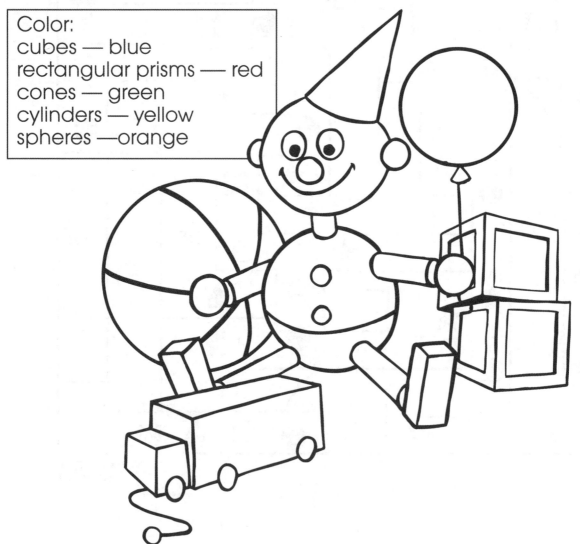

Tangram

Directions: Cut out the tangram below. Use the shapes to make a cat, a chicken, a boat and a large triangle.

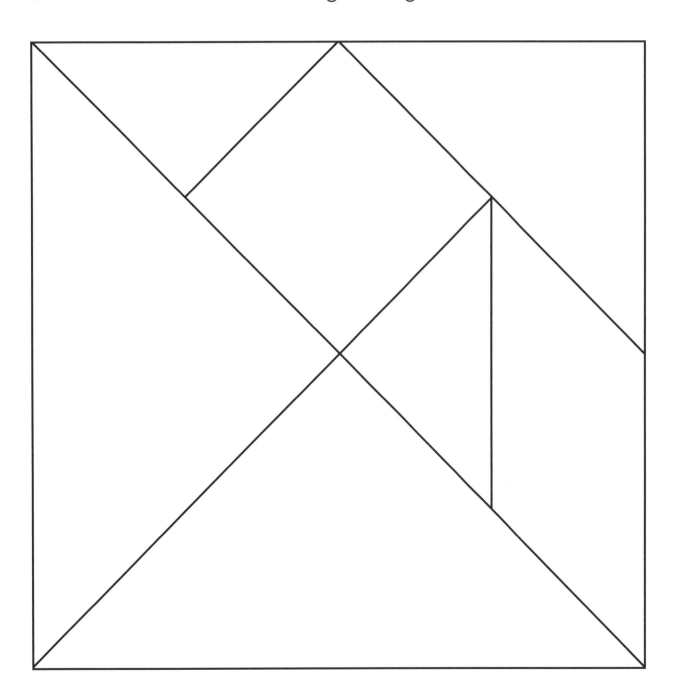

Page is blank for cutting exercise on previous page.

Name: _____

Geometric Coloring

Directions: Color the geometric shapes in the box below.

Geometry: Lines Segments, Rays, Angles

Geometry is the branch of mathematics that has to do with points, lines and shapes.

A **line** goes on and on in both directions. It has no end points.

   Line CD

A **segment** is part of a line. It has two end points.

   Segment AB

A **ray** has a line segment with only one end point. It goes on and on in the other direction.

   Ray EF

An **angle** has two rays with the same end point.

Angle BAC

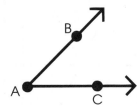

Directions: Write the name for each figure.

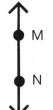   line _____

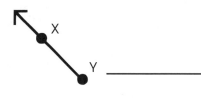 _____

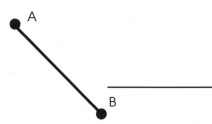 _____

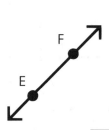 _____

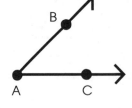 _____

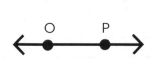 _____

Name: _____

Geometry Game

Directions:

1. Cut out the cards at the bottom of the page. Put them in a pile.

2. Cut out the game boards on the next page.

3. Take turns drawing cards.

4. If you have the figure that the card describes on your gameboard, cover it.

5. The first one to get three in a row, wins.

cube	point	angle	cylinder	rectangular prism
line	square	cone	circle	sphere
triangle	segment	rectangle	tangram	ray

Page is blank for cutting exercise on previous page.

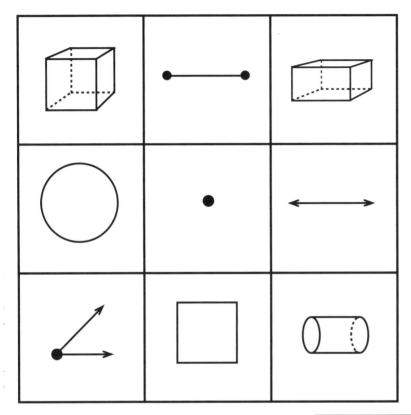

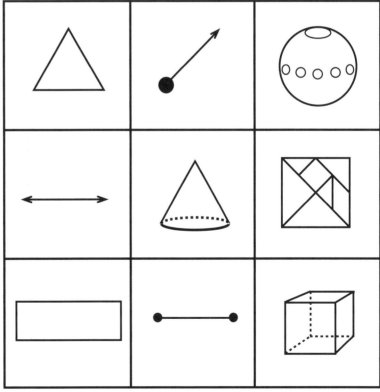

Grade 3 - Comprehensive Curriculum

Name: _____

Geometry: Perimeter

The perimeter is the distance around an object. Find the perimeter by adding the lengths of all the sides.

Directions: Find the perimeter for each object (ft. = feet).

2 ft.

3 ft. 3 ft.

2 ft.

__10 ft.__

6 ft.

6 ft. 6 ft.

6 ft. 6 ft.

6 ft.

_____

4 ft. 4 ft.

3 ft.

_____

2 ft.

5 ft.

5 ft.

2 ft.

_____

10 ft.

3 ft. 3 ft.

10 ft.

_____

1 ft.

1 ft. 1 ft.

1 ft. 1 ft.

1 ft. 1 ft.

1 ft.

_____

7 ft. 5 ft.

5 ft.

_____

1 ft. 3 ft. 1 ft.

5 ft.

_____

Name: _____

Flower Power

Directions: Count the flowers and answer the questions.

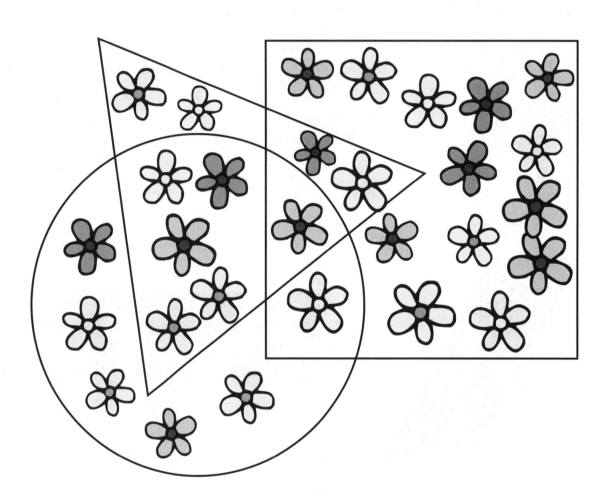

How many s are in the circle? _____

How many s are in the triangle? _____

How many s are in the square? _____

How many s in all? _____

Name: _____

Map Skills: Scale

A **map scale** shows how far one place is from another. This map scale shows that 1 inch on this page equals 1 mile at the real location.

Directions: Use a ruler and the map scale to find out how far it is from Ann's house to other places. Round to the nearest inch.

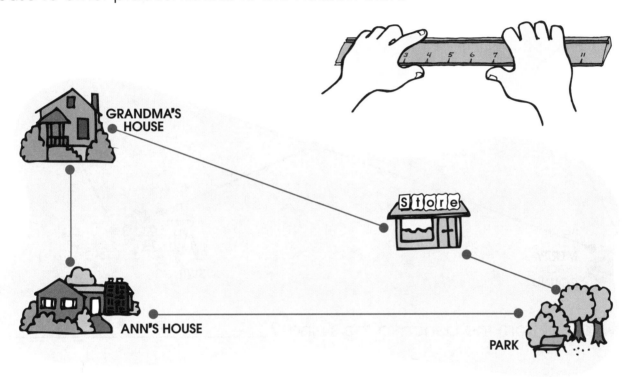

1. How far is it from Ann's house to the park? _____

2. How far is it from Ann's house to Grandma's house? _____

3. How far is it from Grandma's house to the store? _____

4. How far did Ann go when she went from her house to Grandma's and then to the store? _____

Name: _____

Map Skills: Scale

Directions: Use a ruler and the map scale to measure the map and answer the questions. Round to the nearest inch.

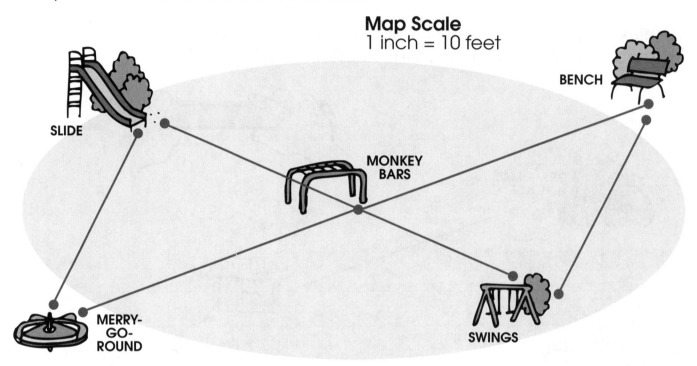

Map Scale
1 inch = 10 feet

BENCH

SLIDE

MONKEY
BARS

MERRY-
GO-
ROUND

SWINGS

1. How far is it from the bench to the swings? _____

2. How far is it from the bench to the monkey bars? _____

3. How far is it from the monkey bars to the merry-go-round? _____

4. How far is it from the bench to the merry-go-round? _____

5. How far is it from the merry-go-round to the slide? _____

6. How far is it from the slide to the swings? _____

Name: _____

Graphs

A graph is a drawing that shows information about numbers.

Directions: Color the picture. Then tell how many there are of each object by completing the graph.

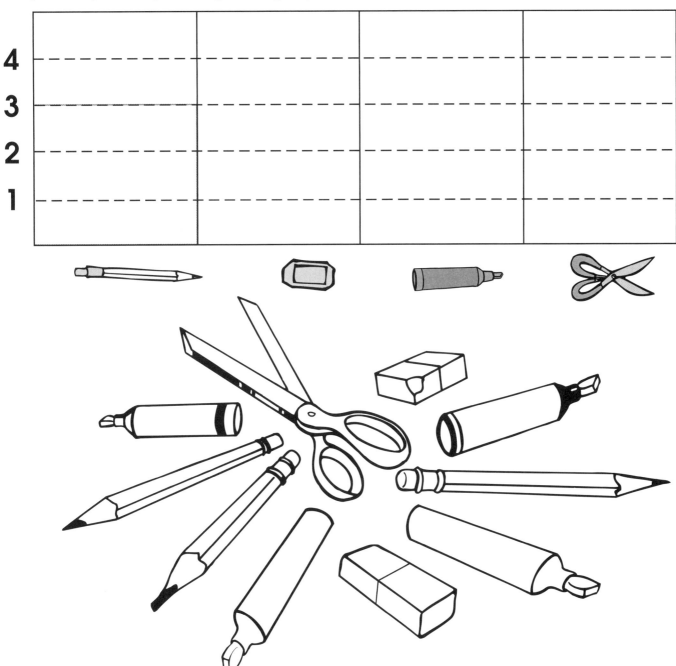

Graphs

Directions: Answer the questions about the graph.

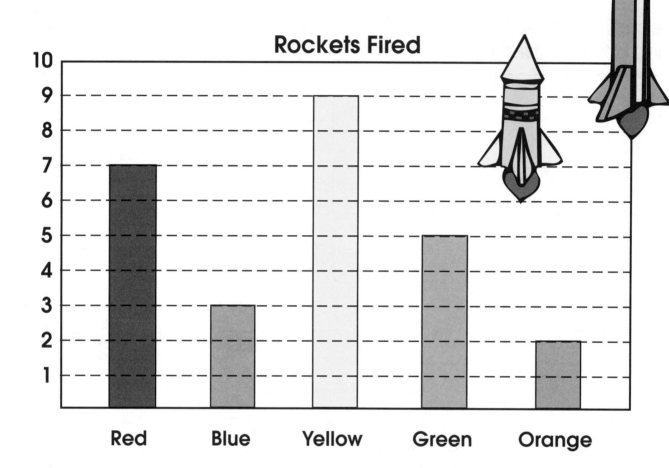

How many rockets did the Red Club fire? _____

How many rockets did the Green Club fire? _____

The Yellow Club fired 9 rockets. How many more rockets
did it fire than the Blue Club? _____

How many rockets were fired in all? _____

Name: _____

Measurement: Ounce and Pound

Ounces and pounds are measurements of weight in the standard measurement system. The ounce is used to measure the weight of very light objects. The pound is used to measure the weight of heavier objects. 16 ounces = 1 pound.

Example:

8 ounces   15 pounds

Directions: Decide if you would use ounces or pounds to measure the weight of each object. Circle your answer.

ounce   pound

ounce   pound

ounce   pound

ounce   pound

a chair: ounce   pound   **a table:**   ounce   pound

a shoe: ounce   pound   **a shirt:**   ounce   pound

Name: _____

Measurement: Inches

An inch is a unit of length in the standard measurement system.

Directions: Use a ruler to measure each object to the nearest $\frac{1}{4}$ inch. Write **in.** to stand for inch.

Example:

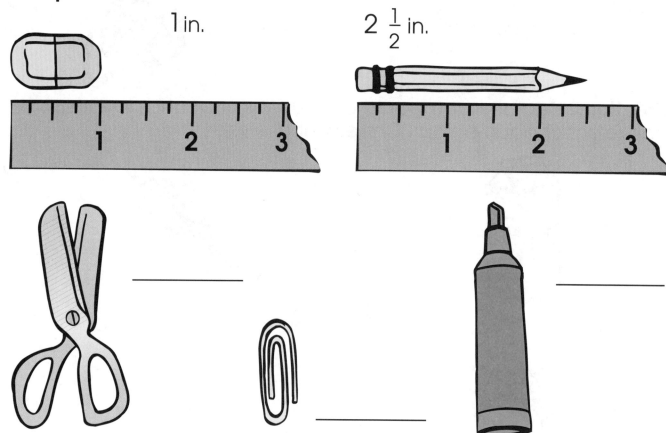

1 in.

$2\frac{1}{2}$ in.

Name: _____

Measurement: Centimeter

A centimeter is a unit of length in the metric system. There are 2.54 centimeters in an inch.

Directions: Use a centimeter ruler to measure each object to the nearest half of a centimeter. Write **cm** to stand for centimeter.

Example:

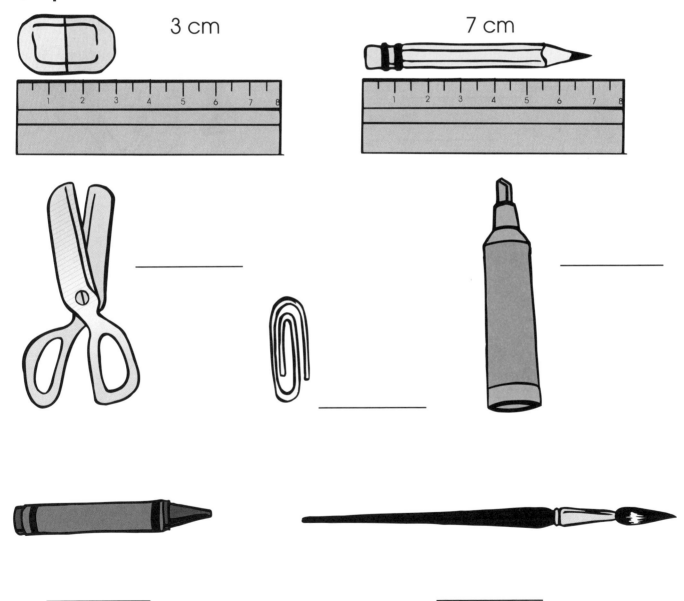

3 cm

7 cm

427

Name: _____

Measurement: Foot, Yard, Mile

Directions: Decide whether you would use foot, yard or mile to measure each object.

1 foot = 12 inches
1 yard = 36 inches or 3 feet
1 mile = 1,760 yards

length of a river ___miles___

height of a tree _____

width of a room _____

length of a football field _____

height of a door _____

length of a dress _____

length of a race _____

height of a basketball hoop _____

width of a window _____

distance a plane travels _____

Directions: Solve the problem.

Tara races Tom in the 100-yard dash. Tara finishes
10 yards in front of Tom. How many feet did Tara finish
in front of Tom?

_____

Name: _____

Measurement: Meter and Kilometer

Meters and kilometers are units of length in the metric system. A meter is equal to 39.37 inches. A kilometer is equal to about $\frac{5}{8}$ of a mile.

Directions: Decide whether you would use meter or kilometer to measure each object.

1 meter = 100 centimeters
1 kilometer = 1,000 meters

length of a river _kilometer_

height of a tree _____

width of a room _____

length of a football field _____

height of a door _____

length of a dress _____

length of a race _____

height of a basketball pole _____

width of a window _____

distance a plane travels _____

Directions: Solve the problem.

Tara races Tom in the 100-meter dash. Tara finishes 10 meters in front of Tom. How many centimeters did Tara finish in front of Tom?

_____

Name: _____

Coordinates

Directions: Locate the points on the grid and color in each box.

What animal did you form?_____

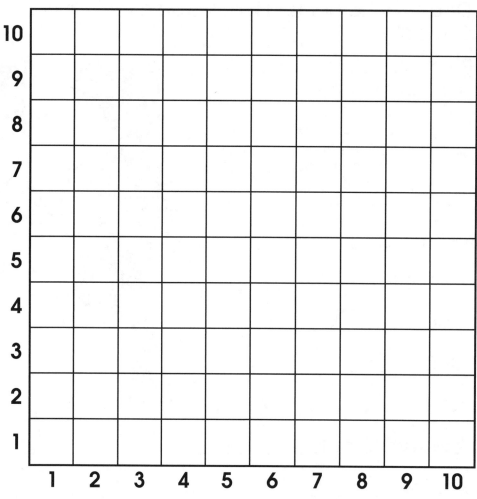

(across, up)

(4, 7)	(4, 1)	(7, 1)	(3, 5)	(2, 8)	(8, 6)	(4, 8)	(3, 7)
(5, 4)	(6, 5)	(5, 5)	(6, 6)	(7, 3)	(8, 5)	(10, 5)	(4, 3)
(7, 6)	(4, 6)	(1, 8)	(6, 4)	(7, 2)	(4, 5)	(9, 6)	(4, 9)
(3, 6)	(7, 5)	(5, 6)	(4, 2)	(4, 4)	(7, 4)	(2, 7)	(3, 8)

Roman Numerals

Another way to write numbers is to use Roman numerals.

I	1	VII	7
II	2	VIII	8
III	3	IX	9
IV	4	X	10
V	5	XI	11
VI	6	XII	12

Directions: Fill in the Roman numerals on the watch.

What time is it on the watch?

_____ o'clock

Name: _____

Roman Numerals

I	1	VII	7
II	2	VIII	8
III	3	IX	9
IV	4	X	10
V	5	XI	11
VI	6	XII	12

Directions: Write the number.

V _____   VII _____

X _____   IX _____

II _____   XII _____

Directions: Write the Roman numeral.

4 _____   5 _____

10 _____   8 _____

6 _____   3 _____

Name: _____

Time: Hour, Half-Hour, Quarter-Hour, 5 Min. Intervals

Directions: Write the time shown on each clock.

Example:

7:15
_____

7:00
_____

_____

_____

_____

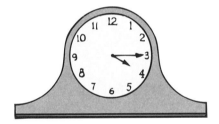

_____

_____

_____

_____

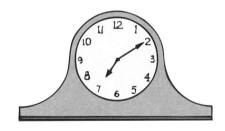

_____

_____

Grade 3 - Comprehensive Curriculum

Time: a.m. and p.m.

In telling time, the hours between 12:00 midnight and 12:00 noon are a.m. hours. The hours between 12:00 noon and 12:00 midnight are p.m. hours.

Directions: Draw a line between the times that are the same.

Example:

7:30 in the morning — 7:30 a.m.
half-past seven a.m.
seven thirty in the morning

9:00 in the evening - - - - - 9:00 p.m.
nine o'clock at night

six o'clock in the evening   8:00 a.m.

3:30 a.m.   six o'clock in the morning

4:15 p.m.   6:00 p.m.

eight o'clock in the morning   eleven o'clock in the evening

quarter past five in the evening   three thirty in the morning

11:00 p.m.   four fifteen in the evening

6:00 a.m.   5:15 p.m.

Name: _____

Time: Minutes

A minute is a measurement of time. There are sixty seconds in a minute and sixty minutes in an hour.

Directions: Write the time shown on each clock.

Example:

Each mark is one minute.
The hand is at mark number 6.

Write: 5:06
Read: six minutes after five.

_____

_____

_____

_____

5:38

_____

_____

2:47

_____

_____

_____

_____

3:18

_____

_____

Grade 3 - Comprehensive Curriculum

Name: _____

Time: Addition

Directions: Add the hours and minutes together.
(Remember, 1 hour equals 60 minutes.)

Example:

```
  2 hours 10 minutes
+ 1 hour  50 minutes
  3 hours 60 minutes
         (1 hour)
  4 hours
```

```
  4 hours 20 minutes
+ 2 hours 10 minutes
  6 hours 30 minutes
```

```
  9 hours
+ 2 hours
```

```
  1 hour
+ 5 hours
```

```
  6 hours
+ 3 hours
```

```
  6 hours 15 minutes
+ 1 hour  15 minutes
```

```
10 hours 30 minutes
+ 1 hour  10 minutes
```

```
  3 hours 40 minutes
+ 8 hours 20 minutes
```

```
11 hours 15 minutes
+ 1 hour  30 minutes
```

```
  4 hours 15 minutes
+ 5 hours 45 minutes
```

```
  7 hours 10 minutes
+ 1 hour  30 minutes
```

Time: Subtraction

Directions: Subtract the hours and minutes.
(Remember, 1 hour equals 60 minutes.)
"Borrow" from the "hours" if you need to.

Example:

```
      5      70
      6̶ hours 1̶0̶ minutes
    - 2 hours 30 minutes
      3 hours 40 minutes
```

```
  12 hours          5 hour          2 hours
 - 2 hours        - 3 hours       - 1 hour
```

```
  5 hours 30 minutes     9 hours 45 minutes     11 hours 50 minutes
- 2 hours 15 minutes   - 3 hours 15 minutes    - 4 hours 35 minutes
```

```
  12 hours             7 hours 15 minutes     8 hours 10 minutes
- 6 hours 30 minutes  - 5 hours 30 minutes   - 4 hours 40 minutes
```

Money: Coins and Dollars

 dollar = 100¢ or $1.00

 penny = 1¢ or $.01

 nickel = 5¢ or $.05

 dime = 10¢ or $.10

 quarter = 25¢ or $.25

 half-dollar = 50¢ or $.50

Directions: Write the amount for each group of money shown. Use a dollar sign and decimal point. The first one is done for you.

   $.07

_____

_____

 _____

 _____

_____

_____

Name: _____

Money: Five-Dollar Bill and Ten-Dollar Bill

Directions: Write the amount for each group of money shown. Use a dollar sign and decimal point. The first one is done for you.

Five-dollar bill =
5 one dollar bills

Ten-dollar bill =
2 five-dollar bills or
10 one-dollar bills

$15.00

_____

_____

_____

7 one-dollar bills, 2 quarters _____

2 five-dollar bills, 3 one-dollar bills, half-dollar _____

3 ten-dollar bills, 1 five-dollar bill, 3 quarters _____

Name: _____

Money: Counting Change

Directions: Subtract the money using decimals to show how much change a person would receive in each of the following.

Example:

Bill had 3 dollars.
He bought a baseball for $2.83.
How much change did he receive?

$3.00
-$2.83
$ .17

Paid 2 dollars.

_____

Paid 1 dollar.

_____

Paid 5 dollars.

_____

Paid 10 dollars.

_____

Paid 4 dollars.

_____

Paid 7 dollars.

_____

Money: Comparing

Directions: Compare the amount of money in the left column with the price of the object in the right column. Is the amount of money in the left column enough to purchase the object in the right column? Circle yes or no.

Example:

Alice has 2 dollars. She wants to buy a box of crayons for $1.75. Does she have enough money? (Yes) No

   Yes No

  Yes No

 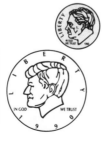  Yes No

Review

Directions: Complete each clock to show the time written below it.

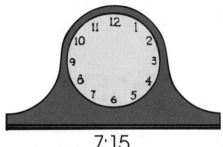

7:15

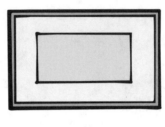

3:07

6:25

Directions: Write the time using a.m. or p.m.

seven twenty-two in the evening _____

three fifteen in the morning _____

eight thirty at night _____

Directions: Write the correct amount of money.

_____

_____

Joey paid $4.67 for a model car. He gave the clerk a five-dollar bill. How much change should he receive?

_____

Review

Directions: Read and solve each of the problems.

The baker sets out 9 baking pans with 6 rolls on each one. How many rolls are there in all? _____

A dozen brownies cost $1.29. James pays for a dozen brownies with a five-dollar bill. How much change does he receive? _____

Theresa has four quarters, a nickel and three pennies. How much more money does she need to buy brownies? _____

The baker made 24 loaves of bread. At the end of the day, he has one-fourth left. How many did he sell? _____

Two loaves of bread weigh a pound. How many loaves are needed to make five pounds? _____

The bakery opens at 8:30 a.m. It closes nine and a half hours later. What time does it close? _____

Name: _____

Review

Place Value

Directions: Write the number's value in each place: **678,421**.

_____ ones   _____ hundred thousands

_____ thousands   _____ hundreds

_____ tens   _____ ten thousands

Addition and Subtraction

Directions: Add or subtract. Remember to regroup, if you need to.

88	46	75	93	76
- 19	+ 39	+ 24	- 68	- 59

		84	97	
683	855	49	54	9,731
- 496	+ 138	+ 62	+ 361	- 4,664

Rounding

Directions: Round to the nearest 10, 100 or 1,000.

72 _____   49 _____   31 _____   66 _____

151 _____   296 _____   917 _____   621 _____

Name: _____

Multiplication and Division

$$\begin{array}{c} 3 \\ \times\,6 \\ \hline \end{array} \qquad \begin{array}{c} 3 \\ \times\,8 \\ \hline \end{array} \qquad \begin{array}{c} 9 \\ \times\,8 \\ \hline \end{array} \qquad \begin{array}{c} 9 \\ \times\,5 \\ \hline \end{array} \qquad \begin{array}{c} 7 \\ \times\,2 \\ \hline \end{array}$$

$$5\overline{)25} \qquad 2\overline{)6} \qquad 3\overline{)18} \qquad 8\overline{)24} \qquad 7\overline{)49}$$

Fractions

$\dfrac{1}{3}$ of 12 = _____ $\dfrac{1}{7}$ of 28 = _____ $\dfrac{1}{9}$ of 45 = _____

Directions: Color parts to match the fractions given.

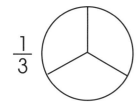

$\dfrac{1}{3}$ $\dfrac{2}{4}$ $\dfrac{2}{6}$

Decimals

Directions: Write the decimal for each fraction.

$\dfrac{4}{10}$ = _____ $3\dfrac{3}{10}$ = _____ $\dfrac{9}{10}$ = _____ $21\dfrac{3}{10}$ = _____

Directions: Add or Subtract.

8.2 + 1.1 = _____   3.6 - 1.8 = _____   3.9 + 2.6 = _____

Geometry

Directions: Write the name for each figure.

      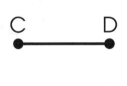   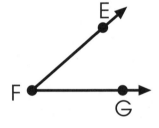

_____   _____   _____   _____

Directions: Find the perimeter of each object.

4 ft.
4 ft. 4 ft.
4 ft.

5 ft.
1 ft. [   ] 1 ft.
5 ft.

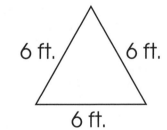
6 ft.   6 ft.
6 ft.

_____   _____   _____

Name: _____

Graphing

Directions: Answer the questions.

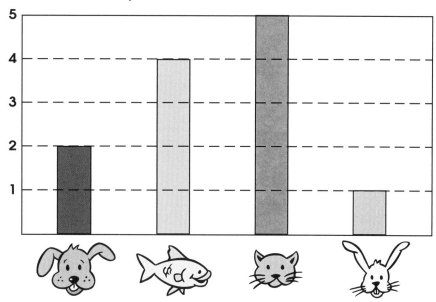

Which animal is there the most of?   _____

Which animal is there the fewest of?   _____

How many animals altogether?   _____

Measurements

Directions: Answer the questions.

What unit of measure would you use to measure...

Example: ...a cow?   <u>pound</u>

...a mouse?   _____

...length of a pencil?   _____

...length of a semi-truck?   _____

...length of a river?   _____

...width of a river?   _____

...height of a flag pole?   _____

Time

Directions: Complete each clock to show the time written below it.

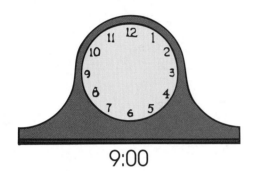

9:00

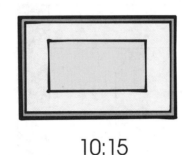

10:15

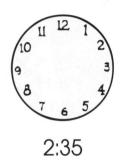

2:35

Directions: Write the time, using a.m. or p.m.

six twenty-two in the evening _____

nine forty-six in the morning _____

Directions: Add or subtract.

```
  2 hours 15 minutes          1 hour  30 minutes
+ 4 hours 30 minutes        + 4 hours 30 minutes
_____        _____
```

```
 12 hours 45 minutes          8 hours 30 minutes
-  4 hours 30 minutes        - 3 hours 45 minutes
_____        _____
```

Name: _____

Problem-Solving: Addition, Subtraction

Directions: Read and solve each problem. The first one is done for you.

The clown started the day with 200 balloons. He gave away 128 of them. Some broke. At the end of the day he had 18 balloons left. How many of the balloons broke?   54

On Monday, there were 925 tickets sold to adults and 1,412 tickets sold to children. How many more children attended the fair than adults?   _____

At one game booth, prizes were given out for scoring 500 points in three attempts. Sally scored 178 points on her first attempt, 149 points on her second attempt and 233 points on her third attempt. Did Sally win a prize?   _____

The prize-winning steer weighed 2,348 pounds. The runner-up steer weighed 2,179 pounds. How much more did the prize steer weigh?   _____

There were 3,418 people at the fair on Tuesday, and 2,294 people on Wednesday. What was the total number of people there for the two days?   _____

Name: _____

Problem-Solving: Multiplication, Division

Directions: Read and solve each problem.

Jeff and Terry are planting a garden. They plant 3 rows of green beans with 8 plants in each row. How many green bean plants are there in the garden? _____

There are 45 tomato plants in the garden. There are 5 rows of them. How many tomato plants are in each row? _____

The children have 12 plants each of lettuce, broccoli and spinach. How many plants are there in all? _____

Jeff planted 3 times as many cucumber plants as Terry. He planted 15 of them. How many did Terry plant? _____

Terry planted 12 pepper plants. He planted twice as many green pepper plants as red pepper plants. How many green pepper plants are there? _____

How many red pepper plants? _____

Name: _____

Problem-Solving: Fractions, Decimals

A fraction is a number that names part of a whole, such as $\frac{1}{2}$ or $\frac{1}{3}$.

Directions: Read and solve each problem.

There are 20 large animals on the Browns' farm. Two-fifths are horses, two-fifths are cows and the rest are pigs. Are there more pigs or cows on the farm? _____

Farmer Brown had 40 eggs to sell. He sold half of them in the morning. In the afternoon, he sold half of what was left. How many eggs did Farmer Brown have at the end of the day? _____

There is a fence running around seven-tenths of the farm. How much of the farm does not have a fence around it? Write the amount as a decimal. _____

The Browns have 10 chickens. Two are roosters and the rest are hens. Write a decimal for the number that are roosters and for the number that are hens. _____ roosters _____ hens

Mrs. Brown spends three-fourths of her day working outside and the rest working inside. Does she spend more time inside or outside? _____

Name: _____

Problem-Solving: Measurement

Directions: Read and solve each problem.

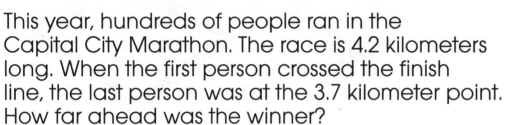

This year, hundreds of people ran in the
Capital City Marathon. The race is 4.2 kilometers
long. When the first person crossed the finish
line, the last person was at the 3.7 kilometer point.
How far ahead was the winner?   _____

Dennis crossed the finish line 10 meters ahead of Lucy.
Lucy was 5 meters ahead of Sam. How far ahead of Sam
was Dennis?   _____

Tony ran 320 yards from school to his home. Then he ran
290 yards to Jay's house. Together Tony and Jay ran 545
yards to the store. How many yards in all did Tony run?   _____

The teacher measured the heights of three children in her
class. Marsha was 51 inches tall, Jimmy was 48 inches tall
and Ted was $52\frac{1}{2}$ inches tall. How much taller is Ted than
Marsha?   _____

How much taller is he than Jimmy?   _____

Problem-Solving

Directions: Read and solve each problem.

Ralph has $8.75. He buys a teddy bear and a puzzle.
How much money does he have left?   _____

Kelly wants to buy a teddy bear and a ball. She has $7.25.
How much more money does she need?   _____

Kim paid a five-dollar bill, two one-dollar bills, two quarters,
one dime and eight pennies for a book.
How much did it cost?   _____

Michelle leaves for school at 7:45 a.m.
It takes her 20 minutes to get there.
On the clock, draw the time that she
arrives at school.

Frank takes piano lessons every
Saturday morning at 11:30.
The lesson lasts for an hour and
15 minutes. On the clock, draw
the time his piano lesson ends.
Is it a.m. or p.m.?
Circle the correct answer.

Abbreviation: A shortened form of a word. Most abbreviations begin with a capital letter and end with a period. Example: Doctor = Dr.

Addition: "Putting together" or adding two or more numbers to find the sum.

Adjectives: Words that describe nouns. Examples: tall, four, cold, happy.

Adverbs: Words that describe verbs. They often tell how, when or where. Examples: here, today, quickly.

Alliteration: The repeated use of beginning sounds. They are also known as tongue twisters. Example: Peter Piper picked a peck of pickled peppers.

Alphabetical Order: Putting letters or words in the order in which they appear in the alphabet.

Analogy: A word pair which compares how things are related to each other.

Angle: Two rays with the same end point.

Antonyms: Words that are opposites. Example: hot and cold.

Apostrophes: Punctuation that is used with contractions in place of the missing letter or used to show ownership. Examples: don't, Susan's.

Articles: Small words that help us better understand nouns. Examples: a, an.

Biography: A type of nonfiction book written about a real person's life.

Capitalization: Letters that are used at the beginning of names of people, places, days, months and holidays. Capital letters are also used at the beginning of sentences.

Cause: The reason for an event.

Centimeter: A measurement of length in the metric system. There are 2.54 centimeters in an inch.

Cinquain: A five-line poem that follows the following form: Line 1: noun; Line 2: adjective, adjective; Line 3: verb + ing, verb + ing, verb + ing; Line 4: four-word phrase; Line 5: synonym for noun in line 1.

Classifying: Putting similar things into categories or groups.

Commands: Sentences that tell someone to do something. They usually begin with a verb or the word "please."

Commas: Punctuation marks which are used to separate words or phrases. They are also used to separate dates from years, cities from states, etc.

Common Nouns: Nouns that name any member of a group of people, places or things rather than specific people, places or things. Example: person.

Compare: To discuss how things are similar.

Compound Predicates: Two or more verbs that have the same subject.

Compound Sentences: Two complete ideas that are joined together into one sentence by a conjunction.

Compound Subject: Two or more nouns that have the same predicate.

Compound Word: Two words that are put together to make one new word. Example: base + ball = baseball.

Comprehension: Understanding what is seen, read or heard.

Consonants: Letters that are not vowels (every letter except a, e, i, o and u).

Contractions: Words that are a short way to write two words together. Example: isn't is short for is not.

Contrast: To discuss how things are different.

Coordinates: Points on a grid. They are named with numbers across, then down.

Decimal: A number with one or more places to the right of a decimal point, such as 6.5 or 3.78. Money amounts are written with two places to the right of a decimal point, such as $1.30.

Detail Sentence: A sentence in a paragraph that supports the main idea.

Dictionary Skills: Learning how to use a dictionary.

Difference: The answer in a subtraction problem.

Digit: The symbols used to write numbers: 0, 1, 2, 3, 4, 5, 6, 7, 8 and 9.

Directions: Sentences that are written as commands, telling someone to do something.

Dividend: The larger number that is divided by the smaller number, or divisor, in a division problem. In the problem $28 \div 7 = 4$, 28 is the dividend.

Division: An operation to find out how many times one number is contained in another number. For example, $28 \div 4 = 7$ means that there are seven groups of four in 28.

Divisor: The smaller number that is divided into the dividend in a division problem. In the problem $28 \div 7 = 4$, 7 is the divisor.

Dollar: A dollar is equal to one hundred cents. It is written $1.00.

Drawing a Conclusion: Using clues to make a final decision about something.

Effect: What happens as a result of a cause.

Ending Sentences: Sentences at the end of a paragraph that tie the story together.

Entry Word: A word defined in a dictionary.

Exclamations: Sentences that express strong feelings. Exclamations often end with an exclamation point. These sentences can be short or long and can be a command. Example: Look at that!

Factors: The numbers multiplied together in a multiplication problem.

Fiction: A type of book about things that are made up or not true.

Following Directions: Doing what the directions say to do.

Fraction: A number that names part of a whole, such as $\frac{1}{2}$ or $\frac{2}{3}$.

Front-End Estimation: The process of using only the first digit in a number and replacing every other place value with a zero to round a number.

Future-Tense Verb: A verb that tells about something that has not happened yet but will happen in the future. "Will" or "shall" are usually used with future tense. Example: We will eat soon.

Geometry: The branch of mathematics that has to do with points, lines and shapes.

Graph: A drawing that shows information about numbers.

Guide Words: Words at the top of a dictionary page. They are the first and last words on that page.

Helping Verb: A word used with an action verb. Example: They are helping.

Homophones: Two words that sound the same but have different meanings and are usually spelled differently. Example: write and right.

Idiom: A saying in which the words do not mean exactly what they say.

Inference: Using logic to figure out what is not directly told.

Irregular Verbs: Verbs that do not change from the present tense to the past tense in the regular way with "d" or "ed." Example: run, ran.

Joining Words: Words that combine ideas in a sentence, such as "and," "but," "or," "because."

Kilometer: A measurement of distance in the metric system. There are 1,000 meters in a kilometer.

Library Skills: Learning how to use the library and its resources.

Line Segment: A part of a line with two end points.

Linking Verbs: Verbs that connect the noun to a descriptive word. Linking verbs are always a form of "to be." Example: I am tired.

Long Vowels: The letters a, e, i, o and u which say the "long" or letter name sound. Long a is the sound you hear in hay. Long e is the sound you hear in me. Long i is the sound you hear in pie. Long o is the sound you hear in no. Long u is the sound you hear in cute.

Making a Deduction: Using reasoning to arrive at a conclusion.

Main Idea: Finding the most important points. The main idea is what the story is mostly about.

Map Scale: Part of a map that shows how far one place is from another.

Meter: A measurement of length in the metric system. A meter is equal to 39.37 inches.

Middle Sentences: Sentences that support the topic sentence in a paragraph.

Mile: A measurement of distance in the standard measurement system. A mile is equal to 1,760 yards or 5,280 feet.

Multiple-Meaning Words: Words that are spelled the same but have different meanings or pronunciations, such as bow (ribbon) and bow (of a ship).

Multiplication: A short way to find the sum of adding the same number a certain amount of times. For example, 7 x 4 = 28 instead of 7 + 7 + 7 + 7 = 28.

Nonfiction: Writing based on facts. It usually gives information about people, places or things.

Nouns: Words that name a person, place or thing.

Ounce: A measurement of weight in the standard measurement system. There are 16 ounces in a pound.

Paragraphs: Groups of sentences that tell about the same thing.

Past-Tense Verb: A verb that tells about something that has already happened. A "d" or "ed" is usually added to the end of the word. Example: walked.

Percentage: The amount of a number out of 100. It uses the sign: %.

Perimeter: The distance around an object. Find the perimeter by adding the lengths of the sides.

Periodical: Writing that is printed regularly within a set period of time. Example: newspaper.

Phonics: Using the sound letters make to decode unknown words.

Place Value: The value of a digit, or numeral, shown by where it is in the number.

Plural Nouns: Nouns which name more than one person, place or thing.

Possessive Nouns: Nouns that tell who or what is the owner of something. Example: the dog's ball.

Possessive Pronouns: Pronouns that show ownership. Example: his dish.

Predicate: The verb in the sentence that tells the main action. It tells what the subject is doing, has done or will do.

Prefixes: Special word parts added to the beginnings of words. Prefixes change the meaning of words. Example: redo.

Prepositions: Words that show the relationship between a noun or pronoun and another word in the sentence. Example: The boy is behind the chair.

Present-Tense Verb: A verb that tells about something that is happening now, happens often or is about to happen. An "s" or "ing" is usually added to the verb. Examples: sings, singing.

Product: The answer of a multiplication problem.

Pronouns: Words that can be used in place of nouns. Example: it.

Proper Nouns: Nouns that name specific people, places or things. Example: Iowa.

Questions: Sentences that ask something. They begin with a capital letter and end with a question mark.

Quotation Marks: Punctuation marks that tell what is said by a person. Quotation marks go before and after a direct quote. Example: She said, "Here I am!"

Quotient: The answer of a division problem.

Ray: A line segment with only one end point. It goes on and on in the other direction.

Recalling Details: Being able to pick out and remember the who, what, when, where, why and how of what is read.

Reference Book: A book that tells basic facts. Example: a dictionary.

Regroup: To use ten ones to form one ten, ten tens to form 100, and so on.

Remainder: The number left over in the quotient of a division problem.

Rhymes: Words with the same ending sounds. Example: lake and cake.

Roman Numerals: Another way to write a number. The system uses Roman letters rather than standard digits.

Root Words: Words before a suffix or prefix is added. Example: Write is the root word of rewritten.

Rounding: Estimating a number by figuring a number using the closest "10" (or "100," "1,000," etc.).

Schedule: A chart with lists of times.

Sentences: A group of words that tell a complete idea, using a noun and a verb. They begin with a capital letter and have end punctuation (a period, question mark or exclamation point).

Sequencing: Putting words or events in a certain order.

Short Vowels: The letters a, e, i, o and u which say the short sound. Short a is the sound you hear in ant. Short e is the sound you hear in elephant. Short i is the sound you hear in igloo. Short o is the sound you hear in octopus. Short u is the sound you hear in umbrella.

Simple Predicate: The main verb of the predicate part of the sentence. Example: Dad will cook for us tonight. "Cook" is the simple predicate.

Simple Subject: The main noun in the complete subject part of the sentence. Example: The silly boy ran around. "Boy" is the simple subject.

Singular Nouns: Words that refer to only one thing.

Statements: Sentences that tell something. They begin with a capital letter and end with a period.

Subject: The noun that does the action. It tells who or what the sentence is about. A noun or pronoun will always be part of the subject.

Subtraction: "Taking away" or subtracting one number from another to find the difference.

Suffixes: Word parts added to the end of a word to change or add to its meaning. Example: statement.

Syllable: Word parts. Each syllable has one vowel sound.

Synonyms: Words that mean the same or nearly the same. Example: small and little.

Topic Sentence: Usually the first sentence in a paragraph. The topic sentence tells what the story is about.

Venn Diagram: A chart that shows comparisons and contrasts.

Verbs: The action words in a sentence. The word that tells what something does or that something exists. Examples: run, is.

Vowels: The letters a, e, i, o, u and sometimes y.

Word Order: The logical order of words in a sentence.

Yard: A measurement of distance in the standard measurement system. There are 3 feet in a yard.

Page 6

My Story

Directions: Fill in the blanks. Use these sentences to write a story about yourself.

Answers will vary.

I feel happy when _____.

I feel sad when _____.

I am good at _____.

Words that describe me: _____ _____

_____ _____ _____

I can help at home by _____.

My friends like me because _____.

I like to _____.

My favorite food is _____.

My favorite animal is _____.

Now . . . take your answers and write a story about **you!**

Page 7

Phonics

Some words are more difficult to read because they have one or more silent letters. Many words you already know are like this.

Examples: wrong and **night**.

Directions: Circle the silent letters in each word. The first one is done for you.

(w)rong   ans(w)er   autum(n)   (w)hole
(k)nife   (h)our   (w)rap   com(b)
si(gh)   strai(gh)t   (k)nee   (k)nown
lam(b)   tau(gh)t   s(c)ent   dau(gh)ter
whis(t)le   (w)rote   (k)new   crum(b)

Directions: Draw a line between the rhyming words. The first one is done for you.

knew --- try
sees --- bowl
taut --- stone
wrote --- true
comb --- song
straight --- trees
sigh --- home
known --- great
wrong --- caught
whole --- boat

Page 8

Phonics

Sometimes letters make sounds you don't expect. Two consonants can work together to make the sound of one consonant. The **f** sound can be made by **ph**, as in the word **elephant**. The consonants **gh** are most often silent, as in the words **night** and **though**. But they also can make the **f** sound as in the word **laugh**.

Directions: Circle the letters that make the **f** sound. Write the correct word from the box to complete each sentence.

| ele(ph)ant | cou(gh) | lau(gh) | tele(ph)one | (ph)onics |
| dol(ph)ins | enou(gh) | tou(gh) | al(ph)abet | rou(gh) |

1. The **dolphins** were playing in the sea.
2. Did you have ____enough____ time to do your homework?
3. A cold can make you ____cough____ and sneeze.
4. The ____elephant____ ate peanuts with his trunk.
5. The road to my school is ____rough____ and bumpy.
6. You had a ____telephone____ call this morning.
7. The ____tough____ meat was hard to chew.
8. Studying ____phonics____ will help you read better.
9. The ____alphabet____ has 26 letters in it.
10. We began to ____laugh____ when the clowns came in.

Page 9

Phonics

There are several consonants that make the **k** sound: **c** when followed by a, o or u as in **cow** or **cup**; the letter **k** as in **milk**; the letters **ch** as in **Christmas** and **ck** as in **black**.

Directions: Read the following words. Circle the letters that make the **k** sound. The first one is done for you.

a(ch)e	s(c)hool	mar(k)et	(c)omb
(c)amera	de(ck)	dar(k)ness	(Ch)ristmas
ne(ck)lace	do(c)tor	stoma(ch)	(c)ra(ck)
ni(ck)el	s(k)in	thi(ck)	es(c)ape

Directions: Use your own words to finish the following sentences. Use words with the **k** sound.

1. If I had a nickel, I would ____Answers will vary.____

2. My doctor is very _____

3. We bought ripe, juicy tomatoes at the _____

4. If I had a camera now, I would take a picture of _____

5. When my stomach aches, _____

Page 10

Phonics

In some word "families," the vowels have a long sound when you would expect them to have a short sound. For example, the **i** has a short sound in **chill**, but a long sound in **child**. The **o** has a short sound in **cost**, but a long sound in **most**.

Directions: Read the words in the word box below. Write the words that have a long vowel sound under the word **LONG**, and the words that have a short vowel sound under the word **SHORT**. (Remember, a long vowel says its name—like **a** in **ate**.)

| old | odd | gosh | gold | sold | soft | toast | frost | lost | most |
| doll | roll | bone | done | kin | mill | mild | wild | blink | blind |

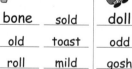 **LONG**   **SHORT**

LONG		SHORT	
bone	sold	doll	soft
old	toast	odd	mill
roll	mild	gosh	frost
most	wild	done	lost
gold	blind	kin	blink

Page 11

Syllables

All words can be divided into **syllables**. Syllables are word parts which have one vowel sound in each part.

Directions: Draw a line between the syllable part and write the word on the correct line below. The first one is done for you.

little	bumble·bee	pil·low
truck	daz·zle	dog
pen·cil	flag	an·gel·ic
re·joic·ing	ant	tel·e·phone

1 SYLLABLE	2 SYLLABLES	3 SYLLABLES
truck	little	rejoicing
flag	pencil	bumblebee
ant	dazzle	angelic
dog	pillow	telephone

Page 12

Syllables

When the letters **le** come at the end of a word, they sometimes have the sound of **ul**, as in raffle.

Directions: Draw a line to match the syllables so they make words. The first one is done for you.

can — gle
tur — cle
pur — ple
cir — kle
spar — zle
raf — dle
ea — fle
siz — tle

Directions: Use the words you made to complete the sentences. One is done for you.

1. Will you buy a ticket for our school <u>raffle</u>?
2. The <u>turtle</u> pulled his head into his shell.
3. We could hear the bacon <u>sizzle</u> in the pan.
4. The baby had one <u>candle</u> on her birthday cake.
5. My favorite color is <u>purple</u>
6. Look at that diamond <u>sparkle</u>!
7. The bald <u>eagle</u> is our national bird.
8. Draw a <u>circle</u> around the correct answer.

Page 13

Compound Words

A compound word is two small words put together to make one new word. Compound words are usually divided into syllables between the two words.

Directions: Read the words. Then divide them into syllables. The first one is done for you.

1. playground <u>play</u> <u>ground</u>
2. sailboat <u>sail</u> <u>boat</u>
3. doghouse <u>dog</u> <u>house</u>
4. dishpan <u>dish</u> <u>pan</u>
5. pigpen <u>pig</u> <u>pen</u>
6. outdoors <u>out</u> <u>doors</u>
7. beehive <u>bee</u> <u>hive</u>
8. airplane <u>air</u> <u>plane</u>
9. cardboard <u>card</u> <u>board</u>
10. nickname <u>nick</u> <u>name</u>
11. hilltop <u>hill</u> <u>top</u>
12. broomstick <u>broom</u> <u>stick</u>
13. sunburn <u>sun</u> <u>burn</u>
14. oatmeal <u>oat</u> <u>meal</u>
15. campfire <u>camp</u> <u>fire</u>
16. somewhere <u>some</u> <u>where</u>
17. starfish <u>star</u> <u>fish</u>
18. birthday <u>birth</u> <u>day</u>
19. sidewalk <u>side</u> <u>walk</u>
20. seashore <u>sea</u> <u>shore</u>

Page 14

Compound Words

Directions: Read the compound words in the word box. Then use them to answer the questions. The first one is done for you.

sailboat	blueberry	bookcase	tablecloth	beehive
dishpan	pigpen	classroom	playground	bedtime
broomstick	treetop	fireplace	newspaper	sunburn

Which compound word means . . .

1. a case for books? — <u>bookcase</u>
2. a berry that is blue? — <u>blueberry</u>
3. a hive for bees? — <u>beehive</u>
4. a place for fires? — <u>fireplace</u>
5. a pen for pigs? — <u>pigpen</u>
6. a room for a class? — <u>classroom</u>
7. a pan for dishes? — <u>dishpan</u>
8. a boat to sail? — <u>sailboat</u>
9. a paper for news? — <u>newspaper</u>
10. a burn from the sun? — <u>sunburn</u>
11. the top of a tree? — <u>treetop</u>
12. a stick for a broom? — <u>broomstick</u>
13. the time to go to bed? — <u>bedtime</u>
14. a cloth for the table? — <u>tablecloth</u>
15. ground to play on? — <u>playground</u>

Page 15

Transportation Vocabulary

Directions: Unscramble the words to spell the names of kinds of transportation. The first one is done for you.

behelwworar — wheel <u>b a r r o w</u>
anirt — <u>t r a i n</u>
moobattor — moto <u>r b o a t</u>
crattor — <u>t r a c t o r</u>
ceicbly — <u>b i c y c l e</u>
tocker — <u>r o c k e t</u>
etobimuloa — aut <u>o m o b i l e</u>
rilanape — <u>a i r p l a n e</u>

Directions: Use a word from above to complete each sentence.

1. My mother uses a <u>wheelbarrow</u> to move dirt to her garden.
2. The <u>rocket</u> blasted the spaceship off the launching pad.
3. We flew on an <u>airplane</u> to visit my aunt in Florida.
4. My grandfather drives a very old <u>automobile</u>.
5. We borrowed Fred's <u>motorboat</u> to go water skiing.
6. You should always look both ways when crossing a <u>train</u> track.
7. I hope I get a new <u>bicycle</u> for my birthday.

Page 16

Space Vocabulary

Directions: Unscramble each word. Use the numbers below the letters to tell you what order they belong in. Write the word by its definition.

i r t b o
4 2 5 3 1

u t o n c w d n o
3 5 7 9 1 8 6 4 2

u l e f
2 4 3 1

a t s r a t n o u
7 9 2 4 1 3 6 5 8

t e h t s u l
5 7 2 4 1 3 6

A member of the team that flies a spaceship. — <u>astronaut</u>

A rocket-powered spaceship that travels between Earth and space. — <u>shuttle</u>

The material, such as gas, used for power. — <u>fuel</u>

The seconds just before take-off. — <u>countdown</u>

The path of a spaceship as it goes around Earth. — <u>orbit</u>

Page 17

Weather Vocabulary

Directions: Use the weather words in the box to complete the sentences.

sunny	temperature	foggy	puddles	rainy
windy	rainbow	cloudy	lightning	snowy

1. My friends and I love <u>snowy</u> days, because we can have snowball fights!
2. On <u>rainy</u> days, we like to stay indoors and play board games.
3. Today was hot and <u>sunny</u>, so we went to the beach.
4. We didn't see the sun at all yesterday. It was <u>cloudy</u> all day.
5. <u>Windy</u> weather is perfect for flying kites.
6. It was so <u>foggy</u>, Mom had to use the headlights in the car so we wouldn't get lost.
7. While it was still raining, the sun began to shine and created a beautiful <u>rainbow</u>.
8. We like to jump in the <u>puddles</u> after it rains.
9. <u>Lightning</u> flashed across the sky during the thunderstorm.
10. The <u>temperature</u> outside was so low, we needed to wear hats, mittens and scarves.

Grade 3 - Comprehensive Curriculum

Page 18

Vocabulary Word Lists

Directions: Complete the vocabulary word lists. Be creative!

Answers may include:

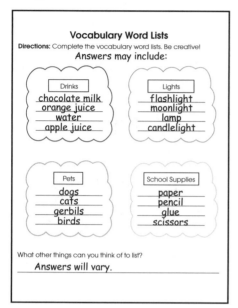

Drinks
- chocolate milk
- orange juice
- water
- apple juice

Lights
- flashlight
- moonlight
- lamp
- candlelight

Pets
- dogs
- cats
- gerbils
- birds

School Supplies
- paper
- pencil
- glue
- scissors

What other things can you think of to list?

Answers will vary.

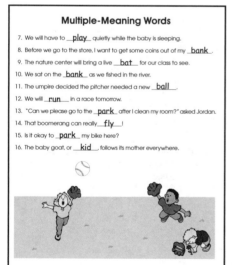

Page 19

Multiple-Meaning Words

Many words have more than one meaning. These words are called **multiple-meaning words**. Think of how the word is used in a sentence or story to determine the correct meaning.

Directions: The following baseball words have multiple meanings. Write the correct word in each baseball below.

| play | bat | ball | fly | run |

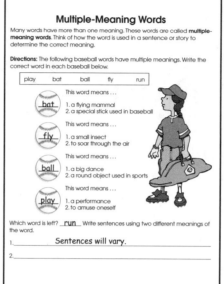

bat — This word means . . .
1. a flying mammal
2. a special stick used in baseball

fly — This word means . . .
1. a small insect
2. to soar through the air

ball — This word means . . .
1. a big dance
2. a round object used in sports

play — This word means . . .
1. a performance
2. to amuse oneself

Which word is left? _run_ Write sentences using two different meanings of the word.

1. _____ Sentences will vary. _____

2. _____

Page 20

Multiple-Meaning Words

Directions: Complete each sentence on pages 40 and 41 using one of the words below. Each word will be used only twice.

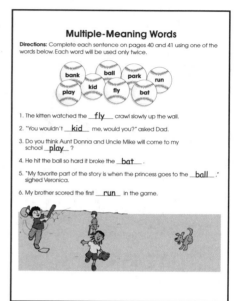

bank ball park run play kid fly bat

1. The kitten watched the _fly_ crawl slowly up the wall.

2. "You wouldn't _kid_ me, would you?" asked Dad.

3. Do you think Aunt Donna and Uncle Mike will come to my school _play_?

4. He hit the ball so hard it broke the _bat_.

5. "My favorite part of the story is when the princess goes to the _ball_," sighed Veronica.

6. My brother scored the first _run_ in the game.

Page 21

Multiple-Meaning Words

7. We will have to _play_ quietly while the baby is sleeping.

8. Before we go to the store, I want to get some coins out of my _bank_.

9. The nature center will bring a live _bat_ for our class to see.

10. We sat on the _bank_ as we fished in the river.

11. The umpire decided the pitcher needed a new _ball_.

12. We will _run_ in a race tomorrow.

13. "Can we please go to the _park_ after I clean my room?" asked Jordan.

14. That boomerang can really _fly_!

15. Is it okay to _park_ my bike here?

16. The baby goat, or _kid_, follows its mother everywhere.

Page 22

Sequencing

Directions: Fill in the blank spaces with what comes next in the series. The first one is done for you.

year	Wednesday	day	sixth	large
twenty	February	night	seventeen	mile
paragraph	winter	ocean		

1. Sunday, Monday, Tuesday, _____ Wednesday

2. third, fourth, fifth, _____ sixth

3. November, December, January, _____ February

4. tiny, small, medium, _____ large

5. fourteen, fifteen, sixteen, _____ seventeen

6. morning, afternoon, evening, _____ night

7. inch, foot, yard, _____ mile

8. day, week, month, _____ year

9. spring, summer, autumn, _____ winter

10. five, ten, fifteen, _____ twenty

11. letter, word, sentence, _____ paragraph

12. second, minute, hour, _____ day

13. stream, lake, river, _____ ocean

Page 23

Sequencing

When words are in a certain order, they are in sequence.

Directions: Complete each sequence using a word from the box. There are extra words in the box. The first one has been done for you.

| below | three | fifteen | December | twenty | above |
| after | go | third | hour | March | yard |

1. January, February, _March_

2. before, during, _after_

3. over, on, _above_

4. come, stay, _go_

5. second, minute, _hour_

6. first, second, _third_

7. five, ten, _fifteen_

8. inch, foot, _yard_

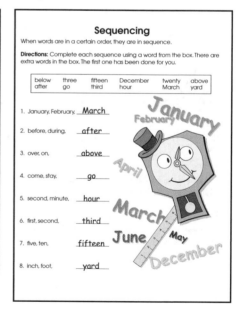

Page 24

Sequencing: Smallest to Largest

Directions: Rearrange each group of words to form a sequence from smallest to largest.

Example:

minute, second, hour — second, minute, hour

1. least, most, more — least, more, most
2. full, empty, half-full — empty, half-full, full
3. month, day, year — day, month, year
4. baseball, golf ball, soccer ball — golf ball, baseball, soccer ball
5. penny, dollar, quarter — penny, quarter, dollar
6. $4.12, $3.18, $3.22 — $3.18, $3.22, $4.12
7. boy, man, infant — infant, boy, man
8. mother, daughter, grandmother — daughter, mother, grandmother

Page 25

Sequencing

Directions: Read each story. Circle the phrase that tells what happened before.

1. Beth is very happy now that she has someone to play with. She hopes that her new sister will grow up quickly!
   A few days ago . . .
   Beth was sick.
   (Beth's mother had a baby.)
   Beth got a new puppy.

2. Sara tried to mend the tear. She used a needle and thread to sew up the hole.
   While playing, Sara had . . .
   broken her bicycle.
   lost her watch.
   (torn her shirt.)

3. The movers took John's bike off the truck and put it in the garage. Next, they moved his bed into his new bedroom.
   John's family . . .
   (bought a new house.)
   went on vacation.
   bought a new truck.

4. Katie picked out a book about dinosaurs. Jim, who likes sports, chose two books about baseball.
   Katie and Jim . . .
   (went to the library.)
   went to the playground.
   went to the grocery.

Page 26

Sequencing

Directions: Read each story. Circle the sentence that tells what might happen next.

1. Sam and Judy picked up their books and left the house. They walked to the bus stop. They got on a big yellow bus.
   What will Sam and Judy do next?
   (They will go to school.)
   They will visit their grandmother.
   They will go to the store.

2. Maggie and Matt were playing in the snow. They made a snowman with a black hat and a red scarf. Then the sun came out.
   What might happen next?
   It will snow again.
   They will play in the sandbox.
   (The snowman will melt.)

3. Megan put on a big floppy hat and funny clothes. She put green make-up on her face.
   What will Megan do next?
   She will go to school.
   (She will go to a costume party.)
   She will go to bed.

4. Mike was eating a hot dog. Suddenly he smelled smoke. He turned and saw a fire on the stove.
   What will Mike do next?
   He will watch the fire.
   (He will call for help.)
   He will finish his hot dog.

Page 27

Sequencing

Directions: Number these sentences from 1 to 5 to show the correct order of the story.

Building a Treehouse
   4 They had a beautiful treehouse!
   2 They got wood and nails.
   1 Jay and Lisa planned to build a treehouse.
   5 Now, they like to eat lunch in their treehouse.
   3 Lisa and Jay worked in the backyard for three days building the treehouse.

A School Play
   5 Everyone clapped when the curtain closed.
   4 The girl who played Snow White came onto the stage.
   2 All the other school children went to the gym to see the play.
   3 The stage curtain opened.
   1 The third grade was going to put on a play about Snow White.

Page 28

Sequencing

Directions: Number these sentences from 1 to 8 to show the correct order of the story.

   4 Jack's father called the family doctor.
   8 Jack felt much better as his parents drove him home.
   1 Jack woke up in the middle of the night with a terrible pain in his stomach.
   5 The doctor told Jack's father to take Jack to the hospital.
   2 Jack called his parents to come help him.
   7 At the hospital, the doctors examined Jack. They said the problem was not serious. They told Jack's parents that he could go home.
   3 Jack's mother took his temperature. He had a fever of 103 degrees.
   6 On the way to the hospital, Jack rested in the backseat. He was worried.

Page 29

Sequencing: A Story

This is a story from *The McGuffey Second Reader*. This is a very old book your great-great-grandparents may have used to learn to read.

Directions: Read the story on pages 29 and 30, then answer the questions on page 31.

The Crow and the Robin

One morning in the early spring, a crow was sitting on the branch of an old oak tree. He felt very ugly and cross and could only say, "Croak! Croak!" Soon, a little robin, who was looking for a place to build her nest, came with a merry song into the same tree. "Good morning to you," she said to the crow.

But the crow made no answer; he only looked at the clouds and croaked something about the cold wind. "I said, 'Good morning to you,'" said the robin, jumping from branch to branch.

"I wonder how you can be so merry this morning," croaked the crow.

"Why shouldn't I be merry?" asked the robin. "Spring has come and everyone ought to be happy."

"I am not happy," said the crow. "Don't you see those black clouds above us? It is going to snow."

"Very well," said the robin, "I shall keep on singing until the snow comes. A merry song will not make it any colder."

"Caw, caw, caw," croaked the crow. "I think you are very foolish."

ANSWER KEY

Page 30

Sequencing: A Story

The Crow and the Robin

The robin flew to another tree and kept on singing, but the crow sat still and made himself very unhappy. "The wind is so cold," he said. "It always blows the wrong way for me."

Very soon the sun came out, warm and bright, and the clouds went away, but the crow was as cross as ever.

The grass began to spring up in the meadows. Green leaves and flowers were seen in the woods. Birds and bees flew here and there in the glad sunshine. The crow sat and croaked on the branch of the old oak tree.

"It is always too warm or too cold," said he. "To be sure, it is a little pleasant just now, but I know that the sun will soon shine warm enough to burn me up. Then before night, it will be colder than ever. I do not see how anyone can sing at such a time as this."

Just then the robin came back to the tree with a straw in her mouth for her nest. "Well, my friend," asked she, "where is your snow?"

"Don't talk about that," croaked the crow. "It will snow all the harder for this sunshine."

"And snow or shine," said the robin, "you will keep on croaking. For my part, I shall always look on the bright side of things and have a song for every day in the year."

Which will you be like—the crow or the robin? __Answers will vary.__

Page 31

Sequencing: The Story

These sentences retell the story of "The Crow and the Robin" but are out of order.

Directions: Write the numbers 1 through 10 on the lines to show the correct sequence. The first one has been done for you.

_7_ Although the sun came out and the clouds went away, the crow was still as cross as ever.

_10_ "I shall always . . . have a song for every day in the year," said the robin.

_1_ The crow sat on the branch of an old oak tree and could only say, "Croak! Croak!"

_6_ "This wind is so cold. It always blows the wrong way," the crow said.

_4_ The crow said, "It is going to snow."

_2_ The robin said good morning to the crow.

_5_ The crow told the robin that he thought she was very foolish.

_8_ The grass began to spring up in the meadows.

_3_ The robin was jumping from branch to branch as she talked to the crow.

_9_ The robin came back with straw in her mouth for her nest.

Page 32

Following Directions

Directions: Learning to follow directions is very important. Use the map to find your way to different houses.

1. Color the start house yellow.
2. Go north 2 houses, and east two houses.
3. Go north 2 houses, and west 4 houses.
4. Color the house green.

5. Start at the yellow house.
6. Go east 1 house, and north 3 houses.
7. Go west 3 houses, and south 3 houses.
8. Color the house blue.

North
West — East
South

Page 33

Following Directions

Directions: Read each sentence and do what it says to do.

1. Count the syllables in each word. Write the number on the line by the word.
2. Draw a line between the two words in each compound word.
3. Draw a circle around each name of a month.
4. Draw a box around each food word.
5. Draw an **X** on each noise word.
6. Draw a line under each day of the week.
7. Write the three words from the list you did not use. Draw a picture of each of those words.

_2_ (April)	_4_ [vegetable]	_3_ table|cloth
_1_ bang	_1_ (June)	_1_ [meat]
_2_ side|walk	_3_ Saturday	_1_ crash
_3_ astronaut	_1_ (March)	_2_ jingle
_1_ moon	_2_ cardboard	_2_ rocket
_2_ Friday	_1_ [fruit]	_2_ Monday

moon	astronaut	rocket

Page 34

Following Directions: A Recipe

Following directions means doing what the directions say to do. Following directions is an important skill to know. When you are trying to find a new place, build a model airplane or use a recipe, you should follow the directions given.

Directions: Read the following recipe. Then answer the questions on page 35.

Fruit Salad

1 fresh pineapple	2 oranges
1 cantaloupe	1 pear
2 bananas	1 cup seedless grapes
1 cup strawberries	lemon juice

- Cut the pineapple into chunks.
- Use a small metal scoop to make balls of the cantaloupe.
- Slice the pear, bananas and strawberries.
- Peel the oranges and divide them into sections. Cut each section into bite-sized pieces.
- Dip each piece of fruit in lemon juice, then combine them in a large bowl.
- Cover and chill.
- Pour a fruit dressing of your choice over the chilled fruit, blend well and serve cold.

Makes 4 large servings.

Page 35

Following Directions: A Recipe

Directions: Using the recipe on page 34, answer the questions below.

1. How many bananas does the recipe require? ___2___

2. Does the recipe explain why you must dip the fruit in lemon juice? __no__
Why would it be important to do this? __It keeps the fruit from turning brown quickly.__

3. Would your fruit salad be as good if you did not cut the pineapple or section the oranges? Why or why not? __No, because it would be harder to eat such big chunks of food.__

4. Which do you do first?
(Check one.)

___ Pour dressing over the fruit.
_✓_ Slice the pear.
___ Serve the fruit salad.

5. Which three fruits do you slice?
__pear__
__bananas__
__strawberries__

Page 36

Main Idea

The main idea of a story is what the story is mostly about.

Directions: Read the story. Then answer the questions.

A tree is more than the enormous plant you see growing in your yard. A large part of the tree grows under the ground. This part is called the roots. If the tree is very big and very old, the roots may stretch down 100 feet!

The roots hold the tree in the ground. The roots do another important job for the tree. They gather minerals and water from the soil to feed the tree so it will grow. Most land plants, including trees, could not live without roots to support and feed them.

1. The main idea of this story is:

   The roots of a tree are underground.

   (The roots do important jobs for the tree.)

2. Where are the roots of a tree? __underground__

Circle the correct answer.

3. The roots help to hold the tree up.   (True)   False

4. Name two things the roots collect from the soil for the tree.

   1) __water__   2) __minerals__

Page 37

Main Idea

Directions: Read about spiders. Then answer the questions.

Many people think spiders are insects, but they are not. Spiders are the same size as insects, and they look like insects in some ways. But there are three ways to tell a spider from an insect. Insects have six legs, and spiders have eight legs. Insects have antennae, but spiders do not. An insect's body is divided into three parts; a spider's body is divided into only two parts.

1. The main idea of this story is:

   Spiders are like insects.

   (Spiders are like insects in some ways, but they are not insects.)

2. What are three ways to tell a spider from an insect?

   1) __Spiders have eight legs; insects have six.__

   2) __Insects have antennae; spiders do not.__

   3) __Insects have three body parts; spiders have two.__

Circle the correct answer.

3. Spiders are the same size as insects.   (True)   False

Page 38

Main Idea

Directions: Read about the giant panda. Then answer the questions.

Giant pandas are among the world's favorite animals. They look like big, cuddly stuffed toys. There are not very many pandas left in the world. You may have to travel a long way to see one.

The only place on Earth where pandas live in the wild is in the bamboo forests of the mountains of China. It is hard to see pandas in the forest because they are very shy. They hide among the many bamboo trees. It also is hard to see pandas because there are so few of them. Scientists think there may be less than 1,000 pandas living in the mountains of China.

1. Write a sentence that tells the main idea of this story:

   __There are very few pandas left in the world.__

2. What are two reasons that it is hard to see pandas in the wild?

   1) __They hide among the bamboo trees.__

   2) __There are very few pandas.__

3. How many pandas are believed to be living in the mountains of China?

   __fewer than 1,000__

Page 39

Main Idea

Directions: Read the story. Then answer the questions.

Because bamboo is very important to pandas, they have special body features that help them eat it. The panda's front foot is like a hand. But, instead of four fingers and a thumb, the panda has five fingers and an extra-long wrist bone. With its special front foot, the panda can easily pick up the stalks of bamboo. It also can hold the bamboo more tightly than it could with a hand like ours.

Bamboo stalks are very tough. The panda uses its big heavy head, large jaws and big back teeth to chew. Pandas eat the bamboo by peeling the outside of the stalk. They do this by moving their front feet from side to side while holding the stalk in their teeth. Then they bite off a piece of the bamboo and chew it with their strong jaws.

1. Write a sentence that tells the main idea of this story.

   __Pandas have special body features to help them eat bamboo.__

2. Instead of four fingers and a thumb, the panda has

   __five fingers and an extra-long wrist bone.__

3. Bamboo is very tender.   True   (False)

Page 40

Main Idea

Directions: Read each main idea sentence on pages 40 and 41. Then read the detail sentences following each main idea. Draw a ✓ on the line in front of each detail that supports the main idea.

Example: Niagara Falls is a favorite vacation spot.

   ✓   There are so many cars and buses that it is hard to get around.
   ___ My little brother gets sick when we go camping.
   ✓   You can see people there from all over the world.

1. Hummingbirds are interesting birds to watch.

   ✓   They look like tiny helicopters as they move around the flowers.

   ✓   One second they are "drinking" from the flower; the next, they are gone!

   ___ It is important to provide birdseed in the winter for our feathered friends.

2. Boys and girls look forward to Valentine's Day parties at school.

   ✓   For days, children try to choose the perfect valentine for each friend.

   ___ The school program is next Tuesday night.

   ✓   Just thinking about frosted, heart-shaped cookies makes me hungry!

Page 41

Main Idea

3. In-line skating has become a very popular activity.

   ___ Bicycles today are made in many different styles.

   ✓   It is hard to spend even an hour at a park without seeing children and adults skating.

   ✓   The stores are full of many kinds and colors of in-line skates.

4. It has been a busy summer!

   ✓   Dad built a new deck off the back of our house, and everyone helped.

   ✓   Our next-door neighbor needed my help to watch her three-year-old twins.

   ___ We will visit my relatives on the East coast for Christmas this year.

Page 42

Main Idea

The **main idea** of a paragraph is the most important point. Often, the first sentence in a paragraph tells the main idea. Most of the other sentences are details that support the main idea. One of the sentences in each paragraph below does not belong in the story.

Directions: Circle the sentence that does not support the main idea.

My family and I went to the zoo last Saturday. It was a beautiful day. The tigers napped in the sun. I guess they liked the warm sunshine as much as we did! Mom and Dad laughed at the baby monkeys. They said the monkeys reminded them of how we act. My sister said the bald eagle reminded her of Dad! I know I'll remember that trip to the zoo for a long time. (My cousin is coming to visit the weekend before school starts.)

Thanksgiving was a special holiday in our classroom. Each child dressed up as either a Pilgrim or a Native American. (My baby sister learned to walk last week.) We prepared food for our "feast" on the last day of school before the holiday. We all helped shake the jar full of cream to make real butter. Our teacher cooked applesauce. It smelled delicious!

Page 43

Main Idea

Directions: Circle the sentence in each paragraph that does not support the main idea.

The school picnic was so much fun! When we arrived, we each made a name tag. Then we signed up for the contests we wanted to enter. My best friend was my partner for every contest. (The hen laid so many eggs that I needed a basket to carry them.) All that exercise made us very hungry. We were glad to see those tables full of food.

The storm howled outside, so we stayed in for an evening of fun. (The colorful rainbow stretched across the sky.) The dining room table was stacked with games and puzzles. The delightful smell of popcorn led us into the kitchen where Dad led a parade around the kitchen table. Then we carried our bowls of popcorn into the dining room. We laughed so hard and ate so much, we didn't care who won the games. It was a great evening!

The city championship game would be played on Saturday at Brookside Park. Coach Metzger called an extra practice Friday evening. He said he knew we were good, because we had made it this far. He didn't want us to get nervous and forget everything we knew. (School starts on Monday, but I'm not ready to go back yet.) After working on some drills, Coach told us to relax, get lots of rest and come back ready to play.

Page 44

Detail Sentences

In most paragraphs, the main idea is stated in the first sentence. The other sentences in the paragraph should give details to support that main idea. These are **detail sentences**.

Example: My calico cat was a good mother to her new kittens.
a. Each day she made sure they were well fed.
b. It was fun to watch her play with them.

Directions: Write two detail sentences to support each main idea.

1. Christopher loved his new bike.
   a. _____
   b. _____

2. Kim ~~Answers will vary.~~ y Day.
   a. _____
   b. _____

3. The picnic was canceled due to rain.
   a. _____
   _____
   b. _____

Page 45

Main Idea: The Inventor

Directions: Read about Thomas Jefferson, then answer the questions.

Thomas Jefferson was the third president of the United States. He was also an inventor. That means he created things that had never been made before. Thomas Jefferson had many inventions. He built a chair that rotated in circles. He created a rotating music stand. He also made a walking stick that unfolded into a chair. Thomas Jefferson even invented a new kind of plow for farming.

1. The main idea is: (Circle one.)

   Thomas Jefferson was very busy when he was president.

   (Thomas Jefferson was a president and an inventor.)

2. What do we call a person who has new ideas and makes things that no one else has made before? **an inventor**

3. List three of Thomas Jefferson's inventions.

1) _____

2) **Answers will vary.**

3) _____

Page 46

Main Idea: Inventing the Bicycle

Directions: Read about the bicycle, then answer the questions.

One of the first bicycles was made out of wood. It was created in 1790 by an inventor in France. The first bicycle had no pedals. It looked like a horse on wheels. The person who rode the bicycle had to push it with his/her legs. Pedals weren't invented until nearly 50 years later.

Bikes became quite popular in the United States during the 1890s. Streets and parks were filled with people riding them. But those bicycles were still different from the bikes we ride today. They had heavier tires, and the brakes and lights weren't very good. Bicycling is still very popular in the United States. It is a great form of exercise and a handy means of transportation.

1. Who invented the bicycle? **an inventor in France**

2. What did it look like? **no pedals, wooden, looked like a horse on wheels**

3. When did bikes become popular in the United States? **during the 1890s**

4. Where did people ride bikes? **streets and parks**

5. How is biking good for you? **good for exercise**

6. How many years have bikes been popular in the United States? **109 years**

Page 47

Main Idea: Chewing Gum

Directions: Read about chewing gum, then answer the questions.

Thomas Adams was an American inventor. In 1870, he was looking for a substitute for rubber. He was working with chicle (chick-ul), a substance that comes from a certain kind of tree in Mexico. Years ago, Mexicans chewed chicle. Thomas Adams decided to try it for himself. He liked it so much he started selling it. Twenty years later, he owned a large factory that produced chewing gum.

1. Who was the American inventor who started selling chewing gum? **Thomas Adams**

2. What was he hoping to invent? **a substitute for rubber**

3. When did he invent chewing gum? **in 1870**

4. Where does the chicle come from? **a tree in Mexico**

5. Why did Thomas Adams start selling chewing gum? **He liked it so much.**

6. How long was it until Adams owned a large factory that produced chewing gum? **20 years**

ANSWER KEY

Page 48

Main Idea: The Peaceful Pueblos

Directions: Read about the Pueblo Native Americans, then answer the questions.

The Pueblo (pooh-eb-low) Native Americans live in the southwestern United States in New Mexico and Arizona. They have lived there for hundreds of years. The Pueblos have always been peaceful Native Americans. They never started wars. They only fought if attacked first.

The Pueblos love to dance. Even their dances are peaceful. They dance to ask the gods for rain or sunshine. They dance for other reasons, too. Sometimes the Pueblos wear masks when they dance.

1. The main idea is: (Circle one.)

Pueblos are peaceful Native Americans who still live in parts of the United States.

Pueblo Native Americans never started wars.

2. Do Pueblos like to fight? __No__

3. What do the Pueblos like to do? __They love to dance.__

Page 49

Main Idea: Clay Homes

Directions: Read about adobe houses, then answer the questions.

Pueblo Native Americans live in houses made of clay. They are called adobe (ah-doe-bee) houses. Adobe is a yellow-colored clay that comes from the ground. The hot sun in New Mexico and Arizona helps dry the clay to make strong bricks. The Pueblos have used adobe to build their homes for many years.

Pueblos use adobe for other purposes, too. The women in the tribes make beautiful pottery out of adobe. While the clay is still damp, they form it into shapes. After they have made the bowls and other containers, they paint them with lovely designs.

1. What is the subject of this story? __adobe__

2. Who uses clay to make their houses? __Pueblo Native Americans__

3. How long have they been building adobe houses? __many years__

4. Why do adobe bricks need to be dried? __to make the clay bricks strong__

5. How do the Pueblos make pottery from adobe? __by forming damp clay__

Page 50

Main Idea: George Washington

Directions: Read about George Washington, then answer the questions.

George Washington was the first president of the United States. An old story proclaimed that he was very honest. It said that when Washington was just six years old, he cut down a cherry tree on the farm where he lived. He told his father he cut down the tree. But George Washington did not chop down a cherry tree. People have since discovered that the story was invented. They say a man named Parson Weems wrote one of the first books about George Washington. He liked Washington so much, he made up that story.

1. The main idea of this story is: (Circle one.)

George Washington cut down a cherry tree.

George Washington did not cut down a cherry tree.

2. Is the story of George Washington chopping down a cherry tree true or false? (Circle one.) True or False

3. Who made up the story about George Washington? __Parson Weems__

4. When did the story say George Washington cut down the tree? __when he was 6__

5. Where was the tree supposedly cut down by Washington? __on the farm where he lived__

6. How did Parson Weems tell people the story? __He wrote a book.__

Page 51

Noting Details

Directions: Read the story. Then answer the questions.

Thomas Edison was one of America's greatest inventors. An **inventor** thinks up new machines and new ways of doing things. Edison was born in Milan, Ohio in 1847. He went to school for only three months. His teacher thought he was not very smart because he asked so many questions.

Edison liked to experiment. He had many wonderful ideas. He invented the light bulb and the phonograph (record player).

Thomas Edison died in 1931, but we still use many of his inventions today.

1. What is an inventor?

__A person who thinks up new machines and new ways of doing things.__

2. Where was Thomas Edison born?

__Milan, Ohio__

3. How long did he go to school?

__three months__

4. What are two of Edison's inventions?

__the light bulb and the phonograph__

Page 52

Noting Details

Directions: Read the story. Then answer the questions.

The giant panda is much smaller than a brown bear or a polar bear. In fact, a horse weighs about four times as much as a giant panda. So why is it called "giant"? It is giant next to another kind of panda called the red panda.

The red panda also lives in China. The red panda is about the size of a fox. It has a long, fluffy, striped tail and beautiful reddish fur. It looks very much like a raccoon.

Many people think the giant pandas are bears. They look like bears. Even the word panda is Chinese for "white bear." But because of its relationship to the red panda, many scientists now believe that the panda is really more like a raccoon!

1. Why is the giant panda called "giant"?

__It is larger than the red panda.__

2. Where does the red panda live?

__in China__

3. How big is the red panda?

__about the size of a fox__

4. What animal does the red panda look like?

__a raccoon__

5. What does the word panda mean?

__"white bear"__

Page 53

Noting Details

Directions: Read the story. Then answer the questions.

Giant pandas do not live in families like people do. The only pandas that live together are mothers and their babies. Newborn pandas are very tiny and helpless. They weigh only five ounces when they are born—about the weight of a stick of butter! They are born with their eyes closed, and they have no teeth.

It takes about three years for a panda to grow up. When full grown, a giant panda weighs about 300 pounds and is five to six feet tall. Once a panda is grown up, it leaves its mother and goes off to live by itself.

1. What pandas live together? __mothers and their babies__

2. How much do pandas weigh when they are born? __about five ounces__

3. Why do newborn pandas live with their mothers? __They are very tiny and helpless.__

4. When is a panda full grown? __at three years old__

5. How big is a grown-up panda? __five to six feet tall and 300 pounds__

Grade 3 - Comprehensive Curriculum

Page 54

Inference

Inference is using logic to figure out what is not directly told.

Directions: Read the story. Then answer the questions.

In the past, thousands of people went to the National Zoo each year to see Hsing-Hsing, the panda. Sometimes, there were as many as 1,000 visitors in one hour! Like all pandas, Hsing-Hsing spent most of his time sleeping. Because pandas are so rare, most people think it is exciting to see even a sleeping panda!

1. Popular means well-liked. Do you think giant pandas are popular?

   Yes.

2. What clue do you have that pandas are popular?

   They had as many as 1,000 visitors an hour.

3. What did most visitors see Hsing-Hsing doing?

   sleeping

Page 55

Inference

Directions: Read the messages on the memo board. Then answer the questions.

1. What kind of lesson does Katie have? _____ dance
2. What time is Amy's birthday party? _____ 1:00 PM
3. What kind of appointment does Jeff have on September 3rd? _____ doctor
4. Who goes to choir practice? _____ mom
5. Where is Dad's meeting? _____ fire station
6. What time does Jeff go to the doctor? _____ 4:00 PM

Page 56

Reading for Information

Directions: Read the story. List the four steps or changes a caterpillar goes through as it becomes a butterfly. Draw the stages in the boxes at the bottom of the page.

The Life Cycle of the Butterfly

One of the most magical changes in nature is the metamorphosis of a caterpillar. There are four stages in the transformation. The first stage is the embryonic stage. This is the stage in which tiny eggs are deposited on a leaf. The second stage is the larvae stage. We usually think of caterpillars at this stage. Many people like to capture the caterpillars hoping that while they have the caterpillar, it will turn into pupa. Another name for the pupa stage is the cocoon stage. Many changes happen inside the cocoon that we cannot see. Inside the cocoon, the caterpillar is changing into an adult. The adult breaks out of the cocoon as a beautiful butterfly!

1. embryonic stage
2. larvae stage
3. pupa stage (cocoon stage)
4. butterfly stage

Life Cycle of the Butterfly

Page 57

Reading for Information

Telephone books contain information about people's addresses and phone numbers. They also list business addresses and phone numbers. The information in a telephone book is listed in alphabetical order.

Directions: Use your telephone book to find the following places in your area. Ask your mom or dad for help if you need it.

Can you find . . .

	Name	Phone number
. . . a pizza place?	Answers will vary.	
. . . a bicycle store?		
. . . a pet shop?		
. . . a toy store?		
. . . a water park?		

What other telephone numbers would you like to have?

_____

Page 58

Reading for Information: Dictionaries

Dictionaries contain meanings and pronunciations of words. The words in a dictionary are listed in alphabetical order. Guide words appear at the top of each dictionary page. They help us know at a glance what words are on each page.

Directions: Place the words in alphabetical order.

APPLE	CRAB	CRIB	FROG
apple	cake	crib	ear
atlas	coat	dog	egg
book	crab	drip	frog

apple	dog	crab	ear
book	atlas	cake	frog
egg	drip	coat	crib

Page 59

Reading for Information: Newspapers

A newspaper has many parts. Some of the parts of a newspaper are:

- banner — the name of the paper
- lead story — the top news item
- caption — sentences under the picture which give information about the picture
- sports — scores and information on current sports events
- comics — drawings that tell funny stories
- editorial — an article by the editor expressing an opinion about something
- ads — paid advertisements
- weather — information about the weather
- advice column — letters from readers asking for help with a problem
- movie guides — a list of movies and movie times
- obituary — information about people who have died

Directions: Match the newspaper sections below with their definitions.

banner	an article by the editor
lead story	sentences under pictures
caption	movies and movie times
editorial	the name of the paper
movies	information about people who have died
obituary	the top news item

Page 60

Newspaper Writing

A good news story gives us important information. It answers the questions:

WHO?   WHY?   WHAT?

WHERE?   HOW?   WHEN?

Directions: Think about the story "Little Red Riding Hood." Answer the following questions about the story.

Who are the characters? <u>Little Red Riding Hood, Grandma, the wolf and the hunter</u>

What is the story about? <u>a girl who visits her sick grandmother</u>

Why does Red go to Granny's house? <u>to bring food to her sick grandmother</u>

Where does the story take place? <u>in the woods, at Grandma's house</u>

When did she go to Granny's house? <u>in the afternoon</u>

Where did the Wolf greet Red? <u>He met her in the woods.</u>

Page 61

Fantasy and Reality

Something that is **real** could actually happen. Something that is **fantasy** is not real. It could not happen.

Examples: Real: Dogs can bark.
Fantasy: Dogs can fly.

Directions: Look at the sentences below. Write **real** or **fantasy** next to each sentence.

1. My cat can talk to me. <u>fantasy</u>
2. Witches ride brooms and cast spells. <u>fantasy</u>
3. Dad can mow the lawn. <u>real</u>
4. I ride a magic carpet to school. <u>fantasy</u>
5. I have a man-eating tree. <u>fantasy</u>
6. My sandbox has toys in it. <u>real</u>
7. Mom can bake chocolate chip cookies. <u>real</u>
8. Mark's garden has tomatoes and corn in it. <u>real</u>
9. Jack grows candy and ice cream in his garden. <u>fantasy</u>
10. I make my bed everyday. <u>real</u>

Write your own **real** sentence. <u>Answers will vary.</u>

Write your own **fantasy** sentence. <u>Answers will vary.</u>

Page 62

Idioms

Idioms are a colorful way of saying something ordinary. The words in idioms do not mean exactly what they say.

Directions: Read the idioms listed below. Draw a picture of the literal meaning. Then match the idiom to its correct meaning.

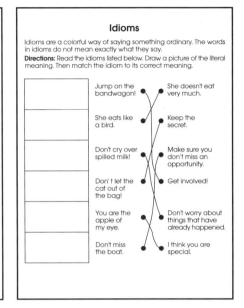

Jump on the bandwagon! — She doesn't eat very much.

She eats like a bird. — Keep the secret.

Don't cry over spilled milk! — Make sure you don't miss an opportunity.

Don't let the cat out of the bag! — Get involved!

You are the apple of my eye. — Don't worry about things that have already happened.

Don't miss the boat. — I think you are special.

Page 63

Analogies

Analogies compare how things are related to each other.

Directions: Complete the other analogies.

Example: Finger is to **hand** as **toe** is to **foot**.

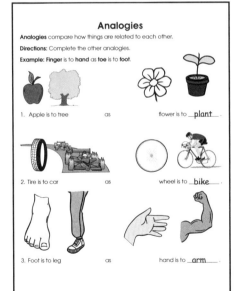

1. Apple is to tree   as   flower is to <u>plant</u>.

2. Tire is to car   as   wheel is to <u>bike</u>.

3. Foot is to leg   as   hand is to <u>arm</u>.

Page 64

Analogies

Directions: Complete each analogy using a word from the box. The first one has been done for you.

week	bottom	month	tiny	sentence	lake	out	eye

1. **Up** is to **down**   as   **in** is to <u>out</u>.
2. **Minute** is to **hour**   as   **day** is to <u>week</u>.
3. **Month** is to **year**   as   **week** is to <u>month</u>.
4. **Over** is to **under**   as   **top** is to <u>bottom</u>.
5. **Big** is to **little**   as   **giant** is to <u>tiny</u>.
6. **Sound** is to **ear**   as   **sight** is to <u>eye</u>.
7. **Page** is to **book**   as   **word** is to <u>sentence</u>.
8. **Wood** is to **tree**   as   **water** is to <u>lake</u>.

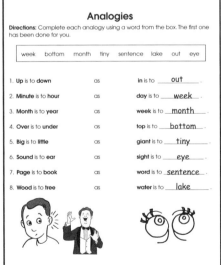

Page 65

Classifying: Seasons

Directions: Each word in the box can be grouped by seasons. Complete the pyramids for each season with a word from the box.

July 4	hot	football	bike rides
kite	froze	sled ride	swimming
snowman	bunnies	ice	jack-o-lantern
windy	baseball	leaves	Thanksgiving

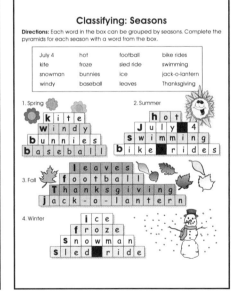

1. Spring
k i t e
w i n d y
b u n n i e s
b a s e b a l l

2. Summer
h o t
J u l y 4
s w i m m i n g
b i k e r i d e s

3. Fall
l e a v e s
f o o t b a l l
T h a n k s g i v i n g
j a c k - o - l a n t e r n

4. Winter
i c e
f r o z e
s n o w m a n
s l e d r i d e

Page 66

Classifying

Directions: Write each word from the box in the correct category.

robin	elm
buckeye	willow
sunflower	bluejay
canary	oak
rose	wren
tulip	morning glory

Trees
- buckeye
- elm
- willow
- oak

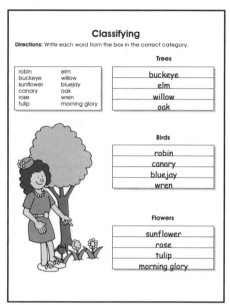

Birds
- robin
- canary
- bluejay
- wren

Flowers
- sunflower
- rose
- tulip
- morning glory

Page 67

Classifying

Directions: Look at the three words in each box and add one more that is like the others. **Answers may include:**

cars	trucks	cows	pigs
airplanes	**trains**	chickens	**horses**
bread	bagels	pens	pencils
muffins	**toast**	paints	**crayons**
square	triangle	violets	tulips
rectangle	**circle**	iris	**roses**
milk	yogurt	mom	dad
cheese	**ice cream**	sister	**brother**
merry-go-round	swings	snowpants	boots
sandbox	**slide**	jacket	**hat**

Challenge: Can you list the theme of each group?
- transportation — farm animals
- grain products — school supplies
- shapes — flowers
- dairy products — family members
- playground equipment — winter clothing

Page 68

Classifying

Directions: Write a word from the word box that is described by the four words in each group.

cake	farm	sick	winter	kite	car
flower	dishes	puppy	storm	ocean	book

leaves	sand	snow	string
petals	shells	wind	tail
stem	waves	cold	wind
roots	fish	ice	fly
flower	**ocean**	**winter**	**kite**

fever	rain	soft	sugar
headache	thunder	furry	butter
pills	wind	playful	flour
sneeze	hail	small	chocolate
sick	**storm**	**puppy**	**cake**

tractor	cup	pages	tires
animals	plate	words	seats
barn	bowl	pictures	windows
plow	platter	cover	trunk
farm	**dishes**	**book**	**car**

Page 69

Classifying

Directions: Write a word from the word box to complete each sentence. If the word you write names an article of clothing, write **1** on the line. If it names food, write **2** on the line. If it names an animal, write **3** on the line. If the word names furniture, write **4** on the line.

jacket	chair	shirt	owl	mice
bed	cheese	dress	bread	chocolate

_1_ 1. Danny tucked his **shirt** into his pants.

_2_ 2. **Chocolate** is my favorite kind of candy.

_3_ 3. The wise old **owl** sat in the tree and said, "Who-o-o."

_4_ 4. We can't sit on the **chair** because it has a broken leg.

_1_ 5. Don't forget to wear your **jacket** because it is chilly today.

_2_ 6. Will you please buy a loaf of **bread** at the store?

_1_ 7. She wore a very pretty **dress** to the dance.

_3_ 8. The cat chased the **mice** in the barn.

_4_ 9. I was so sleepy that I went to **bed** early.

_2_ 10. We put **cheese** in the mouse trap to help catch the mice.

Page 70

Classifying

Directions: Write the word from the word box that tells what kinds of things are in each sentence.

birds	toys	states	insects	women
men	numbers	animals	flowers	letters

1. A father, uncle and king are all **men**.
2. Fred has a wagon, puzzles and blocks. These are all **toys**.
3. Iowa, Ohio and Maine are all **states**.
4. A robin, woodpecker and canary all have wings. They are kinds of **birds**.
5. Squirrels, rabbits and foxes all have tails and are kinds of **animals**.
6. Roses, daisies and violets smell sweet. These are kinds of **flowers**.
7. A, B, C and D are all **letters**. You use them to spell words.
8. Bees, ladybugs and beetles are kinds of **insects**.
9. Mother, aunt and queen are **women**.
10. Seven, thirty and nineteen are all **numbers**.

Page 71

Classifying: Comparisons

Directions: Compare the people of Wackyville to each other. Read the sentences and answer the questions. The first one has been done for you.

1. Wanda cooks fast. Joe cooks faster than Wanda. Who cooks faster? **Joe**

2. Mr. Green plants many flowers. Mrs. Posy plants fewer flowers than Mr. Green. Who plants more flowers? **Mr. Green**

3. Hugo weighs a lot. Edward weighs less. Who weighs more? **Hugo**

4. Sheila has 3 cats. Billy has 2 cats, 1 dog and 1 bird. Who has more pets? **Billy**

5. Ms. Brown has many trees. Mr. Smith has fewer trees than Ms. Brown. Who has more trees? **Ms. Brown**

6. An elephant moves slowly. A snail moves even slower. Which animal moves quicker? **elephant**

Page 72

Classifying

Directions: Read each animal story. Then look at the fun facts. Write an **H** for horse, **P** for panda or **D** for dog next to each fact.

Horses
Horses are fun to ride. You can ride them in the woods or in fields. Horses usually have pretty names. Sometimes, if they are golden, they are called Amber. Horses swish their tails when it is hot. That keeps the flies away from them.

Pandas
Pandas are from China. They like to climb trees. They scratch bark to write messages to their friends in the trees. When pandas get hungry, they gnaw on bamboo shoots.

Dogs
Dogs are good pets. People often call them by names like Spot or Fido. Sometimes they are named after their looks. For example, a brown dog is sometimes named Brownie. Some people have special, small doors for their dogs to use.

Fun Facts
- D 1. My name is often Spot or Fido.
- P 2. I am from China.
- D 3. I make a good house pet.
- H 4. I like to carry people into the fields.
- P 5. My favorite food is bamboo.
- H 6. Flies bother me when I am hot.
- H 7. Amber is often my name when I am golden.
- P 8. I leave messages for my friends by scratching bark.
- D 9. Sometimes I have my own special door on a house.

Page 73

Webs

Webs are another way to classify information. Look at the groups below. Add more words in each group.

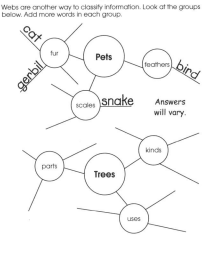

cat fur **Pets** feathers bird
gerbil
scales snake
parts **Trees** kinds
uses

Answers will vary.

Page 74

Story Webs

All short stories have a plot, characters, setting and a theme.
The **plot** is what the story is about.
The **characters** are the people or animals in the story.
The **setting** is where and when the story occurs.
The **theme** is the message or idea of the story.

Directions: Use the story "Snow White" to complete this story web.

plot
The wicked stepmother tries to get rid of Snow White.

characters
Snow White, the seven dwarves, Snow White's stepmother the Prince

title of story: "Snow White"

setting
the palace, the dwarves' cabin in the woods

theme
Good will triumph over evil.

Page 75

Types of Books

A **fiction** book is a book about things that are made up or not true. Fantasy books are fiction. A **nonfiction** book is about things that have really happened. Books can be classified into more types:

Mystery - books that have clues that lead to solving a problem or mystery

Biography - book about a real person's life

Poetry - a collection of poems, which may or may not rhyme

Fantasy - books about things that cannot really happen

Sports - books about different sports or sport figures

Travel - books about going to other places

Directions: Write mystery, biography, poetry, fantasy, sports or travel next to each title.

The Life of Helen Keller	biography
Let's Go to Mexico!	travel
The Case of the Missing Doll	mystery
How to Play Golf	sports
Turtle Soup and Other Poems	poetry
Fred's Flying Saucer	fantasy

Page 76

Fiction and Nonfiction

Fiction writing is a story that has been invented. The story might be about things that could really happen (realistic) or about things that couldn't possibly happen (fantasy). **Nonfiction** writing is based on facts. It usually gives information about people, places or things. A person can often tell while reading whether a story or book is fiction or nonfiction.

Directions: Read the paragraphs below and on page 77. Determine whether each paragraph is fiction or nonfiction. Circle the letter **F** for fiction or the letter **N** for nonfiction.

"Do not be afraid, little flowers," said the oak. "Close your yellow eyes in sleep and trust in me. You have made me glad many a time with your sweetness. Now I will take care that the winter shall do you no harm." **F** N

The whole team watched as the ball soared over the outfield fence. The game was over! It was hard to walk off the field and face parents, friends and each other. It had been a long season. Now, they would have to settle for second place. **F** N

Be careful when you remove the dish from the microwave. It will be very hot, so take care not to get burned by the dish or the hot steam. If time permits, leave the dish in the microwave for 2 or 3 minutes to avoid getting burned. It is a good idea to use a potholder, too. F **N**

Page 77

Fiction and Nonfiction

Megan and Mariah skipped out to the playground at recess. Today, it was Mariah's turn to choose what they would do first. To Megan's surprise, Mariah asked, "What do you want to do, Megan? I'm going to let you pick since it's your birthday!" **F** N

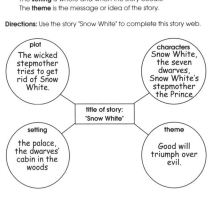

It is easy to tell an insect from a spider. An insect has three body parts and six legs. A spider has eight legs and no wings. Of course, if you see the creature spinning a web, you will know what it is. An insect wouldn't want to get too close to the web or it would be stuck. It might become dinner! F **N**

My name is Lee Chang, and I live in a country that you call China. My home is on the other side of the world from yours. When the sun is rising in my country, it is setting in yours. When it is day at your home, it is night at mine. F **N**

Henry washed the dog's foot in cold water from the brook. The dog lay very still, for he knew that the boy was trying to help him. **F** N

Page 78

Library Skills

A library is a place filled with books. People can borrow the books and take them home. When they are finished reading them, people return the books to the library. Most libraries have two sections: One is for adult books and one is for children's books. A librarian is there to help people find books.

Directions: Read the title of each library book. On each line, write **A** if the book is written for an adult or **C** if it is written for a child.

1. Sam Squirrel Goes to the City — _C_
2. Barney Beagle Plays Baseball — _C_
3. Sammy's Silly Poems — _C_
4. Understanding Your Child . . . — _A_
5. Learn to Play Guitar — _A_
6. Bake Bread in Five Easy Steps — _A_
7. The Selling of the President — _A_
8. Jenny's First Party — _C_

Page 79

Library Skills: Alphabetical Order

Ms. Ling, the school librarian, needs help shelving books. Fiction titles are arranged in alphabetical order by the author's last name. Ms. Ling has done the first set for you.

_3_ Silverstein, Shel   _1_ Bridwell, Norman   _2_ Farley, Walter

Directions: Number the following groups of authors in alphabetical order.

_2_ Bernelmans, Ludwig   _4_ Perkins, Al
_4_ Stein, R.L.   _2_ Dobbs, Rose
_3_ Sawyer, Ruth   _1_ Baldwin, James
_1_ Baum, L. Frank   _3_ Kipling, Rudyard

The content of some books is also arranged alphabetically.

Directions: Circle the books that are arranged in alphabetical order.

T.V. guide   (dictionary)   (encyclopedia)   novel

almanac   science book   (Yellow Pages)   catalog

Write the books you circled in alphabetical order.

1. _dictionary_

2. _encyclopedia_

3. _Yellow Pages_

Page 80

Reference Books

Reference books are books that tell basic facts. They usually cannot be checked out from the library. Dictionaries and encyclopedias are reference books. A dictionary tells you about words. Encyclopedias give you other information, such as when the president was born, what the Civil War was and where Eskimos live. Encyclopedias usually come in sets of more than 20 books. Information is listed in alphabetical order, just like words are listed in the dictionary. There are other kinds of reference books, too, like books of maps called atlases. Reference books are not usually read from cover to cover.

Directions: Draw a line from each sentence to the correct type of book. The first one has been done for you.

1. I can tell you the definition of **divide**.
2. I can tell you when George Washington was born.
3. I can give you the correct spelling for many words.
4. I can tell you where Native Americans live.
5. I can tell you the names of many butterflies.
6. I can tell you what **modern** means.
7. I can give you the history of dinosaurs.
8. If you have to write a paper about Eskimos, I can help you.

A-D
E-G
H-J
K-M
N-P
Q-S
T-V
W-Y
Z

Page 81

Periodicals

Libraries also have periodicals such as magazines and newspapers. They are called **periodicals** because they are printed regularly within a set period of time. There are many kinds of magazines. Some discuss the news. Others cover fitness, cats or other topics of special interest. Almost every city or town has a newspaper. Newspapers usually are printed daily, weekly or even monthly. Newspapers cover what is happening in your town and in the world. They usually include sections on sports and entertainment. They present a lot of information.

Directions: Follow the instructions.   Answers will vary.

1. Choose an interesting magazine.
   What is the name of the magazine? _____
   List the titles of three articles in the magazine.
   _____
   _____
   _____

2. Now, look at a newspaper.
   What is the name of the newspaper? _____
   The title of a newspaper story is called a headline.
   What are some of the headlines in your local newspaper?
   _____
   _____

Page 82

References

Paul and Maria want to learn about the Moon. They go to the library. Where should they look while they are there?

Directions: Answer the questions to help Paul and Maria find information about the Moon.

1. Should they look in the children's section or in the adult's section? — _children's_
2. Should they look for a fiction book or a nonfiction book? — _nonfiction_
3. Who at the library can help them? — _the librarian_
4. What reference books should they look at? — _encyclopedias_
5. Where can they find information that may have been in the news? — _in periodicals_
6. What word would they look up in the encyclopedia to get the information they need? — _moon_

Page 83

Reading a Schedule

There are many different kinds of reading. When reading a magazine, you probably skim over pictures, captions and headlines. You stop to read carefully when you see something of interest. If your teacher assigns a chapter in a science textbook, you read it carefully so you don't miss important details. A **schedule** is a chart with lists of times. Would you read slowly or quickly to get information from a schedule? If you did not read carefully, you might get on the wrong bus or miss the bus altogether!

Directions: Look carefully at the bus schedule, then answer the questions.

City Transit System			
Bus		Leaves	Arrives
#10	Pine Street	7:35 A.M.	Oak Street	7:58 A.M.
#17	James Road	7:46 A.M.	Main Street	8:10 A.M.
#10	Oak Street	8:05 A.M.	Charles Road	8:25 A.M.
#29	Pine Street	9:12 A.M.	Oak Street	9:35 A.M.

1. Which bus goes to Main Street in the morning? _#17_
2. If you miss the #10 bus to Oak Street, could you still get there by noon? _yes_ How? _#29 bus_
3. What time does bus #29 arrive at Oak Street? _9:35 A.M._
4. Can you travel from Pine Street to Charles Road? _yes_ On which bus? _#10_
5. Bus #17 leaves _James Rd._ at 7:46 A.M. and arrives at Main Street at _8:10_ A.M.

Page 84

Reading a Schedule

Here is a schedule for the day's activities at Camp Do-A-Lot. Lisa and Jessie need help to decide what they will do on their last day.

Directions: Use this schedule to answer the questions on page 85.

CAMP DO-A-LOT

Saturday, July 8, 2000

Breakfast	6:30 A.M.	Dining Hall
Archery	7:30 A.M.	Field behind the Hall
Canoeing	7:30 A.M.	Blue Bottom Lake
Landscape Painting	7:30 A.M.	Rainbow Craft Shed
Horseback Riding	8:45 A.M.	Red Barn
Landscape Painting	8:45 A.M.	Rainbow Craft Shed
Scavenger Hunt	8:45 A.M.	Dining Hall
Cabin Clean-up	10:45 A.M.	Assigned Cabins
Lunch	11:45 A.M.	Dining Hall
Canoeing	1:00 P.M.	Blue Bottom Lake
Archery	1:00 P.M.	Field behind the Hall
Scavenger Hunt	1:00 P.M.	Dining Hall
Awards Ceremony	2:45 P.M.	Outdoor Theater
Dismissal	3:30 P.M.	

Page 85

Reading a Schedule

Directions: Use the schedule of activities on page 84 to answer the questions.

1. Where do Lisa and Jessie need to go to take part in archery?
   the field behind the Dining Hall

2. Both girls want to go canoeing. What are the two times that canoeing is offered?   7:30 A.M.   and   1:00 P.M.

3. Lisa and Jessie love to go on scavenger hunts. They agree to go on the hunt at 1:00 P.M. When will they have to go canoeing?   7:30 A.M.

4. Only one activity on the last day of camp takes place at the Outdoor Theater. What is it?   The Awards Ceremony

5. What happens at 10:45 A.M.?   Cabin Clean-up

6. If you went to the Rainbow Craft Shed at 7:30 A.M., what activity would you find there?   Landscape painting

Pretend you are at Camp Do-A-Lot with Lisa and Jessie. On the line next to each time, write which activity you would choose to do.

7:30 A.M.   Answers will vary.

8:45 A.M. _____

1:00 P.M. _____

Page 86

Reading a Schedule

Special Saturday classes are being offered to students of the county schools. They will be given the chance to choose from art, music or gymnastics classes.

Directions: Read the schedule, then answer the questions.

Saturday, November 13

	Art	Music	Gymnastics
8:00 A.M.	Watercolor—Room 350 Clay Sculpting—Room 250	Island Rhythms—Room 54 Orchestra Instruments—Stage	Floor Exercises—W. Gym Parallel Bars—E. Gym
Break (10 minutes)			
10:00 A.M.	Painting Stills—Room 420 Watercolor—Room 350	Percussion—Room 54 Jazz Sounds—Stage	Uneven Bars—N. Gym
Break (10 minutes)			
11:00 A.M.	Oils on Canvas—Room 258	Island Rhythms—Room 54 Create Your Own Music—Room 40	Uneven Bars—N. Gym Balance Beam—W. Gym

1. Where would you meet to learn about Jazz Sounds?   on the stage

2. Could a student sign up for Watercolor and Floor Exercises?   yes
   Explain your answer.   They are offered at different times.

3. Which music class would a creative person enjoy?   Create Your Own Music

4. Could a person sign up for an art class at 11:00?   yes

5. What time is the class on clay sculpting offered?   8:00 A.M.

Page 87

Compare and Contrast

To **compare** means to discuss how things are similar. To contrast means to discuss how things are different.

Directions: Compare and contrast how people grow gardens. Write at least two answers for each question.

Many people in the country have large gardens. They have a lot of space, so they can plant many kinds of vegetables and flowers. Since the gardens are usually quite large, they use a wheelbarrow to carry the tools they need. Sometimes they even have to carry water or use a garden hose.

People who live in the city do not always have enough room for a garden. Many people in big cities live in apartment buildings. They can put in a window box or use part of their balcony space to grow things. Most of the time, the only garden tools they need are a hand trowel to loosen the dirt and a watering can to make sure the plant gets enough water.

1. Compare gardening in the country with gardening in the city.
   Both can plant vegetables and flowers. They both have to use tools and water.

2. Contrast gardening in the country with gardening in the city.
   City gardeners usually have smaller gardens and do not need as many tools as the country gardeners.

Page 88

Compare and Contrast

Directions: Look for similarities and differences in the following paragraphs. Then answer the questions.

Phong and Chris both live in the city. They live in the same apartment building and go to the same school. Phong and Chris sometimes walk to school together. If it is raining or storming, Phong's dad drives them to school on his way to work. In the summer, they spend a lot of time at the park across the street from their building.

Phong lives in Apartment 12-A with his little sister and mom and dad. He has a collection of model race cars that he put together with his dad's help. He even has a bookshelf full of books about race cars and race car drivers.

Chris has a big family. He has two older brothers and one older sister. When Chris has time to do anything he wants, he gets out his butterfly collection. He notes the place he found each specimen and the day he found it. He also likes to play with puzzles.

1. Compare Phong and Chris. List at least three similarities.
   They both live in the city.
   Phong and Chris spend a lot of time at the park.
   They go to the same school.

2. Contrast Phong and Chris. List two differences.
   Phong has a little sister; Chris has two brothers and one sister. Chris has a butterfly collection; Phong collects model race cars.

Page 89

Compare and Contrast: Venn Diagram

Directions: List the similarities and differences you find below on a chart called a **Venn diagram.** This kind of chart shows comparisons and contrasts.

Butterflies and moths belong to the same group of insects. They both have two pairs of wings. Their wings are covered with tiny scales. Both butterflies and moths undergo metamorphosis, or a change, in their lives. They begin their lives as caterpillars.

Butterflies and moths are different in some ways. Butterflies usually fly during the day, but moths generally fly at night. Most butterflies have slender, hairless bodies; most moths have plump, furry bodies. When butterflies land, they hold their wings together straight over their bodies. When moths land, they spread their wings out flat.

1. List three ways that butterflies and moths are alike.
   Both have two pairs of wings.
   Their wings are covered with tiny scales.
   Both begin their lives as caterpillars.

2. List three ways that butterflies and moths are different.
   Butterflies fly during the day; moths fly at night.
   Butterflies' bodies are slender and hairless; moths' plump and furry. Butterflies land wings up and moths land wings spread out.

3. Combine your answers from questions 1 and 2 into a Venn diagram. Write the differences in the circle labeled for each insect. Write the similarities in the intersecting part.

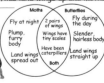

Venn diagram —
Moths: Fly at night, Plump, furry body, Land wings spread out
Both: 2 pairs of wings, Wings have tiny scales, Have been caterpillars
Butterflies: Fly during the day, Slender, hairless body, Land wings straight up

ANSWER KEY

Page 90

Cause and Effect

A **cause** is the reason for an event. An **effect** is what happens as a result of a cause.

Directions: Circle the cause and underline the effect in each sentence. They may be in any order. The first one has been done for you.

1. (The truck hit an icy patch) and skidded off the road.

2. (When the door slammed shut,) the baby woke up crying.

3. Our soccer game was cancelled (when it began to storm.)

4. Dad and Mom are adding a room onto the house (since our family is growing.)

5. (Our car ran out of gas on the way to town,) so we had to walk.

6. (The home run in the ninth inning) helped our team win the game.

7. We had to climb the stairs (because the elevator was broken.)

8. We were late to school (because the bus had a flat tire.)

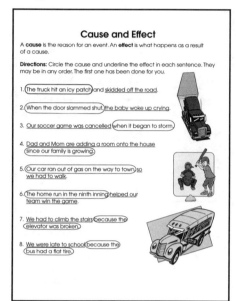

Page 91

Cause and Effect

Cause and effect sentences often use clue words to show the relationship between two events. Common clue words are because, so, when and since.

Directions: Read the sentences on pages 91 and 92. Circle each clue word. The first one has been done for you.

1. I'll help you clean your room, (so) we can go out to play sooner.

2. (Because) of the heavy snowfall, school was closed today.

3. She was not smiling, (so) her mother wanted her school pictures taken again.

4. Mrs. Wilderman came to school with crutches today (because) she had a skating accident.

5. (When) the team began making too many mistakes at practice, the coach told them to take a break.

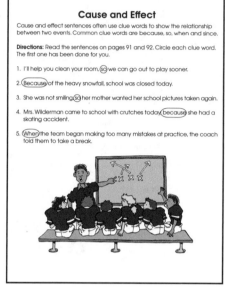

Page 92

Cause and Effect

6. Our telephone was not working, (so) I called the doctor from next door.

7. The police officer began to direct traffic (since) the traffic signal was not working.

8. The class will go out to recess (when) the room is cleaned up.

9. "I can't see you (because) the room is too dark," said Jordan.

10. He has to wash the dishes alone (because) his sister is sick.

11. (Since) the bus had engine trouble, several children were late to school.

12. Monday was a holiday (so) Mom and Dad took us to the park.

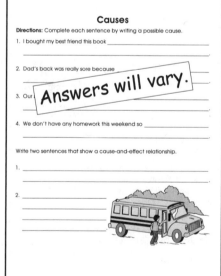

Page 93

Cause and Effect

Directions: Draw a line to match each phrase to form a logical cause and effect sentence.

1. Dad gets paid today, so — because she is sick.
2. When the electricity went out, — we're going out for dinner.
3. Courtney can't spend the night — so she bought a new sweater.
4. Our front window shattered — we grabbed the flashlights.
5. Sophie got $10.00 for her birthday. — when the baseball hit it.

Directions: Read each sentence beginning. Choose an ending from the box that makes sense. Write the correct letter on the line.

1. Her arm was in a cast, because _D_
2. They are building a new house on our street, so _A_
3. Since I'd always wanted a puppy, _E_
4. I had to renew my library book, _C_
5. My parents' anniversary is tomorrow, _B_

A. we all went down to watch.
B. so my sister and I bought them some flowers.
C. since I hadn't finished it.
D. she fell when she was skating.
E. Mom gave me one for my birthday.

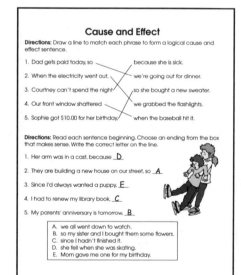

Page 94

Causes

Directions: Complete each sentence by writing a possible cause.

1. I bought my best friend this book _____
2. Dad's back was really sore because _____
3. Our _____
4. We don't have any homework this weekend so _____

Write two sentences that show a cause-and-effect relationship.

1. _____
2. _____

Answers will vary.

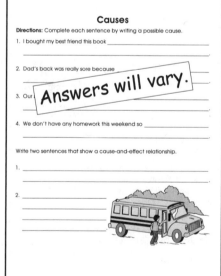

Page 95

Effects

Directions: Complete each sentence by writing a possible effect.

1. The front door was locked, so _____
2. Bec... _____
3. Since I spent all my money, _____
4. When my alarm clock did not wake me this morning, _____

Answers will vary.

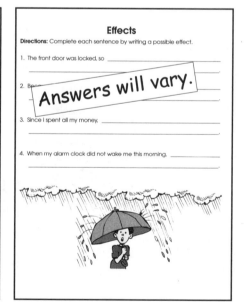

Page 96

Review

Directions: Read the story. Then answer the questions.

There are many different kinds of robots. One special kind of robot takes the place of people in guiding airplanes and ships. They are called "automatic pilots." These robots are really computers programmed to do just one special job. They have the information to control the speed and direction of the plane or ship.

Robots are used for many jobs in which a person can't get too close because of danger, such as in exploding a bomb. Robots can be controlled from a distance. This is called "remote control." These robots are very important in studying space. In the future, robots will be used to work on space stations and on other planets.

1. The main idea of this story is:
   Robots are used for many different jobs.

2. Why are robots good in dangerous jobs?
   They are machines. They can't be hurt the way people can.

3. What is "remote control"?
   controlled from a distance

4. What will robots be used for in the future?
   to work on space stations and on other planets

What would you have a robot do for you?
Answers will vary.

Page 98

Main Idea: Iguanodon

Millions of years ago, many kinds of dinosaurs roamed the Earth. The name of one kind of dinosaur was Iguanodon (ee-gwan-eh-don). The Iguanodon looked like a giant lizard. It had tough skin. The Iguanodon's skin must have felt like leather! Iguanodons ate plants.

Directions: Answer these questions about Iguanodons.

1. Circle the main idea:
   The Iguanodon's skin was like leather.
   (The Iguanodon was a plant-eating dinosaur with tough skin.)

2. What kind of food did Iguanodons eat?
   plants

3. What animal living today did the Iguanodon look like?
   lizard

Page 99

Making Inferences: Dining Dinosaurs

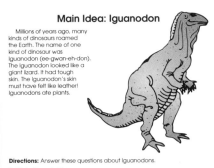

Brontosaurus dinosaurs lived in the swamps. Swamps are water areas where many plants grow. Here are the names of the other kinds of dinosaurs that lived in the swamps. Diplodocus (dip-low-dock-us), Brachiosaurus (bracky-o-saur-us) and Cetiosaurus (set-e-o-saur-us). These dinosaurs had small heads and small brains. They weighed 20 tons or more. They grew to be 60 feet long! These animals did not need to have sharp teeth.

Directions: Answer these questions about Brontosaurus and other big dinosaurs.

1. These big dinosaurs did not have sharp teeth. What did they eat?
   plants

2. Why were swamps a good place for these big dinosaurs to live?
   Many plants grow there.

3. These big dinosaurs had small brains. Do you think they were smart? Why?
   Answers will vary.

4. Name the three kinds of dinosaurs that lived in swamps.
   Diplodocus, Brachiosaurus, Cetiosaurus

Page 100

Comprehension: Tyrannosaurus Rex

One of the biggest dinosaurs was Tyrannosaurus Rex (ty-ran-oh-saur-us recks). This dinosaur walked on its two big back legs. It had two small, short front legs. From the top of its head to the tip of its tail, Tyrannosaurus Rex measured 50 feet long. Its head was 4 feet long! Are you taller than this dinosaur's head? Tyrannosaurus was a meat eater. It had many small, sharp teeth. Its favorite meal was a smaller dinosaur that had a bill like a duck. This smaller dinosaur lived near water.

Directions: Answer these questions about Tyrannosaurus Rex.

1. What is the story about?
   Tyrannosaurus Rex

2. What size was this dinosaur?
   50 feet long; its head was 4 feet long

3. When this dinosaur was hungry, what did it eat?
   Meat. Its favorite meal was a smaller dinosaur with a bill like a duck.

4. Where did this dinosaur find its favorite meal?
   near the water

5. Why did this dinosaur need many sharp teeth?
   It was a meat eater.

Page 101

Comprehension: Triceratops

Triceratops was one of the last dinosaurs to develop. It lived in the Cretaceous (kre-tay-shus) period of history. It was in this time that the dinosaurs became extinct. Triceratops means "three-horned lizard." It was a strong dinosaur and able to defend itself well since it lived during the same time period as Tyrannosaurus Rex.

Triceratops was a plant-eating dinosaur. Its body was 20 feet long, and its head, including the three horns and bony "frill," was another 6½ feet.

Directions: Answer these questions about Triceratops.

1. Dinosaurs became extinct during the __Cretaceous__ period of history.

2. What does **Triceratops** mean?
   three-horned lizard

3. What information above tells you that Triceratops was able to defend itself?
   It was strong; it lived at the same time as Tyrannosaurus Rex; it had three horns and a bony frill.

Page 102

Comprehension: Stegosaurus

The Stegosaurus was a well-equipped fighter. It was covered with large, bony plates and had a spiked tail. As you can probably imagine, this spiked tail was a very important part of its defense. This was another large dinosaur, the same size as Triceratops. It had four legs, but the two front legs were smaller than the two hind legs, and it had a very small head compared to its body. Have you ever seen a walnut? The brain of Stegosaurus was about the same size.

Stegosaurus was one of the many plant-eating dinosaurs. I guess you could call it a vegetarian (veg-e-tair-ee-un). Vegetarians only eat plants like vegetables, leaves and grass! Stegosaurus lived in the Jurassic period, the middle period of dinosaur history.

Directions: Answer these questions about Stegosaurus.

1. Write three things that are the same size as Stegosaurus' brain.
   1) __walnut__ 2) __Answers will vary.__

2. The __spiked tail__ of this dinosaur was a very important part of its defense.

3. Which set of legs, the front legs or the hind ones, do you think the Stegosaurus used more? __the hind legs__
   Why do you think so? __They were bigger and stronger.__

Page 103

Recalling Details: Dinosaur Chart

Directions: Use the pages about Tyrannosaurus Rex, Stegosaurus and Triceratops to help you fill in the chart below.

	Period of History	What It Ate	Size
T-Rex	Cretaceous	meat	50 feet
Triceratops	Cretaceous	plants	20 feet
Stegosaurus	Jurassic	plants	20 feet

Directions: Use the chart to answer these questions.

1. Did Triceratops and Stegosaurus live on Earth at the same time?

   Yes   (No)

2. Which dinosaur was the largest of the three?

   Tyrannosaurus Rex

3. Which two of these dinosaurs were plant eaters?

   1) Triceratops   2) Stegosaurus

Page 104

Comprehension: Cold-Blooded Animals

Like snakes, dinosaurs were cold-blooded. Cold-blooded animals cannot keep themselves warm. Because of this, dinosaurs were not very active when it was cold. In the early morning they did not move much. When the sun grew warm, the dinosaurs became active. When the sun went down in the evening, they slowed down again for the night. The sun warmed the dinosaurs and gave them the energy they needed to move about.

Directions: Answer these questions about dinosaurs.

1. Why were dinosaurs inactive when it was cold?

   They were cold-blooded and could not keep themselves warm.

2. What time of day were the dinosaurs active?

   in the afternoon

3. What times of day were the dinosaurs not active?

   early morning and evening

4. Why did dinosaurs need the sun?

   to warm them up and give them energy

Page 105

Comprehension: Sizes of Dinosaurs

There were many sizes of dinosaurs. Some were as small as dogs. Others were huge! The huge dinosaurs weighed 100,000 pounds. Some dinosaurs ate meat, including other dinosaurs. Some dinosaurs, like the Iguanodon, ate only plants. Meat-eating dinosaurs had sharp teeth. Plant-eating dinosaurs had flat teeth. If you had lived long ago, would you have gotten close enough to look at their teeth?

Directions: Answer these questions about dinosaurs.

1. What size were the small dinosaurs?

   as small as dogs

2. How much did the big dinosaurs weigh?

   100,000 pounds

3. Name two things the different kinds of dinosaurs ate.

   1) meat   2) plants

4. What kind of teeth did meat-eating dinosaurs have?

   sharp teeth

5. What kind of teeth did plant-eating dinosaurs have?

   flat teeth

Page 106

Comprehension: Dinosaur Fossils

Dinosaurs roamed the Earth for 125 million years. Can you imagine that much time? About 40 years ago, some people found fossils of dinosaur tracks in Connecticut. Fossils are rocks that hold the hardened bones, eggs and footprints of animals that lived long ago. The fossil tracks showed that many dinosaurs walked together in herds. The fossils showed more than 2,000 dinosaur tracks!

Directions: Answer these questions about fossils.

1. What did the people find in the fossils?

   dinosaur tracks

2. In what state were the fossils found?

   Connecticut

3. How many tracks were in the fossils?

   more than 2,000 tracks

4. What did the tracks show?

   that many dinosaurs walked together in herds

5. How long did dinosaurs roam the Earth?

   125 million years

Page 107

Main Idea: Dinosaur Models

Some people can build models of dinosaurs. The models are fakes, of course. But they are life-size and they look real! The people who build them must know the dinosaur inside and out. First, they build a skeleton. Then they cover it with fake "skin." Then they paint it. Some models have motors in them. The motors can make the dinosaur's head or tail move. Have you ever seen a life-size model of a dinosaur?

Directions: Answer these questions about dinosaur models.

1. Circle the main idea:

   Some models of dinosaurs have motors in them.

   (Some people can build life-size models of dinosaurs that look real.)

2. What do the motors in model dinosaurs do?

   The motors can make the dinosaur's head or tail move.

3. What is the first step in making a model dinosaur?

   build a skeleton

4. Why do dinosaur models look real?

   They have skin and move like real dinosaurs.

Page 108

Review

There are no dinosaurs alive today. They became extinct (ex-tinkt) millions of years ago. This was before people lived on Earth. When animals are extinct, they are gone forever. No one knows exactly why dinosaurs became extinct. Some scientists say that a disease may have killed them. Other scientists say a huge hot rock called a comet hit the Earth. The comet caused a big fire. The fire killed the dinosaurs' food. Still other scientists believe that the Earth grew very cold. The dinosaurs died because they could not keep warm. Many scientists have ideas, but no one can know for sure exactly what happened.

Directions: Answer these questions about dinosaurs becoming extinct.

1. Why is it not possible to know what caused all the dinosaurs to die?

   Because they died before people lived on Earth.

2. Circle the main idea:

   The dinosaurs died when a comet hit the Earth and caused a big fire.

   (There are many ideas about what killed the dinosaurs, but no one knows for sure.)

3. What does extinct mean?

   when an animal is gone forever

4. Who are the people with ideas about what happened to dinosaurs?

   scientists

ANSWER KEY

Page 109

Comprehension: Kareem Abdul-Jabbar

Have you heard of a basketball star named Kareem Abdul-Jabbar? When he was born, Kareem's name was Lew Alcindor. He was named after his father. When he was in college, Kareem changed his religion from Christianity to Islam. That was when he took the Muslim name of Kareem Abdul-Jabbar.

Directions: Answer these questions about Kareem Abdul-Jabbar.

1. What was Kareem Abdul-Jabbar's name when he was born?
   Lew Alcindor

2. Who was Kareem named after?
   his father

3. When did Kareem become a Muslim?
   when he was in college

4. When did Kareem change his name to Kareem Abdul-Jabbar?
   when he became Muslim

Page 110

Comprehension: Kareem Abdul-Jabbar

Kareem Abdul-Jabbar grew up to be more than 7 feet tall! Kareem's father and mother were both very tall. When he was 9 years old, Kareem was already 5 feet 4 inches tall. Kareem was raised in New York City. He went to Power Memorial High School and played basketball on that team. He went to college at UCLA. He played basketball in college, too. At UCLA, Kareem's team lost only two games in 3 years! After college, Kareem made his living playing basketball.

Directions: Answer these questions about Kareem Abdul-Jabbar.

1. Who is the story about?
   Kareem Abdul-Jabbar

2. For what is this athlete famous?
   playing basketball

3. When did Kareem reach the height of 5 feet 4 inches?
   when he was 9 years old

4. Where did Kareem go to college?
   UCLA

5. Why did Kareem grow so tall?
   His father and mother were both very tall.

6. How did Kareem make his living?
   playing basketball

Page 111

Comprehension: Michael Jordan

Michael Jordan was born February 17, 1963, in Brooklyn, New York. His family moved to North Carolina when he was just a baby. As a young boy, his favorite sport was baseball, but he soon found that he could play basketball as well. At age 17, he began to show people just how talented he really was.

Throughout his basketball career, Michael Jordan has won many scoring titles. Many boys and girls look up to Michael Jordan as their hero. Did you know he had a hero, too, when he was growing up? He looked up to his older brother, Larry.

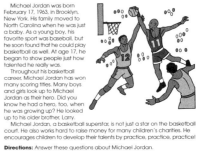

Michael Jordan, a basketball superstar, is not just a star on the basketball court. He also works hard to raise money for many children's charities. He encourages children to develop their talents by practice, practice, practice!

Directions: Answer these questions about Michael Jordan.

1. Michael says children can develop their talents by lots of **practice**.
2. Who was Michael's hero when he was growing up?
   his older brother
3. Where was Michael Jordan born?
   Brooklyn, New York
4. At first, he played **baseball** instead of basketball.

Page 112

Comprehension: Mary Lou Retton

Mary Lou Retton became the first U.S. woman to win Olympic gold in gymnastics. She accomplished this at the 1984 Olympics held in Los Angeles, when she was 16 years old. "Small but mighty" would certainly describe this gymnast.

She was the youngest of five children—all good athletes. She grew up in Fairmont, West Virginia, and began her gymnastic training at the age of 7.

Most women gymnasts are graceful, but Mary Lou helped open up the field of gymnastics to strong, athletic women. Mary Lou was 4 feet 10 inches tall and weighed a mere 95 pounds!

Directions: Answer these questions about Mary Lou Retton.

1. Circle the main idea:

   Mary Lou loved performing.

   (Mary Lou is a famous Olympic gymnast.)

2. She was born in **Fairmont, West Virginia**
3. At what age did she begin her gymnastics training? **7 years old**
4. Mary Lou won a gold medal when she was **16** years old.

Page 113

Comprehension: Troy Aikman

Troy Aikman, Dallas Cowboy, was born on November 21, 1966. As a young boy, he enjoyed doing the usual things, like fishing or hunting with his dad. He also loved playing sports with his friends.

Troy Aikman knows a lot about change. When he was a young boy of 12 living in a city, he knew he wanted to be a baseball player. But when his family moved to a 172-acre ranch near Henryetta, Oklahoma, he felt like he would have to give up that dream. He soon learned that the people of Oklahoma loved football more than any other sport. Troy soon learned to love football, too. And he learned he was very good at it.

You can be a champion, too, in spite of changes in your life. You just have to be willing to make those changes work for you!

Directions: Answer these questions about Troy Aikman.

1. Why did Troy Aikman change from playing baseball to playing football?
   People in Oklahoma loved football more than baseball.
2. How old was he when his family moved?
   12 years old
3. For what NFL team does he play?
   Dallas Cowboys
4. How can changes in your life be a good thing?
   You can make them work for you.

Page 114

Comprehension: Babe Ruth

A great baseball champion, Babe Ruth, was born in Baltimore, Maryland, on February 6, 1895. He could hit a ball farther than most major-league players when he was only 13 years old. He did not have a very good home life, so he spent most of his early years living in a school for boys. He played baseball whenever he could, so he became very good at it.

George Ruth (his real name) was given the nickname, Babe, when he was 19 years old. A minor-league team manager, Jack Dunn, became his legal guardian. The other players on the team called him "Jack's Babe." Later, it was shortened to "Babe."

Directions: Answer these questions about Babe Ruth.

1. When was Babe Ruth born?
   February 6, 1895
2. Where was he born?
   Baltimore, Maryland
3. What was Babe's original nickname?
   Jack's Babe
4. How old was Babe when he got his nickname?
   19 years old

Grade 3 - Comprehensive Curriculum

Page 115

Comprehension: Babe Ruth

Babe Ruth began playing as a pitcher for the Boston Red Sox in 1915. He switched to the outfield in 1918 because his manager wanted him to bat more often. Everyone soon found out what a good hitter he was!

Yankee Stadium became known as "The House That Ruth Built" because he was such a popular player and so many people came to the baseball games. New York City was able to have a new baseball stadium because he was so popular. This left-handed baseball superstar drew large crowds to ballparks wherever his team played. Even if he didn't hit a home run, the fans were just excited to have the chance to see him.

Directions: Answer these questions about Babe Ruth.

1. Does the story let you know whether Babe is still living? _____no_____
   How old would he be if he were still alive?
   Answers will vary, depending on the year.

2. What is another name for Yankee Stadium?
   The House That Ruth Built

3. In 1915, he began playing for the ____Boston Red Sox____ as a pitcher.

4. Why did his manager switch him to the outfield?
   because he wanted him to bat more often

Page 116

Recalling Details: The Home Run Race

The summer of 1998 was exciting for the sport of baseball. Even if you were not a big fan of this sport, you couldn't help but hear about two great sluggers—Mark McGwire and Sammy Sosa. By mid-summer, many baseball fans realized that several men were getting close to the home run record. The record of 61 home runs in a single season had been set by Roger Maris 37 years before!

On Tuesday, September 8, 1998, that record was broken. Mark McGwire, who plays for the St. Louis Cardinals, hit his 62nd home run in a game with the Chicago Cubs.

To make the home run race more interesting, a player for the Chicago Cubs, Sammy Sosa, was also close to breaking the 61 home run record. On Sunday, September 13, Sammy Sosa also hit his 62nd home run.

Directions: Write the letter of the correct answer in the blanks.

A. Sept. 13   B. McGwire   C. 37   D. Maris   E. Chicago Cubs

1. Had the home run record   __D__
2. First to hit 62 home runs   __B__
3. Sosa broke the home run record   __A__
4. Years record had stood   __C__
5. Sosa's team   __E__

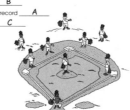

Page 117

Recalling Details: Venn Diagram

A **Venn diagram** is a diagram used to compare two things. The Venn diagram below is comparing a cat and a dog.

Cat	Both	Dog
meows	4 legs	barks
catches mice	tail	chases rabbits
	furry	

Directions: Use **The Home Run Race** (page 116) to complete the Venn diagram comparing Mark McGwire and Sammy Sosa.

McGwire	Both	Sosa
St. Louis Cardinals	Broke home run record	Chicago Cubs
Broke home run record on Sept. 8, 1998	Great baseball player	Broke home run record on Sept. 13, 1998

Page 118

Comprehension: Christopher Columbus

What do you know about Christopher Columbus? He was a famous sailor and explorer. Columbus was 41 years old when he sailed from southern Spain on August 3, 1492, with three ships. On them was a crew of 90 men. Thirty-three days later, he landed on Watling Island in the Bahamas. The Bahamas are islands located in the West Indies. The West Indies are a large group of islands between North America and South America.

Directions: Answer these questions about Christopher Columbus.

1. How old was Columbus when he set sail from southern Spain?
   41 years old

2. How many ships did he take?
   three ships

3. How many men were with him?
   90 men

4. How long did it take him to reach land?
   33 days

5. Where did Columbus land?
   Watling Island in the Bahamas

6. What are the West Indies?
   a large group of islands between North and South America

Page 119

Comprehension: Christopher Columbus

Columbus was an explorer. He wanted to find out what the rest of the world looked like. He also wanted to make money! He would sail to distant islands and trade with the people there. He would buy their silks, spices and gold. Then he would sell these things in Spain. In Spain, people would pay high prices for them. Columbus got the queen of Spain to approve his plan. She would pay for his ships and his crew. He would keep 10 percent of the value of the goods he brought back. She would take the rest. Columbus and the queen had a business deal.

Directions: Answer these questions about Christopher Columbus.

1. Which statement is correct?
   Columbus and the queen of Spain were friends.
   (Columbus and the queen of Spain were business partners.)

2. Write two reasons why Columbus was an explorer.
   1) _He wanted to find out what the rest of the world looked like._
   2) _He wanted to make money._

3. What was Columbus' business deal with the queen of Spain?
   1) Columbus would get _Ships and a crew, and he would keep 10 percent of the value of the goods he brought back._
   2) In return for paying his expenses, the queen would get
   90 percent of the value of the goods Columbus brought back

Page 120

Comprehension: Lewis and Clark

In 1801, President Thomas Jefferson chose an army officer named Meriwether Lewis to lead an expedition through our country's "new frontier." He knew Lewis would not be able to make the journey by himself, so he chose William Clark to travel with him. The two men had known each other in the army. They decided to be co-leaders of the expedition.

The two men and a group of about 45 others made the trip from the state of Missouri, across the Rocky Mountains all the way to the Pacific Coast. They were careful in choosing the men who would travel with them. They wanted men who were strong and knew a lot about the wilderness. It was also important that they knew some of the Native American languages.

Directions: Answer these questions about Lewis and Clark.

1. Which president wanted an expedition through the "new frontier"?
   Thomas Jefferson

2. Look at a United States map or a globe. In what direction did Lewis and Clark travel? (Circle one.)
   north   south   east   (west)

3. About how many people made up the entire expedition, including Lewis and Clark?
   47 people

LOUISIANA TERRITORY

Lewis and Clark Expedition
1804-1806

Page 121

Comprehension: Lewis and Clark

The two explorers and their men began their trip in 1804. They had camped all winter across the river from St. Louis, Missouri. While camping, they built a special boat they would need for the first part of their trip. This boat, called a keelboat, was 55 feet long. It could be rowed or sailed. If the men needed to use it like a raft, they could do that, too.

Besides flour, salt and cornmeal, they took along medicines and weapons. They knew they would meet Native Americans as they traveled to the "new frontier," so they also brought colored beads and other small gifts to give to them.

Directions: Answer these questions about Lewis and Clark.

1. Lewis, Clark and the others began their trip in ___1804___.

2. What is the name of the special boat that they built for their trip?
   keelboat

3. Why did they take along small gifts and colored beads?
   to give to the Native Americans they met along the way

Page 122

Comprehension: Boats for the Expedition

The men were not able to take the keelboat the whole way on their trip. The Missouri River became too narrow for this boat, so Lewis and Clark had to send some of the men back to St. Louis with it. More canoes were built with the help of some friendly Native Americans. These were used for travel since they no longer had the keelboat.

Directions: Answer these questions about Lewis and Clark's boats.

1. Why couldn't Lewis and Clark use the keelboat for the entire trip?
   The Missouri River became too narrow for the boat.

2. What did they do with it?
   They sent men back to St. Louis with it.

3. Why did they need to build more canoes?
   because they no longer had the keelboat

Find a picture of a keelboat or canoe. Draw a picture of it below.

Page 123

Comprehension: Hardships of the Expedition

Lewis and Clark and their men had seen large grizzly bears as they traveled through the West. They were thankful they had their weapons with them. But meeting the grizzlies was not the hardest part of the journey. It was also hard to cross the Rocky Mountains. It took the explorers and their men a month to make this part of their trip. The friendly Shoshone tribe was very helpful in telling them how they could cross the mountains.

There were many reasons why this part of the trip was difficult. The steep, narrow pathways sometimes caused the horses to fall over the cliffs to their deaths. Many times the men had to lead the horses. There were also fewer wild animals for the men to hunt for food.

Directions: Answer these questions about the hardships of the expedition.

1. What was the hardest part of the trip?
   crossing the Rocky Mountains

2. Lewis and Clark got help from which friendly Native American tribe?
   the Shoshone tribe

3. What word in the story means "a group of people traveling together"?
   party

4. What caused some of the horses to fall to their deaths?
   the steep, narrow pathways in the Rocky Mountains

Page 124

Comprehension: End of the Journey

New canoes had to be built for the last part of the trip. The men traveled along the Clearwater River to get to the Columbia River, and finally the Pacific Coast. They reached the Northwest Coast in November 1805.

President Jefferson was glad he had chosen Lewis and Clark to lead the expedition. They were able to make the trip successfully and could now claim the Oregon region for the United States.

Directions: Answer these questions about Lewis and Clark's expedition.

1. What two rivers did Lewis and Clark travel on the last part of their journey?
   1) _Clearwater River_
   2) _Columbia River_

2. When did they reach the Pacific Coast? ___November 1805___

3. What season of the year is that? _fall_

4. Circle the words below that would describe the journey:
   (dangerous)   quick   not planned   (successful)

5. This expedition allowed the United States to claim _____
   Oregon region

Page 125

Comprehension: George Washington

George Washington was the first president of the United States. He was born in Wakefield, Virginia, on February 22, 1732. His father was a wealthy Virginia planter. As he grew up, George Washington became interested in surveying and farming. When George was only 11 years old, his father died. George moved in with his older brother, Lawrence.

Even if he had not become the country's first president, he would have been well known because of his strong military leadership. Washington was a good leader because of his patience and his ability to survive hardships.

George Washington became president in 1789. At that time there were only 11 states in the United States. He served two terms (4 years each) as our first president. After his second term, he returned to a former home at Mt. Vernon. He died there in 1799 after catching a cold while riding around his farm in the wind and snow.

Directions: Answer these questions about George Washington.

1. In what year did George Washington become president? ___1789___

2. Besides being our country's first president, how else did he serve our country?
   as a strong military leader

3. Where was he born?
   Wakefield, Virginia

Page 126

Comprehension: Robin Hood

Long ago in England there lived a man named Robin Hood. Robin lived with a group of other men in the woods. These woods were called Sherwood Forest.

Robin Hood was a thief—a different kind of thief. He stole from the rich and gave what he stole to the poor. Poor people did not need to worry about going into Sherwood Forest. In fact, Robin Hood often gave them money. Rich people were told to beware. If you were rich, would you stay out of Sherwood Forest?

Directions: Answer these questions about Robin Hood.

1. What was the name of the woods where Robin Hood lived?
   Sherwood Forest

2. What did Robin Hood do for a living?
   He was a thief.

3. What was different about Robin Hood?
   He stole from the rich and gave to the poor.

4. Did poor people worry about going into Sherwood Forest? Why or why not?
   No. Because Robin Hood wouldn't steal from them.

5. Do you think rich people worried about going into Sherwood Forest? Why?
   Yes. Because Robin Hood might steal from them.

Page 127

Making Inferences: Robin Hood and the King

Everyone in England knew about Robin Hood. The king was mad! He did not want a thief to be a hero. He sent his men to Sherwood Forest to catch Robin Hood. But they could not catch him. Robin Hood outsmarted the king's men every time!

One day, Robin Hood sent a message to the king. The message said, "Come with five brave men. We will see who is stronger." The king decided to fool Robin Hood. He wanted to see if what people said about Robin Hood was true. The king dressed as a monk. A monk is a poor man who serves God. Then he went to Sherwood Forest to see Robin Hood.

Directions: Circle the correct answer to these questions about the king's meeting with Robin Hood.

1. If the stories about Robin Hood were true, what happened when the king met Robin Hood?

   Robin Hood robbed the king and took all his money.

   (Robin Hood helped the king because he thought he was a poor man.)

2. Why didn't the king want Robin Hood to know who he was?

   He was afraid of Robin Hood.

   (He wanted to find out what Robin Hood was really like.)

3. Why couldn't the king's men find Robin Hood?

   (Robin Hood outsmarted them.)

   They didn't look in Sherwood Forest.

Page 128

Making Inferences: Robin Hood and the King

The king liked Robin Hood. He said, "Here is a man who likes a good joke." He told Robin Hood who he really was. Robin Hood was not mad. He laughed and laughed. The king invited Robin Hood to come and live in the castle. The castle was 20 miles away. Robin had to walk south, cross a river and make two left turns to get there. He stayed inside the castle grounds for a year and a day.

Then Robin grew restless and asked the king for permission to leave. The king did not want him to go. He said Robin Hood could visit Sherwood Forest for only one week. Robin said he missed his men but promised to return. The king knew Robin Hood never broke his promises.

Directions: Answer these questions about Robin Hood and the king.

1. Do you think Robin Hood returned to the castle? ___yes___

2. Why do you think Robin Hood laughed when the king told him the truth?

   because he enjoyed a good joke

3. Give directions from Sherwood Forest to the king's castle.

   Walk south, cross a river and make two left turns.

4. Circle the main idea:

   (The king liked Robin Hood, but Robin missed his life in Sherwood Forest.)

   Robin Hood thought the castle was boring.

Page 129

Comprehension: Benjamin Franklin

Benjamin Franklin was born in Boston, Massachusetts, on January 17, 1706. Even though he only attended school to age 10, he worked hard to improve his mind and character. He taught himself several foreign languages and learned many skills that would later be a great help to him.

Ben Franklin played a very important part in our history. One of his many accomplishments was as a printer. He was a helper (apprentice) to his half-brother, James, and later moved to the city of Philadelphia where he worked in another print shop.

Another skill that he developed was writing. He wrote and published Poor Richard's Almanac in December 1732. Franklin was also a diplomat. He served our country in many ways, both in the United States and in Europe. As an inventor he experimented with electricity. Have you heard about the kite and key experiment? Benjamin Franklin was able to prove that lightning has an electrical discharge.

Directions: Answer these questions about Benjamin Franklin.

1. Circle the main idea:

   (Benjamin Franklin was a very important part of our history.)

   Benjamin Franklin wrote Poor Richard's Almanac.

   He flew a kite with a key on the string.

2. How old was Ben Franklin when he left school? ___10 years old___

3. Write three of Ben Franklin's accomplishments.

   1) He wrote Poor Richards Almanac.

   2) He was a diplomat.

   3) He proved lightning has an electrical discharge.

Page 130

Comprehension: Morning Glories

Have you ever seen morning glories? They begin to bloom in mid-May. Morning glory flowers grow on vines. They trail over the ground. Sometimes the vines twine over other plants. They will grow over walls and fences. The vines on morning glory plants can grow to be 10 feet long! Morning glory flowers are bell-shaped. The flowers are white, pink or blue. There are more than 200 different kinds of morning glory flowers!

Directions: Answer these questions about morning glories.

1. When do morning glories begin to bloom?

   in mid-May

2. Morning glories grow on

   stems.

   (vines.)

3. What shape are morning glory flowers?

   bell-shaped

4. How many different kinds of morning glory flowers are there?

   more than 200 different kinds

Page 131

Following Directions: How Plants Get Food

Every living thing needs food. Did you ever wonder how plants get food? They do not sit down and eat a bowl of soup! Plants get their food from the soil and from water. To see how, cut off some stalks of celery. Put the stalks in a clear glass. Fill the glass half full of water. Add a few drops of red food coloring to the water. Leave it overnight. The next day you will see that parts of the celery have turned red! The red lines show how the celery "sucked up" water.

Directions: Answer these questions about how plants get food.

1. Name two ways plants get food.

   1) from soil

   2) from water

2. Complete the four steps for using celery to see how plants get food.

   1) Cut off some stalks of __celery__.

   2) Put the stalks in __a clear glass__.

   3) Fill the glass __half full of water__.

   4) Add a few drops of __red food coloring to the water__.

3. What do the red lines in the celery show?

   how the celery "sucked up" the water

Page 132

Making Inferences: Fig Marigolds

Fig marigolds are beautiful! The flowers stay closed unless the light is bright. These flowers are also called by another name—the "mid-day flower." Mid-day flowers have very long leaves. The leaves are as long as your finger! There is something else unusual about mid-day flowers. They change color. When the flowers bloom, they are light yellow. After two or three days, they turn pink.

Mid-day flowers grow in California and South America where it is hot. They do not grow in other parts of the United States.

Directions: Answer these questions about fig marigolds.

1. Why do you think fig marigolds are also called mid-day flowers?

   because the flowers stay closed unless the light is bright

2. How long are the leaves of the mid-day flower?

   as long as your finger

3. Why do you think mid-day flowers do not grow all over the United States?

   because they need hot weather to grow

ANSWER KEY

Page 133

Main Idea: Unusual Plants

Do you have a cat? Do you have catnip growing around your home? If you don't know, your cat probably does. Cats love the catnip plant and can be seen rolling around in it. Some cat toys have catnip inside them because cats love it so much.

People can enjoy catnip, too. Some people make catnip tea with the leaves of the plant. It is like the mint with which people make tea.

Another refreshing drink can be made with the berries of the sumac bush or tree. Native Americans would pick the red berries, crush them and add water to make a thirst-quenching drink. The berries were sour, but they must have believed that the cool, tart drink was refreshing. Does this remind you of lemonade?

Directions: Answer these questions about unusual plants.

1. What is the main idea of the first two paragraphs above?

   Cats and people can both enjoy catnip.

2. Write two ways cats show that they love catnip.

   1) by rolling around in it
   2) by playing with a catnip toy

3. How can people use catnip?

   They can make tea with it.

Page 134

Comprehension: Dangerous Plants

You may have been warned about some plants. Poison ivy and poison oak are plants we usually learn about at an early age. The itching and burning some people get from touching or even being around these plants is enough to make them extra careful. Have you ever walked through a field and felt like you had been stung? You probably touched the stinging nettle. This plant with jagged edges is a good one to avoid, too.

Other plants can be more dangerous. You should not pick and eat any berries, seeds or nuts without first checking to make sure they are safe. You could get very sick or even die if you ate from one of these poisonous plants. Rhubarb and cherries are two common pie-making ingredients, but never eat the leaves of the rhubarb plant. The cherry leaves and branches have poison in them.

Directions: Answer these questions about dangerous plants.

1. You should not pick and eat any ___berries___ , ___seeds___
   or ___nuts___ without first making sure they are safe.

2. ___Poisin ivy___ and ___poisin oak___ might make your skin itch and burn.

3. What would happen if you touched a stinging nettle plant?

   It would feel like you had been stung.

Page 135

Comprehension: Rainforests

The soil in rainforests is very dark and rich. The trees and plants that grow there are very green. People who have seen one say a rainforest is "the greenest place on Earth." Why? Because it rains a lot. With so much rain, the plants stay very green. The earth stays very wet. Rainforests cover only 6 percent of the Earth. But they are home to 66 percent of all the different kinds of plants and animals on Earth! Today, rainforests are threatened by such things as acid rain from factory smoke emissions around the world and from farm expansion. Farmers living near rainforests cut down many trees each year to clear the land for farming. I wish I could see a rainforest. Do you?

Directions: Answer these questions about rainforests.

1. What do the plants and trees in a rainforest look like?

   They are very green.

2. What is the soil like in a rainforest?

   very dark and rich

3. How much of the Earth is covered by rainforests?

   6 percent

4. What percentage of the Earth's plants and animals live there?

   66 percent

Page 136

Comprehension: The Rainforest Lizard

Many strange animals live in the rainforest. One kind of strange animal is a very large lizard. This lizard grows as large as a dog! It has scales on its skin. It has a very wide mouth. It has spikes sticking out of the top of its head. It looks scary, but don't be afraid! This lizard eats mostly weeds. This lizard does not look very tasty, but other animals think it tastes good. Snakes eat these lizards. So do certain birds. Some people in the rainforest eat them, too! Would you like to eat a lizard for lunch?

Directions: Answer these questions about the rainforest lizard.

1. What is the size of this rainforest lizard?

   as large as a dog

2. Where do its scales grow?

   on its skin

3. Which kind of food does the lizard eat?

   mostly weeds

4. Who likes to eat these lizards?

   snakes, birds and some people

5. Would you like to see this lizard?

   Answers will vary.

Page 137

Comprehension: The Sloth

The sloth spends most of its life in the trees of the rainforest. The three-toed sloth, for example, is usually hanging around, using its claws to keep it there. Because it is in the trees so much, it has trouble moving on the ground. Certainly it could be caught easily by other animals of the rainforest if it was being chased. The sloth is a very slow-moving animal. Do you have any idea what the sloth eats? The sloth eats mostly leaves it finds in the treetops.

Have you ever seen a three- or two-toed sloth? If you see one in a zoo, you don't have to get close enough to count the toes. You can tell these two "cousins" apart in a different way—the three-toed sloth has some green mixed in with its fur because of the algae it gets from the trees.

Directions: Answer these questions about the sloth.

1. How does the three-toed sloth hang around the rainforest?

   a. by its tail, like a monkey

   (b. by its claws, or toes)

2. The main diet of the sloth is ___leaves___

3. Why does the sloth have trouble moving around on the ground?

   because it is in the trees so much

Page 138

Comprehension: The Kinkajou

If you have ever seen a raccoon holding its food by its "hands" and carefully eating it, you would have an idea of how the kinkajou (king-kuh-joo) eats. This animal of the rainforest is a "cousin" of the raccoon. Unlike its North American cousin, though, it is a golden-brown color.

The kinkajou's head and body are 17 to 22 inches long. The long tail of the kinkajou comes in handy for hanging around its neighborhood! If you do some quick mental math you can get a good idea of its size. It weighs very little—about 5 pounds. (You may have a 5-pound bag of sugar or flour in your kitchen to help you get an idea of the kinkajou's weight.)

This rainforest animal eats a variety of things. It enjoys nectar from the many rainforest flowers, insects, fruit, honey, birds and other small animals. Because it lives mostly in the trees, the kinkajou has a ready supply of food.

Directions: Answer these questions about the kinkajou.

1. The kinkajou is a "cousin" to the ___raccoon___

2. Do you weigh more or less than the kinkajou? ___more___

3. Write three things th Answers will vary but may include:

   1) nectar
   2) insects
   3) fruit

Grade 3 - Comprehensive Curriculum

Page 139

Comprehension: The Jaguar

The jaguar weighs between 100 and 250 pounds. It can be as long as 6 feet! This is not your ordinary house cat!

One strange feature of the jaguar is its living arrangements. The jaguar has its own territory. No other jaguar lives in its "home range." It would be very unusual for one jaguar to meet another in the rainforest. One way they mark their territory is by scratching trees.

Have you ever seen your pet cat hide in the grass and carefully and quietly sneak up on an unsuspecting grasshopper or mouse? Like its gentler, smaller "cousin," the jaguar stalks its prey in the high grass. It likes to eat small animals, such as rodents, but can attack and kill larger animals such as tapirs, deer and cattle. It is good at catching fish as well.

Directions: Answer these questions about the jaguar.

1. The jaguar lives:
   a. in large groups
   (b. alone)
   c. under water
2. This large cat marks its territory by:
   a. black marker
   b. roaring
   (c. scratching trees)
3. What does the jaguar eat?
   small animals, tapirs, deer and cattle
4. How much does it weigh?
   between 100 and 250 pounds

Page 140

Comprehension: The Toucan

One interesting bird of the rainforest is the toucan. This bird has a very large bill which is shaped like a canoe. Sometimes the toucan's bill can be as large as its body! The toucan's bill is colorful and hard, but flexible. You can also tell a toucan by its colorful feathers. They are mostly blue or black but also include red, yellow and orange.

The heavy growth in the rainforest provides protective covering for this colorful bird. The toucan lives in the layer of the rainforest called the "canopy." Here, high in the trees, it can use its large, hooked bill to find the berries and fruits that it loves to eat.

Directions: Answer these questions about the toucan.

1. Circle three characteristics of the toucan's bill.
   (colorful) (large)
   brittle (pointed)
   small soft
   hooked
2. In what layer of the rainforest does the toucan live?
   canopy
3. What does the toucan love to eat?
   1) berries
   2) fruits
4. What colors are the toucan's feathers?
   blue, black, red, yellow and orange

Page 141

Comprehension: Visiting the Rainforest

Many people travel to the rainforest each year. Some go by car, some go by train and some go by school bus! You don't even need a passport—the only thing you need is a field-trip permission slip.

If you are lucky enough to live in the Cleveland, Ohio area, you might get to take a class trip to the rainforest there. It is next to the Cleveland Zoo. This "rainforest" is a building that contains all the sights, sounds, smells and temperatures of the real rainforest. You will get to see many of the animals, big and small, that you could see if you went to Central or South America. The plants that grow there also grow in the rainforest. It is an interesting way to get an idea of what life is like in that part of the world!

Directions: Answer these questions about visiting the "rainforest."

1. If you lived in northern Ohio, name three ways you could get to the "rainforest." by car, train or school bus
2. In this "rainforest" you can see ___animals___ and ___plants___ that are found in the real rainforest.
3. Do you think it would be hot or cold in this "rainforest" building?
   (hot) cold
4. The real rainforest is located in both ___Central America___ and ___South America___

Page 142

Making Inferences: Unusual Flowers

You can grow many kinds of flowers in a garden. Here are the names of some—trumpet vine, pitcher plant and bird-of-paradise. The flowers that grow on these plants form seeds. The seeds can be used to grow new plants. The bird-of-paradise looks as if it has wings! The pitcher plant is very strange. It eats insects! The trumpet vine grows very long. It trails around fences and other plants. These plants are very different. Together, they make a pretty flower garden.

Bird of Paradise

Directions: Answer these questions about unusual flowers.

1. What do you think a pitcher plant looks like?
   a pitcher
2. What do you think a trumpet vine looks like?
   long like a trumpet
3. Name two of the three plants that grow seeds in their flowers.
   1) trumpet vine or pitcher plant
   2) bird of paradise
4. What can the seeds be used for?
   The seeds can be used to grow new plants.
5. What could you plant in a garden to get rid of insects?
   the pitcher plant

Page 143

Making Inferences: State Bird — Arizona

Have you ever traveled through Arizona or other southwestern states of the United States? One type of plant you may have seen is the cactus. This plant and other desert thickets are homes to the cactus wren, the state bird of Arizona. It is interesting how this bird (which is the size of a robin) can roost on this prickly plant and keep from getting stuck on the sharp spines. The cactus wren builds its nest on top of these thorny desert plants.

The cactus wren's "song" is not a beautiful, musical sound. Instead, it is compared to the grating sound of machinery. You can also identify the bird by its coloring. It has white spots on its outer tail feathers and white eyebrows. The crown (head) of the cactus wren is a rusty color.

Directions: Answer these questions about the cactus wren.

1. In what part of the United States would you find the cactus wren?
   the southwestern states
2. What does **prickly** mean?
   a. soft   b. green   (c. having sharp points)
3. Do you think you would like to hear the "song" of the cactus wren? Why or why not?
   Answers will vary.

Page 144

Comprehension: State Bird — Louisiana

Along the sandy coastline of Louisiana you may see the brown pelican. It is not hard to identify this large bird with a throat pouch. When it is young, the brown pelican has a dark-brown body and head. If you see this bird with a brown body and a white head, you are looking at an adult.

Do you know what the brown pelican uses its large throat pouch for? If you said the pouch is used for carrying the fish it catches, you would be wrong. Many people think that is how the pouch is used, but the pouch is really used for separating the fish from the water. Just imagine how much water the brown pelican can scoop up as it fishes!

Directions: Answer these questions about the brown pelican.

1. The brown pelican is found mostly along the ___sandy coastline___ of Louisiana.
2. How does it catch its food?
   by scooping out fish from the water with its beak and throat pouch
3. How is a young pelican's coloring different from the adult pelican?
   The young pelican has a brown body and head; the adult has a brown body and a white head.
4. What does **pouch** mean?
   a. catch   (b. pocket)   c. fish

Page 145

Comprehension: State Bird — Maine

The chickadee may visit your bird feeder on a regular basis if you live in Maine. This bird seems to have a feeding schedule so it doesn't miss a meal! The chickadee can be tamed to eat right out of your hand. If this bird sees some insect eggs on a tree limb, it even will hang upside down to get at this treat.

The chickadee lives in forests and open woodlands throughout most of the year, but when winter comes, it moves into areas populated by people. It is colored gray with a black cap and white on its underside and cheeks.

The chickadee lives in the northern half of the United States and in southern and western Canada. The western part of Alaska is also home to this curious and tame little bird.

Directions: Answer these questions about the chickadee.

1. What does **curious** mean?
   a. underside   c. tame
   b. questioning   d. schedule
2. What does the chickadee do when winter comes?
   It moves into areas populated by people.

3. One of the chickadee's favorite treats is _____ insect eggs
4. Where does the chickadee live?
   in forests and open woodlands in the northern
   half of the United States and in southern and
   western Canada

Page 146

Comprehension: State Bird — Ohio

The cardinal is the state bird of Ohio. You probably know that the cardinal is red, but do you know how this bright red bird (males are red; females are brown with some red) got its name? Its name came from the bright red robes of the Roman Catholic cardinals.

Cardinals live in gardens as well as brushy swamps, thickets and the edges of woodlands. This bird can be found, year-round, in the eastern half of the United States. Some parts of southern California and Arizona are also home to this bird.

If you have a bird feeder, you have probably seen a cardinal there. Its main diet is seeds, but it also sometimes eats insects. The song of the cardinal can be heard throughout the year, so you don't have to wait for the warmer weather of spring.

Directions: Answer these questions about the cardinal.

1. Which paragraph tells you where the cardinal lives?
   a. paragraph 1
   b. paragraph 2
   c. paragraph 3
2. What do cardinals eat?
   seeds and insects
3. How did this bird get its name?
   from the bright red robes of Roman
   Catholic cardinals
4. Which is red in color, the male or female cardinal?
   the male

Page 147

Main Idea: Hawks

Hawks are birds of prey. They "prey upon" birds and animals. This means they kill other animals and eat them. The hawk has long pointed wings. It uses them to soar through the air as it looks for prey. It looks at the ground while it soars.

When it sees an animal or bird to eat, the hawk swoops down. It grabs the animal in its beak and and claws then carries it off and eats it. The hawk eats birds, rats, ground squirrels and other pests.

Directions: Answer these questions about hawks.

1. Circle the main idea:

   Hawks are mean because they swoop down from the sky and eat animals and birds.

   Hawks are helpful because they eat sick birds, rats, ground squirrels and other pests.

2. What kind of wings does a hawk have?
   long pointed wings

3. How does the hawk pick up its prey?
   It swoops down and grabs the prey in its beak and claws.

4. What does "prey upon" mean?
   to kill other animals and eat them

Page 148

Comprehension: Birds' Homing Instinct

What is instinct (in-stinkt)? Instinct is knowing how to do something without being told how. Animals have instincts. Birds have an amazing instinct. It is called the "homing instinct." The homing instinct is birds' inner urge to find their way somewhere. When birds fly south in the winter, how do they know where to go? How do they know how to get there? When they return in the spring, what makes them return to the same place they left? It is birds' homing instinct. People do not have a homing instinct. That is why we get lost so often!

Directions: Answer these questions about birds' homing instinct.

1. What word means knowing how to do something without being told?
   instinct

2. What is birds' inner urge to find their way somewhere called?
   the homing instinct

3. Which direction do birds fly in the winter?
   south

4. Do people have a homing instinct?
   no

5. When do birds return home?
   spring

Page 149

Comprehension: Pet Crickets

Did you know that some people keep crickets as pets? These people always keep two crickets together. That way, the crickets do not get lonely!

Crickets are kept in a flowerpot filled with dirt. The dirt helps the crickets feel at home. They are used to being outside. Over the flowerpot is a covering that lets air inside. It also keeps the crickets in! Some people use a small net; others use cheesecloth. They make sure there is room under the covering for crickets to hop!

Pet crickets like to eat bread and lettuce. They also like raw hamburger meat. Would you like to have a pet cricket?

Directions: Answer these questions about pet crickets.

1. Where do pet crickets live?
   in a flowerpot filled with dirt

2. Why should you put dirt in with the crickets?
   It helps them feel at home.

3. What is placed over the flowerpot?
   a covering that lets air inside

4. Write three things pet crickets like to eat.
   bread, lettuce, raw hamburger meat

Page 150

Making Inferences: Pussy Willow Poem

Directions: Read the poem about the pussy willow plant. Then answer the questions.

I have a little pussy,
Her coat is silver gray.
She's in a great wide meadow,
She never runs away.
She'll always be a pussy,
She'll never be a cat,
'Cause she's a pussy willow!
What do you think of that?

1. Why does a pussy willow never run away?
   because it is a plant
2. Why will this pussy never grow to be a cat?
   because it's a pussy willow
3. Really, what is the "coat of silver gray"?
   the buds on the plant

Page 151

Comprehension: Our Solar System

There are nine planets in our solar system. All of them circle the Sun. The planet closest to the Sun is named Mercury. The Romans said Mercury was the messenger of the gods. The second planet from the Sun is named Venus. Venus shines the brightest. Venus was the Roman goddess of beauty. Earth is the third planet from the Sun. It is about the same size as Venus. After Earth is Mars, which is named after the Roman god of war. The other five planets are Jupiter, Saturn, Uranus, Neptune and Pluto. They, too, are named after Roman gods.

Directions: Answer these questions about our solar system.

1. How many planets are in our solar system?
   nine planets
2. What do the planets circle?
   the Sun
3. What are the planets named after?
   Roman gods and goddesses
4. Which planet is closest to the Sun?
   Mercury
5. Which planet is about the same size as Earth?
   Venus
6. Which planet comes after Earth in the solar system?
   Mars

Page 152

Comprehension: Mercury

In 1974, for the first time, a U.S. spacecraft passed within 400 miles of the planet Mercury. The name of the spacecraft was Mariner 10. There were no people on the spacecraft, but there were cameras that could take clear pictures from a long distance. What the pictures showed was interesting. They showed that Mercury's surface was a lot like the surface of the Moon. The surface of Mercury is filled with huge holes called craters. A layer of fine dust covers Mercury. This, too, is like the dust on the Moon. There is no life on either Mercury or the Moon.

Directions: Answer these questions about Mercury.

1. What was the name of the spacecraft that went near Mercury?
   Mariner 10
2. What was on the spacecraft?
   cameras
3. Write two ways that Mercury is like the Moon.
   1) It has craters.
   2) A layer of fine dust covers its surface.
4. Is there life on Mercury?
   No

Page 153

Main Idea: Venus

For many years, no one knew much about Venus. When people looked through telescopes, they could not see past Venus' clouds. Long ago, people thought the clouds covered living things. Spacecraft radar has shown this is not true. Venus is too hot for life to exist. The temperature on Venus is about 900 degrees! Remember how hot you were the last time it was 90 degrees? Now imagine it being 10 times hotter. Nothing could exist in that heat. It is also very dry on Venus. For life to exist, water must be present. Because of the heat and dryness, we know there are no people, plants or other life on Venus.

Directions: Answer these questions about Venus.

1. Circle the main idea:
   We cannot see past Venus' clouds to know what the planet is like.
   [Spacecraft radar shows it is too hot and dry for life to exist on Venus.]
2. What is the temperature on Venus? 900 degrees
3. This temperature is how many times hotter than a hot day on Earth?
   6 times hotter
   (10 times hotter)
4. In the past, why did people think life might exist on Venus?
   They couldn't see past the clouds.

Page 154

Comprehension: Earth

One planet in our solar system certainly supports life—Earth. Our planet is the third planet from the Sun and takes 365 days, or 1 year, to orbit the Sun. This rotation makes it possible for most of our planet to have four seasons—winter, spring, summer and fall.

Besides being able to support life, our planet is unique in another way—Earth is 75% covered by water. No other planet has that much, if any, liquid on its surface. This liquid and its evaporation help provide the cloud cover and climate patterns.

Earth has one natural satellite—the Moon. Scientists and other experts all over the world have created and sent into orbit other satellites used for a variety of purposes—communication, weather forecasting, and so on.

Directions: Answer these questions about Earth.

1. How much of Earth is covered by water? 75%
2. The Moon is a natural satellite of Earth.
3. How long does it take Earth to orbit the Sun? 365 days or 1 year
4. How does water make Earth the "living planet"?
   Its evaporation helps provide the cloud cover and climate
   patterns that enable life to exist.

Page 155

Comprehension: Mars

The U.S. has sent many unmanned spacecrafts to Mars since 1964. (**Unmanned** means there are no people on the spacecraft.) That's why scientists know a lot about this planet. Mars has low temperatures. There is no water on Mars. There is only a gas called water vapor. There is also ice on Mars. Scientists have also learned that there is fog on Mars in the early morning! Do you remember when you last saw fog here on Earth? Scientists say the fog on Mars looks the same. As on Earth, the fog occurs in low-lying areas of the ground.

Another interesting thing about Mars is that it is very windy. The wind blows up many dust storms on this planet. A spacecraft called Mariner 9 was the first to take pictures of dust storms. Later, the unmanned Viking spacecraft landed on the surface of Mars.

Directions: Answer these questions about Mars.

1. On Mars, it is (cold.)
   hot.
2. When there are no people on a spacecraft, it is unmanned .
3. Mars and Earth both have fog in the early morning in low-lying areas.
4. These are caused by all the wind on Mars.
   dust storms
5. This spacecraft took pictures of dust storms on Mars.
   Mariner 9

Page 156

Comprehension: Jupiter

Jupiter, the fifth planet from the Sun, is circled by a ring of dark particles. It takes this planet almost 12 years to orbit the Sun. Jupiter's ring is very difficult to see from Earth without using special equipment. Jupiter is the largest planet in our solar system. It is 11 times bigger than Earth!

Scientists have been able to learn much about this planet because of the information received from Voyager 1 in 1979. They know that we cannot send a spacecraft to land on the surface of Jupiter as we have done with the Moon. The surface of Jupiter is not solid. The outer "shell" of Jupiter is gas.

Directions: Answer these questions about Jupiter.

1. In what year did Voyager 1 send us more information about Jupiter?
   1979
2. Why can't we send a spacecraft to land on Jupiter?
   because the surface is not solid; it is made of gas
3. The ring that circles Jupiter is made of dark particles
4. What is the largest planet in our solar system?
   Jupiter
5. Jupiter is the fifth planet from the Sun.

ANSWER KEY

Page 157

Comprehension: Saturn

Have you looked at Saturn through a strong telescope? If you have, you know it has rings. Saturn is the most beautiful planet to see! It is bright yellow. It is circled by four rings. Two bright rings are on the outside of the circle. Two dark rings are on the inside of the circle. The rings of Saturn are made of billions of tiny bits of ice and rock. The ice and rocks travel around the planet in a swarm. They keep their ring shape as the planet travels around the Sun. These rings shine brightly, and so does the planet Saturn. Both reflect the rays of the Sun.
The Sun is 885 million miles away from Saturn. It takes Saturn 29½ years to travel around the Sun!

Directions: Answer these questions about Saturn.

1. How many rings does Saturn have? __four__
2. Where are Saturn's dark rings?
   __on the inside of the circle__
3. Where are Saturn's bright rings?
   __on the outside of the circle__
4. What are Saturn's rings made of?
   __billions of tiny bits of ice and rock__
5. What causes Saturn and its rings to shine?
   __They reflect the rays of the Sun.__
6. How far away from the Sun is Saturn?
   __885 million miles away__

Page 158

Comprehension: Uranus

William Herschel discovered the planet Uranus in 1781. As has happened many times throughout history with other scientists, inventors and explorers, he didn't realize he had found a planet—he thought it was a comet. Scientists didn't know too much about this planet, though, until 1986 when the U.S. spacecraft Voyager 2 flew past it.
Do you think the planet Earth is big? Well, the planet Uranus is four times bigger! Uranus is another planet that has rings. While Saturn's rings are made of ice and rock, the rings of Uranus are made of dark particles the size of boulders. Earth has one natural satellite—the Moon—but Uranus has 15 natural satellites. It takes Earth 1 year to circle the Sun, but Uranus takes 84 years! Uranus is the seventh planet from the Sun.

Directions: Answer these questions about Uranus.

1. This story tells about two planets that have rings. They are:
   1) __Uranus__   2) __Saturn__
2. Who was William Herschel?
   __the scientist who discovered Uranus__
3. Which planet is bigger, Earth or Uranus? How much bigger?
   __Uranus/four times bigger__

Page 159

Comprehension: Neptune

Neptune is the eighth planet from the Sun. Because of its location, it takes Neptune 168 years to orbit the Sun. It is closely related to Uranus, one of its neighbors in the solar system. Scientists have noticed that its coloring and appearance look very similar to that of Uranus.
Neptune was discovered by Galle in 1846. It is almost four times bigger than Earth. Neptune has two known satellites—the larger is named Triton and the smaller is named Nereid. Some scientists have noticed that the orbit of the larger satellite s getting closer and closer to the planet. It will eventually crash into the surface of Neptune. However, you and I won't be able to watch this happen. Scientists predict it will happen in 100 million years!

Directions: Answer these questions about Neptune.

1. Why does it take Neptune 168 years to orbit the Sun?
   __because it is so far from the Sun__
2. What are the names of Neptune's two satellites?
   1) __Triton__   2) __Nereid__
3. Which word in the last paragraph means "to tell about something that will happen"?
   __predict__
4. Who discovered the planet Neptune?
   __Galle__

Page 160

Comprehension: Pluto

Pluto is the ninth planet in our solar system. It is 3,700 million miles from the Sun. It cannot be seen from Earth without a telescope. Maybe that is why it was named Pluto. Pluto was the Roman god of the underworld. For years, scientists suspected there was a ninth planet. But it was not until 1930 that a young scientist proved Pluto existed. His name was Clyde Tombaugh. He compared pictures of the sky near Pluto taken at different times. He noticed one big "star" was in a different place in different pictures. He realized it was not a star. It was a planet moving around the Sun.

Directions: Answer these questions about Pluto.

1. Who discovered Pluto? __Clyde Tombaugh__
2. When did he discover Pluto? __1930__
3. Why was the new planet named Pluto?
   __because it couldn't be seen without a telescope, and Pluto is the Roman god of the underworld__
4. How was Pluto discovered? __Tombaugh compared pictures of the sky taken at different times. One big star was in a different place in different pictures.__
5. What is Pluto's distance from the sun? __3,700 millions miles__

Page 161

Comprehension: Moon

Our moon is not the only moon in the solar system. Some other planets have moons also. Saturn has 10 moons! Our moon is Earth's closest neighbor in the solar system. Sometimes our moon is 225,727 miles away. Other times, it is 252,002 miles away. Why? Because the Moon revolves around Earth. It does not go around Earth in a perfect circle. So, sometimes its path takes it further away from our planet.
When our astronauts visited the Moon, they found dusty plains, high mountains and huge craters. There is no air or water on the Moon. That is why life cannot exist there. The astronauts had to wear space suits to protect their skin from the bright Sun. They had to take their own air to breathe. They had to take their own food and water. The Moon was an interesting place to visit. Would you want to live there?

Directions: Answer these questions about the Moon.

1. Circle the main idea:
   > The Moon travels around Earth, and the astronauts visited the Moon.

   Astronauts found that the Moon—Earth's closest neighbor— has no air or water and cannot support life.
2. Write three things our astronauts found on the Moon.
   1) __dusty plains__ 2) __high mountains__ 3) __huge craters__
3. Make a list of what to take on a trip to the Moon.
   __Answers will vary, but can include: space suits, food, water, and air.__

Page 162

Comprehension: Your Heart

Make your hand into a fist. Now look at it. That is about the size of your heart! Your heart is a strong pump. It works all the time. Right now it is beating about 90 times a minute. When you run, it beats about 150 times a minute.
Inside, your heart has four spaces. The two spaces on the top are called atria. This is where blood is pumped into the heart. The two spaces on the bottom are called ventricles. This is where blood is pumped out of the heart. The blood is pumped to every part of your body. How? Open and close your fist. See how it tightens and loosens? The heart muscle tightens and loosens, too. This is how it pumps blood.

Directions: Answer these questions about your heart.

1. How often does your heart work?
   __all the time__
2. How fast does it beat when you are sitting?
   __about 90 times a minute__
3. How fast does it beat when you are running?
   __about 150 times a minute__
4. How many spaces are inside your heart? __four__
5. What are the heart's upper spaces called? What are the lower spaces called?
   __atria__   __ventricles__

Grade 3 - Comprehensive Curriculum

Page 163

Making Inferences: Your Bones

Are you scared of skeletons? You shouldn't be. There is a skeleton inside of you! The skeleton is made up of all the bones in your body. These 206 bones give you your shape. They also protect your heart and everything else inside. Your bones come in many sizes. Some are short. Some are long. Some are rounded. Some are very tiny. The outside of your bones looks solid. Inside, they are filled with a soft material called marrow. This is what keeps your bones alive. Red blood cells and most white blood cells are made here. These cells help feed the body and fight disease.

Directions: Answer these questions about your bones.

1. Do you think your leg bone is short, long or rounded?

   long

2. Do you think the bones in your head are short, long or rounded?

   rounded

3. What is the size of the bones in your fingers?

   small

4. What is the "something soft" inside your bones?

   marrow

5. How many bones are in your skeleton?

   206 bones

Page 164

Comprehension: Your Muscles

Can you make a fist? You could not do this without muscles. You need muscles to make your body move. You have muscles everywhere. There are muscles in your legs. There are even muscles in your tongue!

Remember, your heart is a muscle. It is called an "involuntary muscle" because it works without help from you. Your stomach muscles are also involuntary. You don't need to tell your stomach to digest food. Other muscles are called "voluntary muscles." You must tell these muscles to move. Most voluntary muscles are hooked to bones. When the muscles squeeze, they cause the bone to move. Without your muscles, you would be nothing but a "bag of bones"!

Directions: Answer these questions about your muscles.

1. What are involuntary muscles?

   muscles that work without help from you

2. What are voluntary muscles?

   muscles you must tell to move

3. These muscles are usually hooked to bones:

   involuntary muscles

   [voluntary muscles]

4. What causes bones to move?

   when muscles squeeze

Page 165

Comprehension: Your Hands

Wiggle your fingers. Now clap your hands. That was easy, wasn't it? But it wasn't as easy as you think! Each of your hands has 27 bones. Eight of the 27 bones are in your wrist. There are five bones in each of your palms. Your hands have many muscles, too. It takes 30 muscles to wiggle your fingers. When you use your hands, the bones and muscles work together. Remember this the next time you cut your meat. You will use your wrist bones and muscles. You will use your finger bones and muscles. Cutting your meat seems easy. It is—thanks to your muscles and bones!

Directions: Answer these questions about your hands.

1. How many bones are in each of your wrists?

   8 bones

2. How many bones are in each of your hands?

   27 bones

3. How many muscles does it take to wiggle your fingers?

   30 muscles

4. How many bones are in each of your palms?

   5 bones

5. Add together the palm bones and wrist bones. Subtract from the total number of bones in the hand. How many bones are left?

   5 + 8 = 13   27 - 13 = 14

Page 166

Comprehension: Your Digestive System

The digestive system begins in your mouth. (And you thought you were just enjoying that salad and slice of pizza!) The teeth begin the process by slicing and chewing the food you eat. Usually adults have 32 teeth to help do this. Saliva enters the mouth, too, and helps soften the food so it can be swallowed easily. Now, your salad and pizza move through a short tube called the esophagus onward to the stomach.

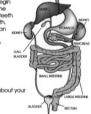

Directions: Answer these questions about your digestive system.

1. What does saliva do?

   It helps soften the food so it can be swallowed easily.

2. Where does the digestive system begin?

   in your mouth

3. What do your teeth do?

   They slice and chew food.

4. The ___esophagus___ is a short tube that brings food to the stomach.

Page 167

Comprehension: Your Digestive System

It's here in the stomach that food is stored long enough to let it mix with 6 pints of gastric juices. These important juices help kill bacteria and break down food into nutrients that your body needs.

Next, the food moves into the small intestine. This section of the digestive system helps to continue breaking down the food into nutrients needed by your body. From here, most of the nutrients needed are absorbed.

The final stage of the digestive system takes place in the large intestine, or colon. The colon helps send into the body any leftover usable products, water and salt.

Directions: Answer these questions about your digestive system.

1. How do the gastric juices help digestion?

   They help kill bacteria and break food down.

   What is their function?

   To break food down into nutrients.

2. Where does the final stage of digestion take place?

   It takes place in the colon.

3. Number the order of where digestion takes place.

   5 large intestine   1 mouth   2 esophagus

   4 small intestine   3 stomach

Page 168

Main Idea: Your Lungs

Imagine millions of teeny, tiny balloons joined together. That is what your lungs are like. When you breathe, the air goes to your two lungs. One lung is located on each side of your chest. The heart is located between the two lungs. The lungs are soft, spongy and delicate. That is why there are bones around the lungs. These bones are called the rib cage. The rib cage protects the lungs so they can do their job. The lungs bring oxygen (ox-i-gin) into the body. They also take waste out of the body. This waste is called carbon dioxide. We could not live without our lungs!

Directions: Answer these questions about your lungs.

1. Circle the main idea:

   The lungs are spongy and located in the chest. They are like small balloons.

   [The lungs bring in oxygen and take out carbon dioxide. We could not live without our lungs.]

2. What is the name of the bones around your lungs?

   the rib cage

3. What is located between the lungs?

   the heart

4. What goes into your lungs when you breathe?

   oxygen

5. Why are there bones around your lungs?

   to protect them

ANSWER KEY

Page 169

Comprehension: Your Brain

When you are grown, your brain will weigh only 3 pounds. But what an important 3 pounds! Billions of brain cells are packed into your brain. The cells make up the three areas of the brain. One part does your thinking and feeling. Another part of the brain helps you move your body. It also helps you keep your balance. A third part of the brain keeps you alive! It keeps your heart beating and your lungs working so you don't have to think about these things. This part of your brain is called the medulla (ma-dool-la). As long as you are alive, the medulla never rests.

Directions: Answer these questions about your brain.

1. What do you think would happen if the medulla stopped working?

   You would die.

2. What do you think would happen if something happened to the part of your brain that helps you move your body?

   You wouldn't be able to move.

3. Circle the main idea:

   The brain has lots of cells. Three billion cells are packed into the brain.

   (The brain has three areas. Each area has a very important job to do.)

4. What directions does the medulla give the heart and lungs?

   to keep working so you don't have to think about it

Page 170

Comprehension: Horseless Carriage

Do you know how people traveled before cars? They rode horses! Often the horses were hooked up to wagons. Some horses were hooked up to carriages. Wagons were used to carry supplies. Carriages had covered tops. They were used to carry people. Both wagons and carriages were pulled by horses.

The first cars in the United States were invented shortly before the year 1900. These cars looked a lot like carriages. The seats were high off the ground. They had very thin wheels. The difference was that they were powered by engines. Carriages were pulled by horses. Still, they looked alike. People called the first cars "horseless carriages."

Directions: Answer these questions about "horseless carriages."

1. Write one way wagons and carriages were the same.

   both were pulled by horses.

2. When were the first cars invented?

   shortly before 1900

3. Why were the first cars called "horseless carriages"?

   because they looked like carriages without a horse

4. What was the difference between a carriage and a "horseless carriage"?

   A horseless carriage had an engine and didn't need a horse to pull it.

Page 171

Comprehension: Giant Snowblower

A snowblower is used to blow snow off sidewalks and driveways. It is faster than using a shovel. It is also easier! Airports use snowblowers, too. They use them to clear the runways that planes use. Many airports use a giant snowblower. It is a type of truck. This snowblower weighs 30,000 pounds! It can blow 100,000 pounds of snow every minute. It cuts through the snow with huge blades. The blades are over 6 feet tall.

Directions: Answer these questions about snowblowers.

1. Why do people use snowblowers instead of shovels?

   It is faster and easier.

2. What do airports use snowblowers for?

   They use them to clear the runways.

3. How much do some airport snowblowers weigh?

   30,000 pounds

4. How much snow can the airport snowblower blow every minute?

   100,000 pounds

5. What does the snowblower use to cut through snow?

   huge blades over 6 feet tall

Page 172

Comprehension: Early Trucks

What would we do without trucks? Your family may not own a truck, but everyone depends on trucks. Trucks bring our food to stores. Trucks carry new clothes to shopping centers. The goods of the world move on trucks.

Trucks are harder to make than cars. They must be sturdy. They carry heavy loads. They cannot break down.

The first trucks were on the road in 1900. Like trains, they were powered by steam engines. They did not use gasoline. The first trucks did not have heavy wheels. Their engines often broke down.

Trucks changed when the U.S. entered World War I in 1917. Big, heavy tires were put on trucks. Gasoline engines were used. Trucks used in war had to be sturdy. Lives were at stake!

Directions: Answer these questions about the first trucks.

1. What powered the first trucks?

   steam engines

2. When did early trucks begin using gasoline engines?

   in 1917 during World War I

3. How do trucks serve us?

   They deliver food, furniture and other goods of the world.

4. Why did trucks used in war have to be sturdy?

   because lives were at stake

Page 173

Comprehension: The First Trains

Trains have been around much longer than cars or trucks. The first train used in the United States was made in England. It was brought to the U.S. in 1829. Because it was light green, it was nicknamed the Grasshopper. Unlike a real grasshopper, this train was not fast. It only went 10 miles an hour.

That same year, another train was built by an American. Compared to the Grasshopper, the American train was fast. It went 30 miles an hour. People were amazed. This train was called the Rocket. Can you guess why?

Directions: Answer these questions about the first trains.

1. Where was the first train made that was used in the U.S.?

   England

2. What did people call this train?

   the Grasshopper

3. How fast did it travel?

   10 miles an hour

4. What year did the Grasshopper arrive in the U.S.?

   1829

5. What American train was built that same year?

   the Rocket

Page 174

Comprehension: Beavers

Have you ever been called a "busy beaver"? You may not know what this expression means, but read the paragraphs below to find out.

Most animals cannot change where they live. A bird can build a nest and a mole can burrow into the ground, but the beaver can do more than that. If it likes a certain area but finds that the water is not deep enough, do you know what it can do? The beaver "gets busy" and starts cutting down trees to build a dam so that the area covered by water is deeper and larger.

The beaver does this using its sharp teeth. After it gnaws on a tree, it cuts away until the tree starts to fall. The beaver makes sure to get out of the way! It then trims off the branches and bark. Without using a chainsaw, as a person would do, the beaver cuts the wood into smaller pieces.

Directions: Answer these questions about the beaver.

1. What does the beaver use to chop down a tree?

   its sharp teeth

2. After the tree has fallen, what does the beaver do?

   It trims off the branches and bark.

3. How did the term **busy beaver** come about?

   because beavers are always busy cutting down trees

Grade 3 - Comprehensive Curriculum

Page 175

Comprehension: Beavers

The beaver is not only a great lumberjack, it can also swim quite well. Its special fur helps to keep it warm; its hind legs work like fins; its tail is used as a rudder to steer it through the water. The beaver can hold its breath under water for 15 minutes, and its special eyelids are transparent, so they work like goggles!

Even though the beaver is a very good swimmer and can stay under water for a long time, it does not live under water. When the beaver builds a dam it also builds a lodge. A lodge is a dome-shaped structure above water level in which the beaver lives. The beaver enters its lodge through underwater tunnels. The lodge provides a place for the beaver to rest, eat and raise young.

Directions: Answer these questions about the beaver.

1. What is the main idea of the first paragraph?

   The beaver has many qualities that make it a very good swimmer.

2. Which word in the first paragraph means "able to see through"?

   transparent

3. How long can the beaver hold its breath under water?

   15 minutes

4. How does a beaver enter his lodge?

   through underwater tunnels

Page 176

Comprehension: Cows

Thousands of years ago, people domesticated (tamed) cows. If you live on or near a farm, you may see cows every day. You may know what it is like to hear their mooing sounds when they are ready to be fed or milked.

Cows are raised for meat and milk. If a cow is raised for the sole purpose of providing milk, it is called a dairy cow. Some common breeds of dairy cows are Holstein-Friesians (hole-steen free-zhunz), Jerseys, Brown Swiss and Guernseys (gurn-zeez). Cows raised for their meat are Herefords (her-ferdz).

Cows use their long tails to swat flies and other bothersome bugs. Cows chew cud. This is a portion of their food that has already been chewed a little. It is swallowed, then brought back up after it has been combined with liquid. The cow has four stomachs which make this possible. What do you think of chewing cud? Yuck!

Directions: Answer these questions about cows.

1. Holstein-Friesians and Guernseys are two kinds of __dairy__ cows.

2. Cows have __four__ stomachs.

3. Another word for tamed is __domesticated__.

4. A common breed of cow raised for meat is __Herefords__.

Page 177

Making Inferences: Sheep

Sheep like to stay close together. They do not run off. They move together in a flock. They live on sheep ranches. Some sheep grow 20 pounds of fleece each year. After it is cut off, the fleece is called wool. Cutting off the wool is called "shearing." It does not hurt the sheep to be sheared. The wool is very warm and is used to make clothing.

Female sheep are called ewes ("yous"). Some types of ewes have only one baby each year. The baby is called a lamb. Other types of ewes have two or three lambs each year.

Directions: Answer these questions about sheep.

1. Why is sheep's behavior helpful to sheep ranchers?

   Sheep like to stay close together.

2. If you were a sheep farmer, would you rather own the kind of sheep that has one baby each year, or one that has two or three?

   the kind that has two or three babies

   Why?

   because then you would have more sheep

3. When it is still on the sheep, what is wool called?

   fleece

4. What is a group of sheep called?

   flock

Page 178

Making Inferences: Sheep

Farmers shear sheep at the time of the year when the climate is warm. Shearing is usually done in May in the northern states and as early as February or March in the warmer southern states.

Whether in a small or large flock, sheep must be watched more carefully than cattle. Herders take care of sheep on the open range. The herders live in tents, campers or camp wagons and take care of 500–2,000 sheep. As the sheep get larger, the herder must make sure that there is plenty of grass for the herd to graze.

Directions: Answer these questions about sheep.

1. What does **graze** mean?

   a. run

   b. eat ⓑ

   c. like

2. Why do you think shearing takes place when the climate is warm?

   After sheep are sheared, their skin is bare with nothing to keep them warm.

3. What do you think an "open range" is?

   a large area of land without fences

Page 179

Comprehension: Rhinos

Rhinos are the second largest land animal. Only elephants are bigger.

Most people think rhinos are ugly. Their full name is "rhinoceros" (rhy-nos-ur-us). There are five kinds of rhinos—the square-lipped rhino, black rhino, great Indian rhino, Sumatran (sue-ma-trahn) rhino and Javan rhino.

Rhinos have a great sense of smell, which helps protect them. They can smell other animals far away. They don't eat them, though. Rhinos do not eat meat. They are vegetarians.

Directions: Answer these questions about rhinos.

1. What is the largest land animal?

   the elephant

2. What are the five kinds of rhinos?

   1) square-lipped rhino
   2) black rhino
   3) great Indian rhino
   4) Sumatran rhino
   5) Javan rhino

3. What is a "vegetarian"?

   Someone who does not eat meat, only plants.

Page 180

Comprehension: Robins

Have you ever heard this old song? "Oh, the red, red robin goes bob-bob-bobbin' along!" It's hard not to smile when you see a robin. Robins were first called "redbreasts." If you have seen why! The fronts of their bodies are red. Robins are cheerful-looking birds.

Robins sing a sweet, mellow song. That is another reason why people like robins. The female robin lays two to six eggs. She sits on them for 2 weeks. Then the father and mother robin both bring food to the baby birds. Robins eat spiders, worms, insects and small seeds. Robins will also eat food scraps people put out for them.

Directions: Answer these questions about robins.

1. Write one reason people like robins. Sample answer:

   Robins are cheerful-looking birds.

2. How many eggs does a mother robin lay?

   two to six eggs

3. What do robins eat?

   spiders, worms, insects, small seeds and food scraps

4. Who sits on the robin's eggs?

   the female

ANSWER KEY

Page 181

Comprehension: Rodents

You are surrounded by rodents (row-dents)! There are 1,500 different kinds of rodents. One of the most common rodents is the mouse. Rats, gophers (go-furs) and beavers are also rodents. So are squirrels and porcupines (pork-you-pines).

All rodents have long, sharp teeth. These sharp teeth are called incisors (in-size-ors). Rodents use these teeth to eat their food. They eat mostly seeds and vegetables. There is one type of rodent some children have as a pet. No, it is not a rat! It is the guinea (ginney) pig.

Directions: Answer these questions about rodents.

1. How many different kinds of rodents are there?
   _1,500_

2. Name seven kinds of rodents.
   1) _mice_
   2) _rats_
   3) _gophers_
   4) _beavers_
   5) _squirrels_
   6) _porcupines_
   7) _guinea pigs_

3. What are rodents' sharp teeth called?
   incisors

4. What rodent is sometimes a pet?
   guinea pig

Page 182

Making Inferences: Dictionary Mystery

Directions: Below are six dictionary entries with pronunciations and definitions. The only things missing are the entry words. Write the correct entry words. Be sure to spell each word correctly.

Entry word:
rose
(rōz)
A flower that grows on bushes and vines.

Entry word:
rabbit
(ra bet)
A small animal that has long ears.

Entry word:
fox
(fäks)
A wild animal that lives in the woods.

Entry word:
piano
(pē ân ō)
A musical instrument that has many keys.

Entry word:
lake
(lāk)
A body of water that is surrounded by land.

Entry word:
baseball
(bās bol)
A game played with a bat and a ball.

Directions: Now write the entry words in alphabetical order.

1. _baseball_
2. _fox_
3. _lake_
4. _piano_
5. _rabbit_
6. _rose_

Page 183

Drawing Conclusions

Drawing a conclusion means to use clues to make a final decision about something. To draw a conclusion, you must read carefully.

Directions: Read each story carefully. Use the clues given to draw a conclusion about the story.

The boy and girl took turns pushing the shopping cart. They went up and down the aisles. Each time they stopped the cart, they would look at things on the shelf and decide what they needed. Jody asked her older brother, "Will I need a box of 48 crayons in Mrs. Charles' class?"

"Yes, I think so," he answered. Then he turned to their mother and said, "I need some new notebooks. Can I get some?"

1. Where are they? _at the store_
2. What are they doing there? _buying school supplies_
3. How do you know? Write at least two clue words that helped you.
   Mrs. Charles's class, notebooks, box of 48 crayons

Eric and Randy held on tight. They looked around them and saw that they were not the only ones holding on. The car moved slowly upward. As they turned and looked over the side, they noticed that the people far below them seemed to be getting smaller and smaller. "Hey, Eric, did I tell you this is my first time on one of these?" asked Randy. As they started down the hill at a frightening speed, Randy screamed, "And it may be my last!"

1. Where are they? _on a roller coaster_
2. How do you know? Write at least two clue words that helped you.
   car moved slowly upward, down at frightening speed

Page 184

Drawing Conclusions: The Jitterbug

Directions: Read about the jitterbug, then answer the questions.

The music is playing loudly. Paul and Mary are facing each other. They hold hands. They are going to do something called the jitterbug. Paul starts bouncing back and forth, first on one foot, then on the other. Mary starts doing the same thing. They are "keeping time" to the beat of the music. Then they start moving around a lot. Mary ducks under Paul's arm. They are laughing because they are having fun.

1. What are Paul and Mary doing? _dancing_

2. What clue words helped you to know? _music, "keeping time"_

3. Why are Paul and Mary laughing? _They are having fun._

Page 185

Drawing Conclusions: A Colorful Yard

Directions: Read the story, then answer the questions.

Mrs. Posy plants roses everywhere. She plants yellow roses near her front porch. She plants red roses near the back door. There are also pink roses and white roses in her yard. Every time the postal carrier comes to her house, he sneezes. "You should not plant so many flowers," he tells Mrs. Posy. Mrs. Posy just smiles.

1. What are Mrs. Posy's favorite flowers? _roses_

2. Why do you think the postal carrier tells Mrs. Posy, "You should not plant so many flowers"? _He sneezes every time he comes near her house._

3. Why does Mrs. Posy smile? _She thinks it's funny that her beautiful roses make the postal carrier sneeze._

Page 186

Drawing Conclusions: Mrs. Posy's Roses

Directions: Read more about Mrs. Posy, then answer the questions.

Mrs. Posy is working in her rose garden. She is trimming the branches so that the plants will grow better. Mrs. Posy is careful, because rose bushes have thorns on them. "Hello, Mrs. Posy!" calls Ann as she rides her bicycle down the street. "Hi, Ann!" replies Mrs. Posy. Then she yells, "Ouch!" She runs inside the house and stays there for a few minutes. When Mrs. Posy comes back outside, she has a bandage on one finger.

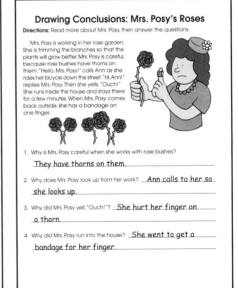

1. Why is Mrs. Posy careful when she works with rose bushes?
   They have thorns on them.

2. Why does Mrs. Posy look up from her work? _Ann calls to her so she looks up._

3. Why did Mrs. Posy yell, "Ouch!"? _She hurt her finger on a thorn._

4. Why did Mrs. Posy run into the house? _She went to get a bandage for her finger._

Grade 3 - Comprehensive Curriculum

Page 187

Drawing Conclusions: What's Hiding?

Directions: Read about caterpillars, then answer the questions.

Some people do not like caterpillars. Caterpillars look like fuzzy worms. They have many legs and they creep and crawl on trees and leaves. But a caterpillar is really the beginning of something else. After the caterpillar is very large, it spins a cocoon. It stays inside the cocoon for a few months. When the cocoon opens, something else is inside. It is very beautiful. It flies away.

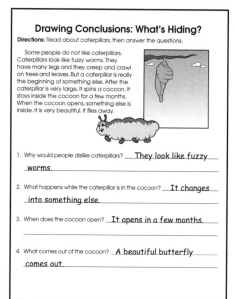

1. Why would people dislike caterpillars? __They look like fuzzy worms.__

2. What happens while the caterpillar is in the cocoon? __It changes into something else.__

3. When does the cocoon open? __It opens in a few months.__

4. What comes out of the cocoon? __A beautiful butterfly comes out.__

Page 188

Drawing Conclusions: Butterflies

Directions: Read about butterflies, then answer the questions.

Butterflies are many different colors. They have different designs on them, too. These colors and designs help them. When some butterflies are resting, they look like leaves. Animals cannot see them. Other butterflies smell funny. Animals do not like the smell.

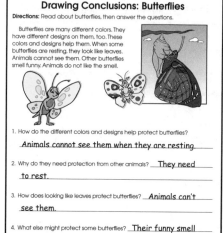

1. How do the different colors and designs help protect butterflies? __Animals cannot see them when they are resting.__

2. Why do they need protection from other animals? __They need to rest.__

3. How does looking like leaves protect butterflies? __Animals can't see them.__

4. What else might protect some butterflies? __Their funny smell might protect them.__

Page 189

Drawing Conclusions: Eskimos

Directions: Read about the traditional lives of Eskimos, then answer the questions.

Eskimos live in Alaska. A long time ago, Eskimos lived in houses made of snow, dirt or animal skins. They moved around from place to place. The Eskimos hunted and fished. They often ate raw meat because they had no way to cook it. When they ate meat raw, they liked it dried or frozen. Eskimos used animal skins for their clothes. They used fat from whales, seals and other animals to heat their houses.

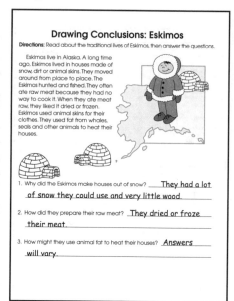

1. Why did the Eskimos make houses out of snow? __They had a lot of snow they could use and very little wood.__

2. How did they prepare their raw meat? __They dried or froze their meat.__

3. How might they use animal fat to heat their houses? __Answers will vary.__

Page 190

Drawing Conclusions: Eskimos

Directions: Read about today's Eskimos, then answer the questions.

Today, many Eskimos live in villages or towns instead of moving from place to place. They work at jobs, instead of hunting and fishing. Eskimo children go to school, too. Their houses are heated by oil from the ground instead of animal oil. Many Eskimos use snowmobiles instead of dogs and sleds. In the winter, they wear coats that are very warm.

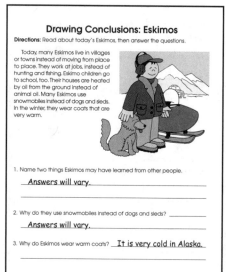

1. Name two things Eskimos may have learned from other people. __Answers will vary.__

2. Why do they use snowmobiles instead of dogs and sleds? __Answers will vary.__

3. Why do Eskimos wear warm coats? __It is very cold in Alaska.__

Page 192

Alphabetical Order

Alphabetical order (or ABC order) is the order of letters in the alphabet. When putting words in alphabetical order, use the first letter of each word.

Directions: Number the words in each list from 1 to 5 in alphabetical order.

3 happy	5 zebra	2 banana
4 scared	1 gorilla	3 kiwi
5 worried	4 monkey	1 apple
1 amused	2 hyena	5 peach
2 excited	3 kangaroo	4 lemon

Page 193

Alphabetical Order

Directions: Alphabetical order is putting words in the order in which they appear in the alphabet. Put the eggs in alphabetical order. The first and last words are done for you.

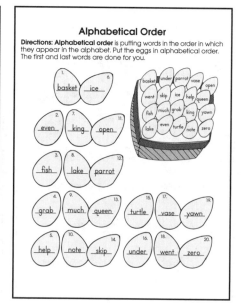

1. basket   6. ice
2. even   7. king   11. open
3. fish   8. lake   12. parrot
4. grab   9. much   13. queen   15. turtle   17. vase   19. yawn
5. help   10. note   14. skip   16. under   18. went   20. zero

Page 194

Alphabetical Order

The words in these lists begin with the same letter.

Directions: Use the second or third letters of each word to put the lists in alphabetical order.

Example:

tiger	3	tiger
tape	1	tape
tide	2	tide

All three words begin with the same letter (t), so look at the second letters. The letter **a** comes before **i**, so **tape** comes first. Then look at the third letters in **tiger** and **tide** to see which word comes next.

3	glad
4	goat
1	gasoline
2	gentle
5	grumble

3	answer
1	about
5	ask
4	around
2	against

3	tape
4	taste
1	table
2	talent
5	taught

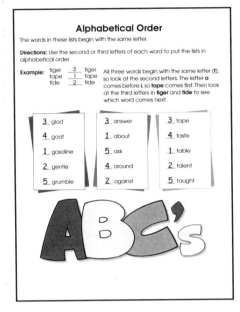

Page 195

Alphabetical Order

Alphabetical order is the order in which letters come in the alphabet.

Directions: Write the words in alphabetical order. If the first letter is the same, use the second letter of each word to decide which word comes first. If the second letter is also the same, look at the third letter of each word to decide.

Example: wish wasp won't

1. wasp
2. wish
3. won't

bench   flag   bowl

1. bench
2. bowl
3. flag

dog   dart   drag

1. dart
2. dog
3. drag

egg   nod   neat

1. egg
2. neat
3. nod

skipped   stairs   stones

1. skipped
2. stairs
3. stones

Page 196

Antonyms

An **antonym** is a word that means the opposite of another word.

Examples:

child   adult   hot   cold

Directions: Match the words that have opposite meanings. Draw a line between each pair of antonyms.

thaw	same
huge	sad
crying	friend
happy	open
enemy	freeze
asleep	thin
closed	hide
fat	tiny
seek	awake
different	laughing

Page 197

Antonyms

Directions: Complete each sentence with an antonym pair from page 196. Some pairs will not be used.

Example: Usually we wear <u>different</u> clothes, but today we are dressed the <u>same</u>.

1. A <u>child</u> is allowed in the museum if he/she is with an <u>adult</u>.
2. Mom was <u>happy</u> it rained since her garden was very dry, but I was <u>sad</u> because I had to stay inside.
3. The <u>huge</u> crowd of people tried to fit into the <u>tiny</u> room.
4. The <u>crying</u> baby was soon <u>laughing</u> and playing in the crib.
5. We'll <u>freeze</u> the meat for now, and Dad will <u>thaw</u> it when we need it.
6. The windows were wide <u>open</u>, but the door was <u>closed</u>.

Now, write your own sentence using one of the antonym pairs.

<u>Sentences will vary.</u>

Page 198

Antonyms

Antonyms are words that are opposites.

Example: hairy   bald

Directions: Choose a word from the box to complete each sentence below.

open	right	light	full	late	below
hard	clean	slow	quiet	old	nice

Example:
My car was **dirty**, but now it's **clean**.

1. Sometimes my cat is naughty, and sometimes she's <u>nice</u>.
2. The sign said, "Closed," but the door was <u>open</u>.
3. Is the glass half empty or half <u>full</u>?
4. I bought new shoes, but I like my <u>old</u> ones better.
5. Skating is easy for me, but <u>hard</u> for my brother.
6. The sky is dark at night and <u>light</u> during the day.
7. I like a noisy house, but my mother likes a <u>quiet</u> one.
8. My friend says I'm wrong, but I say I'm <u>right</u>.
9. Jason is a fast runner, but Adam is a <u>slow</u> runner.
10. We were supposed to be early, but we were <u>late</u>.

Page 199

Antonyms

Directions: Write the antonym pairs from each sentence in the boxes.

Example: Many things are bought and sold at the market.

bought	sold

1. I thought I lost my dog, but someone found him.

lost	found

2. The teacher will ask questions for the students to answer.

ask	answer

3. Airplanes arrive and depart from the airport.

arrive	depart

4. The water in the pool was cold compared to the warm water in the whirlpool.

cold	warm

5. The tortoise was slow, but the hare was fast.

slow	fast

Grade 3 - Comprehensive Curriculum

ANSWER KEY

Page 200

Synonyms

Synonyms are words with nearly the same meaning.

Directions: Draw a line to match each word on the left with its synonym on the right.

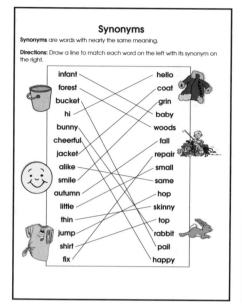

infant	hello
forest	coat
bucket	grin
hi	baby
bunny	woods
cheerful	fall
jacket	repair
alike	small
smile	same
autumn	hop
little	skinny
thin	top
jump	rabbit
shirt	pail
fix	happy

Page 201

Synonyms

Directions: Read each sentence. Choose a word from the box that has the same meaning as the bold word. Write the synonym on the line next to the sentence. The first one has been done for you.

skinniest	biggest	jacket	little		quickly	woods	joyful
grin	alike	trip	rabbit	fix	autumn	infant

1. The deer ran through the **forest**. __woods__
2. White mice are very **small** pets. __little__
3. Goldfish move **fast** in the water. __quickly__
4. The twins look exactly the **same**. __alike__
5. Trees lose their leaves in the **fall**. __autumn__
6. The blue whale is the **largest** animal on Earth. __biggest__
7. We will go to the ocean on our next **vacation**. __trip__
8. The **bunny** hopped through the tall grass. __rabbit__
9. The **baby** was crying because it was hungry. __infant__
10. Put on your **coat** before you go outside. __jacket__
11. Does that clown have a big **smile** on his face? __grin__
12. That is the **thinnest** man I have ever seen. __skinniest__
13. I will **repair** my bicycle as soon as I get home. __fix__
14. The children made **happy** sounds when they won. __joyful__

Page 202

Synonyms

Directions: Match the pairs of synonyms.

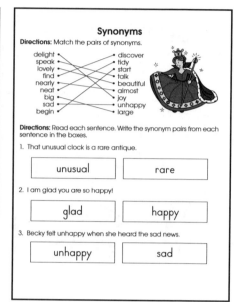

delight	discover
speak	tidy
lovely	start
find	talk
nearly	beautiful
neat	almost
big	joy
sad	unhappy
begin	large

Directions: Read each sentence. Write the synonym pairs from each sentence in the boxes.

1. That unusual clock is a rare antique.

unusual	rare

2. I am glad you are so happy!

glad	happy

3. Becky felt unhappy when she heard the sad news.

unhappy	sad

Page 203

Homophones

Homophones are words that sound the same but are spelled differently and have different meanings.
Example:

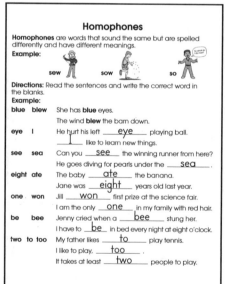

sew   sow   so

Directions: Read the sentences and write the correct word in the blanks.
Example:

blue	blew	She has __blue__ eyes.
		The wind __blew__ the barn down.
eye	I	He hurt his left __eye__ playing ball. __I__ like to learn new things.
see	sea	Can you __see__ the winning runner from here? He goes diving for pearls under the __sea__.
eight	ate	The baby __ate__ the banana. Jane was __eight__ years old last year.
one	won	Jill __won__ first prize at the science fair. I am the only __one__ in my family with red hair.
be	bee	Jenny cried when a __bee__ stung her. I have to __be__ in bed every night at eight o'clock.
two	to	too	My father likes __to__ play tennis. I like to play, __too__. It takes at least __two__ people to play.

Page 204

Homophones

Directions: Circle the correct word to complete each sentence. Then write the word on the line.

1. I am going to __write__ a letter to my grandmother. right (write)
2. Draw a circle around the __right__ answer. (right) write
3. Wait an __hour__ before going swimming. our, (hour)
4. This is __our__ house. (our) hour
5. He got a __beet__ from his garden. beat, (beet)
6. Our football team __beat__ that team. (beat) beet
7. Go to the store and __buy__ a loaf of bread. by, (buy)
8. We will drive __by__ your house. (by) buy
9. It will be trouble if the dog __sees__ the cat. seas, (sees)
10. They sailed the seven __seas__. (seas) sees
11. We have __two__ cars in the garage. to, too, (two)
12. I am going __to__ the zoo today. (to) too, two
13. My little brother is going, __too__. to, (too), two

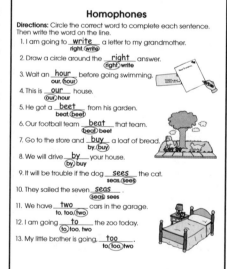

Page 205

Homophones

Homophones are words that sound the same but have different spellings and meanings.

Directions: Complete each sentence using a word from the box.

blew	night	blue	knight	hour	in	ant	inn
our	aunt	meet	too	two	to	meat

1. A red __ant__ crawled up the wall.
2. It will be one __hour__ before we can go back home.
3. Will you __meet__ us later?
4. We plan to stay at an __inn__ during our trip.
5. The king had a __knight__ who fought bravely.
6. The wind __blew__ so hard that I almost lost my hat.
7. His jacket was __blue__.
8. My __aunt__ plans to visit us this week.
9. I will come __in__ when it gets too cold outside.
10. It was late at __night__ when we finally got there.
11. __Two__ of us will go with you.
12. I will mail a note __to__ someone at the bank.
13. Do you eat red __meat__?
14. We would like to join you, __too__.
15. Come over to see __our__ new cat.

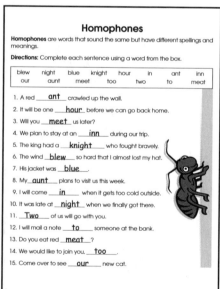

Grade 3 - Comprehensive Curriculum

Page 206

Homophones

Directions: Circle the words that are not used correctly. Write the correct word above the circled word. Use the words in the box to help you. The first one has been done for you.

road	see	one	be	so	I	brakes	piece	there
wait	not	some	hour	would	no	deer	you	heard

Jake and his family were getting close to Grandpa's. It had taken them

nearly an **hour** ~~out~~ to get ~~their~~ but Jake knew it was worth it. In his mind, he could **there**

already ~~sea~~ **see** the pond and could almost feel the cool water. It had been ~~sew~~ **so**

hot this summer in the apartment.

"~~Wood~~ **Would** ~~ewe~~ **you** like a ~~peace~~ **piece** of my apple, Jake?" asked his big sister Clare.

"~~Eye~~ **I** can't eat any more."

"~~No~~ **No**, thank you," Jake replied. "I still have ~~sum~~ **some** of my fruit left."

Suddenly, Dad slammed on the ~~brakes~~ **brakes**. "Did you see that ~~dear~~ **deer** on the ~~rode~~ **road**?"

I always ~~herd~~ **heard** that if you see ~~won~~ **one** there might ~~bee~~ **be** more."

"Good thinking, Dad. I'm glad you are a safe **not**

driver. We're ~~knot~~ very far from **wait**

Grandpa's now. I can't ~~weight~~ **wait**!"

Page 207

Nouns

Nouns are words that tell the names of people, places or things.
Directions: Read the words below. Then write them in the correct column.

goat	Mrs. Jackson	girl
beach	tree	song
mouth	park	Jean Rivers
finger	flower	New York
Kevin Jones	Elm City	Frank Gates
Main Street	theater	skates
River Park	father	boy

Person	Place	Thing
Kevin Jones	beach	goat
Mrs. Jackson	Main Street	mouth
father	River Park	finger
girl	park	tree
Jean Rivers	Elm City	flower
Frank Gates	theater	song
boy	New York	skates

Page 208

Common Nouns

Common nouns are nouns that name any member of a group of people, places or things, rather than specific people, places or things.

Directions: Read the sentences below and write the common noun found in each sentence.

Example: __socks__ My socks do not match.

1. __bird__ The bird could not fly.
2. __jelly beans__ Ben likes to eat jelly beans.
3. __mother__ I am going to meet my mother.
4. __lake__ We will go swimming in the lake tomorrow.
5. __flowers__ I hope the flowers will grow quickly.
6. __eggs__ We colored eggs together.
7. __bicycle__ It is easy to ride a bicycle.
8. __cousin__ My cousin is very tall.
9. __boat__ Ted and Jane went fishing in their boat.
10. __prize__ They won a prize yesterday.
11. __ankle__ She fell down and twisted her ankle.
12. __brother__ My brother was born today.
13. __slide__ She went down the slide.
14. __doctor__ Ray went to the doctor today.

Page 209

Proper Nouns

Proper nouns are names of specific people, places or things. Proper nouns begin with a capital letter.

Directions: Read the sentences below and circle the proper nouns found in each sentence.

Example: (Aunt Frances) gave me a puppy for my birthday.

1. We lived on (Jackson Street) before we moved to our new house.
2. (Angela's) birthday party is tomorrow night.
3. We drove through (Cheyenne, Wyoming) on our way home.
4. (Dr. Charles) always gives me a treat for not crying.
5. (George Washington) was our first president.
6. Our class took a field trip to the (Johnson Flower Farm).
7. (Uncle Jack) lives in (New York City).
8. (Amy) and (Elizabeth) are best friends.
9. We buy doughnuts at the (Grayson Bakery).
10. My favorite movie is (E.T.).
11. We flew to (Miami, Florida) in a plane.
12. We go to (Riverfront Stadium) to watch the baseball games.
13. (Mr. Fields) is a wonderful music teacher.
14. My best friend is (Tom Dunlap).

Page 210

Proper Nouns

Directions: Rewrite each sentence, capitalizing the proper nouns.

1. mike's birthday is in september.

Mike's birthday is in September.

2. aunt katie lives in detroit, michigan.

Aunt Katie lives in Detroit, Michigan.

3. in july, we went to canada.

In July, we went to Canada.

4. kathy jones moved to utah in january.

Kathy Jones moved to Utah in January.

5. My favorite holiday is valentine's day in february.

My favorite holiday is Valentine's Day in February.

6. On friday, mr. polzin gave the smith family a tour.

On Friday, Mr. Polzin gave the Smith family a tour.

7. saturday, uncle cliff and I will go to the mall of america in minnesota.

Saturday, Uncle Cliff and I will go to the Mall of America in Minnesota.

Page 211

Proper Nouns

Directions: Write about you! Write a proper noun for each category below. Capitalize the first letter of each proper noun.

1. Your first name: _____
2. Your last name: _____
3. Your street: _____
4. Your city: _____
5. Your state: _____
6. Your school: _____
7. Your best friend's name: _____
8. Your teacher: _____
9. Your favorite book character: _____
10. Your favorite vacation place: _____

Answers will vary.

ANSWER KEY

Page 212

Common and Proper Nouns

Directions: Look at the list of nouns in the box. Write the common nouns under the kite. Write the proper nouns under the balloons. Remember to capitalize the first letter of each proper noun.

lisa smith
cats
shoelace
saturday
dr. martin
whistle
teddy bears
main street
may
boy
lawn chair
mary stewart
bird
florida
school
apples
washington, d.c.
pine cone
elizabeth jones
charley reynolds

cats
shoelace
whistle
teddy bears
boy
lawn chair
bird
school
apples
pine cone

Lisa Smith
Saturday
Dr. Martin
Main Street
Mary Stewart
Florida
Washington, D.C.
May
Elizabeth Jones
Charley Reynolds

Page 213

Plural Nouns

A **plural** is more than one person, place or thing. We usually add an **s** to show that a noun names more than one. If a noun ends in **x, ch, sh** or **s**, we add an **es** to the word.

Example: pizza   pizzas

Directions: Write the plural of the words below.

Example: dog + s = dogs
cat — cats
boot — boots
house — houses

Example: peach + es = peaches
lunch — lunches
bunch — bunches
punch — punches

Example: ax + es = axes
fox — foxes
tax — taxes
box — boxes

Example: glass + es = glasses
mess — messes
guess — guesses
class — classes

Example: dish + es = dishes
bush — bushes
ash — ashes
brush — brushes

walrus
walruses

Page 214

Plural Nouns

To write the plural forms of words ending in **y**, we change the **y** to **ie** and add **s**.

Example: pony   ponies

Directions: Write the plural of each noun on the lines below.

berry — berries
cherry — cherries
bunny — bunnies
penny — pennies
family — families
candy — candies
party — parties

Now, write a story using some of the words that end in **y**. Remember to use capital letters and periods.

Answers will vary.

Page 215

Plural Nouns

Directions: Write the plural of each noun to complete the sentences below. Remember to change the y to ie before you add s!

1. I am going to two birthday **parties** this week.
(party)

2. Sandy picked some **cherries** for Mom's pie.
(cherry)

3. At the store, we saw lots of **bunnies**.
(bunny)

4. My change at the candy store was three **pennies**.
(penny)

5. All the **ladies** baked cookies for the bake sale.
(lady)

6. Thanksgiving is a special time for **families** to gather together.
(family)

7. Boston and New York are very large **cities**.
(city)

Page 216

Plural Nouns

Some words have special plural forms.

Example: leaf   leaves

tooth	teeth
child	children
foot	feet
mouse	mice
woman	women
man	men

Directions: Some of the words in the box are special plurals. Complete each sentence with a plural from the box. Then write the letters from the boxes in the blanks below to solve the puzzle.

1. I lost my two front t e e[t] h!

2. My sister has two pet m i c e.

3. Her favorite book is Little W o m e n.

4. The circus clown had big f e e[t].

5. The teacher played a game with the
c h[i] l d r e n.

Take good care of this pearly plural!
t e e t h
1 2 3 4 5

Page 217

Plural Nouns

Directions: The **singular form** of a word shows one person, place or thing. Write the singular form of each noun on the lines below.

cherries — cherry
lunches — lunch
countries — country
leaves — leaf
churches — church
arms — arm
boxes — box
men — man
wheels — wheel
pictures — picture
cities — city
places — place
ostriches — ostrich
glasses — glass

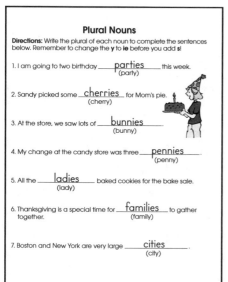

Grade 3 - Comprehensive Curriculum

494

Page 218

Possessive Nouns

Possessive nouns tell who or what is the owner of something. With singular nouns, we use an apostrophe **before** the s. With plural nouns, we use an apostrophe **after** the s.

Example:
singular: one elephant
The **elephant's** dance was wonderful.
plural: more than one elephant
The **elephants'** dance was wonderful.

Directions: Put the apostrophe in the correct place in each bold word. Then write the word in the blank.

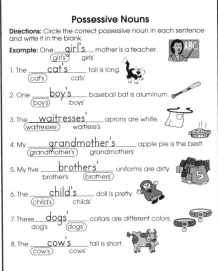

1. The **lion's** cage was big. _lion's or lions'_
2. The **bears'** costumes were purple. _bears'_
3. One **boy's** laughter was very loud. _boy's_
4. The **trainer's** dogs were dancing about. _trainer's or trainers'_
5. The **man's** popcorn was tasty and good. _man's_
6. **Mark's** cotton candy was delicious. _Mark's_
7. A little **girl's** balloon burst in the air. _girl's_
8. The big **clown's** tricks were very funny. _clown's or clowns'_
9. **Laura's** sister clapped for the clowns. _Laura's_
10. The **woman's** money was lost in the crowd. _woman's_
11. **Kelly's** mother picked her up early. _Kelly's_

Page 219

Possessive Nouns

Directions: Circle the correct possessive noun in each sentence and write it in the blank.

Example: One ___girl's___ mother is a teacher.
(girl's) girls'

1. The ___cat's___ tail is long.
(cat's) cats'
2. One ___boy's___ baseball bat is aluminum.
(boy's) boys'
3. The ___waitresses'___ aprons are white.
(waitresses') waitress's
4. My ___grandmother's___ apple pie is the best!
(grandmother's) grandmothers'
5. My five ___brothers'___ uniforms are dirty.
brother's (brothers')
6. The ___child's___ doll is pretty.
(child's) childs'
7. These ___dogs'___ collars are different colors.
dog's (dogs')
8. The ___cow's___ tail is short.
(cow's) cows'

Page 220

Pronouns

Pronouns are words that are used in place of nouns.
Examples: he, she, it, they, him, them, her, him

Directions: Read each sentence. Write the pronoun that takes the place of each noun.

Example:
The **monkey** dropped the banana. _It_

1. **Dad** washed the car last night. _He_
2. **Mary and David** took a walk in the park. _They_
3. **Peggy** spent the night at her grandmother's house. _She_
4. The baseball **players** lost their game. _they_
5. **Mike Van Meter** is a great soccer player. _He_
6. The **parrot** can say five different words. _It_
7. **Megan** wrote a story in class today. _She_
8. They gave a party for **Teresa**. _her_
9. Everyone in the class was happy for **Ted**. _him_
10. The children petted the **giraffe**. _it_
11. Linda put the **kittens** near the warm stove. _them_
12. **Gina** made a chocolate cake for my birthday. _She_
13. **Pete and Matt** played baseball on the same team. _They_
14. Give the books to **Herbie**. _him_

Page 221

Pronouns

Singular Pronouns	Plural Pronouns
I me my mine	we us our ours
you your yours	you your yours
he she it her	they them their theirs
hers his its him	

Directions: Underline the pronouns in each sentence.

1. Mom told <u>us</u> to wash <u>our</u> hands.
2. Did <u>you</u> go to the store?
3. <u>We</u> should buy <u>him</u> a present.
4. <u>I</u> called <u>you</u> about <u>their</u> party.
5. <u>Our</u> house had damage on <u>its</u> roof.
6. <u>They</u> want to give <u>you</u> a prize at <u>our</u> party.
7. <u>My</u> cat ate <u>her</u> sandwich.
8. <u>Your</u> coat looks like <u>his</u> coat.

Page 222

Pronouns

We use the pronouns **I** and **we** when talking about the person or people doing the action.
Example: I can roller skate. **We** can roller skate.
We use **me** and **us** when talking about something that is happening to a person or people.
Example: They gave **me** the roller skates.
They gave **us** the roller skates.

Directions: Circle the correct pronoun and write it in the blank.

Example:
___We___ are going to the picnic together. (We) Us

1. ___I___ am finished with my science project. (I) Me
2. Eric passed the football to ___me___. (me) I
3. They ate dinner with ___us___ last night. we (us)
4. ___I___ like spinach better than ice cream. (I) Me
5. Mom came in the room to tell ___me___ good night. (me) I
6. ___We___ had a pizza party in our backyard. Us (We)
7. They told ___us___ the good news. (us) we
8. Tom and ___I___ went to the store. me (I)
9. She is taking ___me___ with her to the movies. I (me)
10. Katie and ___I___ are good friends. (I) me

Page 223

Possessive Pronouns

Possessive pronouns show ownership.
Example: his hat, **her** shoes, **our** dog
We can use these pronouns before a noun:
my, our, you, his, her, its, their
Example: That is **my** bike.
We can use these pronouns on their own:
mine, yours, ours, his, hers, theirs, its
Example: That is **mine**.

Directions: Write each sentence again, using a pronoun instead of the words in bold letters. Be sure to use capitals and periods.

Example:
My **dog's** bowl is brown.   **Its** bowl is brown.

1. That is **Lisa's** book. _That is her book._
2. This is **my pencil**. _This is mine._
3. This hat is **your hat**. _This hat is yours._
4. Fifi is **Kevin's** cat. _Fifi is his cat._
5. That beautiful house is **our home**.
That beautiful house is ours.
6. The **gerbil's** cage is too small.
Its cage is too small.

Grade 3 - Comprehensive Curriculum

Page 224

Abbreviations

An **abbreviation** is the shortened form of a word. Most abbreviations begin with a capital letter and end with a period.

Mr.	Mister	St.	Street
Mrs.	Missus	Ave.	Avenue
Dr.	Doctor	Blvd.	Boulevard
A.M.	before noon	Rd.	Road
P.M.	after noon		

Days of the week: Sun. Mon. Tues. Wed. Thurs. Fri. Sat.
Months of the year: Jan. Feb. Mar. Apr. Aug. Sept. Oct. Nov. Dec.

Directions: Write the abbreviations for each word.

street	St.	doctor	Dr.	Tuesday	Tues.
road	Rd.	mister	Mr.	avenue	Ave.
missus	Mrs.	October	Oct.	Friday	Fri.
before noon	A.M.	March	Mar.	August	Aug.

Directions: Write each sentence using abbreviations.

1. On Monday at 9:00 before noon Mister Jones had a meeting.

On Mon. at 9:00 A.M., Mr. Jones had a meeting.

2. In December Doctor Carlson saw Missus Zuckerman.

In Dec., Dr. Carlson saw Mrs. Zuckerman.

3. One Tuesday in August Mister Wood went to the park.

One Tues. in Aug., Mr. Wood went to the park.

Page 225

Adjectives

Adjectives are words that tell more about nouns, such as a **happy** child, a **cold** day or a **hard** problem. Adjectives can tell how many (**one** airplane) or which one (**those** shoes).
Directions: The nouns are in bold letters. Circle the adjectives that describe the nouns.

Example: Some people have (unusual) **pets.**

1. Some people keep (wild) **animals**, like lions and bears.
2. (These) **pets** need special care.
3. (These) **animals** want to be free when they get older.
4. Even (small) **animals** can be difficult if they are wild.
5. Raccoons and squirrels are not (tame) **pets.**
6. Never touch a (wild) **animal** that may be sick.

Complete the story below by writing in your own adjectives. Use your imagination.

My Cat

My cat is a very _____ animal. She ha__

and _____ fur. Her _____ ball.

She has _____ ___ a _____ tail.

She has a _____ face and _____ whiskers.

I think she is the _____ cat in the world!

Answers will vary.

Page 226

Adjectives

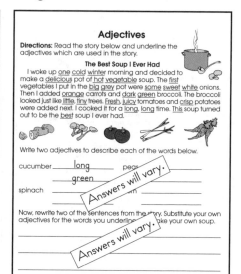

Directions: Read the story below and underline the adjectives which are used in the story.

The Best Soup I Ever Had

I woke up one cold winter morning and decided to make a delicious pot of hot vegetable soup. The first vegetables I put in the big grey pot were some sweet white onions. Then I added orange carrots and dark green broccoli. The broccoli looked just like little, tiny trees. Fresh, juicy tomatoes and crisp potatoes were added next. I cooked it for a long, long time. This soup turned out to be the best soup I ever had.

Write two adjectives to describe each of the words below.

cucumber _____ long _____ peas _____
_____ green _____
spinach _____ _____

Answers will vary.

Now, rewrite two of the sentences from the story. Substitute your own adjectives for the words you underline. Make your own soup.

Answers will vary.

Page 227

Adjectives and Nouns

Directions: Underline the nouns in each sentence below. Then draw an arrow from each adjective to the noun it describes.
Example:

A platypus is a furry animal that lives in Australia.

1. This animal likes to swim.
2. The nose looks like a duck's bill.
3. It has a broad tail like a beaver.
4. Platypuses are great swimmers.
5. They have webbed feet which help them swim.
6. Their flat tails also help them move through the water.
7. The platypus is an unusual mammal because it lays eggs.
8. The eggs look like reptile eggs.
9. Platypuses can lay three eggs at a time.
10. These babies do not leave their mothers for one year.
11. This animal spends most of its time hunting near streams.

Page 228

Adjectives

A chart of adjectives can also be used to help describe nouns.

Directions: Look at the pictures. Complete each chart.

Example:

Noun	What Color?	What Size?	What Number?
flower	red	small	two

Noun	What Color?	What Size?	What Number?
elephants	gray	large	two

Noun	What Color?	What Size?	What Number?
turtles	green	small	four

Noun	What Color?	What Size?	What Number?
tree	green	large	one

Page 229

Prefixes

Prefixes are special word parts added to the beginnings of words. Prefixes change the meaning of words.

Prefix	Meaning	Example
un	not	**un**happy
re	again	**re**do
pre	before	**pre**view
mis	wrong	**mis**understanding
dis	opposite	**dis**obey

Directions: Circle the word that begins with a prefix. Then write the prefix and the root word.

1. The dog was (unfriendly). __un__ + __friendly__
2. The movie (preview) was interesting. __pre__ + __view__
3. The referee called an (unfair) penalty. __un__ + __fair__
4. Please do not (misbehave). __mis__ + __behave__
5. My parents (disapprove) of that show. __dis__ + __approve__
6. I had to (redo) the assignment. __re__ + __do__

Page 230

Suffixes

Suffixes are word parts added to the ends of words. Suffixes change the meaning of words.

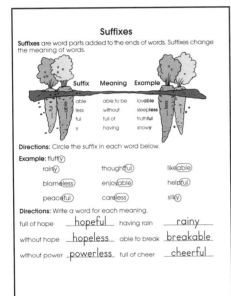

	Suffix	Meaning	Example
	able	able to be	lov**able**
	less	without	sleep**less**
	ful	full of	truth**ful**
	y	having	snow**y**

Directions: Circle the suffix in each word below.

Example: fluff(y)

rain(y)   thought(ful)   like(able)

blame(less)   enjoy(able)   help(ful)

peace(ful)   care(less)   silk(y)

Directions: Write a word for each meaning.

full of hope __hopeful__   having rain __rainy__

without hope __hopeless__   able to break __breakable__

without power __powerless__ full of cheer __cheerful__

Page 231

Verbs

A **verb** is the action word in a sentence, the word that tells what something does or that something exists. **Examples: run, jump, skip.**

Directions: Draw a box around the verb in each sentence below.

1. Spiders [spin] webs of silk.
2. A spider [waits] in the center of the web for its meals.
3. A spider [sinks] its sharp fangs into insects.
4. Spiders [eat] many insects.
5. Spiders [make] their nests with silk.
6. Female spiders [wrap] silk around their eggs to [protect] them.

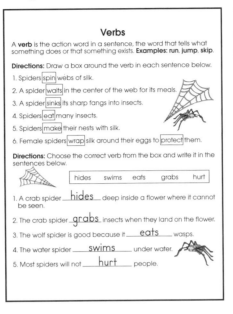

Directions: Choose the correct verb from the box and write it in the sentences below.

| hides | swims | eats | grabs | hurt |

1. A crab spider __hides__ deep inside a flower where it cannot be seen.
2. The crab spider __grabs__ insects when they land on the flower.
3. The wolf spider is good because it __eats__ wasps.
4. The water spider __swims__ under water.
5. Most spiders will not __hurt__ people.

Page 232

Verbs

When a verb tells what one person or thing is doing now, it usually ends in **s. Example:** She sing**s**.

When a verb is used with **you, I** or **we,** we do not add an **s.**

Example: I **sing.**

Directions: Write the correct verb in each sentence.

Example:

I __write__ a newspaper about our street.   **writes, write**

1. My sister __helps__ me sometimes.   **helps, help**
2. She __draws__ the pictures.   **draw, draws**
3. We __deliver__ them together.   **delivers, deliver**
4. I __tell__ the news about all the people. **tell, tells**
5. Mr. Macon __grows__ the most beautiful flowers. **grow, grows**
6. Mrs. Jones __talks__ to her plants.   **talks, talk**
7. Kevin Turner __lets__ his dog loose everyday. **lets, let**
8. Little Mikey Smith __gets__ lost once a week. **get, gets**
9. You may __think__ I live on an interesting street. **thinks, think**
10. We __say__ it's the best street in town. **say, says**

Page 233

Helping Verbs

A **helping verb** is a word used with an action verb.

Examples: might, shall and **are**

Directions: Write a helping verb from the box with each action verb.

can	could	must	might
may	would	should	will
shall	did	does	do
had	have	has	am
are	were	is	
be	being	been	

Example: Answers will vary but may include:

Tomorrow, I __might__ play soccer.

1. Mom __may__ buy my new soccer shoes tonight.
2. Yesterday, my old soccer shoes __were__ ripped by the cat.
3. I __am__ going to ask my brother to go to the game.
4. He usually __does__ not like soccer.
5. But, he __will__ go with me because I am his sister.
6. He __has__ promised to watch the entire soccer game.
7. He has __been__ helping me with my homework.
8. I __can__ spell a lot better because of his help.
9. Maybe I __could__ finish the semester at the top of my class.

Page 234

Past-Tense Verbs

The **past tense** of a verb tells about something that has already happened. We add a **d** or an **ed** to most verbs to show that something has already happened.

Directions: Use the verb from the first sentence to complete the second sentence.

Example:

Please **walk** the dog.   I already __walked__ her.

1. The flowers look good.   They __looked__ better yesterday.
2. Please accept my gift.   I __accepted__ it for my sister.
3. I wonder who will win.   I __wondered__ about it all night.
4. He will saw the wood.   He __sawed__ some last week.
5. Fold the paper neatly.   She __folded__ her paper.
6. Let's cook outside tonight. We __cooked__ outside last night.
7. Do not block the way.   They __blocked__ the entire street.
8. Form the clay this way.   He __formed__ it into a ball.
9. Follow my car.   We __followed__ them down the street.
10. Glue the pages like this. She __glued__ the flowers on.

Page 235

Present-Tense Verbs

The **present tense** of a verb tells about something that is happening now, happens often or is about to happen. These verbs can be written two ways: The bird sing**s**. The bird is sing**ing**.

Directions: Write each sentence again, using the verb **is** and writing the **ing** form of the verb.

Example: He cooks the cheeseburgers.

__He is cooking the cheeseburgers.__

1. Sharon dances to that song.

__Sharon is dancing to that song.__

2. Frank washed the car.

__Frank is washing the car.__

3. Mr. Benson smiles at me.

__Mr. Benson is smiling at me.__

Write a verb for the sentences below that tells something that is happening now. Be sure to use the verb **is** and the **ing** form of the verb.

Example: The big, brown dog __is barking__

1. The little baby _____

2. Most nine-year-olds _____

3. The monster on television _____

Answers will vary.

Page 236

Future-Tense Verbs

The **future tense** of a verb tells about something that has not happened yet but will happen in the future. **Will** or **shall** are usually used with future tense.

Directions: Change the verb tense in each sentence to future tense.

Example: She cooks dinner.
She will cook dinner.

1. He plays baseball.
He will play baseball.

2. She walks to school.
She will walk to school.

3. Bobby talks to the teacher.
Bobby will talk to the teacher.

4. I remember to vote.
I will remember to vote.

5. Jack mows the lawn every week.
Jack will mow the lawn every week.

6. We go on vacation soon.
We will go on vacation soon.

Page 237

Review

Verb tenses can be in the past, present or future.

Directions: Match each sentence with the correct verb tense. (Think: When did each thing happen?)

It will rain tomorrow. — past
He played golf. — present
Molly is sleeping. — future

Jack is singing a song. — past
I shall buy a kite. — present
Dad worked hard today. — future

Past
Present
Future

Directions: Change the verb to the tense shown.

1. Jenny played with her new friend. (present)
Jenny is playing with her new friend.

2. Bobby is talking to him. (future)
Bobby will talk to him.

3. Holly and Angie walk here. (past)
Holly and Angie walked here.

Page 238

Irregular Verbs

Irregular verbs are verbs that do not change from the present tense to the past tense in the regular way with **d** or **ed**.

Example: sing, **sang**

Directions: Read the sentence and underline the verbs. Choose the past-tense form from the box and write it next to the sentence.

blow — blew	fly — flew
come — came	give — gave
take — took	wear — wore
make — made	sing — sang
grow — grew	

Example:
Dad will <u>make</u> a cake tonight. — made

1. I will probably <u>grow</u> another inch this year. — grew
2. I will <u>blow</u> out the candles. — blew
3. Everyone will <u>give</u> me presents. — gave
4. I will <u>wear</u> my favorite red shirt. — wore
5. My cousins will <u>come</u> from out of town. — came
6. It will <u>take</u> them four hours. — took
7. My Aunt Betty will <u>fly</u> in from Cleveland. — flew
8. She will <u>sing</u> me a song when she gets here. — sang

Page 239

Irregular Verbs

Directions: Circle the verb that completes each sentence.

1. Scientists will try to (find) found the cure.

2. Eric brings (brought) his lunch to school yesterday.

3. Everyday, Betsy (sings) sang all the way home.

4. Jason breaks (broke) the vase last night.

5. The ice had freezes (frozen) in the tray.

6. Mitzi has swims (swum) in that pool before.

7. Now I (choose) chose to exercise daily.

8. The teacher has rings (rung) the bell.

9. The boss speaks (spoke) to us yesterday.

10. She says (said) it twice already.

Page 240

Irregular Verbs

The verb **be** is different from all other verbs. The present-tense forms of **be** are **am, is** and **are**. The past-tense forms of **be** are **was** and **were**. The verb **to be** is written in the following ways:

singular: I am, you are, he is, she is, it is
plural: we are, you are, they are

Directions: Choose the correct form of **be** from the words in the box and write it in each sentence.

are	am	is	was	were

Example: Answers will vary, but may include:
I **am** feeling good at this moment.

1. My sister **is** a good singer.
2. You **are** going to the store with me.
3. Sandy **was** at the movies last week.
4. Rick and Tom **are** best friends.
5. He **is** happy about the surprise.
6. The cat **is** hungry.
7. I **am** going to the ball game.
8. They **are** silly.
9. I **am** glad to help my mother.

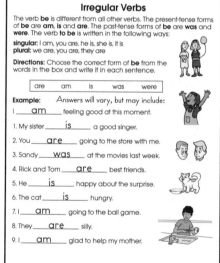

Page 241

Linking Verbs

Linking verbs connect the noun to a descriptive word. Linking verbs are often forms of the verb **be**.

Directions: The linking verb is underlined in each sentence. Circle the two words that are being connected.

Example: The (cat) <u>is</u> (fat).

1. My favorite (food) <u>is</u> (pizza).

2. The (car) <u>was</u> (red).

3. (I) <u>am</u> (tired).

4. (Books) <u>are</u> (fun).

5. The (garden) <u>is</u> (beautiful).

6. (Pears) <u>taste</u> (juicy).

7. The (airplane) <u>looks</u> (large).

8. (Rabbits) <u>are</u> (furry).

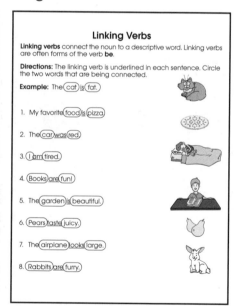

Page 242

Adverbs

Adverbs are words that describe verbs. They tell where, how or when.

Directions: Circle the adverb in each of the following sentences.

Example: The doctor worked (carefully.)

1. The skater moved (gracefully) across the ice.
2. Their call was returned (quickly.)
3. We (easily) learned the new words.
4. He did the work (perfectly.)
5. She lost her purse (somewhere.)

Directions: Complete the sentences below by writing your own adverbs in the blanks.

Example: The bees worked _____ busily

1. The dog barked _____
2. The baby smiled _____
3. She wrote her name _____ *Answers may vary.*
4. The horse ran _____

Page 243

Adverbs

Directions: Read each sentence. Then answer the questions on the lines below.

Example: Charles ate hungrily.

who? __Charles__
what? __ate__
how? __hungrily__

1. She dances slowly.

who? __She__
what? __dances__
how? __slowly__

2. The girl spoke carefully.

who? __girl__
what? __spoke__
how? __carefully__

3. My brother ran quickly.

who? __brother__
what? __ran__
how? __quickly__

4. Jean walks home often.

who? __Jean__
what? __walks__
when? __often__

5. The children played there.

who? __children__
what? __played__
where? __there__

Page 244

Prepositions

Prepositions show relationships between the noun or pronoun and another noun in the sentence. The preposition comes before that noun.

Example: The book is (on) the table.

Common Prepositions				
above	behind	by	near	over
across	below	in	off	through
around	beside	inside	on	under

Directions: Circle the prepositions in each sentence.

1. The dog ran fast (around) the house.
2. The plates (in) the cupboard were clean.
3. Put the card (inside) the envelope.
4. The towel (on) the sink was wet.
5. I planted flowers (in) my garden.
6. My kite flew high (above) the trees.
7. The chair (near) the counter was sticky.
8. (Under) the ground, worms lived (in) their homes.
9. I put the bow (around) the box.
10. (Beside) the pond, there was a playground.

Page 245

Articles

Articles are words used before nouns. **A**, **an** and **the** are articles. We use **a** before words that begin with a consonant. We use **an** before words that begin with a vowel.

Example: a peach   an apple

Directions: Write **a** or **an** in the sentences below.

Example: My bike had ___a___ flat tire.

1. They brought ___a___ goat to the farm.
2. My mom wears ___an___ old pair of shoes to mow the lawn.
3. We had ___a___ party for my grandfather.
4. Everybody had ___an___ ice-cream cone after the game.
5. We bought ___a___ picnic table for our backyard.
6. We saw ___a___ lion sleeping in the shade.
7. It was ___an___ evening to be remembered.
8. He brought ___a___ blanket to the game.
9. ___An___ exit sign was above the door.
10. They went to ___an___ orchard to pick apples.
11. He ate ___an___ orange for lunch.

Page 246

Commas

Commas are used to separate words in a series of three or more.

Example: My favorite fruits are apples, bananas and oranges.

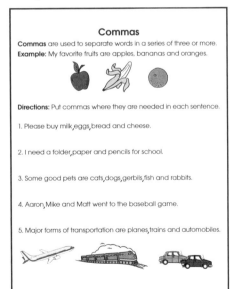

Directions: Put commas where they are needed in each sentence.

1. Please buy milk, eggs, bread and cheese.

2. I need a folder, paper and pencils for school.

3. Some good pets are cats, dogs, gerbils, fish and rabbits.

4. Aaron, Mike and Matt went to the baseball game.

5. Major forms of transportation are planes, trains and automobiles.

Page 247

Commas

We use commas to separate the day from the year.
Example: May 13, 1950

Directions: Write the dates in the blanks. Put the commas in and capitalize the name of each month.

Example:

Jack and Dave were born on february 22 1982.
_____ February 22, 1982

1. My father's birthday is may 19 1948.
_____ May 19, 1948

2. My sister was fourteen on december 13 1994.
_____ December 13, 1994

3. Lauren's seventh birthday was on november 30 1998.
_____ November 30, 1998

4. october 13 1996 was the last day I saw my lost cat.
_____ October 13, 1996

5. On april 17 1997, we saw the Grand Canyon.
_____ April 17, 1997

6. Our vacation lasted from april 2 1998 to april 26 1998.
_____ April 2, 1998   _____ April 26, 1998

7. Molly's baby sister was born on august 14 1991.
_____ August 14, 1991

8. My mother was born on june 22 1959.
_____ June 22, 1959

Page 248

Articles and Commas

Directions: Write **a** or **an** in each blank. Put commas where they are needed in the paragraphs below.

Owls

<u>An</u> owl is <u>a</u> bird of prey. This means it hunts small animals. Owls catch insects, fish and birds. Mice are <u>an</u> owl's favorite dinner. Owls like protected places, such as trees, burrows or barns. Owls make noises that sound like hoots, screeches or even barks. <u>An</u> owl's feathers may be black, brown, gray or white.

A Zoo for You

<u>A</u> zoo is <u>an</u> excellent place for keeping animals. Zoos have mammals, birds, reptiles and amphibians. Some zoos have domestic animals, such as rabbits, sheep and goats. Another name for this type of zoo is <u>a</u> petting zoo. In some zoos, elephants, lions and tigers live in open country. This is because <u>an</u> enormous animal needs open space for roaming.

Page 249

Capitalization

The names of **people**, **places** and **pets**, the **days of the week**, the **months of the year** and **holidays** begin with a capital letter.

Directions: Read the words in the box. Write the words in the correct column with capital letters at the beginning of each word.

ron polsky	tuesday	march	april
presidents' day	saturday	woofy	october
blackie	portland, oregon	corning, new york	molly yoder
valentine's day	fluffy	harold edwards	arbor day
bozeman, montana	sunday		

People	Places	Pets
Ron Polsky	Bozeman, Montana	Blackie
Harold Edwards	Portland, Oregon	Fluffy
Molly Yoder	Corning, New York	Woofy

Days	Months	Holidays
Tuesday	March	Valentine's Day
Saturday	April	Presidents' Day
Sunday	October	Arbor Day

Page 250

Capitalization and Commas

We capitalize the names of cities and states. We use a comma to separate the name of a city and a state.

Directions: Use capital letters and commas to write the names of the cities and states correctly.

Example:
sioux falls south dakota — <u>Sioux Falls, South Dakota</u>

1. plymouth massachusetts — <u>Plymouth, Massachusetts</u>
2. boston massachusetts — <u>Boston, Massachusetts</u>
3. philadelphia pennsylvania — <u>Philadelphia, Pennsylvania</u>
4. white plains new york — <u>White Plains, New York</u>
5. newport rhode island — <u>Newport, Rhode Island</u>
6. yorktown virginia — <u>Yorktown, Virginia</u>
7. nashville tennessee — <u>Nashville, Tennessee</u>
8. portland oregon — <u>Portland, Oregon</u>
9. mansfield ohio — <u>Mansfield, Ohio</u>

Page 251

Parts of Speech

Nouns, pronouns, verbs, adjectives, adverbs and prepositions are all **parts of speech**.

Directions: Label the words in each sentence with the correct part of speech.

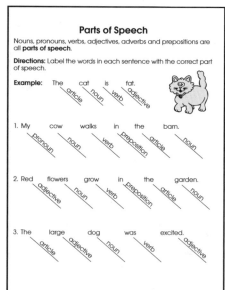

Example: The (article) cat (noun) is (verb) fat. (adjective)

1. My (pronoun) cow (noun) walks (verb) in (preposition) the (article) barn. (noun)

2. Red (adjective) flowers (noun) grow (verb) in (preposition) the (article) garden. (noun)

3. The (article) large (adjective) dog (noun) was (verb) excited. (adjective)

Page 252

Parts of Speech

Directions: Ask someone to give you nouns, verbs, adjectives and pronouns where shown. Write them in the blanks. Read the story to your friend when you finish.

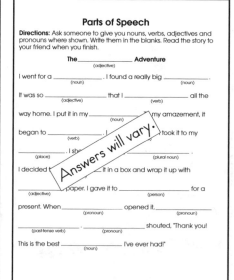

The _____ (adjective) Adventure

I went for a _____ (noun). I found a really big _____ (noun).

It was so _____ (adjective) that I _____ (verb) all the way home. I put it in my _____ (noun) my amazement, it began to _____ (verb) _____ took it to my _____ (place). I sh_____ _____ (plural noun)

I decided _____ it in a box and wrap it up with _____ (adjective) paper. I gave it to _____ (person) for a present. When _____ (pronoun) opened it, _____ (pronoun) _____ (past-tense verb) _____ (pronoun) shouted, "Thank you!

This is the best _____ (noun) I've ever had!"

Answers will vary.

Page 253

Parts of Speech

Directions: Write the part of speech of each underlined word.

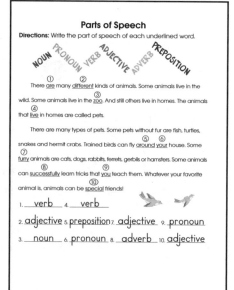

NOUN PRONOUN VERB ADJECTIVE ADVERB PREPOSITION

① There ②are many different kinds of animals. Some animals live in the wild. Some animals live in the ③zoo. And still others live in homes. The animals ④that live in homes are called pets.

There are many types of pets. Some pets without fur are fish, turtles, snakes and hermit crabs. Trained birds can fly ⑤around ⑥your house. Some ⑦furry animals are cats, dogs, rabbits, ferrets, gerbils or hamsters. Some animals can ⑧successfully learn tricks that ⑨you teach them. Whatever your favorite animal is, animals can be ⑩special friends!

1. <u>verb</u>   4. <u>verb</u>
2. <u>adjective</u> 5. <u>preposition</u> 7. <u>adjective</u> 9. <u>pronoun</u>
3. <u>noun</u> 6. <u>pronoun</u> 8. <u>adverb</u> 10. <u>adjective</u>

Page 254

And and But

We can use **and** or **but** to make one longer sentence from two short ones.

Directions: Use **and** or **but** to make two short sentences into a longer, more interesting one. Write the new sentence on the line below the two short sentences.

Example:
The skunk has black fur. The skunk has a white stripe.

The skunk has black fur and a white stripe.

1. The skunk has a small head. The skunk has small ears.

The skunk has a small head and small ears.

2. The skunk has short legs. Skunks can move quickly.

The skunk has short legs but can move easily.

3. Skunks sleep in hollow trees. Skunks sleep underground.

Skunks sleep in hollow trees and underground.

4. Skunks are chased by animals. Skunks do not run away.

Skunks are chased by animals but do not run away.

5. Skunks sleep during the day. Skunks hunt at night.

Skunks sleep during the day and hunt at night.

Page 255

Subjects

A **subject** tells who or what the sentence is about.

Directions: Underline the subject in the following sentences.

Example:
The zebra is a large animal.

1. Zebras live in Africa.
2. Zebras are related to horses.
3. Horses have longer hair than zebras.
4. Zebras are good runners.
5. Their feet are protected by their hooves.
6. Some animals live in groups.
7. These groups are called herds.
8. Zebras live in herds with other grazing animals.
9. Grazing animals eat mostly grass.
10. They usually eat three times a day.
11. They often travel to water holes.

Page 256

Simple Subjects

A **simple subject** is the main noun or pronoun in the complete subject.

Directions: Draw a line between the subject and the predicate. Circle the simple subject.

Example: The black (bear) lives in the zoo.

1. (Penguins) look like they wear tuxedos.
2. The (seal) enjoys raw fish.
3. The (monkeys) like to swing on bars.
4. The beautiful (peacock) has colorful feathers.
5. (Bats) like dark places.
6. Some (snakes) eat small rodents.
7. The orange and brown (giraffes) have long necks.
8. The baby (zebra) is close to his mother.

Page 257

Compound Subjects

Compound subjects are two or more nouns that have the same predicate.

Directions: Combine the subjects to create one sentence with a compound subject.

Example: Jill can swing
Whitney can swing.
Luke can swing.
Jill, Whitney and Luke can swing.

1. Roses grow in the garden. Tulips grow in the garden.

Roses and tulips grow in the garden.

2. Apples are fruit. Oranges are fruit. Bananas are fruit.

Apples, oranges and bananas are fruit.

3. Bears live in the zoo. Monkeys live in the zoo.

Bears and monkeys live in the zoo.

4. Jackets keep us warm. Sweaters keep us warm.

Jackets and sweaters keep us warm.

Page 258

Compound Subjects

Directions: Underline the simple subjects in each compound subject.

Example: Dogs and cats are good pets.

1. Blueberries and strawberries are fruit.
2. Jesse, Jake and Hannah like school.
3. Cows, pigs and sheep live on a farm.
4. Boys and girls ride the bus.
5. My family and I took a trip to Duluth.
6. Fruits and vegetables are good for you.
7. Katarina, Lexi and Mandi like to go swimming.
8. Petunias, impatiens, snapdragons and geraniums are all flowers.
9. Coffee, tea and milk are beverages.
10. Dave, Karla and Tami worked on the project together.

Page 259

Predicates

A **predicate** tells what the subject is doing, has done or will do.

Directions: Underline the predicate in the following sentences.

Example: Woodpeckers live in trees.

1. They hunt for insects in the trees.
2. Woodpeckers have strong beaks.
3. They can peck through the bark.
4. The pecking sound can be heard from far away.

Directions: Circle the groups of words that can be predicates.

(have long tongues)   (pick up insects)
hole in bark   sticky substance
(help it to climb trees) tree bark

Now, choose the correct predicates from above to finish these sentences.

1. Woodpeckers ___ have long tongues
2. They use their tongues to ___ pick up insects
3. Its strong feet ___ help it to climb trees

Page 260

Simple Predicates

A **simple predicate** is the main verb or verbs in the complete predicate.

Directions: Draw a line between the complete subject and the complete predicate. Circle the simple predicate.

Example: The ripe apples (fell) to the ground.

1. The farmer scattered feed for the chickens.

2. The horses galloped wildly around the corral.

3. The baby chicks were staying warm by the light.

4. The tractor was baling hay.

5. The silo was full of grain.

6. The cows were being milked.

7. The milk truck drove up to the barn.

8. The rooster woke everyone up.

Page 261

Compound Predicates

Compound predicates have two or more verbs that have the same subject.

Directions: Combine the predicates to create one sentence with a compound predicate.

Example: We went to the zoo.
We watched the monkeys.
We went to the zoo and watched the monkeys.

1. Students read their books. Students do their work.

Students read their books and do their work.

2. Dogs can bark loudly. Dogs can do tricks.

Dogs can bark loudly and do tricks.

3. The football player caught the ball. The football player ran.

The football player caught the ball and ran.

4. My dad sawed wood. My dad stacked wood.

My dad sawed and stacked wood.

5. My teddy bear is soft. My teddy bear likes to be hugged.

My teddy bear is soft and likes to be hugged.

Page 262

Compound Predicates

Directions: Underline the simple predicates (verbs) in each predicate.

Example: The fans clapped and cheered at the game.

1. The coach talks and encourages the team.

2. The cheerleaders jump and yell.

3. The basketball players dribble and shoot the ball.

4. The basketball bounces and hits the backboard.

5. The ball rolls around the rim and goes into the basket.

6. Everyone leaps up and cheers.

7. The team scores and wins!

Page 263

Subjects and Predicates

Directions: Write the words for the subject to answer the **who** or **what** questions. Write the words for the predicate to answer the **does**, **did**, **is** or **has** questions.

Example:

My friend has two pairs of sunglasses. who? __My friend__
has? __has two pairs of sunglasses.__

1. John's dog went to school with him. what? __John's dog__
did? __went to school with him.__

2. The Eskimo traveled by dog sled. who? __The Eskimo__
did? __traveled by dog sled.__

3. Alex slept in his treehouse last night. who? __Alex__
did? __slept in his treehouse last night__

4. Cherry pie is my favorite kind of pie. what? __Cherry pie__
is? __is my favorite kind of pie.__

5. The mail carrier brings the mail to the door. who? __The mail carrier__
does? __brings the mail to the door.__

6. We have more than enough bricks to build the wall. who? __We__
has? __have more than enough bricks to build the wall.__

7. The bird has a worm in its beak. what? __The bird__
has? __has a worm in its beak.__

Page 264

Subjects and Predicates

Directions: Every sentence has two main parts—the subject and the predicate. Draw one line under the subject and two lines under the predicate in each sentence below.

Example:
Porcupines are related to mice and rats.

1. They are large rodents.

2. Porcupines have long, sharp quills.

3. The quills stand up straight when it is angry.

4. Most animals stay away from porcupines.

5. Their quills hurt other animals.

6. Porcupines sleep under rocks or bushes.

7. They sleep during the day.

8. Porcupines eat plants at night.

9. North America has some porcupines.

10. They are called New World porcupines.

11. New World porcupines can climb trees.

Page 265

Subjects and Predicates

Directions: Draw one line under the subjects and two lines under the predicates in the sentences below.

1. My mom likes to plant flowers.

2. Our neighbors walk their dog.

3. Our car needs gas.

4. The children play house.

5. Movies and popcorn go well together.

6. Peanut butter and jelly is my favorite kind of sandwich.

7. Bill, Sue and Nancy ride to the park.

8. We use pencils, markers and pens to write on paper.

9. Trees and shrubs need special care.

Page 266

Subjects

Directions: Use your own words to write the subjects in the sentences below.

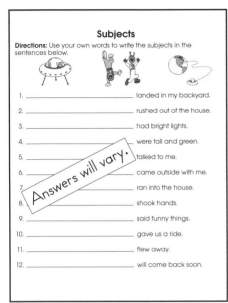

1. _____ landed in my backyard.
2. _____ rushed out of the house.
3. _____ had bright lights.
4. _____ were tall and green.
5. _____ talked to me.
6. _____ came outside with me.
7. _____ ran into the house.
8. _____ shook hands.
9. _____ said funny things.
10. _____ gave us a ride.
11. _____ flew away.
12. _____ will come back soon.

Answers will vary.

Page 267

Predicates

Directions: Use your own words to write the predicates in the sentences below.

1. The swimming pool _____
2. The water _____
3. The sun _____
4. I always _____
5. My friends _____
6. We always _____
7. The lifeguard _____
8. The rest periods _____
9. The lunch _____
10. My favorite food _____
11. The diving board _____
12. We never _____

Answers will vary.

Page 268

Review

Directions: Use **and** or **but** to make longer, more interesting sentences from two shorter sentences.

1. I have a dog. I have a cat.
   I have a dog and a cat.

2. The sun is shining. The weather is cold.
   The sun is shining, but the weather is cold.

Directions: Draw one line under the subjects in the sentences. Draw two lines under the predicates.

1. We went on a white water rafting trip.
2. Sam and Ben won the best prize.
3. She painted a picture for me.
4. Those flowers are beautiful.
5. She is a great babysitter.
6. My shoes got wet in the creek.
7. The cows are not in the barn.
8. He has a new shirt for the party.

Page 269

Word Order

Word order is the logical order of words in sentences.

Directions: Put the words in order so that each sentence tells a complete idea.

Example: outside put cat the

Put the cat outside.

1. mouse the ate snake the
   The snake ate the mouse.

2. dog John his walk took a for
   John took his dog for a walk.

3. birthday Maria the present wrapped
   Maria wrapped the birthday present.

4. escaped parrot the cage its from
   The parrot escaped from its cage.

5. to soup quarts water three of add the
   Add three quarts of water to the soup.

6. bird the bushes into the chased cat the
   The cat chased the bird into the bushes.

Page 270

Sentences and Non-Sentences

A **sentence** tells a complete idea.

Directions: Circle the groups of words that tell a complete idea.

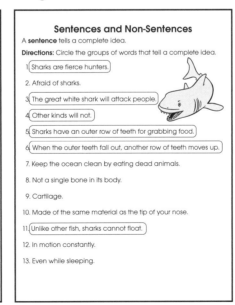

1. (Sharks are fierce hunters.)
2. Afraid of sharks.
3. (The great white shark will attack people.)
4. (Other kinds will not.)
5. (Sharks have an outer row of teeth for grabbing food.)
6. (When the outer teeth fall out, another row of teeth moves up.)
7. Keep the ocean clean by eating dead animals.
8. Not a single bone in its body.
9. Cartilage.
10. Made of the same material as the tip of your nose.
11. (Unlike other fish, sharks cannot float.)
12. In motion constantly.
13. Even while sleeping.

Page 271

Completing a Story

Directions: Complete the story, using sentences that tell complete ideas.

One morning, my friend asked me to take my first bus trip downtown. I was so excited I _____

At the bus stop, we saw _____ Our bus driver _____

When we got off the bus _____ . I'd never seen so many

My favorite part was when we _____

We stopped to eat _____
_____ . I bought a _____
_____

When we got home, I told my friend, "_____
_____ ."

Answers will vary.

Page 272

Complete the Sentences

Directions: Write your own endings to make the sentences tell a complete idea.

Example:
The Wizard of Oz is a story about __Dorothy and her dog, Toto__.

1. Dorothy and Toto live on _____
2. A big storm _____
3. Dorothy and Toto are carried off to _____
4. Dorothy meets _____
5. Dorothy, Toto and their friends follow the _____
6. Dorothy tries to find _____
7. The Wizard turns out to be _____
8. A scary person in the story is _____
9. The wicked witch is killed by _____
10. The hot air balloon leaves without _____
11. Dorothy uses her magic shoes to _____

Answers will vary.

Page 273

Complete the Sentences

Directions: Write your own endings to make the sentences tell a complete idea.

Example:
Cinderella is a story about __Cinderella, her stepmother, stepsisters and the prince.__

1. Cinderella lives with _____
2. Her stepmother and her stepsisters _____
3. Cinderella's stepsisters receive _____
4. Cinderella cannot go to the ball because _____
_____
5. The fairy godmother comes _____
6. The prince dances with _____
7. When the clock strikes midnight, _____
8. The prince's men look for _____
9. The slipper fits _____
10. Cinderella and the prince live _____

Answers will vary.

Page 274

Statements and Questions

Statements are sentences that tell about something. Statements begin with a capital letter and end with a period. **Questions** are sentences that ask about something. Questions begin with a capital letter and end with a question mark.

Directions: Rewrite the sentences using capital letters and either a period or a question mark.

Example: walruses live in the Arctic
__Walruses live in the Arctic.__

1. are walruses large sea mammals or fish
__Are walruses large sea mammals or fish?__

2. they spend most of their time in the water and on ice
__They spend most of their time in the water and on ice.__

3. are floating sheets of ice called ice floes
__Are floating sheets of ice called ice floes?__

4. are walruses related to seals
__Are walruses related to seals?__

5. their skin is thick, wrinkled and almost hairless
__Their skin is thick, wrinkled and almost hairless.__

Page 275

Statements and Questions

Directions: Change the statements into questions and the questions into statements.

Example: Jane is happy.   Is Jane happy?
Were you late?   You were late.

1. The rainbow was brightly colored.
__Is the rainbow brightly colored?__

2. Was the sun coming out?
__The sun was coming out.__

3. The dog is doing tricks.
__Is the dog doing tricks?__

4. Have you washed the dishes today?
__You have washed the dishes today.__

5. Kurt was the circus ringmaster.
__Was Kurt the circus ringmaster?__

6. Were you planning on going to the library?
__You were planning on going to the library.__

Page 276

Exclamations

Exclamation points are used for sentences that express strong feelings. These sentences can have one or two words or be very long.

Example: Wait! or **Don't forget to call!**

Directions: Add an exclamation point at the end of sentences that express strong feelings. Add a period at the end of the statements.

1. My parents and I were watching television.
2. The snow began falling around noon.
3. Wow!
4. The snow was really coming down!
5. We turned the television off and looked out the window.
6. The snow looked like a white blanket.
7. How beautiful!
8. We decided to put on our coats and go outside.
9. Hurry!
10. Get your sled.
11. All the people on the street came out to see the snow.
12. How wonderful!
13. The children began making a snowman.
14. What a great day!

Page 277

Review

There are three kinds of sentences.

Statements: Sentences that tell something. Statements end with a period (.).
Questions: Sentences that ask a question. Questions end with a question mark (?).
Exclamations: Sentences that express a strong feeling. Exclamations end with an exclamation point (!).

Directions: Write what kind of sentence each is.

1. __Exclamation__ What a super day to go to the zoo!
2. __Question__ Do you like radishes?
3. __Statement__ I belong to the chess club.
4. __Statement__ Wash the dishes.
5. __Question__ How much does that cost?
6. __Statement__ Apples grow on trees.
7. __Statement__ Look out the window.
8. __Exclamation__ Look at the colorful rainbow!

Page 278

Contractions

Contractions are shortened forms of two words. We use apostrophes to show where letters are missing.

Example: It is = it's

Directions: Write the words that are used in each contraction.

we're __we__ + __are__
you'll __you__ + __will__
I'm __I__ + __am__

they'll __they__ + __will__
aren't __are__ + __not__
isn't __is__ + __not__

Directions: Write the contraction for the two words shown.

you have __you've__
had not __hadn't__
they are __they're__
she had __she'd__
I am __I'm__

have not __haven't__
we will __we'll__
he is __he's__
it will __it'll__
is not __isn't__

Page 279

Apostrophes

Apostrophes are used to show ownership by placing an **s** at the end of a single person, place or thing.

Example: Mary**'s** cat

Directions: Write the apostrophes in the contractions below.

Example: We shouldn't be going to their house so late at night.

1. We didn't think that the ice cream would melt so fast.
2. They're never around when we're ready to go.
3. Didn't you need to make a phone call?
4. Who's going to help you paint the bicycle red?

Directions: Add an apostrophe and an **s** to the words to show ownership of a person, place or thing.

Example: Jill**'s** bike is broken.

1. That is Holly's flower garden.
2. Mark's new skates are black and green.
3. Mom threw away Dad's old shoes.
4. Buster's food dish was lost in the snowstorm.

Page 280

Quotation Marks

Quotation marks are punctuation marks that tell what is said by a person. Quotation marks go before the first word and after the punctuation of a direct quote. The first word of a direct quote begins with a capital letter.

Example: Katie said, "Never go in the water without a friend."

Directions: Put quotation marks around the correct words in the sentences below.

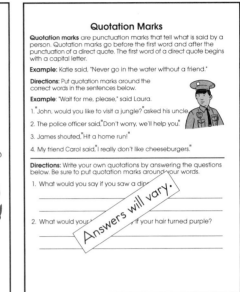

Example: "Wait for me, please," said Laura.

1. "John, would you like to visit a jungle?" asked his uncle.
2. The police officer said, "Don't worry, we'll help you."
3. James shouted, "Hit a home run!"
4. My friend Carol said, "I really don't like cheeseburgers."

Directions: Write your own quotations by answering the questions below. Be sure to put quotation marks around your words.

1. What would you say if you saw a di_____

_____

2. What would your _____ if your hair turned purple?

_____

Answers will vary.

Page 281

Quotation Marks

Directions: Put quotation marks around the correct words in the sentences below.

1. Can we go for a bike ride? asked Katrina.

   "Can we go for a bike ride?" asked Katrina.

2. Yes, said Mom.

   "Yes," said Mom.

3. Let's go to the park, said Mike.

   "Let's go to the park," said Mike.

4. Great idea! said Mom.

   "Great idea!" said Mom.

5. How long until we get there? asked Katrina.

   "How long until we get there?" asked Katrina.

6. Soon, said Mike.

   "Soon," said Mike.

7. Here we are! exclaimed Mom.

   "Here we are!" exclaimed Mom.

Page 282

Parts of a Paragraph

A **paragraph** is a group of sentences that all tell about the same thing. Most paragraphs have three parts: a **beginning**, a **middle** and an **end**.

Directions: Write **beginning**, **middle** or **end** next to each sentence in the scrambled paragraphs below. There can be more than one middle sentence.

Example:

__middle__ We took the tire off the car.
__beginning__ On the way to Aunt Louise's, we had a flat tire.
__middle__ We patched the hole in the tire.
__end__ We put the tire on and started driving again.

__middle__ I took all the ingredients out of the cupboard.
__beginning__ One morning, I decided to bake a pumpkin pie.
__end__ I forgot to add the pumpkin!
__middle__ I mixed the ingredients together, but something was missing.

__middle__ The sun was very hot and our throats were dry.
__end__ We finally decided to turn back.
__beginning__ We started our hike very early in the morning.
__middle__ It kept getting hotter as we walked.

Page 283

Topic Sentences

A **topic sentence** is usually the first sentence in a paragraph. It tells what the story will be about.

Directions: Read the following sentences. Circle the topic sentence that should go first in the paragraph that follows.

(Rainbows have seven colors.)
There's a pot of gold.
I like rainbows.

The colors are red, orange, yellow, green, blue, indigo and violet. Red forms the outer edge, with violet on the inside of the rainbow.

He cut down a cherry tree.

His wife was named Martha.

(George Washington was a good president.)

He helped our country get started. He chose intelligent leaders to help him run the country.

(Mark Twain was a great author.)

Mark Twain was unhappy sometimes.

Mark Twain was born in Missouri.

One of his most famous books is *Huckleberry Finn*. He wrote many other great books.

Page 284

Middle Sentences

Middle sentences support the topic sentence. They tell more about it.

Directions: Underline the middle sentences that support each topic sentence below.

Topic Sentence:

Penguins are birds that cannot fly.

Pelicans can spear fish with their sharp bills.
Many penguins waddle or hop about on land.
Even though they cannot fly, they are excellent swimmers.
Pelicans keep their food in a pouch.

Topic Sentence:

Volleyball is a team sport in which the players hit the ball over the net.

There are two teams with six players on each team.
My friend John would rather play tennis with Lisa.
Players can use their heads or their hands.
I broke my hand once playing handball.

Topic Sentence:

Pikes Peak is the most famous of all the Rocky Mountains.

Some mountains have more trees than other mountains.
Many people like to climb to the top.
Many people like to ski and camp there, too.
The weather is colder at the top of most mountains.

Page 285

Ending Sentences

Ending sentences are sentences that tie the story together.

Directions: Choose the correct ending sentence for each story from the sentences below. Write it at the end of the paragraph.
A new pair of shoes!
All the corn on the cob I could eat!
A new eraser!

Corn on the Cob

Corn on the cob used to be my favorite food. That is, until I lost my four front teeth. For one whole year, I had to sit and watch everyone else eat my favorite food without me. Mom gave me creamed corn, but it just wasn't the same. When my teeth finally came in, Dad said he had a surprise for me. I thought I was going to get a bike or a new C.D. player or something. I was just as happy to get what I did.

All the corn on the cob I could eat!

I would like to take a train ride every year.
Trains move faster than I thought they would.
She had brought her new gerbil along for the ride.

A Train Ride

When our family took its first train ride, my sister brought along a big box. She would not tell anyone what she had in it. In the middle of the trip, we heard a sound coming from the box. "Okay, Jan, now you have to open the box," said Mom. When she opened the box we were surprised.

She had brought her new gerbil along for the ride.

Page 286

Alliteration

Alliteration is the repeated use of beginning sounds. Alliterative sentences are sometimes referred to as tongue twisters.

Example:
She sells sea shells by the seashore.
Peter Piper picked a peck of pickled peppers.

Directions: Use alliteration to write your own tongue twisters.

1. _____

2. _____ _Answers will vary._

3. _____

Page 287

Poetry

Shape poems are words that form the shape of the thing being written about.

Example:

Directions: Create your own shape poem below.

Page 288

Poetry: Cinquains

A cinquain is a type of poetry. The form is:

Noun
Adjective, adjective
Verb + ing, verb + ing, verb + ing
Four-word phrase
Synonym for noun in line 1.

Example:

Books
Creative, fun
Reading, choosing, looking
I love to read!
Novels

Directions: Write your own cinquain!

Results will vary.

_____
noun

_____ , _____
adjective   adjective

_____ _____ _____
verb + ing   verb + ing   verb + ing

_____
four-word phrase

_____
synonym for noun in first line

Page 290

Vocabulary: Beginning and Ending Sounds

Directions: Use the words in the box to answer the questions below.

ax	mix
beach	church
class	kiss
brush	crash

Which word:

begins with the same sound as **breakfast** and ends with the same sound as **fish**? _brush_

begins with the same sound as **children** and ends with the same sound as **catch**? _church_

begins and ends with the same sound as **cuts**? _kiss_

sounds like **acts**? _ax_

begins with the same sound as **coconut** and ends with the same sound as **splash**? _crash_

rhymes with **tricks**? _mix_

has **each** in it? _beach_

Page 291

Vocabulary: Sentences

Directions: Use a word from the box to complete each sentence. Use each word only once.

| ax | mix | beach | church | class | kiss | brush | crash |

1. Those two cars are going to __crash__ .
2. He chopped the wood with an __ax__ .
3. Grandma gave me a __kiss__ on my cheek.
4. Before you go, __brush__ your hair.
5. How many students are in your __class__ at school?
6. The waves bring sand to the __beach__ .
7. To make orange, you __mix__ yellow and red.
8. On Sunday, we always go to __church__ .

Page 292

Vocabulary: Plurals

A word that names one thing is **singular**, like **house**. A word that names more than one thing is **plural**, like **houses**.

To make a word plural, we usually add **s**.

Examples: one book — two book**s**   one tree — four tree**s**

To make plural words that end in **s, ss, x, sh** and **ch**, we add **es**.

Examples: one fox — two fox**es**   one bush — three bush**es**

Directions: Write the word that is missing from each pair below. Add **s** or **es** to make the plural words. The first one is done for you.

Singular	Plural
table	tables
beach	beaches
class	classes
ax	axes
brush	brushes
crash	crashes

Page 293

Vocabulary: Spelling

Directions: Circle the word in each sentence which is not spelled correctly. Then write the word correctly.

1. How many (clases) are in your school? __classes__
2. Our town has six (chirches). __churches__
3. Have you been to Maryland's (beechs?) __beaches__
4. Water (mixs) with dirt to make mud. __mixes__
5. We need two (axs) for this tree. __axes__
6. That car has been in three (crashs). __crashes__
7. She gave the baby lots of (kises). __kisses__
8. I lost both of my (brushs) at school. __brushes__

Page 294

Vocabulary: Nouns and Verbs

A **noun** names a person, place or thing. A **verb** tells what something does or what something is. Some words can be a noun one time and a verb another time.

Directions: Complete each pair of sentences with a word from the box. The word will be a noun in the first sentence and a verb in the second sentence.

| mix | kiss | brush | crash |

1. Did your dog ever give you a __kiss__ ?
   (noun)

   I have a cold, so I can't __kiss__ you today.
   (verb)

2. I brought my comb and my __brush__ .
   (noun)

   I will __brush__ the leaves off your coat.
   (verb)

3. Was anyone hurt in the __crash__ ?
   (noun)

   If you aren't careful, you will __crash__ into me.
   (verb)

4. We bought a cake __mix__ at the store.
   (noun)

   I will __mix__ the eggs together.
   (verb)

Page 295

Vocabulary: Nouns and Verbs

Directions: Write the correct word in each sentence. Use each word once. Write **N** above the words that are used as nouns (people, places and things). Write **V** above the words that are used as verbs (what something does or what something is).

Example:

I need a __drink__ (N). I will __drink__ (V) milk.

| mix | beach | church | class | kiss | brush | crash |

1. It's hot today, so let's go to the __beach__ (N).
2. The __church__ (N) was crowded.
3. I can't find my paint __brush__ (N).
4. Will you __kiss__ (V) my finger and make it stop hurting?
5. I will __mix__ (V) the red and yellow paint to get orange.
6. The teacher asked our __class__ (N) to get in line.
7. If you move that bottom can, the rest will __crash__ (V) to the floor.

Page 296

Vocabulary: Sentences

Every sentence must have two things: a **noun** that tells who or what is doing something and a **verb** that tells what the noun is doing.

Directions: Add a **noun** or a **verb** to complete each sentence. Be sure to begin your sentences with capital letters and end them with periods.

Example: reads after school. (needs a noun)

Brandy reads after school.

1. brushes her dog every day
2. at the beach, we
3. k...
4. i... class
5. stopped with a crash

Answers will vary.

Page 297

Vocabulary

Directions: Find the picture that matches each sentence below. Then complete each sentence with the word under the picture.

list · search · spill · toast · pound · load

1. I will __search__ until I find it.

2. Be careful you don't __spill__ the paint.

3. Is that __load__ too heavy for you?

4. They made __toast__ for breakfast.

5. Please go to the store and buy a __pound__ of butter.

6. Is my name on the __list__ ?

Page 298

Vocabulary

Directions: Find the picture that matches each sentence below. Then complete the sentence with the word under the picture.

hug · plan · clap · stir · drag · grab

1. She will __plan__ where to go on her trip.

2. __Drag__ that big box over here, please.

3. My little brother always tries to __grab__ my toys.

4. May I help you __stir__ the soup?

5. I like to __hug__ my dog because he is so soft.

6. After she played, everyone started to __clap__ .

Page 299

Vocabulary: Beginning and Ending Sounds

Directions: Write the words from the box that begin or end with the same sound as the pictures.

| stir | clap | drag | hug | plan | grab |

1. Which word **begins** with the same sound as each picture?

- clap
- hug
- grab
- drag
- stir
- plan

2. Which word (or words) **ends** with the same sound as each picture?

- stir
- clap
- plan
- grab
- drag
- hug

Page 300

Vocabulary: Explaining Sentences

Directions: Complete each sentence, explaining why each event might have happened.

She hugged me because _____

_____

He didn't want to play with us because _____

_____

We planned to go to the _____

Answers will vary.

We ____ loudly because _____

_____

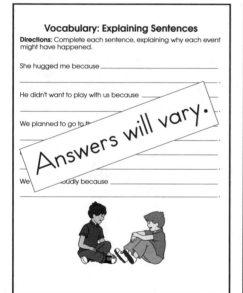

Page 301

Vocabulary: Verbs

Directions: Write the verb that answers each question. Write a sentence using that verb.

| stir | clap | drag | hug | plan | grab |

Which verb means to put your arms around someone?

__hug__

Answers will vary.

Which verb means to mix something with a spoon?

__stir__

Answers will vary.

Which verb means to pull something along the ground?

__drag__

Answers will vary.

Which verb means to take something suddenly?

__grab__

Answers will vary.

Page 302

Vocabulary: Past-Tense Verbs

The past tense of a verb tells that something already happened. To tell about something that already happened, add **ed** to most verbs. If the verb already ends in **e**, just add **d**.

Examples:

We enter**ed** the contest last week. · We tast**ed** the cupcakes.
I fold**ed** the paper wrong. · They decid**ed** quickly.
He add**ed** two boxes to the pile. · She shar**ed** her cupcake.

Directions: Use the verb from the first sentence to complete the second sentence. Add **d** or **ed** to show that something already happened.

Example:

My mom looks fine today. Yesterday, she __looked__ tired.

1. You enter through the middle door.
   We __entered__ that way last week.

2. Please add this for me. I already __added__ it twice.

3. Will you share your cookie with me?
   I __shared__ my apple with you yesterday.

4. It's your turn to fold the clothes. I __folded__ them yesterday.

5. May I taste another one? I already __tasted__ one.

6. You need to decide. We __decided__ this morning.

Page 303

Vocabulary: Past-Tense Verbs

When you write about something that already happened, you add **ed** to most verbs. For some verbs that have a short vowel and end in one consonant, you double the consonant before adding ed.

Examples:

He hug**ged** his pillow. The dog grab**bed** the stick.
She sti**rred** the carrots. We pla**nned** to go tomorrow.
They clap**ped** for me. They drag**ged** their bags on the ground.

Directions: Use the verb from the first sentence to complete the second sentence. Change the verb in the second part to the past tense. Double the consonant and add **ed**.

Example:

We skip to school. Yesterday, we __skipped__ the whole way.

1. It's not nice to grab things.
   When you __grabbed__ my cookie, I felt angry.
2. Did anyone hug you today? Dad __hugged__ me this morning.
3. We plan our vacations every year. Last year, we __planned__ to go to the beach.
4. Is it my turn to stir the pot? You __stirred__ it last time.
5. Let's clap for Andy, just like we __clapped__ for Amy.
6. My sister used to drag her blanket everywhere.
   Once, she __dragged__ it to the store.

Page 304

Vocabulary: Past-Tense Verbs

When you write about something that already happened, you add **ed** to most verbs. Here is another way to write about something in the past tense.

Examples: The dog walked. The dog was walking.
The cats played. The cats were playing.

Directions: Write each sentence again, writing the verb a different way.

Example: The baby pounded the pans.

The baby was pounding the pans.

1. Gary loaded the car by himself.

Gary was loading the car by himself.

2. They searched for a long time.

They were searching for a long time.

3. The water spilled over the edge.

The water was spilling over the edge.

4. Dad toasted the rolls.

Dad was toasting the rolls.

Page 305

Vocabulary: Past-Tense Verbs

Directions: Write sentences that tell about each picture using the words **is**, **are**, **was** and **were**. Use words from the box as either nouns or verbs.

pound	spill	toast	list	load	search

Answers will vary.

Page 306

Vocabulary: Present-Tense Verbs

When something is happening right now, it is in the **present tense**. There are two ways to write verbs in the present tense:

Examples: The dog walks. The cats play.
The dog is walking. The cats are playing.

Directions: Write each sentence again, writing the verb a different way.

Example:

He lists the numbers.

He is listing the numbers.

1. She is pounding the nail.
She pounds the nail.
2. My brother toasts the bread.
He is toasting the bread.
3. They search for the robber.
They are searching for the robber.
4. The teacher lists the pages.
The teacher is listing the pages.
5. They are spilling the water.
They spill the water.
6. Ken and Amy load the packages.
They are loading the packages.

Page 307

Vocabulary: Sentences

Directions: Write a word from the box to complete each sentence. Use each word only once.

glue	enter	share	add	decide	fold

1. I know how to __add__ 3 and 4.
2. Which book did you __decide__ to read?
3. Go in the door that says "__Enter__."
4. I will __glue__ a yellow circle for the sun onto my picture.
5. I help __fold__ the clothes after they are washed.
6. She will __share__ her banana with me.

Page 308

Vocabulary

Directions: Follow the directions below.

glue	enter	share	add	decide	fold

1. Add letters to these words to make words from the box.

old __fold__ are __share__

2. Write the two words from the box that begin with vowels.

__enter__ __add__

3. Change one letter of each word to make a word from the box.

food __fold__ clue __glue__

4. Change two letters of this word to make a word from the box.

beside __decide__

Page 309

Vocabulary: Statements

A **statement** is a sentence that tells something.

Directions: Use the words in the box to complete the statements below. Write the words on the lines.

glue	decide	add
share	enter	fold

1. It took ten minutes for Kayla to _____add_____ the numbers.

2. Ben wants to _____share_____ his cookies with me.

3. "I can't _____decide_____ which color to choose," said Rocky.

4. _____Glue_____ can be used to make things stick together.

5. "This is how you _____fold_____ your paper in half," said Mrs. Green.

6. The opposite of **leave** is _____enter_____.

Write your own statement on the line.

Answers will vary.

Page 310

Vocabulary: Questions

Questions are asking sentences. They begin with a capital letter and end with a question mark. Many questions begin with the words **who, what, why, when, where** and **how**. Write six questions using the question words below. Make sure to end each question with a question mark.

1. Who _____

2. What _____

3. _____

4. _____

5. Where _____

6. How _____

Answers will vary.

Page 311

Vocabulary: Commands

A **command** is a sentence that tells someone to do something.

Directions: Use the words in the box to complete the commands below. Write the words on the lines.

glue	decide	add	share	enter	fold

1. _____Add_____ a cup of flour to the cake batter.

2. _____Decide_____ how much paper you will need to write your story.

3. Please _____glue_____ the picture of the apple onto the paper.

4. _____Enter_____ through this door and leave through the other door.

5. Please _____fold_____ the letter and put it into an envelope.

6. _____Share_____ your toys with your sister.

Write your own command on the lines.

Answers will vary.

Page 312

Vocabulary: Directions

A **direction** is a sentence written as a command.

Directions: Write the missing directions for these pictures. Begin each direction with one of the verbs below.

glue	enter	share	add	decide	fold

How To Make a Peanut Butter and Jelly Sandwich:

1. Spread peanut butter on bread.

2. _____

3. Cut th_____

_____ to Make a Valentine:

2. Draw half a heart.

3. Cut along the line you drew.

4. _____

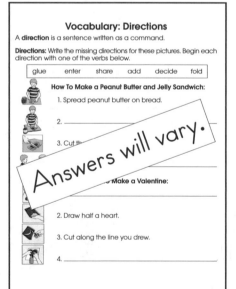

Answers will vary.

Page 313

Kinds of Sentences

A **statement** is a sentence that tells something.
A **question** is a sentence that asks something.
A **command** is a sentence that tells someone to do something.

Commands begin with a verb or **please**. They usually end with a period. The noun is **you** but does not need to be part of the sentence.

Example: "Come here, please." means "**You** come here, please."

Examples of commands: Stand next to me.
                          Please give me some paper.

Directions: Write **S** in front of the statements, **Q** in front of the questions and **C** in front of the commands. End each sentence with a period or a question mark.

Example:

_C_ Stop and look before you cross the street.
_Q_ 1. Did you do your math homework?
_S_ 2. I think I lost my math book.
_Q_ 3. Will you help me find it?
_S_ 4. I looked everywhere.
_C_ 5. Please open your math books to page three.
_Q_ 6. Did you look under your desk?
_S_ 7. I looked, but it's not there.
_Q_ 8. Who can add seven and four?
_C_ 9. Come up and write the answer on the board.
_Q_ 10. Chris, where is your math book?
_S_ 11. I don't know for sure.
_C_ 12. Please share a book with a friend.

Page 314

Kinds of Sentences

Remember: a **statement** tells something, a **question** asks something and a **command** tells someone to do something.

Directions: On each line, write a statement, question or command. Use a word from the box in each sentence.

glue	share	decide
enter	add	fold

Example:
Question:
Can he add anything else?

1. Statement: _____

2. Questi_____

3. _____

4. Statement: _____

5. Question: _____

Answers will vary.

Page 315

Kinds of Sentences

Directions: Use the group of words below to write three sentences: a **statement**, a **question** and a **command**.

| add | can | these | he | quickly | numbers |

Example:

Statement:

He can add these numbers quickly.

Question:

Can he can add these numbers quickly?

Command:

Add these numbers quickly.

| fold | here | should |

1. Statement:

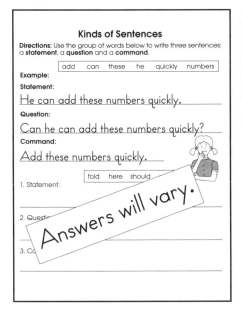

Answers will vary.

2. Question:

3. Command:

Page 316

Vocabulary: Completing a Story

Directions: Use verbs to complete the story below. The verbs that tell about things that happened in the past will end in **ed**.

Answers may vary.

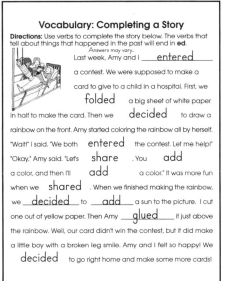

Last week, Amy and I ___entered___ a contest. We were supposed to make a card to give to a child in a hospital. First, we ___folded___ a big sheet of white paper in half to make the card. Then we ___decided___ to draw a rainbow on the front. Amy started coloring the rainbow all by herself. "Wait!" I said. "We both ___entered___ the contest. Let me help!" "Okay," Amy said. "Let's ___share___ . You ___add___ a color, and then I'll ___add___ a color." It was more fun when we ___shared___ . When we finished making the rainbow, we ___decided___ to ___add___ a sun to the picture. I cut one out of yellow paper. Then Amy ___glued___ it just above the rainbow. Well, our card didn't win the contest, but it did make a little boy with a broken leg smile. Amy and I felt so happy! We ___decided___ to go right home and make some more cards!

Page 317

Homophones

Homophones are words that sound the same but are spelled differently and have different meanings.

Directions: Use the homophones in the box to answer the riddles below.

| main | meat | peace | dear | to |
| mane | meet | piece | deer | too |

1. Which word has the word **pie** in it? ___piece___
2. Which word rhymes with **ear** and is an animal? ___deer___
3. Which word rhymes with **shoe** and means **also**? ___too___
4. Which word has the word **eat** in it and is something you might eat? ___meat___
5. Which word has the same letters as the word **read** but in a different order? ___dear___
6. Which word rhymes with **train** and is something on a pony? ___mane___
7. Which word, if it began with a capital letter, might be the name of an important street? ___main___
8. Which word sounds like a number but has only two letters? ___to___
9. Which word rhymes with and is a synonym for **greet**? ___meet___
10. Which word rhymes with the last syllable in **police** and can mean quiet? ___peace___

Page 318

Homophones: Sentences

Directions: Write a word from the box to complete each sentence.

| main | meat | peace | dear | two |
| mane | meet | piece | deer | too |

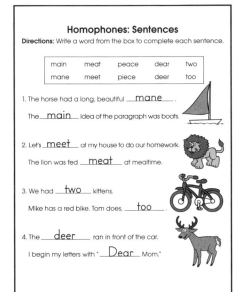

1. The horse had a long, beautiful ___mane___ .

The ___main___ idea of the paragraph was boats.

2. Let's ___meet___ at my house to do our homework.

The lion was fed ___meat___ at mealtime.

3. We had ___two___ kittens.

Mike has a red bike. Tom does, ___too___ .

4. The ___deer___ ran in front of the car.

I begin my letters with " ___Dear___ Mom."

Page 319

Homophones

Directions: Cut out each honeybee at the bottom of the page and glue it on the flower with its homophone.

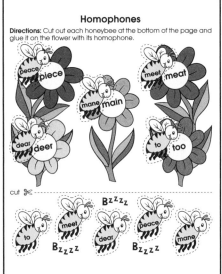

cut ✂ - - - - - - - - - - - - - - -

Page 321

Homophones: Spelling

Directions: Circle the word in each sentence which is not spelled correctly. Then write the word correctly.

1. Please (meat) me at the park. ___meet___

2. I would like a (peace) of pie. ___piece___

3. There were (too) cookies left. ___two___

4. The horse's (main) needed to be brushed. ___mane___

5. We saw a (dear) in the forest. ___deer___

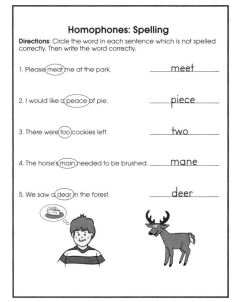

Page 322

Homophones: Rhymes

Directions: Use homophones to create two-lined rhymes.

Example: I found it a **pain**
To comb the horse's **mane**!

1. _____

_____

Answers will vary.

2. _____

_____

3. _____

_____

Page 323

Short Vowels

Short vowel patterns usually have a single vowel followed by a consonant sound.

Short a is the sound you hear in the word **can**.
Short e is the sound you hear in the word **men**.
Short i is the sound you hear in the word **pig**.
Short o is the sound you hear in the word **pot**.
Short u is the sound you hear in the word **truck**.

fast	stop
spin	track
wish	lunch
bread	block

Directions: Use the words in the box to answer the questions below.

Which word:

begins with the same sound as **blast** and ends with the same sound as **look**? _____block_____

rhymes with **stack**? _____track_____

begins with the same sound as **phone** and ends with the same sound as **lost**? _____fast_____

has the same vowel sound as **hen**? _____bread_____

rhymes with **crunch**? _____lunch_____

begins with the same sound as **spot** and ends with the same sound as **can**? _____spin_____

begins with the same sound as **win** and ends with the same sound as **crush**? _____wish_____

has the word **top** in it? _____stop_____

Page 324

Short Vowels: Sentences

Directions: Use the words in the box to complete each sentence.

fast	wish	truck	bread	sun
best	stop	track	lunch	block

Race cars can go very _____fast_____.

Carol packs a _____lunch_____ for Ted before school.

Throw a penny in the well and make a _____wish_____.

The _____truck_____ had a flat tire.

My favorite kind of _____bread_____ is whole wheat.

Page 325

Short Vowels: Spelling

Directions: Circle the word in each sentence which is not spelled correctly. Then write the word correctly.

1. Be sure to (stopp) at the red light. _____stop_____

2. The train goes down the (trak.) _____track_____

3. Please put the (bred) in the toaster. _____bread_____

4. I need another (blok) to finish. _____block_____

5. The (beasst) player won a trophy. _____best_____

6. Blow out the candles and make a (wiish.) _____wish_____

7. The (truk) blew its horn. _____truck_____

Page 326

Long Vowels

Long vowels are the letters **a, e, i, o** and **u** which say the letter name sound.

Long a is the sound you hear in **cane**.
Long e is the sound you hear in **green**.
Long i is the sound you hear in **pie**.
Long o is the sound you hear in **bowl**.
Long u is the sound you hear in **cube**.

lame	goal
pain	few
street	fright
nose	gray
bike	fuse

Directions: Use the words in the box to answer the questions below.

1. Add one letter to each of these words to make words from the box.

ray _____gray_____   use _____fuse_____   right _____fright_____

2. Change one letter from each word to make a word from the box.

pail _____pain_____   goat _____goal_____

late _____lame_____   bite _____bike_____

3. Write the word from the box that . . .

has the long e sound. _____street_____

rhymes with **you**. _____few_____

is a homophone for **knows**. _____nose_____

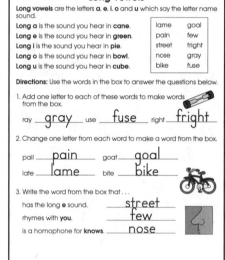

Page 327

Long Vowels: Sentences

Directions: Use the words in the box to complete each sentence.

lame	goal	pain	few	bike
street	fright	nose	gray	fuse

1. Look both ways before crossing the _____street_____.

2. My _____bike_____ had a flat tire.

3. Our walk through the haunted house gave us such a _____fright_____.

4. I kicked the soccer ball and scored a _____goal_____.

5. The _____gray_____ clouds mean rain is coming.

6. Cover your _____nose_____ when you sneeze.

7. We blew a _____fuse_____ at my house last night.

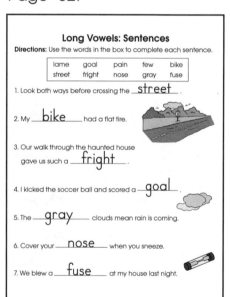

Page 328

Long Vowels

Directions: Use long vowel words from the box to answer the clues below. Write the letters of the words on the lines.

few bike dime goal fuse lame street nose fright pain

1. f r i g h [t] (rhymes with **night**)
2. s t r e e [t] (could be Main or Maple)
3. f [e] w (synonym for **a couple**)
4. l [a] m e (rhymes with **tame**)
5. b i [k] e (can be ridden on a trail)
6. p a i [n] (homophone for **pane**)
7. [d] i m e (ten of these make a dollar)
8. [g] o a l (changing one letter of this word makes **goat**)
9. [f] u s e (has the word **use** in it)
10. n [o] s e (homophone for **knows**)

Now, read the letters in the boxes from top to bottom to find out what kind of a job you did! **tremendous**

Page 329

Adjectives

Directions: Use the words in the box to answer the questions below. Use each word only once.

polite   careless   neat   shy   selfish   thoughtful

1. Someone who is quiet and needs some time to make new friends is ___shy___.

2. A person who says "please" and "thank you" is ___polite___.

3. Someone who always puts all the toys away is ___neat___.

4. A person who won't share with others is being ___selfish___.

5. A person who leaves a bike out all night is being ___careless___.

6. Someone who thinks of others is ___thoughtful___.

Page 330

Adjectives

Directions: Use the adjectives in the box to answer the questions below.

polite   careless   neat   shy   selfish   thoughtful

1. Change a letter in each word to make an adjective.

near ___neat___

why ___shy___

2. Write the word that rhymes with each of these.

fell dish ___selfish___

not full ___thoughtful___

hair mess ___careless___

3. Find these words in the adjectives. Write the adjective.

at ___neat___

are ___careless___

it ___polite___

Page 331

Adjectives: Spelling

Directions: Circle the word in each sentence which is not spelled correctly. Then write the word correctly.

1. John isn't (shelfish) at all. ___selfish___
2. He (sharred) his lunch with me today. ___shared___
3. I was (careles) and forgot to bring mine. ___careless___
4. My father says if I (planed) better, that wouldn't happen all the time. ___planned___
5. John is kind of quiet, and I used to think he was (shie.) ___shy___
6. Now, I know he is really (thotful.) ___thoughtful___
7. He's also very (polyte) and always asks before he (borrows) anything. ___polite___
8. He would never just reach over and (grabb) something he wanted. ___grab___
9. I'm glad John (desided) to be my friend. ___decided___

Page 332

Adjectives: Explaining Sentences

Directions: Use a word from the box to tell about a person in each picture below. Then write a sentence that explains why you chose that word.

polite neat careless shy selfish thoughtful

Sample answers given.
The word I picked: ___shy___

I think so because . . .

the girl is standing alone and looks sad.

The word I picked: ___thoughtful___

I think so because . . .

it is thoughtful to give someone flowers.

The word I picked: ___selfish___

I think so because . . .

the boy is not sharing his cookies.

Page 333

Adjectives

Directions: Look at each picture. Then add adjectives to the sentences. Use colors, numbers, words from the box and any other words you need to describe each picture.

polite neat careless shy selfish thoughtful

Example:

The boy shared his pencil.

The polite boy shared his red pencil.

The girl dropped her coat.

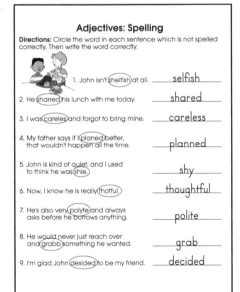

The boy put books away.

Answers will vary.

ANSWER KEY

Page 334

C, K, CK Words: Spelling

Directions: Write the words from the box that answer the questions.

| crowd | keeper | cost | pack | kangaroo | thick |

1. Which words spell the **k** sound with a **k**?
keeper   kangaroo

2. Which words spell the **k** sound with a **c**?
crowd   cost

3. Which words spell the **k** sound with **ck**?
pack   thick

4. Circle the letters that spell **k** in these words:
cook   black   cool   kite
cake   pocket   poke

5. Which words from the box rhyme with each of these?
tossed cost   deeper keeper
proud crowd   all in blue kangaroo

Page 335

C, K, CK Words: Sentences

The **k** sound can be spelled with a **c, k** or **ck** after a short vowel sound.

Directions: Use the words from the box to complete the sentences. Use each word only once.

crowd	keeper
cost	pack
kangaroo	thick

1. On sunny days, there is always a crowd of people at the zoo.

2. It doesn't cost much to get into the zoo.

3. We always get hungry, so we pack a picnic lunch.

4. We like to watch the kangaroo.

5. Its thick tail helps it jump and walk.

6. The keeper always makes sure the cages are clean.

Page 336

C, K, CK Words: Sentences

Remember: every sentence must have a noun that tells who or what is doing something and a verb that tells what the noun is doing.

Directions: Parts of each sentence below are missing. Rewrite each sentence, adding a noun or a verb, periods and capital letters.

Example:
read a book every day (needs a noun)
Leon reads a book every day.

1. packed a lunch

2. the crowd at the beach

3. cost

Answers will vary.

4. kan... their babies

5. was too thick to chew

Page 337

C, K, CK Words: Joining Sentences

Joining words are words that make two sentences into one longer sentence. Here are some words that join sentences:

and — if both sentences are about the same noun or verb.
Example: Tom is in my class at school, **and** he lives near me.

but — if the second sentence says something different from the first sentence.
Example: Julie walks to school with me, **but** today she is sick.

or — if each sentence names a different thing you could do.
Example: We could go to my house, **or** we could go to yours.

Directions: Join each set of sentences below using the words **and, but** or **or**.

1. Those socks usually cost a lot. This pack of ten socks is cheaper.
Those socks usually cost a lot, but this pack of ten socks is cheaper.

2. The kangaroo has a pouch. It lives in Australia.
The kangaroo has a pouch, and it lives in Australia.

3. The zoo keeper can start to work early. She can stay late.
The zoo keeper can start to work early, or she can stay late.

Page 338

C, K, CK Words: Joining Sentences

If and **when** can be joining words, too.

Directions: Read each set of sentences. Then join the two sentences to make one longer sentence.

Example: The apples will need to be washed. The apples are dirty.
The apples will need to be washed if they are dirty.

1. The size of the crowd grew. It grew when the game began.
The size of the crowd grew when the game began.

2. Be careful driving in the fog. The fog is thick.
Be careful driving in the fog if the fog is thick.

3. Pack your suitcases. Do it when you wake up in the morning.
Pack your suitcases when you wake up in the morning.

Page 339

C, K, CK Words: Joining Sentences

Some words that can join sentences are:
when — **When** we got there, the show had already started.
after — **After** I finished my homework, I watched TV.
because — You can't go by yourself, **because** you are too young.

Directions: Use the joining words to make the two short sentences into one longer one.

1. when — The keeper opened the door. The bear got out.
When the keeper opened the door, the bear got out.

2. because — I didn't buy the tickets. They cost too much.
I didn't buy the tickets because they cost too much.

3. after — The kangaroo ate lunch. He took a nap.
After the kangaroo ate lunch, he took a nap.

4. when — The door opened. The crowd rushed in.
When the door opened, the crowd rushed in.

5. after — I cut the bread. Everyone had a slice.
After I cut the bread, everyone had a slice.

Page 340

C, K, CK Words: Joining Sentences

Directions: Use **because**, **after** or **when** to join each set of sentences into one longer sentence.

1. I pack my own lunch. I always put in some fruit.

When I pack my lunch, I always put in some fruit.

2. I would like to be a zoo keeper. I love animals.

I would like to be a zoo keeper, because I love animals.

3. I was surprised there was such a crowd. It cost a lot.

I was surprised there was such a crowd because it cost a lot.

4. I beat the eggs for two minutes. They were thick and yellow.

After I beat the eggs for two minutes, they were thick and yellow.

Page 341

C, K, CK Words: Completing a Story

Directions: Use **c**, **k**, or **ck** words to complete this story. Some of the verbs are past tense and need to end with **ed**.

One day, Kevin and I __packed__ a lunch and went to the zoo. There was a big __crowd__ of people. Kevin wanted to see the __kangaroos__. When we got to the kangaroos cage, we met the __zookeeper__ whose name was Carla. "How much does it __cost__ $ to keep a kangaroo?" Kevin asked the __zookeeper__.

"Our grass at home is really __thick__ [NOT THIN], and that's what kangaroos eat, right?"

"You must have a big cage and clean it every day," Carla the zookeeper told Kevin. Kevin got quiet very quickly.

"I'll just keep coming here to see __kangaroos__ in the cage you clean," he said.

Page 342

S Words: Spelling

The **s** sound can be spelled with an **s**, **ss**, **c** or **ce**.

Directions: Use the words from the box to complete the sentences below. Write each word only once.

center	pencil	space
address	police	darkness

1. I drew a circle in the __center__ of the page.

2. I'll write to you if you tell me your __address__.

3. She pushed too hard and broke the point on her __pencil__.

4. If you hear a noise at night, call the __police__.

5. It was night, and I couldn't see him in the __darkness__.

6. There's not enough __space__ for me to sit next to you.

Page 343

S Words: Spelling

Directions: Write the words from the box that answer the questions.

center	pencil	space	address	police	darkness

1. Which words spell the **s** sound with **ss**?

address   darkness

2. Which words spell **s** with a **c**?

center   pencil

3. Which words spell **s** with **ce**?

space   police

4. Write two other words you know that spell **s** with an **s**.

Answers will vary.

5. Circle the letters that spell **s** in these words.

de**c**ide   ki**ss**   careless   i**ce**

cost   fier**ce**   **s**enten**ce**

6. Put these letters in order to make words from the box.

sdsdera __address__   sdserakn __darkness__

clipoe __police__   clipne __pencil__

capse __space__   retnce __center__

Page 344

C Words: Spelling

The letter **c** can make the **k** sound or the **s** sound.

Example: count, city

Directions: Write **k** or **s** to show how the **c** in each word sounds.

cave	k	copy	k	force	s
become	k	dance	s	city	s
certain	s	contest	k	cool	k

Directions: Use the words from the box to answer these questions.

center	pencil	space	address	police	darkness

1. Which word begins with the same sound as **simple** and ends with the same sound as **fur**? __center__

2. Which word begins with the same sound as **average** and ends with the same sound as **circus**? __address__

3. Which word begins with the same sound as **popcorn** and ends with the same sound as **glass**? __police__

4. Which word begins and ends with the same sound as **pool**? __pencil__

5. Which word begins with the same sound as **city** and ends with the same sound as **kiss**? __space__

6. Which word begins and ends with the same sound as **delicious**? __darkness__

Page 345

Review

Directions: Circle the words which are not spelled correctly in the story. Then write each word correctly on the lines below.

One day, Peter and I were sitting on a bench at the park. A (polise) woman came and sat in the empty (spase) beside us. "Have you seen a little dog with (thik) black fur?" she asked. She was very (poolite). "Remember that dog?" I asked Peter. "He was just here!" Peter nodded. He was too (shie) to say anything.

"Give us his (adress)," I said. "We'll find him and take him home." She got out a (pensil) and wrote the (addres) in the (senter) of a piece of paper. Peter and I (desided) to walk down the street the way the dog had gone. There was a (krowd) of people at a (cherch) we passed, but no dog.

Then it started getting late. "We better go home," Peter said. "I can't see in this (drakness) anyway."

As we turned around to go back, there was the little dog! He had been following us! We took him to the (adress). The girl who came to the door (grabed) him and (huged) him tight. "I'm sorry I let you wander away," she told the dog. "I'll never be so (carless) again." I thought she was going to (kis) us, too. We left just in time!

police	space	thick
polite	shy	address
pencil	address	center
decided	crowd	church
darkness	address	grabbed
hugged	careless	kiss

Page 346

Suffixes

A **suffix** is a word part added to the end of a word. Suffixes add to or change the meaning of the word.

Example: sad + ly = sadly

Below are some suffixes and their meanings.

ment	state of being, quality of, act of
ly	like or in a certain way
ness	state of being
ful	full of
less	without

Directions: The words in the box have suffixes. Use the suffix meanings above to match each word with its meaning below. Write the words on the lines.

friendly	cheerful	safely	sleeveless	speechless
kindness	amazement	sickness	peaceful	excitement

1. in a safe way   s a f e l y
2. full of cheer   c h e e r f u l
3. full of peace   p e a c e f u l
4. state of being amazed   a m a z e m e n t
5. state of being excited   e x c i t e m e n t
6. without speech   s p e e c h l e s s

Use the numbered letters to find the missing word below.

You are now on your way to becoming a

m a s t e r of suffixes!

Page 347

Suffixes: Adverbs

Adverbs are words that describe ... tell where, when or how. Most adverbs e ...

Directions: Com ... with the correct part of speech.

Example:

Hank   wrote   here.
who? (noun)   what? (verb)   where? (adverb)

1. _____ was lost _____
who? (noun)   what? (verb)   where? (adverb)

2. _____ quickly.
who? (noun)   what? (verb)   how? (adverb)

3. _____ felt _____
who? (noun)   what? (verb)   how? (adverb)

4. My brother _____
who? (noun)   what? (verb)   when? (adverb)

5. _____ woke up _____
who? (noun)   what? (verb)   when? (adverb)

6. _____ gladly.
who? (noun)   what? (verb)   how? (adverb)

Page 348

Suffixes: Sentences

Directions: Use a word from the box to complete each sentence.

cheerful	softness	encouragement
kindness	safely	friendly

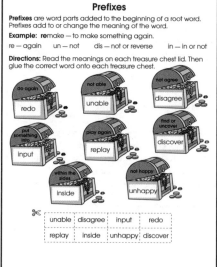

1. The __friendly__ dog licked me and wagged his tail.

2. Jeff is happy and __cheerful__ .

3. To ride your bike __safely__ , you should wear a helmet.

4. My aunt is known for her thoughtfulness and __kindness__ .

5. I love the __softness__ of my cat's fur.

6. The teacher gave her class a lot of __encouragement__

Page 349

Suffixes: Root Words

A **root word** is a word before a suffix is added.

Example: In the word hope**ful**, the root word is **hope**.

Directions: Each egg contains a root word. Cut out each egg and match it with a basket so that it forms a new word. Write the new word on the lines on the basket.

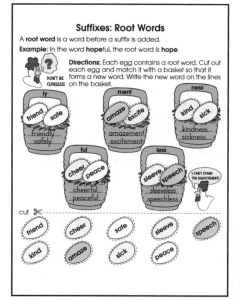

ly — friend + safe — friendly, safely
ment — amaze + excite — amazement, excitement
ness — kind + sick — kindness, sickness
ful — cheer + peace — cheerful, peaceful
less — sleeve + speech — sleeveless, speechless

cut ✂------------------

friend   cheer   safe   sleeve   speech
kind   amaze   sick   peace

Page 351

Prefixes

Prefixes are word parts added to the beginning of a root word. Prefixes add to or change the meaning of the word.

Example: re**make** — to make something again.

re — again   un — not   dis — not or reverse   in — in or not

Directions: Read the meanings on each treasure chest lid. Then glue the correct word onto each treasure chest.

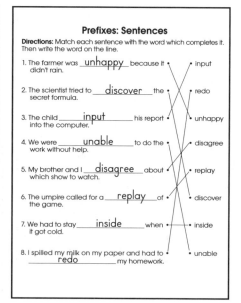

do again — redo
not able — unable
not agree — disagree
put something into — input
play again — replay
find or uncover — discover
within the sides — inside
not happy — unhappy

✂ | unable | disagree | input | redo |
| replay | inside | unhappy | discover |

Page 353

Prefixes: Sentences

Directions: Match each sentence with the word which completes it. Then write the word on the line.

1. The farmer was __unhappy__ because it didn't rain. • • input

2. The scientist tried to __discover__ the • • redo secret formula.

3. The child __input__ his report • • unhappy into the computer.

4. We were __unable__ to do the • • disagree work without help.

5. My brother and I __disagree__ about • • replay which show to watch.

6. The umpire called for a __replay__ of • • discover the game.

7. We had to stay __inside__ when • • inside it got cold.

8. I spilled my milk on my paper and had to • • unable __redo__ my homework.

Page 354

Synonyms

Synonyms are words which mean almost the same thing.

Example: sick — ill

Directions: Use words from the box to help you complete the sentences below.

| glad | fast | noisy | filthy | angry |

1. When I am mad, I could also say I am ___angry___ .

2. To be ___glad___ is the same as being happy.

3. After playing outside, I thought I was dirty, but Mom said I was ___filthy___ !

4. I tried not to be too loud, but I couldn't help being a little ___noisy___ .

5. If you're too ___fast___ , or speedy, you may not do a careful job.

Think of another pair of synonyms. ~~Answers will vary.~~ on the lines.

Page 355

Synonyms

Directions: Cut out the sails below. Glue each one to the boat whose synonym matches it.

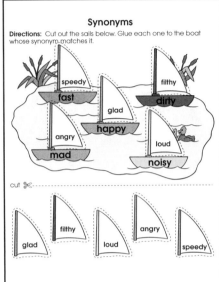

cut ✂- - - - - - - - - - - - - - - - -

glad   filthy   loud   angry   speedy

Page 357

Antonyms

Antonyms are words that have opposite meanings.

Example: neat — sloppy

Directions: Cut out each frog below and glue it to the lily pad with its antonym.

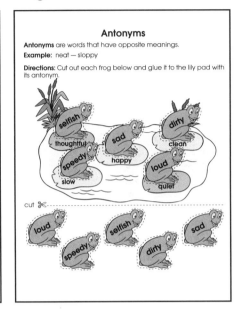

cut ✂- - - - - - - - - - - - - - - - -

loud   speedy   selfish   dirty   sad

Page 359

Antonyms

Directions: Use antonyms from the box to complete the sentences below.

| speedy | clean | quiet | thoughtful | happy |

1. If we get too loud, the teacher will ask us to get ___quiet___

2. She was sad to lose her puppy, but she was ___happy___ to find it again.

3. Mark got dirty, so he had to scrub himself ___clean___ .

4. Janna was too ___speedy___ when she did her homework, so she tried to be slow when she did it over.

5. Dave was too selfish to share his cookies, but Deborah was ___thoughtful___ enough to share hers.

Think of another pair of antonyms. ~~Answers will vary.~~ on the lines.

Page 360

Contractions

A **contraction** is a short way to write two words together. Some letters are left out, but an apostrophe takes their place.

Directions: Write the words from the box that answer the questions.

| hasn't | you've | aren't | we've | weren't |

1. Write the correct contractions below.

Example:

I have ___I've___   was not ___wasn't___

we have ___we've___   you have ___you've___

are not ___aren't___   were not ___weren't___

has not ___hasn't___

2. Write two words from the box that are contractions using **have**.

___you've___   ___we've___

3. Write three words from the box that are contractions using **not**.

___hasn't___   ___aren't___   ___weren't___

Page 361

Contractions

Directions: In each sentence below, underline the two words that could be made into a contraction. Write the contraction on the line. Use each contraction from the box only once.

Example: The boys have not gone camping in a long time.

___haven't___

| hasn't | you've | aren't |
| we've | weren't | |

1. After a while, we <u>were not</u> sure it was the right direction.   ___weren't___

2. I think <u>we have</u> been this way before.   ___we've___

3. We have been waiting, but our guide <u>has not</u> come yet.   ___hasn't___

4. Did you say <u>you have</u> been here with your sister?   ___you've___

5. You <u>are not</u> going to give up and go back, are you?   ___aren't___

Page 362

Review

Directions: Circle the two words in each sentence that are not spelled correctly. Then write the words correctly.

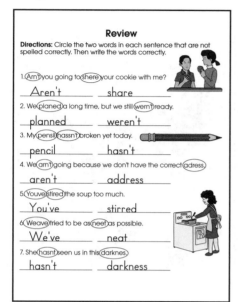

1. (Arn't) you going to (shere) your cookie with me?
   Aren't _____ share _____

2. We (planed) a long time, but we still (wern't) ready.
   planned _____ weren't _____

3. My (pensil) (hassn't) broken yet today.
   pencil _____ hasn't _____

4. We (arn't) going because we don't have the correct (adress.)
   aren't _____ address _____

5. (Youve) (stired) the soup too much.
   You've _____ stirred _____

6. (Weave) tried to be as (neet) as possible.
   We've _____ neat _____

7. She (hasnt) seen us in this (darknes.)
   hasn't _____ darkness _____

Page 364

Addition

Directions: Add.
Example:

Add the ones.	Add the tens.
26 +21 = 7	26 +21 = 47

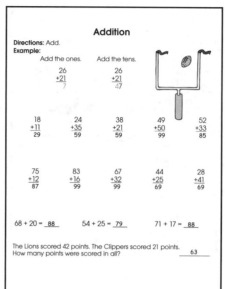

18 +11 = 29	24 +35 = 59	38 +21 = 59	49 +50 = 99	52 +33 = 85

75 +12 = 87	83 +16 = 99	67 +32 = 99	44 +25 = 69	28 +41 = 69

68 + 20 = __88__   54 + 25 = __79__   71 + 17 = __88__

The Lions scored 42 points. The Clippers scored 21 points. How many points were scored in all?   __63__

Page 365

Subtraction

Subtraction means "taking away" or subtracting one number from another to find the difference. For example, 10 - 3 = 7.

Directions: Subtract.
Example:

Subtract the ones.	Subtract the tens.
39 -24 = 5	39 -24 = 5

48 -35 = 13	95 -22 = 73	87 -16 = 71	55 -43 = 12

37 -14 = 23	69 -57 = 12	44 -23 = 21	99 -78 = 21

66 - 44 = __22__   57 - 33 = __24__

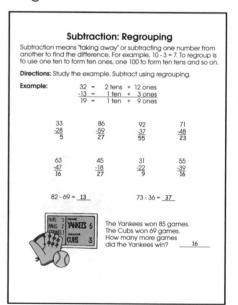

The yellow car traveled 87 miles per hour. The orange car traveled 66 miles per hour. How much faster was the yellow car traveling?   __21 m.p.h.__

Page 366

Place Value

The place value of a digit, or numeral, is shown by where it is in the number. For example, in the number 1,234, 1 has the place value of thousands, 2 is hundreds, 3 is tens and 4 is ones.

Hundred Thousands	Ten Thousands	Thousands	Hundreds	Tens	Ones
9	4	3	8	5	2

943,852

Directions: Match the numbers in Column A with the words in Column B.

A	B
62,453	two hundred thousand
7,641	three thousand
486,113	four hundred thousand
11,277	eight hundreds
813,463	seven tens
594,483	five ones
254,089	six hundreds
79,841	nine ten thousands
27,115	five tens

Page 367

Addition: Regrouping

Addition means "putting together" or adding two or more numbers to find the sum. For example, 3 + 5 = 8. To regroup is to use ten ones to form one ten, ten tens to form one 100 and so on.

Directions: Add using regrouping.
Example:

Add the ones.	Add the tens with regrouping.
88 +21 = 9	88 +21 = 109

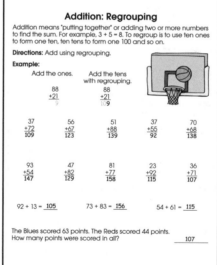

37 +72 = 109	56 +67 = 123	51 +88 = 139	37 +55 = 92	70 +68 = 138

93 +54 = 147	47 +82 = 129	81 +77 = 158	23 +92 = 115	36 +71 = 107

92 + 13 = __105__   73 + 83 = __156__   54 + 61 = __115__

The Blues scored 63 points. The Reds scored 44 points. How many points were scored in all?   __107__

Page 368

Subtraction: Regrouping

Subtraction means "taking away" or subtracting one number from another to find the difference. For example, 10 - 3 = 7. To regroup is to use one ten to form ten ones, one 100 to form ten tens and so on.

Directions: Study the example. Subtract using regrouping.
Example:

32	=	2 tens	+	12 ones
-13	=	1 ten	+	3 ones
19	=	1 ten	+	9 ones

33 -28 = 5	86 -59 = 27	92 -37 = 55	71 -48 = 23

63 -47 = 16	45 -18 = 27	31 -22 = 9	55 -39 = 16

82 - 69 = __13__   73 - 36 = __37__

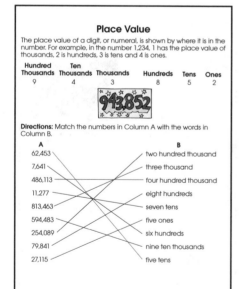

The Yankees won 85 games. The Cubs won 69 games. How many more games did the Yankees win?   __16__

Page 369

Addition and Subtraction: Regrouping

Addition means "putting together" or adding two or more numbers to find the sum. Subtraction means "taking away" or subtracting one number from another to find the difference. To regroup is to use one ten to form ten ones, one 100 to form ten tens and so on.

Directions: Add or subtract. Regroup when needed.

92 −47 = 45	58 +26 = 84	63 +18 = 81	77 −38 = 39
27 −17 = 10	31 +42 = 73	56 −29 = 27	67 +33 = 100
72 +19 = 91	87 −58 = 29	93 −89 = 4	54 +27 = 81

The soccer team scored 83 goals this year. The soccer team scored 68 goals last year. How many goals did they score in all? **151**

How many more goals did they score this year than last year? **15**

Page 370

Addition: Regrouping

Directions: Study the example. Add using regrouping.

Examples:

Add the ones. Regroup.
1
156
+267
3

Add the tens. Regroup.
11
156
+267
23

Add the hundreds.
1
156
+267
423

6
+7
13

5
+6
12

1
156
+267
3

29 46 +12 = 87	81 78 +33 = 192	52 67 +23 = 142	49 37 +19 = 105	162 +349 = 511
273 +198 = 471	655 +297 = 952	783 +148 = 931	385 +169 = 554	428 +122 = 550

Sally went bowling. She had scores of 115, 129 and 103. What was her total score for three games? **347**

Page 371

Addition: Regrouping

Directions: Add using regrouping. Then use the code to discover the name of a United States president.

348 +752 = 1,100	642 +277 = 919	386 +787 = 1,173	184 +875 = 1,059	578 +874 = 1,452
653 +768 = 1,421	653 +359 = 1,012	946 +239 = 1,185	393 +257 = 650	199 +843 = 1,042
721 +679 = 1,400				

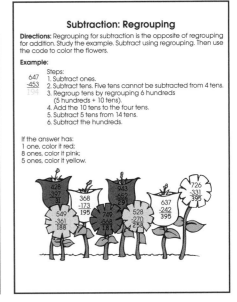

G W A S H I N G T O N

1012	1173	1059	1421	919	650	1452	1042	1100	1400	1185
N	A	S	I	W	T	H	O	G	N	G

Page 372

Addition: Regrouping

Directions: Study the example. Add using regrouping.

Example:

5,356
+3,976
9,332

Steps:
1. Add the ones.
2. Regroup the tens. Add the tens.
3. Regroup the hundreds. Add the hundreds.
4. Add the thousands.

6,849 +3,276 = 10,125	1,846 +8,384 = 10,230	9,221 +6,769 = 15,990
2,758 +3,663 = 6,421	5,299 +8,764 = 14,063	7,932 +6,879 = 14,811

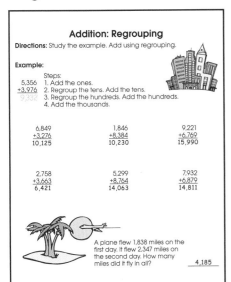

A plane flew 1,838 miles on the first day. It flew 2,347 miles on the second day. How many miles did it fly in all? **4,185**

Page 373

Addition: Mental Math

Directions: Try to do these addition problems in your head without using paper and pencil.

7 +4 = 11	6 +3 = 9	8 +1 = 9	10 +2 = 12	2 +9 = 11	6 +6 = 12
10 +20 = 30	40 +20 = 60	80 +100 = 180	60 +30 = 90	50 +70 = 120	100 +40 = 140
350 +150 = 500	300 +500 = 800	400 +800 = 1,200	450 +10 = 460	680 +100 = 780	900 +70 = 970
1,000 +200 = 1,200	4,000 400 +30 = 4,430	300 200 +80 = 580	8,000 500 +60 = 8,560	9,800 +150 = 9,950	7,000 300 +30 = 7,330

Page 374

Subtraction: Regrouping

Directions: Regrouping for subtraction is the opposite of regrouping for addition. Study the example. Subtract using regrouping. Then use the code to color the flowers.

Example:

647
−453
194

Steps:
1. Subtract ones.
2. Subtract tens. Five tens cannot be subtracted from 4 tens.
3. Regroup tens by regrouping 6 hundreds (5 hundreds + 10 tens).
4. Add the 10 tens to the four tens.
5. Subtract 5 tens from 14 tens.
6. Subtract the hundreds.

If the answer has:
1 one, color it red;
8 ones, color it pink;
5 ones, color it yellow.

428 −397 = 31
368 −173 = 195
943 −652 = 291
726 −331 = 395
549 −361 = 188
749 −568 = 181
528 −270 = 258
637 −242 = 395

ANSWER KEY

Page 375

Subtraction: Regrouping

Directions: Study the example. Follow the steps. Subtract using regrouping.

Example:

```
 634   Steps:
-455   1. Subtract ones. You cannot subtract five ones from 4 ones.
 179   2. Regroup ones by regrouping 3 tens to 2 tens + 10 ones.
       3. Subtract 5 ones from 14 ones.
       4. Regroup tens by regrouping hundreds
          (5 hundreds + 10 tens).
       5. Subtract 5 tens from 12 tens.
       6. Subtract hundreds.
```

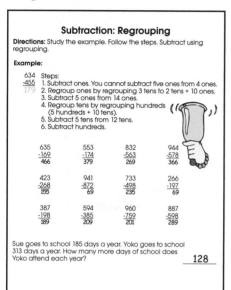

635	553	832	944
-169	-174	-563	-578
466	379	269	366

423	941	733	266
-268	-872	-498	-197
155	69	235	69

387	594	960	887
-198	-385	-759	-598
189	209	201	289

Sue goes to school 185 days a year. Yoko goes to school 313 days a year. How many more days of school does Yoko attend each year?   **128**

Page 376

Subtraction: Regrouping

Directions: Study the example. Follow the steps. Subtract using regrouping. If you have to regroup to subtract ones and there are no tens, you must regroup twice.

Example:

```
 300   Steps:
-182   1. Subtract ones. You cannot subtract 2 ones from 0 ones.
 118   2. Regroup. No tens. Regroup hundreds
          (2 hundreds + 10 tens).
       3. Regroup tens (9 tens + 10 ones).
       4. Subtract 2 ones from ten ones.
       5. Subtract 8 tens from 9 tens.
       6. Subtract 1 hundred from 2 hundreds.
```

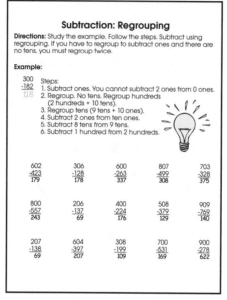

602	306	600	807	703
-423	-128	-263	-499	-328
179	178	337	308	375

800	206	400	508	909
-557	-137	-224	-379	-769
243	69	176	129	140

207	604	308	700	900
-138	-397	-199	-531	-278
69	207	109	169	622

Page 377

Subtraction: Regrouping

Directions: Subtract. Regroup when necessary. The first one is done for you.

7,354	4,214	8,437	6,837
-5,295	-3,185	-5,338	-4,318
2,059	1,029	3,099	2,519

5,735	1,036	6,735	3,841
-3,826	- 947	-6,646	-1,953
1,909	89	89	1,888

Columbus discovered America in 1492. The pilgrims landed in America in 1620. How many years difference was there between these two events?

```
 1620
-1492
```
128 years

Page 378

Subtraction: Mental Math

Directions: Try to do these subtraction problems in your head without using paper and pencil.

9	12	7	5	15	2
-3	-6	-6	-1	-5	-0
6	6	1	4	10	2

40	90	100	20	60	70
-20	-80	-50	-20	-10	-40
20	10	50	0	50	30

450	500	250	690	320	900
-250	-300	-20	-100	-20	-600
200	200	230	590	300	300

1,000	8,000	7,000	4,000	9,500	5,000
-400	-500	-900	-2,000	-4,000	-2,000
600	7,500	6,100	2,000	5,500	3,000

Page 379

Review

Directions: Add or subtract using regrouping.

28	82	33	67
56	49	75	94
+93	+51	+128	+248
177	182	236	409

683	756	818	956
-495	+139	-387	+267
188	895	431	1,223

1,588	4,675	8,732	2,938
- 989	-2,976	-5,664	+3,459
599	1,699	3,068	6,397

To drive from New York City to Los Angeles is 2,832 miles. To drive from New York City to Miami is 1,327 miles. How much farther is it to drive from New York City to Los Angeles than from New York City to Miami?

```
 2,832
-1,327
 1,505
```

Page 380

Rounding: The Nearest Ten

If the ones number is 5 or greater, "round up" to the nearest 10. If the ones number is 4 or less, the tens number stays the same and the ones number becomes a zero.

Examples: **15** round up to 20   **23** round down to 20   **47** round up to 50

7	**10**		58	**60**
12	**10**		81	**80**
33	**30**		94	**90**
27	**30**		44	**40**
73	**70**		88	**90**
25	**30**		66	**70**
39	**40**		70	**70**

Page 381

Rounding: The Nearest Hundred

If the tens number is 5 or greater, "round up" to the nearest hundred. If the tens number is 4 or less, the hundreds number remains the same.

REMEMBER... Look at the number directly to the right of the place you are rounding to.

Example:

230 round down to 200   **470** round up to 500

150 round up to 200   **732** round down to 700

456 **500**   120 **100**

340 **300**   923 **900**

867 **900**   550 **600**

686 **700**   231 **200**

770 **800**   492 **500**

Page 382

Front-End Estimation

Front-end estimation is useful when you don't need to know the exact amount, but a close answer will do.

When we use front-end estimation, we use only the first number, and then add the numbers together to get the estimate.

Example:

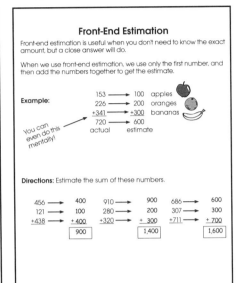

$$\begin{array}{ll}153 \longrightarrow & 100 \quad \text{apples}\\226 \longrightarrow & 200 \quad \text{oranges}\\+341 \longrightarrow & +300 \quad \text{bananas}\\720 & 600\\\text{actual} & \text{estimate}\end{array}$$

You can even do this mentally!

Directions: Estimate the sum of these numbers.

$$\begin{array}{ccc}456 \longrightarrow 400 & 910 \longrightarrow 900 & 686 \longrightarrow 600\\121 \longrightarrow 100 & 280 \longrightarrow 200 & 307 \longrightarrow 300\\+438 \longrightarrow +400 & +320 \longrightarrow +300 & +711 \longrightarrow +700\\\boxed{900} & \boxed{1,400} & \boxed{1,600}\end{array}$$

Page 383

Multiplication

Multiplication is a short way to find the sum of adding the same number a certain amount of times. For example, we write 7 x 4 = 28 instead of 7 + 7 + 7 + 7 = 28.

Directions: Study the example. Multiply.

Example:

There are two groups of seashells. There are 3 seashells in each group. How many seashells are there in all?   2 x 3 = 6

4 + 4 = **8**   3 + 3 + 3 = **9**
2 x 4 = **8**   3 x 3 = **9**

$$\begin{array}{ccccc}2 & 3 & 4 & 6 & 7\\\underline{\times 3} & \underline{\times 5} & \underline{\times 3} & \underline{\times 2} & \underline{\times 3}\\6 & 15 & 12 & 12 & 21\end{array}$$

$$\begin{array}{ccccc}5 & 6 & 4 & 7 & 8\\\underline{\times 2} & \underline{\times 3} & \underline{\times 2} & \underline{\times 2} & \underline{\times 3}\\10 & 18 & 8 & 14 & 24\end{array}$$

$$\begin{array}{ccccc}5 & 9 & 8 & 6 & 9\\\underline{\times 5} & \underline{\times 4} & \underline{\times 5} & \underline{\times 6} & \underline{\times 3}\\25 & 36 & 40 & 36 & 27\end{array}$$

Page 384

Multiplication

Directions: Multiply.

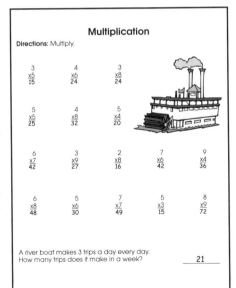

$$\begin{array}{ccc}3 & 4 & 3\\\underline{\times 5} & \underline{\times 6} & \underline{\times 8}\\15 & 24 & 24\end{array}$$

$$\begin{array}{ccc}5 & 4 & 5\\\underline{\times 5} & \underline{\times 8} & \underline{\times 4}\\25 & 32 & 20\end{array}$$

$$\begin{array}{ccccc}6 & 3 & 2 & 7 & 9\\\underline{\times 7} & \underline{\times 9} & \underline{\times 8} & \underline{\times 6} & \underline{\times 4}\\42 & 27 & 16 & 42 & 36\end{array}$$

$$\begin{array}{ccccc}6 & 5 & 7 & 5 & 8\\\underline{\times 8} & \underline{\times 6} & \underline{\times 7} & \underline{\times 3} & \underline{\times 9}\\48 & 30 & 49 & 15 & 72\end{array}$$

A river boat makes 3 trips a day every day. How many trips does it make in a week?   **21**

Page 385

Multiplication

Factors are the numbers multiplied together in a multiplication problem. The answer is called the product. If you change the order of the factors, the product stays the same.

Example:

There are 4 groups of fish. There are 3 fish in each group. How many fish are there in all?
4 x 3 = 12
factor x factor = product

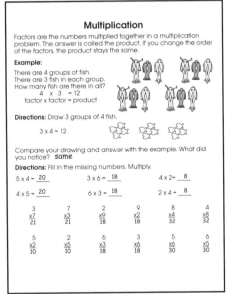

Directions: Draw 3 groups of 4 fish.

3 x 4 = 12

Compare your drawing and answer with the example. What did you notice? **same**

Directions: Fill in the missing numbers. Multiply.

5 x 4 = **20**   3 x 6 = **18**   4 x 2 = **8**

4 x 5 = **20**   6 x 3 = **18**   2 x 4 = **8**

$$\begin{array}{ccccc}3 & 7 & 2 & 9 & 8 \quad 4\\\underline{\times 7} & \underline{\times 3} & \underline{\times 9} & \underline{\times 2} & \underline{\times 4} \quad \underline{\times 8}\\21 & 21 & 18 & 18 & 32 \quad 32\end{array}$$

$$\begin{array}{ccccc}5 & 2 & 6 & 3 & 5 \quad 6\\\underline{\times 2} & \underline{\times 5} & \underline{\times 3} & \underline{\times 6} & \underline{\times 6} \quad \underline{\times 5}\\10 & 10 & 18 & 18 & 30 \quad 30\end{array}$$

Page 386

Multiplication: Zero and One

Any number multiplied by zero equals zero. One multiplied by any number equals that number. Study the example. Multiply.

Example:

How many full sails are there in all?

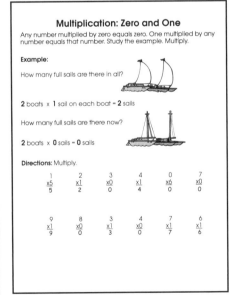

2 boats **x 1** sail on each boat **= 2** sails

How many full sails are there now?

2 boats **x 0** sails **= 0** sails

Directions: Multiply.

$$\begin{array}{cccccc}1 & 2 & 3 & 4 & 0 & 7\\\underline{\times 5} & \underline{\times 1} & \underline{\times 0} & \underline{\times 1} & \underline{\times 6} & \underline{\times 0}\\5 & 2 & 0 & 4 & 0 & 0\end{array}$$

$$\begin{array}{cccccc}9 & 8 & 3 & 4 & 7 & 6\\\underline{\times 1} & \underline{\times 0} & \underline{\times 1} & \underline{\times 0} & \underline{\times 1} & \underline{\times 1}\\9 & 0 & 3 & 0 & 7 & 6\end{array}$$

Page 387

Multiplication

Directions: Time yourself as you multiply. How quickly can you complete this page?

3 x2 6	8 x7 56	1 x0 0	1 x6 6	3 x4 12	0 x4 0
4 x1 4	4 x4 16	2 x5 10	9 x3 27	9 x9 81	5 x3 15
0 x8 0	2 x6 12	9 x6 54	8 x5 40	7 x3 21	4 x2 8
3 x5 15	2 x0 0	4 x6 24	1 x3 3	0 x0 0	3 x3 9

Page 388

Multiplication Table

Directions: Complete the multiplication table. Use it to practice your multiplication facts.

X	0	1	2	3	4	5	6	7	8	9	10
0	0	0	0	0	0	0	0	0	0	0	0
1	0	1	2	3	4	5	6	7	8	9	10
2	0	2	4	6	8	10	12	14	16	18	20
3	0	3	6	9	12	15	18	21	24	27	30
4	0	4	8	12	16	20	24	28	32	36	40
5	0	5	10	15	20	25	30	35	40	45	50
6	0	6	12	18	24	30	36	42	48	54	60
7	0	7	14	21	28	35	42	49	56	63	70
8	0	8	16	24	32	40	48	56	64	72	80
9	0	9	18	27	36	45	54	63	72	81	90
10	0	10	20	30	40	50	60	70	80	90	100

Page 389

Division

Division is a way to find out how many times one number is contained in another number. For example, 28 ÷ 4 = 7 means that there are seven groups of four in 28.

Directions: Study the example. Divide.

Example:

There are 6 oars.
Each canoe needs 2 oars.
How many canoes can be used?

Circle groups of 2.
There are 3 groups of 2.

$$\underset{\text{oars}}{6} + \underset{\substack{\text{number}\\\text{of oars}\\\text{needed}\\\text{per canoe}}}{2} = \underset{\text{canoes}}{3}$$

9 ÷ 3 = **3**   8 ÷ 2 = **4**   16 ÷ 4 = **4**

15 ÷ 5 = **3**   18 ÷ 2 = **9**   20 ÷ 4 = **5**

21 ÷ 7 = **3**   24 ÷ 6 = **4**   12 ÷ 2 = **6**

Page 390

Division

Directions: Divide. Draw a line from the boat to the sail with the correct answer.

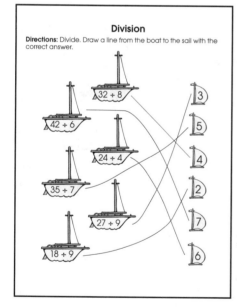

- 32 ÷ 8
- 42 ÷ 6
- 24 ÷ 4
- 35 ÷ 7
- 27 ÷ 9
- 18 ÷ 9

Sails: 3, 5, 4, 2, 7, 6

Page 391

Order of Operations

When you solve a problem that involves more than one operation, this is the order to follow:

- ( ) Parentheses first
- x Multiplication
- ÷ Division
- + Addition
- − Subtraction

Example:

2 + (3 x 5) - 2 = 15
2 + 15 - 2 = 15
17 - 2 = 15

Directions: Solve the problems using the correct order of operations.

(5 - 3) + 4 x 7 = **30**
2   28

6 x 3 - 1 = **17**
18

9 ÷ 3 x 3 + 0 = **1**
9

1 + 2 x 3 + 4 = **11**
6

(8 + 2) x 4 = **16**
4

5 - 2 x 1 + 2 = **1**
2

Page 392

Order of Operations

Directions: Use +, −, x and ÷ to complete the problems so the number sentence is true.

Example: 4 **+** 2 **−** 1 = 5

(8 **÷** 2) **+** 4 = 8

(1 **+** 2) **÷** 3 = 1

9 **÷** 3 **−** 9 = 3

(7 **−** 5) **x** 1 = 2

8 **x** 5 **÷** 4 = 10

5 **−** 4 **+** 1 = 1

REMEMBER...
USE THE ORDER OF OPERATIONS

Page 393

Review

Directions: Multiply or divide. Fill in the blanks with the missing numbers or x or ÷ signs. The first one is done for you.

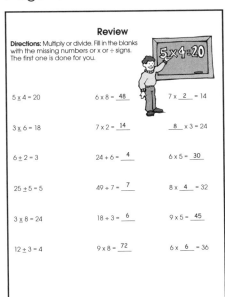

5 x 4 = 20

6 x 8 = __48__

7 x __2__ = 14

3 x 6 = 18

7 x 2 = __14__

__8__ x 3 = 24

6 ÷ 2 = 3

24 ÷ 6 = __4__

6 x 5 = __30__

25 ÷ 5 = 5

49 ÷ 7 = __7__

8 x __4__ = 32

3 x 8 = 24

18 ÷ 3 = __6__

9 x 5 = __45__

12 ÷ 3 = 4

9 x 8 = __72__

6 x __6__ = 36

Page 394

Division

Division is a way to find out how many times one number is contained in another number. The ÷ sign means "divided by." Another way to divide is to use ⌐. The dividend is the larger number that is divided by the smaller number, or divisor. The answer of a division problem is called the quotient.

Directions: Study the example. Divide.

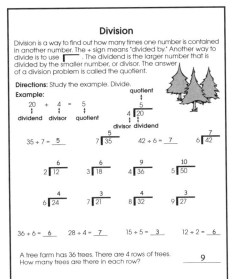

Example:

20 ÷ 4 = 5
dividend ÷ divisor = quotient

5
4⌐20
divisor dividend

35 ÷ 7 = __5__   7⌐35 (5)   42 ÷ 6 = __7__   6⌐42 (7)

2⌐12 (6)   3⌐18 (6)   4⌐36 (9)   5⌐50 (10)

6⌐24 (4)   7⌐21 (3)   8⌐32 (4)   9⌐27 (3)

36 ÷ 6 = __6__   28 ÷ 4 = __7__   15 ÷ 5 = __3__   12 ÷ 2 = __6__

A tree farm has 36 trees. There are 4 rows of trees. How many trees are there in each row?   __9__

Page 395

Division: Zero and One

Directions: Study the rules of division and the examples. Divide, then write the number of the rule you used to solve each problem.

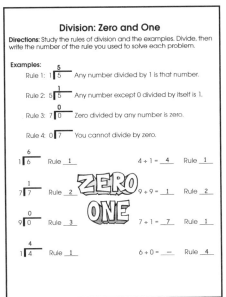

Examples:

Rule 1: 1⌐5 (5)   Any number divided by 1 is that number.

Rule 2: 5⌐5 (1)   Any number except 0 divided by itself is 1.

Rule 3: 7⌐0 (0)   Zero divided by any number is zero.

Rule 4: 0⌐7   You cannot divide by zero.

1⌐6 (6)   Rule __1__   4 ÷ 1 = __4__   Rule __1__

7⌐7 (1)   Rule __2__   9 ÷ 9 = __1__   Rule __2__

9⌐0 (0)   Rule __3__   7 ÷ 1 = __7__   Rule __1__

1⌐4 (4)   Rule __1__   6 ÷ 0 = __—__   Rule __4__

Page 396

Division: Remainders

Division is a way to find out how many times one number is contained in another number. For example, 28 ÷ 4 = 7 means that there are seven groups of four in 28. The dividend is the larger number that is divided by the smaller number, or divisor. The quotient is the answer in a division problem. The remainder is the amount left over. The remainder is always less than the divisor.

Directions: Study the example. Find each quotient and remainder.

Example:
There are 11 dog biscuits. Put them in groups of 3. There are 2 left over.

3⌐11 (3)
-9
2 remainder

3⌐11 (3 r 2)

Remember: The remainder must be less than the **divisor!**

3⌐13 (4 r1)   4⌐17 (4 r1)   6⌐32 (5 r2)   5⌐26 (5 r1)

9 ÷ 4 = __2 r1__   12 ÷ 5 = __2 r2__   26 ÷ 4 = __6 r2__   49 ÷ 9 = __5 r4__

The pet store has 7 cats. Two cats go in each cage. How many cats are left over?   __1__

Page 397

Divisibility Rules

A number is divisible... by 2 if the last digit is 0 or even (2, 4, 6, 8).
by 3 if the sum of all digits is divisible by 3.
by 4 if the last two digits are divisible by 4.
by 5 if the last digit is a 0 or 5.
by 10 if the last digit is 0.

Example: 250 is divisible by __2, 5, 10__

Directions: Tell what numbers each of these numbers is divisible by.

3,732 __2, 3, 4__   439 __—__

50 __2, 5, 10__   444 __2, 3, 4__

7,960 __2, 4, 5, 10__   8,212 __2, 4__

104,924 __2, 4__   2,345 __5__

Page 398

Factor Trees

Factors are the smaller numbers multiplied together to make a larger number. Factor trees are one way to find all the factors of a number.

Example:

24
6 x 4
2 x 3 x 2 x 2

40
8 x 5
4 x 2 x 5
2 x 2 x 2 x 5

36
6 x 6
3 x 2 x 3 x 2

439 __—__

12
3 x 4
3 x 2 x 2

81
9 x 9
3 x 3 x 3 x 3

Grade 3 - Comprehensive Curriculum

Page 399

Percentages

A percentage is the amount of a number out of 100. This is the percent sign: %

Directions: Fill in the blanks.

Example: 70% = $\frac{70}{100}$ $\underline{40}$ % = $\frac{40}{100}$

30% = $\frac{30}{100}$ 10% = $\frac{10}{100}$

90% = $\frac{90}{100}$ 40% = $\frac{40}{100}$

70% = $\frac{70}{100}$ 80% = $\frac{80}{100}$

$\underline{20}$ % = $\frac{20}{100}$ $\underline{60}$ % = $\frac{60}{100}$

$\underline{30}$ % = $\frac{30}{100}$ $\underline{10}$ % = $\frac{10}{100}$

$\underline{50}$ % = $\frac{50}{100}$ $\underline{90}$ % = $\frac{90}{100}$

Page 400

Fractions

A fraction is a number that names part of a whole, such as $\frac{1}{2}$ or $\frac{1}{3}$.

Directions: Write the fraction that tells what part of each figure is colored. The first one is done for you.

Example:
2 parts shaded
5 parts in the whole figure

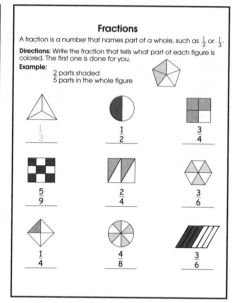

$\frac{1}{3}$ $\frac{1}{2}$ $\frac{3}{4}$

$\frac{5}{9}$ $\frac{2}{4}$ $\frac{3}{6}$

$\frac{1}{4}$ $\frac{4}{8}$ $\frac{3}{6}$

Page 401

Fractions: Equivalent

Fractions that name the same part of a whole are equivalent fractions.

Example:

$\frac{1}{2}$ = $\frac{2}{4}$

Directions: Fill in the numbers to complete the equivalent fractions.

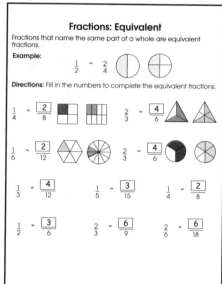

$\frac{1}{4}$ = $\frac{2}{8}$ $\frac{2}{3}$ = $\frac{4}{6}$

$\frac{1}{6}$ = $\frac{2}{12}$ $\frac{2}{3}$ = $\frac{4}{6}$

$\frac{1}{3}$ = $\frac{4}{12}$ $\frac{1}{5}$ = $\frac{3}{15}$ $\frac{1}{4}$ = $\frac{2}{8}$

$\frac{1}{2}$ = $\frac{3}{6}$ $\frac{2}{3}$ = $\frac{6}{9}$ $\frac{2}{6}$ = $\frac{6}{18}$

Page 402

Fractions: Division

A fraction is a number that names part of an object. It can also name part of a group.

Directions: Study the example. Divide by the bottom number of the fraction to find the answers.

Example:
There are 6 cheerleaders.
$\frac{1}{3}$ of the cheerleaders are boys.
How many cheerleaders are boys?

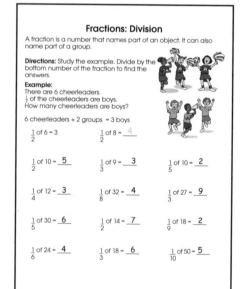

6 cheerleaders ÷ 2 groups = 3 boys

$\frac{1}{2}$ of 6 = 3 $\frac{1}{2}$ of 8 = 4

$\frac{1}{2}$ of 10 = $\underline{5}$ $\frac{1}{3}$ of 9 = $\underline{3}$ $\frac{1}{5}$ of 10 = $\underline{2}$

$\frac{1}{4}$ of 12 = $\underline{3}$ $\frac{1}{8}$ of 32 = $\underline{4}$ $\frac{1}{3}$ of 27 = $\underline{9}$

$\frac{1}{5}$ of 30 = $\underline{6}$ $\frac{1}{2}$ of 14 = $\underline{7}$ $\frac{1}{9}$ of 18 = $\underline{2}$

$\frac{1}{6}$ of 24 = $\underline{4}$ $\frac{1}{3}$ of 18 = $\underline{6}$ $\frac{1}{10}$ of 50 = $\underline{5}$

Page 403

Fractions: Comparing

Directions: Circle the fraction in each pair that is larger.

Example:

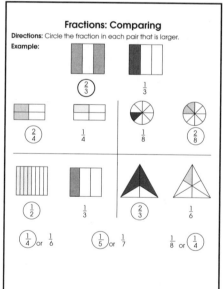

$\boxed{\frac{2}{3}}$ $\frac{1}{3}$

$\frac{2}{4}$ $\frac{1}{4}$ $\frac{1}{8}$ $\boxed{\frac{2}{8}}$

$\boxed{\frac{1}{2}}$ $\frac{1}{3}$ $\boxed{\frac{2}{3}}$ $\frac{1}{6}$

$\boxed{\frac{1}{4}}$ or $\frac{1}{6}$ $\boxed{\frac{1}{5}}$ or $\frac{1}{7}$ $\frac{1}{8}$ or $\boxed{\frac{1}{4}}$

Page 404

Decimals

A decimal is a number with one or more numbers to the right of a decimal point. A decimal point is a dot placed between the ones place and the tens place of a number, such as 2.5.

Example:

$\frac{3}{10}$ can be written as .3   They are both read as three-tenths.

Directions: Write the answer as a decimal for the shaded parts.

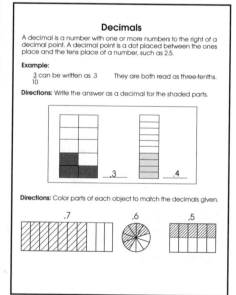

.3   .4

Directions: Color parts of each object to match the decimals given.

.7   .6   .5

Page 405

Decimals

A decimal is a number with one or more numbers to the right of a decimal point, such as 6.5 or 2.25. Equivalent means numbers that are equal.

Directions: Draw a line between the equivalent numbers.

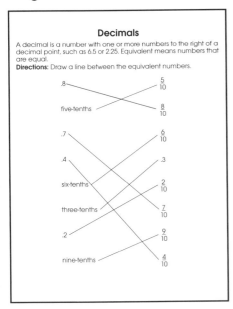

Page 406

Decimals Greater Than 1

Directions: Write the decimal for the part that is shaded.

Example:

$2\frac{4}{10}$

Write: 2.4   Read: two and four-tenths

$1\frac{2}{10}$ = **1.2** $3\frac{6}{10}$ = **3.6**

$2\frac{3}{10}$ = **2.3** $2\frac{7}{10}$ = **2.7**

Directions: Write each number as a decimal.

four and two-tenths = **4.2**   seven and one-tenth = **7.1**

$3\frac{4}{10}$ = **3.4** $6\frac{9}{10}$ = **6.9** $8\frac{3}{10}$ = **8.3** $7\frac{5}{10}$ = **7.5**

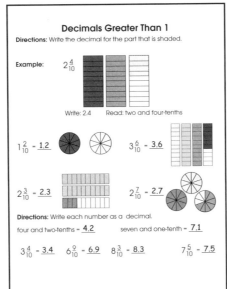

Page 407

Decimals: Addition and Subtraction

Decimals are added and subtracted in the same way as other numbers. Simply carry down the decimal point to your answer.

Directions: Add or subtract.

Examples:

$$\begin{array}{r} 1.3 \\ +2.8 \\ \hline \end{array}\quad \begin{array}{r} 4.5 \\ -2.2 \\ \hline \end{array}$$

$$\begin{array}{r} 1.3 \\ +2.2 \\ \hline 3.5 \end{array}\quad \begin{array}{r} 4.6 \\ -3.4 \\ \hline 1.2 \end{array}\quad \begin{array}{r} 5.1 \\ +8.8 \\ \hline 13.9 \end{array}\quad \begin{array}{r} 6.7 \\ -4.3 \\ \hline 2.4 \end{array}$$

$$\begin{array}{r} 7.9 \\ -3.7 \\ \hline 4.2 \end{array}\quad \begin{array}{r} 6.4 \\ +8.7 \\ \hline 15.1 \end{array}\quad \begin{array}{r} 11.4 \\ -9.5 \\ \hline 1.9 \end{array}\quad \begin{array}{r} 0.5 \\ +3.6 \\ \hline 4.1 \end{array}$$

9.3 + 1.2 = **10.5**   2.5 - 0.7 = **1.8**   1.2 + 5.0 = **6.2**

Bob jogs around the school every day. The distance for one time around is .7 of a mile. If he jogs around the school two times, how many miles does he jog each day? **1.4**

Page 408

Patterns

Directions: Write the one that would come next in each pattern.

0 2 0 4 0 6   0

1 3 5 7 9 11   13

5 10 20 40 80   160

▽ □ ▷ □ ▽ □   ▷

◇ □ ▽ ◇ □ ▽   ◇

○ ◯ ● ⬤ ○ ◯   ●

1 A 2 B 3 C   4

A B C 1 2 3   D

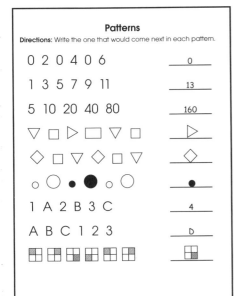

Page 409

Pattern Maze

Directions: Follow the pattern: ●■▲☆ to get through the maze.

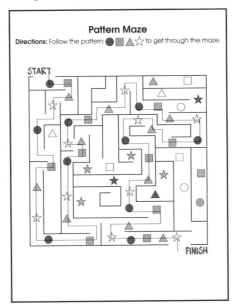

Page 410

Geometry

Geometry is the branch of mathematics that has to do with points, lines and shapes.

cube   rectangular prism   cone   cylinder   sphere

Directions: Use the code to color the picture.

Color:
cubes — blue
rectangular prisms — red
cones — green
cylinders — yellow
spheres —orange

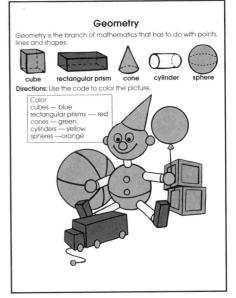

Page 411

Tangram

Directions: Cut out the tangram below. Use the shapes to make a cat, a chicken, a boat and a large triangle.

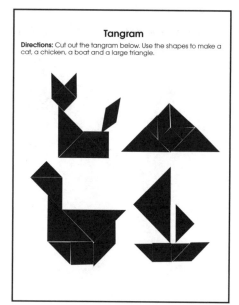

Page 413

Geometric Coloring
Directions: Color the geometric shapes in the box below.

Page 414

Geometry: Lines Segments, Rays, Angles

Geometry is the branch of mathematics that has to do with points, lines and shapes.

A **line** goes on and on in both directions. It has no end points.

Line CD

A **segment** is part of a line. It has two end points.

Segment AB

A **ray** has a line segment with only one end point. It goes on and on in the other direction.

Ray EF

An **angle** has two rays with the same end point.

Angle BAC

Directions: Write the name for each figure.

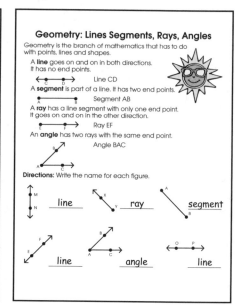

line   ray   segment

line   angle   line

Page 415

Geometry Game

Directions: 1. Cut out the cards at the bottom of the page. Put them in a pile.
2. Cut out the game boards on the next page.
3. Take turns drawing cards.
4. If you have the figure that the card describes on your gameboard, cover it.
5. The first one to get three in a row, wins.

cube	point	angle	cylinder	rectangular prism
line	square	cone	circle	sphere
triangle	segment	rectangle	tangram	ray

Page 417

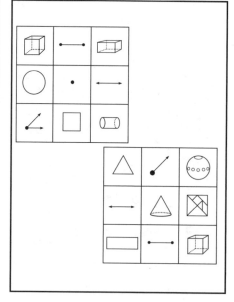

Page 419

Geometry: Perimeter
The perimeter is the distance around an object. Find the perimeter by adding the lengths of all the sides.

Directions: Find the perimeter for each object (ft. = feet).

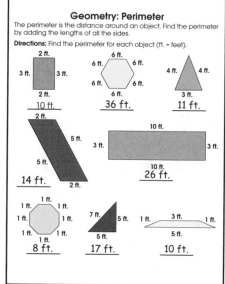

10 ft.   36 ft.   11 ft.

14 ft.   26 ft.

8 ft.   17 ft.   10 ft.

ANSWER KEY

Page 420

Flower Power

Directions: Count the flowers and answer the questions.

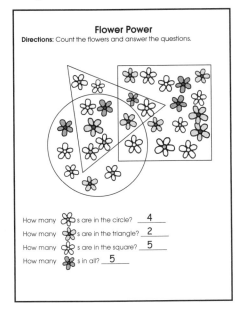

How many 🌼 s are in the circle? __4__

How many 🌼 s are in the triangle? __2__

How many 🌼 s are in the square? __5__

How many 🌼 s in all? __5__

Page 421

Map Skills: Scale

A **map scale** shows how far one place is from another. This map scale shows that 1 inch on this page equals 1 mile at the real location.

Directions: Use a ruler and the map scale to find out how far it is from Ann's house to other places. Round to the nearest inch.

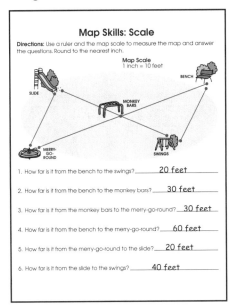

1. How far is it from Ann's house to the park? __4 miles__

2. How far is it from Ann's house to Grandma's house? __1 mile__

3. How far is it from Grandma's house to the store? __3 miles__

4. How far did Ann go when she went from her house to Grandma's and then to the store? __4 miles__

Page 422

Map Skills: Scale

Directions: Use a ruler and the map scale to measure the map and answer the questions. Round to the nearest inch.

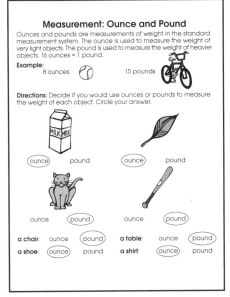

1. How far is it from the bench to the swings? __20 feet__

2. How far is it from the bench to the monkey bars? __30 feet__

3. How far is it from the monkey bars to the merry-go-round? __30 feet__

4. How far is it from the bench to the merry-go-round? __60 feet__

5. How far is it from the merry-go-round to the slide? __20 feet__

6. How far is it from the slide to the swings? __40 feet__

Page 423

Graphs

A graph is a drawing that shows information about numbers.

Directions: Color the picture. Then tell how many there are of each object by completing the graph.

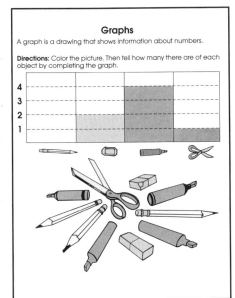

Page 424

Graphs

Directions: Answer the questions about the graph.

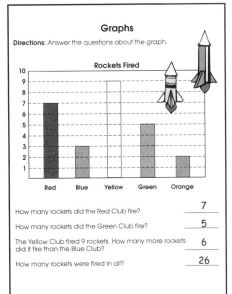

Rockets Fired

How many rockets did the Red Club fire? __7__

How many rockets did the Green Club fire? __5__

The Yellow Club fired 9 rockets. How many more rockets did it fire than the Blue Club? __6__

How many rockets were fired in all? __26__

Page 425

Measurement: Ounce and Pound

Ounces and pounds are measurements of weight in the standard measurement system. The ounce is used to measure the weight of very light objects. The pound is used to measure the weight of heavier objects. 16 ounces = 1 pound.

Example:

8 ounces   15 pounds

Directions: Decide if you would use ounces or pounds to measure the weight of each object. Circle your answer.

(ounce)   pound   (ounce)   pound

ounce   (pound)   ounce   (pound)

a chair: ounce (pound)   **a table:** ounce (pound)

a shoe: (ounce) pound   **a shirt:** (ounce) pound

Page 426

Measurement: Inches

An inch is a unit of length in the standard measurement system.

Directions: Use a ruler to measure each object to the nearest $\frac{1}{4}$ inch. Write **in.** to stand for inch.

Example:

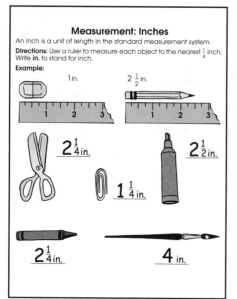

$2\frac{1}{4}$ in.

$2\frac{1}{2}$ in.

$1\frac{1}{4}$ in.

$2\frac{1}{4}$ in.

4 in.

Page 427

Measurement: Centimeter

A centimeter is a unit of length in the metric system. There are 2.54 centimeters in an inch.

Directions: Use a centimeter ruler to measure each object to the nearest half of a centimeter. Write **cm.** to stand for centimeter.

Example:

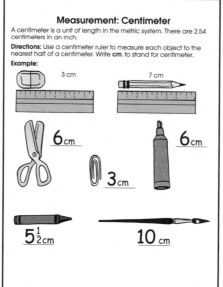

6 cm

6 cm

3 cm

$5\frac{1}{2}$ cm

10 cm

Page 428

Measurement: Foot, Yard, Mile

Directions: Decide whether you would use foot, yard or mile to measure each object.

1 foot = 12 inches
1 yard = 36 inches or 3 feet
1 mile = 1,760 yards

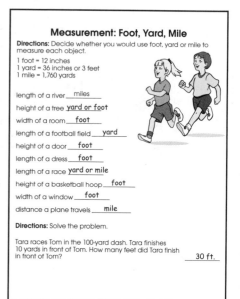

length of a river ___miles___
height of a tree ___yard or foot___
width of a room ___foot___
length of a football field ___yard___
height of a door ___foot___
length of a dress ___foot___
length of a race ___yard or mile___
height of a basketball hoop ___foot___
width of a window ___foot___
distance a plane travels ___mile___

Directions: Solve the problem.

Tara races Tom in the 100-yard dash. Tara finishes 10 yards in front of Tom. How many feet did Tara finish in front of Tom? ___30 ft.___

Page 429

Measurement: Meter and Kilometer

Meters and kilometers are units of length in the metric system. A meter is equal to 39.37 inches. A kilometer is equal to about $\frac{5}{8}$ of a mile.

Directions: Decide whether you would use meter or kilometer to measure each object.

1 meter = 100 centimeters
1 kilometer = 1,000 meters

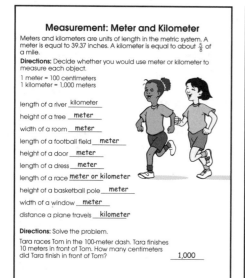

length of a river ___kilometer___
height of a tree ___meter___
width of a room ___meter___
length of a football field ___meter___
height of a door ___meter___
length of a dress ___meter___
length of a race ___meter or kilometer___
height of a basketball pole ___meter___
width of a window ___meter___
distance a plane travels ___kilometer___

Directions: Solve the problem.

Tara races Tom in the 100-meter dash. Tara finishes 10 meters in front of Tom. How many centimeters did Tara finish in front of Tom? ___1,000___

Page 430

Coordinates

Directions: Locate the points on the grid and color in each box.

What animal did you form? ___Answers will vary.___

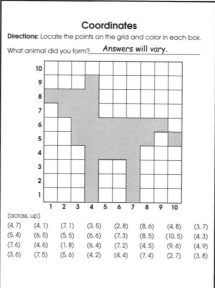

(across, up)

(4, 7) (4, 1) (7, 1) (3, 5) (2, 8) (8, 6) (4, 8) (3, 7)
(5, 4) (6, 5) (5, 5) (6, 6) (7, 3) (8, 5) (10, 5) (4, 3)
(7, 6) (4, 6) (1, 8) (6, 4) (7, 2) (4, 5) (9, 6) (4, 9)
(3, 6) (7, 5) (5, 6) (4, 2) (4, 4) (7, 4) (2, 7) (3, 8)

Page 431

Roman Numerals

Another way to write numbers is to use Roman numerals.

I	1	VII	7
II	2	VIII	8
III	3	IX	9
IV	4	X	10
V	5	XI	11
VI	6	XII	12

Directions: Fill in the Roman numerals on the watch.

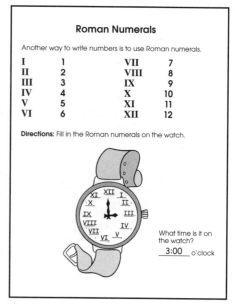

What time is it on the watch?
___3:00___ o'clock

Page 432

Roman Numerals

I	1	VII	7
II	2	VIII	8
III	3	IX	9
IV	4	X	10
V	5	XI	11
VI	6	XII	12

Directions: Write the number.

V	5	VII	7
X	10	IX	9
II	2	XII	12

Directions: Write the Roman numeral.

4	IV	5	V
10	X	8	VIII
6	VI	3	III

Page 433

Time: Hour, Half-Hour, Quarter-Hour, 5 Min. Intervals
Directions: Write the time shown on each clock.

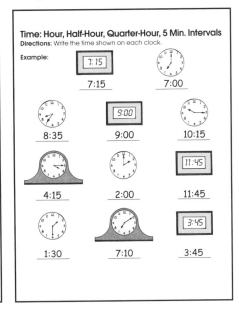

Example: 7:15

7:15   7:00

8:35   9:00   10:15

4:15   2:00   11:45

1:30   7:10   3:45

Page 434

Time: a.m. and p.m.

In telling time, the hours between 12:00 midnight and 12:00 noon are a.m. hours. The hours between 12:00 noon and 12:00 midnight are p.m. hours.

Directions: Draw a line between the times that are the same.

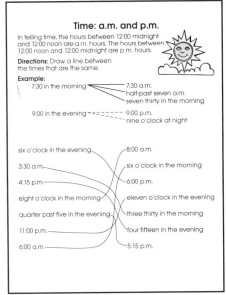

Example:
7:30 in the morning — 7:30 a.m. / half-past seven a.m. / seven thirty in the morning

9:00 in the evening — 9:00 p.m. / nine o'clock at night

six o'clock in the evening — 8:00 a.m.
3:30 a.m. — six o'clock in the morning
4:15 p.m. — 6:00 p.m.
eight o'clock in the morning — eleven o'clock in the evening
quarter past five in the evening — three thirty in the morning
11:00 p.m. — four fifteen in the evening
6:00 a.m. — 5:15 p.m.

Page 435

Time: Minutes

A minute is a measurement of time. There are sixty seconds in a minute and sixty minutes in an hour.

Directions: Write the time shown on each clock.

Example:
Each mark is one minute.
The hand is at mark number 6.

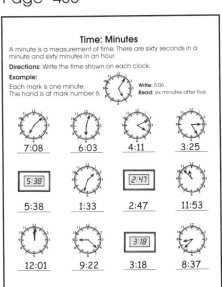

Write: 5:06
Read: six minutes after five.

7:08   6:03   4:11   3:25

5:38   1:33   2:47   11:53

12:01   9:22   3:18   8:37

Page 436

Time: Addition
Directions: Add the hours and minutes together.
(Remember, 1 hour equals 60 minutes.)

Example:

```
  2 hours 10 minutes
+ 1 hour  50 minutes
  3 hours (60 minutes)
         (1 hour)
  4 hours
```

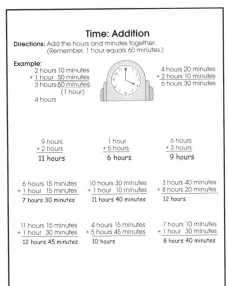

```
  4 hours 20 minutes
+ 2 hours 10 minutes
  6 hours 30 minutes
```

```
  9 hours        1 hour        6 hours
+ 2 hours      + 5 hours     + 3 hours
  11 hours       6 hours       9 hours
```

```
  6 hours 15 minutes    10 hours 30 minutes    3 hours 40 minutes
+ 1 hour  15 minutes   + 1 hour  10 minutes   + 8 hours 20 minutes
  7 hours 30 minutes    11 hours 40 minutes    12 hours
```

```
  11 hours 15 minutes    4 hours 15 minutes    7 hours 10 minutes
+ 1 hour  30 minutes   + 5 hours 45 minutes  + 1 hour  30 minutes
  12 hours 45 minutes    10 hours              8 hours 40 minutes
```

Page 437

Time: Subtraction
Directions: Subtract the hours and minutes.
(Remember, 1 hour equals 60 minutes.)
"Borrow" from the "hours" if you need to.

Example:

```
  5    70
  6 hours 10 minutes
- 2 hours 30 minutes
  3 hours 40 minutes
```

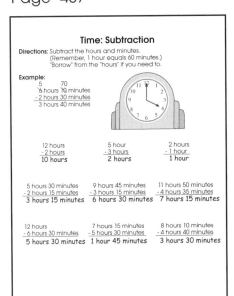

```
  12 hours      5 hour        2 hours
- 2 hours     - 3 hours     - 1 hour
  10 hours      2 hours       1 hour
```

```
  5 hours 30 minutes    9 hours 45 minutes    11 hours 50 minutes
- 2 hours 15 minutes   - 3 hours 15 minutes   - 4 hours 35 minutes
  3 hours 15 minutes    6 hours 30 minutes    7 hours 15 minutes
```

```
  12 hours              7 hours 15 minutes    8 hours 10 minutes
- 6 hours 30 minutes   - 5 hours 30 minutes  - 4 hours 40 minutes
  5 hours 30 minutes    1 hour 45 minutes     3 hours 30 minutes
```

Grade 3 - Comprehensive Curriculum

Page 438

Money: Coins and Dollars

penny = 1¢ or $.01
nickel = 5¢ or $.05
dollar = 100¢ or $1.00
dime = 10¢ or $.10
quarter = 25¢ or $.25
half-dollar = 50¢ or $.50

Directions: Write the amount for each group of money shown. Use a dollar sign and decimal point. The first one is done for you.

$.07 or 7¢

$.11 or 11¢

$.36 or 36¢

$.32 or 32¢

$2.55

$1.16

Page 439

Money: Five-Dollar Bill and Ten-Dollar Bill
Directions: Write the amount for each group of money shown. Use a dollar sign and decimal point. The first one is done for you.

Five-dollar bill = 5 one dollar bills

Ten-dollar bill = 2 five-dollar bills or 10 one-dollar bills

$15.00

$6.00

$6.35

$16.31

7 one-dollar bills, 2 quarters $7.50

2 five-dollar bills, 3 one-dollar bills, half-dollar $13.50

3 ten-dollar bills, 1 five-dollar bill, 3 quarters $35.75

Page 440

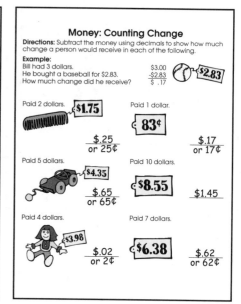

Money: Counting Change
Directions: Subtract the money using decimals to show how much change a person would receive in each of the following.

Example:
Bill had 3 dollars.
He bought a baseball for $2.83.
How much change did he receive?

$3.00
−$2.83
$ .17

$2.83

Paid 2 dollars. $1.75

$.25 or 25¢

Paid 1 dollar. 83¢

$.17 or 17¢

Paid 5 dollars. $4.35

$.65 or 65¢

Paid 10 dollars. $8.55

$1.45

Paid 4 dollars. $3.98

$.02 or 2¢

Paid 7 dollars. $6.38

$.62 or 62¢

Page 441

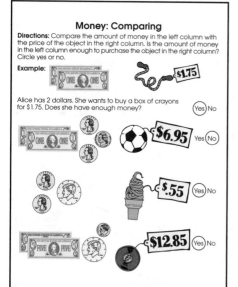

Money: Comparing
Directions: Compare the amount of money in the left column with the price of the object in the right column. Is the amount of money in the left column enough to purchase the object in the right column? Circle yes or no.

Example: $1.75

Alice has 2 dollars. She wants to buy a box of crayons for $1.75. Does she have enough money? **Yes** No

$6.95 Yes **No**

$.55 **Yes** No

$12.85 **Yes** No

Page 442

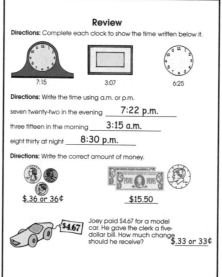

Review
Directions: Complete each clock to show the time written below it.

7:15

3:07

6:25

Directions: Write the time using a.m. or p.m.

seven twenty-two in the evening ___7:22 p.m.___

three fifteen in the morning ___3:15 a.m.___

eight thirty at night ___8:30 p.m.___

Directions: Write the correct amount of money.

$.36 or 36¢

$15.50

$4.67 Joey paid $4.67 for a model car. He gave the clerk a five-dollar bill. How much change should he receive? ___$.33 or 33¢___

Page 443

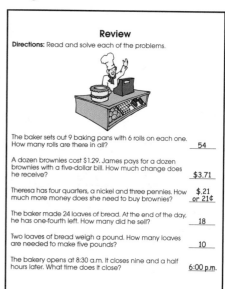

Review
Directions: Read and solve each of the problems.

The baker sets out 9 baking pans with 6 rolls on each one. How many rolls are there in all? ___54___

A dozen brownies cost $1.29. James pays for a dozen brownies with a five-dollar bill. How much change does he receive? ___$3.71___

Theresa has four quarters, a nickel and three pennies. How much more money does she need to buy brownies? ___$.21 or 21¢___

The baker made 24 loaves of bread. At the end of the day, he has one-fourth left. How many did he sell? ___18___

Two loaves of bread weigh a pound. How many loaves are needed to make five pounds? ___10___

The bakery opens at 8:30 a.m. It closes nine and a half hours later. What time does it close? ___6:00 p.m.___

Page 444

Review
Place Value
Directions: Write the number's value in each place: **678,421**.

1 ones		**6** hundred thousands	
8 thousands		**4** hundreds	
2 tens		**7** ten thousands	

Addition and Subtraction
Directions: Add or subtract. Remember to regroup, if you need to.

88 − 19 = 69   46 + 39 = 85   75 + 24 = 99   93 − 68 = 25   76 − 59 = 17

683 − 496 = 187   855 + 138 = 993   84/49 + 62 = 195   97/54 + 361 = 512   9,731 − 4,664 = 5,067

Rounding
Directions: Round to the nearest 10, 100 or 1,000.

72 **70**   49 **50**   31 **30**   66 **70**
151 **200**   296 **300**   917 **900**   621 **600**

Page 445

Multiplication and Division

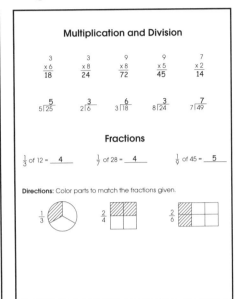

3 × 6 = 18   3 × 8 = 24   9 × 8 = 72   9 × 5 = 45   7 × 2 = 14

5√25 = 5   2√6 = 3   3√18 = 6   8√24 = 3   7√49 = 7

Fractions

$\frac{1}{3}$ of 12 = **4** $\frac{1}{7}$ of 28 = **4** $\frac{1}{9}$ of 45 = **5**

Directions: Color parts to match the fractions given.

$\frac{1}{3}$ $\frac{2}{4}$ $\frac{2}{6}$

Page 446

Decimals
Directions: Write the decimal for each fraction.

$\frac{4}{10}$ = **.4** $3\frac{3}{10}$ = **3.3** $\frac{9}{10}$ = **.9** $21\frac{3}{10}$ = **21.3**

Directions: Add or Subtract.

8.2 + 1.1 = **9.3**   3.6 − 1.8 = **1.8**   3.9 + 2.6 = **6.5**

Geometry
Directions: Write the name for each figure.

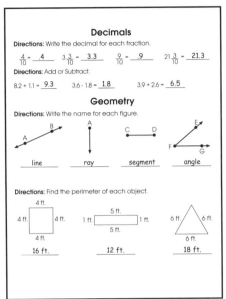

line   ray   segment   angle

Directions: Find the perimeter of each object.

4 ft square: 16 ft.   5 ft × 1 ft rectangle: 12 ft.   6 ft triangle: 18 ft.

Page 447

Graphing
Directions: Answer the questions.

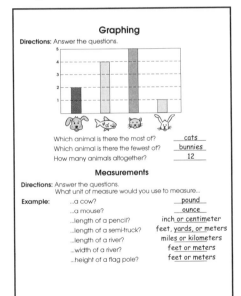

Which animal is there the most of? **cats**
Which animal is there the fewest of? **bunnies**
How many animals altogether? **12**

Measurements
Directions: Answer the questions.
What unit of measure would you use to measure...

Example: ...a cow? **pound**
...a mouse? **ounce**
...length of a pencil? **inch or centimeter**
...length of a semi-truck? **feet, yards, or meters**
...length of a river? **miles or kilometers**
...width of a river? **feet or meters**
...height of a flag pole? **feet or meters**

Page 448

Time
Directions: Complete each clock to show the time written below it.

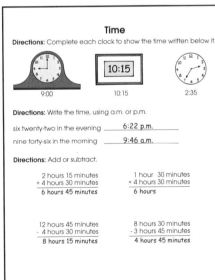

9:00   10:15   2:35

Directions: Write the time, using a.m. or p.m.

six twenty-two in the evening **6:22 p.m.**
nine forty-six in the morning **9:46 a.m.**

Directions: Add or subtract.

2 hours 15 minutes + 4 hours 30 minutes = 6 hours 45 minutes
1 hour 30 minutes + 4 hours 30 minutes = 6 hours

12 hours 45 minutes − 4 hours 30 minutes = 8 hours 15 minutes
8 hours 30 minutes − 3 hours 45 minutes = 4 hours 45 minutes

Page 449

Problem-Solving: Addition, Subtraction
Directions: Read and solve each problem. The first one is done for you.

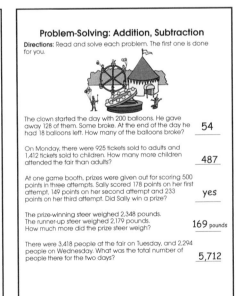

The clown started the day with 200 balloons. He gave away 128 of them. Some broke. At the end of the day he had 18 balloons left. How many of the balloons broke? **54**

On Monday, there were 925 tickets sold to adults and 1,412 tickets sold to children. How many more children attended the fair than adults? **487**

At one game booth, prizes were given out for scoring 500 points in three attempts. Sally scored 178 points on her first attempt, 149 points on her second attempt and 233 points on her third attempt. Did Sally win a prize? **yes**

The prize-winning steer weighed 2,348 pounds. The runner-up steer weighed 2,179 pounds. How much more did the prize steer weigh? **169** pounds

There were 3,418 people at the fair on Tuesday, and 2,294 people on Wednesday. What was the total number of people there for the two days? **5,712**

Page 450

Problem-Solving: Multiplication, Division

Directions: Read and solve each problem.

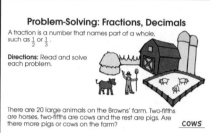

Jeff and Terry are planting a garden. They plant 3 rows of green beans with 8 plants in each row. How many green bean plants are there in the garden? **24**

There are 45 tomato plants in the garden. There are 5 rows of them. How many tomato plants are in each row? **9**

The children have 12 plants each of lettuce, broccoli and spinach. How many plants are there in all? **36**

Jeff planted 3 times as many cucumber plants as Terry. He planted 15 of them. How many did Terry plant? **5**

Terry planted 12 pepper plants. He planted twice as many green pepper plants as red pepper plants. How many green pepper plants are there? **8**

How many red pepper plants? **4**

Page 451

Problem-Solving: Fractions, Decimals

A fraction is a number that names part of a whole, such as $\frac{1}{2}$ or $\frac{1}{3}$.

Directions: Read and solve each problem.

There are 20 large animals on the Browns' farm. Two-fifths are horses, two-fifths are cows and the rest are pigs. Are there more pigs or cows on the farm? **cows**

Farmer Brown had 40 eggs to sell. He sold half of them in the morning. In the afternoon, he sold half of what was left. How many eggs did Farmer Brown have at the end of the day? **10**

There is a fence running around seven-tenths of the farm. How much of the farm does not have a fence around it? Write the amount as a decimal. **.3**

The Browns have 10 chickens. Two are roosters and the rest are hens. Write a decimal for the number that are roosters and for the number that are hens. **.2** roosters **.8** hens

Mrs. Brown spends three-fourths of her day working outside and the rest working inside. Does she spend more time inside or outside? **outside**

Page 452

Problem-Solving: Measurement

Directions: Read and solve each problem.

This year, hundreds of people ran in the Capital City Marathon. The race is 4.2 kilometers long. When the first person crossed the finish line, the last person was at the 3.7 kilometer point. How far ahead was the winner? **.5**

Dennis crossed the finish line 10 meters ahead of Lucy. Lucy was 5 meters ahead of Sam. How far ahead of Sam was Dennis? **15**

Tony ran 320 yards from school to his home. Then he ran 290 yards to Jay's house. Together Tony and Jay ran 545 yards to the store. How many yards in all did Tony run? **1,155**

The teacher measured the heights of three children in her class. Marsha was 51 inches tall, Jimmy was 48 inches tall and Ted was $52\frac{1}{2}$ inches tall. How much taller is Ted than Marsha? **$1\frac{1}{2}$ in.**

How much taller is he than Jimmy? **$4\frac{1}{2}$ in.**

Page 453

Problem-Solving

Directions: Read and solve each problem.

$2.45 $1.59 $4.99

Ralph has $8.75. He buys a teddy bear and a puzzle. How much money does he have left? **$2.17**

Kelly wants to buy a teddy bear and a ball. She has $7.25. How much more money does she need? **$.19 or 19¢**

Kim paid a five-dollar bill, two one-dollar bills, two quarters, one dime and eight pennies for a book. How much did it cost? **$7.68**

Michelle leaves for school at 7:45 a.m. It takes her 20 minutes to get there. On the clock, draw the time that she arrives at school.

Frank takes piano lessons every Saturday morning at 11:30. The lesson lasts for an hour and 15 minutes. On the clock, draw the time his piano lesson ends. Is it a.m. or p.m.? Circle the correct answer.

ADDITION, SUBTRACTION, MULTIPLICATION, DIVISION

Have your child compute his/her age in years, in months and in days. Then try your age!

Purchase a blank book or notebook to serve as your child's Math Journal. As you complete math pages together, your child can write his/her reflections about what he/she has learned. If your child wants, you can write comments to him/her in the book to give your child positive feedback and reinforce the skill learned.

Talk with your child about how math is used in your profession. Make a list of other occupations, and talk about how math is used in these professions as well.

Imagine that "National Math Day" has become a holiday. Ask your child: If you were in charge of the celebration, what "Math Events" would you plan?

ADJECTIVES

Blindfold your child so he/she can touch, smell and hear but cannot see. Seal a scoop of ice cream in a plastic bag. Hand the bag to your child to touch without opening the bag. Ask your child to describe the ice cream using several adjectives. Write down your child's words. Repeat this activity with other objects which allow your child to describe what he/she can see, hear, smell, touch or taste.

ALPHABETICAL ORDER

Alphabetical order is a skill used every day. Have your child look up phone numbers or find videos at the local video store. (Note: Not all stores arrange their movies alphabetically.)

ANTONYMS/SYNONYMS/HOMOPHONES

If you notice your child using a homophone incorrectly in his/her writing ("there" for "their"), make sure to correct him/her before it becomes a habit.

As your child communicates in writing or speech, he/she will need to increase his/her vocabulary. Many words are overused and can be replaced with synonyms. Challenge your child to think of words that could replace over-used ones: "I'm thinking of a word that means the same as . . . ." Then have your child try to challenge you.

Have your child write a list of antonym word pairs, such as light, dark; silent, noisy; neat, sloppy; etc. Encourage him/her to use a variety of words. The list should contain about 10–12 word pairs. With this list, help your child make an Antonym Tree. Have on hand scissors, glue, some colored markers or crayons and several sheets of construction paper of different sizes and colors. Have your child cut out a tree trunk and branches and glue them onto large white background paper. Cut out leaves of various colors. Your child can then print the antonym pairs on the different leaves and glue them onto the tree branches. Synonym or homophone pairs could also be used.

COMPOUND WORDS

Give your child a section of the newspaper. Ask him/her to find and circle as many compound words as possible. This could also be done with other parts of speech, such as adjectives, verbs, pronouns, etc.

COMPREHENSION

While cause-effect relationships are learned in real-life situations—e.g., if I touch the hot stove, I will burn my hand—those same cause-effect relationships in reading are not as easy to see. Present a situation, such as "All the food in the freezer has thawed." Ask your child to think of possible causes for the occurrence. Then give your child practice imagining effects. "Jim wrecked his bicycle. What happened next?"

At this age, your child is or may soon be reading "chapter books." These books have very few pictures. Check your child's comprehension by having him/her draw pictures representing the action or the problem for each chapter. Before starting each new chapter, ask your child to predict what will happen.

As you read with your child, encourage him/her to picture in his/her mind what is happening. This will help your child recall the story using the "mind's eye" as well as the ear. Ask him/her to retell the story, noting details from the beginning, middle and end.

When you read with your child, take turns asking each other questions about the story. Your child may find it more difficult to think of a question to ask than to answer a question, so give him/her clues from the story to help.

Invite your child to write a different ending or new chapter to a story. If your child can do this in a logical manner, he/she has grasped the plot or ideas presented.

Encourage your child to become a "thinker." Use the activities and lessons in this book as a springboard for related lessons. As you work with your child on classifying, for example, you are helping him/her develop the skills needed to determine the main idea and details. Give your child a group of words and ask him/her to tell you the category in which they belong. Your child should also be able to look at a group of three to four words and decide which word does not belong. As your child writes, help him/her use these skills to group related sentences into good paragraphs. Discuss whether a book is fiction or nonfiction. Guide your child to understand the difference and to read a variety of literature.

If your child is able to place story events in the proper sequence, he/she probably understands the events of the story. Name an event from the story and ask if it happened near the beginning, middle or end.

Save the Sunday comics and cut out strips with interesting pictures or ones that tell a simple story. Cut the frames apart and challenge your child to reorder the story. Take this a step further by suggesting that your child create an extra frame to show what might happen next. For another activity, cut out or cover the text in the speech balloons and challenge your child to create a story that fits the pictures.

DETAILS

Write ideas on index cards, such as summer vacation. Then invite your child to write three or four details about the idea, such as lots of fun, no school, playing with friends, camping, riding bikes, and so on.

Write a simple sentence for your child. Example: The cat ran down the street. Show your child how adding details makes the sentence more interesting. Example: The fluffy white cat ran quickly down the quiet street.

Take this idea one step further and have your child write a story about a family trip or a day at the mall, the beach or at Grandma's. Encourage him/her to include lots of details about what happened.

Place some items on a table and give your child 10 to 30 seconds to memorize them. Then, as your child's back is turned, remove one of the items. Have your child see if he/she can tell you what is missing. Increase the difficulty by removing two or more items.

DICTIONARY SKILLS

Dictionary skills will be used more and more often as your child progresses through school, so encourage him/her to become familiar with this resource. Don't look up a word for your child but assist if he/she asks for your help. Play dictionary games with your child. Time your child to see how quickly he/she can look up a word or see who can open up the dictionary closer to the page on which a given word is found.

FOLLOWING DIRECTIONS

Your child may find it difficult to understand oral directions. This usually happens because he/she is not "really" listening. Make sure you have eye contact and the full attention of your child when giving directions.

Check out a book on origami, the ancient art of Japanese paper-folding. Challenge your child to read the directions to create figures from paper.

Encourage your child to follow directions with fun activities like scavenger hunts, mazes and puzzles. Ask your child to help with recipes and have him/her follow the directions given on boxes from your cupboard or freezer.

Written directions need to be understood before they can be followed. Check his/her understanding before he/she attempts an activity.

Show your child the importance of following directions by preparing a simple recipe together. Point out how the steps must be followed in order. Then invite him/her to write a recipe for making a sandwich, chocolate milk or another simple food. Encourage your child to include all the necessary steps, then see if you can create the recipe from your child's directions.

INFERENCE

Guide your child to "figure out" what an author means even when it is not stated directly. Practice by describing a situation to your child and having him/her tell you what is happening. Example: I got some baby shampoo and a big towel. I went outside, got the hose and turned on the water. The dog took one look at me and tried to run out the gate. What is happening? (I am getting ready to wash the dog.)

MAIN IDEA

Set up a group of items and have your child locate something else that would fit in that group. You may want to provide several items from which he/she can choose. As your child's skill level increases, invite him/her to locate something on his/her own.

Invite your child to group things into categories such as color, shape, size or idea to see if the concept, or main idea, is understood. Examples: round things, wild animals, sports played outside, board games.

Ask your child questions while reading together, such as "What is the most important thing the author is saying in this paragraph?"

MONEY

Talk with your child about different things he/she can do to earn money.

Pose this question to your child: If we did not have money, what would we use to buy things? Tell your child about the Native American system of using wampum as "money." Do research together about other monetary systems.

QUOTATION MARKS

From the newspaper, cut out your child's favorite comic strip. Have your child rewrite the comic strip conversations, using sentences with quotation marks. Check your child's sentences for proper use of quotation marks and discuss what you find with your child.

READING

Read to and with your child, and let him/her see you reading for enjoyment. Encourage your child to read for enjoyment and make sure to provide many opportunities for your child to discuss what he/she is reading.

Ask your child: What if you couldn't read? Challenge him/her to make a list of as many kinds of reading as he/she thinks he/she does in a day. Then together keep track of every time you use reading throughout the day—reading directions on packages while cooking dinner, reading road signs, looking up information in a telephone book, reading mail, etc. Your child will be impressed by the important role reading plays in your lives!

When your child finishes a book, create fun ways to share the information in the book with you or with a friend. Some ways to do this might be to have your child write a letter from one character to another, create a comic strip illustrating the events of the book or write a journal entry one of the characters might write.

Before you take your child to a movie or buy a new video, suggest that your child read the book first, or read it aloud to him/her. Talk with your child about the similarities and differences between the book and the movie and discuss which he/she likes better and why.

Encourage your child to dress up as a character from one of his/her favorite books and to act out events from the book for members of your family.

Encourage your child to keep a "reading log" of books he/she has read, and write his/her reflections about each book. After your child has read several books, challenge him/her to go through the journal and classify the book titles by genre. Add symbols to indicate the types of books your child has read: F for fiction and N for nonfiction. To make this activity more challenging, further extend these classifications, indicating M for mystery, B for biography, P for poetry, etc.

When you vacation with your child, purchase postcards from the various locations you visit. Let your child write important information about your trip on the postcards. Use a hole punch to make a hole in each postcard and fasten them together for a unique travel memory book!

Make sure your child has a current library card and plan a weekly time to visit the library together. Each time, take a few moments to teach your child about different parts of the library. For example, on one visit, you can show him/her where fiction and nonfiction books are located. Regular library visits will help you to expose your child to many genres of books and help him/her to develop a life-long love of learning.

SPELLING

Review with your child how to study a word:

1) Look at the word.
2) Say the word.
3) Write the word.
4) Check yourself.

Repeat the steps if the word is incorrect.

Every day, write one sentence with errors in it. Have your child correct it. Focus on spelling, punctuation, capitalization and word order. Example: the dag and cat fite.

Help your child create his/her own spelling dictionary.

Discuss the origins of words with your child. Latin and Greek influences are most common. For example, "cent" in money or "century" means 100 and comes from the Latin word centum. Many dictionaries list word origins.

Teach your child more words with multiple meanings using a dictionary.

Other things to do besides write a word for practice:

- Chant the spelling.
- Write the word in the air.
- Use frosting or a condiment to write the word on food.
- Fill an empty mustard container with water and write the words on your sidewalk or driveway.
- Write the word in the snow with a stick or umbrella.
- Put the word to a song (i.e., sing the tune of "Bingo" for a 5-letter word).
- Spell the word aloud, tapping on consonants, clapping on vowels.

Have a word poster or folder for your child to keep a list of new words. Then he/she can study and review the words independently.

Play charades with your child using spelling words. Each guess must be spelled out.

SUBJECTS AND PREDICATES

Give your child 20 index cards. He/she should write ten subjects on the first ten cards, and ten predicates on the remaining cards. Punch holes in the upper right-hand corner of each stack and fasten with a notebook ring. Have your child flip through the stack of cards, mixing subjects and predicates to form a variety of sentences.

TIME

Talk with your child about different methods of keeping time, such as with clocks, stopwatches, calendars, etc. Let your child make a list of as many ways to keep time as he/she can.

Have your child time how long it takes the family to eat dinner. Have him/her write down the start time and the stop time, and subtract.

Have your child make a "time management" chart to plan his/her time from after school until bedtime.

VERBS

Write some action verbs, such as run, talk, jump, watch, read, wave, drive, slide, bend, etc., on paper. Put the pieces of paper into a hat or can. Let your child choose a piece of paper and pantomime the word for you to guess. Take turns doing this until you've both had several turns.

WRITING

Review the Writing Process:

1) prewriting and brainstorming
2) first (or rough) draft
3) revision
4) proofreading
5) publish final edited copy

Encourage your child to write in a daily journal. Provide a spiral notebook with wide-spaced lines. Journal entries are usually anecdotal and personal. Encourage your child to ask questions, describe dreams or write accounts of his/her day in the journal. Following are some suggestions for journal starters:

I'd like to go . . .	I want to know more about . . .
My birthday is . . .	Did you know . . .
Sometimes I feel . . .	My favorite . . .
I laughed and laughed . . .	My best friend is . . .
I went to . . .	When I got to the party, . . .
I felt silly . . .	Was I ever mad when . . .
I really miss . . .	I feel _____ when . . .
I try hard to . . .	Last night when I went to bed . . .
I can't wait until . . .	I felt so proud when . . .

Encourage your child to compose poems, copying the patterns of the following poetry:

Couplet (a two-line rhyme)
Example: I saw a cloud way up high,
          Soaring gently in the sky.

Limerick (a humorous poem that has the rhyme scheme AABBA)
Example: There was a young man from Maine (A)
          Who liked to stand out in the rain. (A)
          Although he's all wet, (B)
          He's standing there yet. (B)
          That crazy young man from Maine. (A)

Quatrain (a four-line poem with rhymes AABB or ABAB)
Examples: AABB   ABAB
          I asked a small boy, (A)   As I watched a waterfall, (A)
          Who played with a toy, (A)   Water splashed upon my face. (B)
          Why trees do not rain. (B)   Although I was quite small, (A)
          He could not explain. (B)   I knew it was a grand place. (B)

Abbreviations 224

Addition 364, 367, 369–373,
379, 444

Adjectives 225–228, 329–333

Adverbs 242, 243

Alliteration 286

Alphabetical Order 79, 192–195

Analogies 63, 64

Antonyms 196–199, 357–359

Articles 245, 248

Capitalization 249, 250

Cause and Effect 90–95

Classifying 65–74

Commas 246–248, 250

Common Nouns 208, 212

Compare and Contrast 87–89

Compound Predicates 261, 262

Compound Subjects 257, 258

Compound Words 13, 14

Comprehension 100–102, 104–106,
108–115, 118–126,
129, 130, 134–141,
144–146, 148, 149,
151, 152, 154–162,
164–167, 169–176,
179–181

Contractions 278, 360–362

Coordinates 430

Decimals 404–407, 446

Detail Sentences 44

Dictionary Skills 58

Division 389–397, 445

Drawing Conclusions 182–190

Exclamations 276, 277

Factors 398

Fantasy and Reality 61

Fiction and Nonfiction 75, 76

Following Directions 32–35, 131

Fractions 400–403, 445

Front-End Estimation 382

Future-Tense Verbs 236, 237

Geometry 410–419, 446

Graphs 423, 424, 430, 447

Helping Verbs 233

Homophones 203–206, 317–322

Idioms 62

Inferences 54, 99, 127, 128,
132, 142, 143, 150,
163, 177, 178, 182

Irregular Verbs 238–240

Library Skills 78–82

Linking Verbs 241

Long Vowel Words 326–328

Making Inferences 54, 99, 127, 128,
132, 142, 143, 150,
163, 177, 178, 182

Main Idea 36–50, 96, 98,
107, 108, 133,
147, 153, 168

Map Scales 421, 422

Measurement 425–429, 447

Money 438–443

Multiple-Meaning Words 19–21

Multiplication 383–388, 391–393, 398, 445

Noting Details 51–53, 103, 116, 117

Nouns 207–219, 227

Parts of a Paragraph 282–285

Parts of Speech 244, 251–254

Past-Tense Verbs 234, 237–240

Patterns 408, 409

Percentages 399

Phonics 7–10

Place Value 366, 444

Plural Nouns 213–219

Poetry 286–288

Possessive Nouns 218, 219, 279

Possessive Pronouns 223

Predicates 259–265, 267, 268

Prefixes 229, 351, 353

Prepositions 244

Present-Tense Verbs 235, 237

Problem-Solving 449–453

Pronouns 220–223

Proper Nouns 209–212

Punctuation 224, 246–248, 277–281

Questions 274, 275, 277

Quotation Marks 280, 281

Reading for Information 56–60, 83–86

Recalling Details 51–53, 103, 116, 117

References 80–82

Regrouping 367–372, 374–377, 444

Remainders 396

Review Section 442–448

Roman Numerals 431, 432

Rounding 380–382, 444

Sentences 269–277

Sequencing 22–31

Short Vowel Words 323–325

Simple Predicates 260

Simple Subjects 256

Spelling C, K, CK Words 334–341

Spelling S Words 342–345

Statements 274, 275, 277

Subjects 255–258, 263–266, 268

Subtraction 365, 368, 369, 374–379, 444

Suffixes 230, 346–349

Syllables 11, 12

Synonyms 200–202, 354, 355

Tangram 411

Time 431, 433–437, 448

Topic Sentences 283

Types of Sentences 274–277

Verbs 231–241

Vocabulary 15–18, 290–316

Writing 6, 60